Leisure and Ethics

Reflections on the Philosophy of Leisure

Gerald S. Fain
Editor

Kimberly A. Gillespie
Contributing Editor

American Association for Leisure and Recreation
an association of the
American Alliance for Health,
Physical Education, Recreation and Dance

American Alliance for Health,
Physical Education, Recreation and Dance
1900 Association Drive
Reston, Virginia 22091

ISBN 0-88314-489-1

Purposes of the American Alliance for Health, Physical Education, Recreation and Dance

The American Alliance is an educational organization, structured for the purposes of supporting, encouraging, and providing assistance to member groups and their personnel throughout the nation as they seek to initiate, develop, and conduct programs in health, leisure, and movement-related activities for the enrichment of human life.

Alliance objectives include:

1. Professional growth and development—to support, encourage, and provide guidance in the development and conduct of programs in health, leisure, and movement-related activities which are based on the needs, interests, and inherent capacities of the individual in today's society.

2. Communication—to facilitate public and professional understanding and appreciation of the importance and value of health, leisure, and movement-related activities as they contribute toward human well-being.

3. Research—to encourage and facilitate research which will enrich the depth and scope of health, leisure, and movement-related activities; and to disseminate the findings to the profession and other interested and concerned publics.

4. Standards and guidelines—to further the continuous development and evaluation of standards within the profession for personnel and programs in health, leisure, and movement-related activities.

5. Public affairs—to coordinate and administer a planned program of professional, public, and governmental relations that will improve education in areas of health, leisure, and movement-related activities.

6. To conduct such other activities as shall be approved by the Board of Governors and the Alliance Assembly, provided that the Alliance shall not engage in any activity which would be inconsistent with the status of an educational and charitable organization as defined in Section 501(c)(3) of the Internal Revenue Code of 1954 or any successor provision thereto, and none of the said purposes shall at any time be deemed or construed to be purposes other than the public benefit purposes and objectives consistent with such educational and charitable status.

Bylaws, Article III

Dedication

To my wife Jane and our children
Lucas and Ellice.

Contents

Section Three—Epilogue

Preface

This book was written for those interested in the study of leisure and ethics. Most of the chapters are grounded in either moral philosophy or leisure theory. The reader will find that this is not a study of professional codes of ethics and it is not devoted to the examination or analysis of particular moral dilemmas related to leisure behavior or leisure services. This is a book thought to be particularly useful in the academic setting where the liberal discussion of leisure and philosophy has long been enjoyed.

The original conceptualization for this book came from the 1989 Leisure and Ethics Symposium, sponsored by the American Association for Leisure and Recreation. The primary purpose of this symposium was to provide a meeting place for scholars interested in leisure philosophy and ethics. The international call for papers was initiated through professional journals and organizations two years in advance of the meeting. Despite the anticipation that a meeting of this type, with exclusive specificity on the topic of leisure and ethics, might attract relatively few individuals, AALR leadership sustained its continuing commitment. The symposium was held in Boston, Massachusetts, at Boston University on April 18 and 19, 1989, in conjunction with the national convention of the American Alliance for Health, Physical Education, Recreation and Dance. Participants came from across the United States, Canada, the United Kingdom, and as far away as China. In review of the presenters' backgrounds, one cannot help but be impressed by the diversity of experiences and disciplines represented.

The symposium, which allowed thoughtful discussion of the papers presented, generated ideas and interests that went beyond many of the original papers. It was not, therefore, the intention to simply publish a set of selected papers in the form of proceedings. The purpose of the book evolved into a text designed to capture the character and content of thoughts that flowed from the actual meeting. All of the participants were invited to submit their original papers, or revised versions of original papers, for publication. In addition, several original works, not presented at the symposium, have been included. The reader will also note the inclusion of "Selected Thoughts" in Section Two. These contributions, primarily condensed versions of formal symposium presentations, provide insights and ideas that evidence expanded directions for continuing thought and reflection. As a result of this process, much of what is included in this text represents scholarship that extends well beyond the presentations and discussion at the original symposium.

The final section includes the 1989 Jay B. Nash Lecture and "Reflections." The lecture elaborates the notion of moral leisure with particular regard to professional life. "Reflections" serves as a reminder that the study of leisure and ethics began long ago, belongs to no one in particular, and will, in one form or another, continue.

Acknowledgments

This project represents the sustained commitment of a number of individuals. More than seven years ago I presented the idea of an ethics committee to the leadership of AALR. In response, President Ron Mendell established the first Committee on Leisure and Ethics, which was supported by each subsequent president of AALR, including L. Dale Cruse, Larry Neal, and S. Harold Smith. During this same period, Barbara Sampson of AALR provided essential support to the committee along with ensuring the successful operation of the symposium.

I wish to express appreciation to those individuals who worked directly on the symposium. Victor Kestenbaum provided advice and guidance in the early stages of conceptualization and planning for the symposium and this text. He also served on the panel that selected papers. Moreover, he has helped to guide and shape my pursuit of the philosophic. Larry Neal and Barbara Sampson assisted with the review and selection of papers along with providing the satisfaction found in our mutual friendships. Kim Gillespie, Sally Sutherland, and Lesley Sturt worked to construct the program along with ensuring the successful operation of the two-day meeting. Later, Kim worked at my side as contributing editor and in that role assumed responsibilities and made comments that are evidenced on nearly every page. I am also grateful to Edwin Delattre who, toward the end of this project, provided thoughtful review and discussion of my work on moral leisure.

I particularly wish to note the contribution of both critical comments and thoughtful insight provided to me by Albert Murphy. His influence on my thinking over the past few years continues to provide a valued source of enrichment.

Howard Gray, along with the other members of the AALR publications committee, deserve recognition for their continuing interest and support. The highly skilled and reasoned support of the AAHPERD production staff, led by Nancy Rosenberg, is reflected in the final preparation of the text and is sincerely appreciated.

Finally, I wish to express my gratitude to the 31 individuals who contributed to this volume. Each of these authors put a measure of trust in this project by sharing their work. The presentation of one's ideas in formal writing is a serious matter. I hope that each individual will be proud to note the association with this text.

Gerald S. Fain

Section One

Reflections on the
Philosophy of Leisure

Introduction: Leisure and the "Perfection of Importance"

Victor Kestenbaum

Importance" is the title of the first chapter of Alfred North Whitehead's book, *Modes of Thought* (1938). Early in that chapter he says:

> Philosophy can exclude nothing. Thus it should never start from systematization. Its primary stage can be termed "assemblage." (p. 2)

What is the advantage or value of this process? In Whitehead's view it helps us "to avoid the narrowness inherent in all finite systems." Seen in this way, it is fitting that the reflections on the philosophy of leisure collected in this volume should cover such a remarkable range of topics and orientations: liberty, democracy, Islam, management, feminism, theology, sports, and many more. Such a variety of frameworks and viewpoints will help assure that the philosophy of leisure studies avoids the "narrowness" lamented by Whitehead, but which has become a distinguishing feature of American higher education. What, however, does this collection, this "assemblage," accomplish? What does it make possible that was not possible before its publication or at least not as easily accomplished?

My sense is that this collection significantly helps to clarify the importance of leisure, provided one has an adequate concept of importance. Whitehead says: "Importance, limited to a finite individual occasion, ceases to be important. In some sense or other, importance is derived from the immanence of infinitude in the finite" (p. 28). Individual occasions of sailing, jogging, going to the museum on Sunday morning, camping, gardening, collecting Toscanini recordings, are commendable leisure activities. What, however, constitutes their importance? Are these finite expressions of leisure responses to something which transcends their own individual occasions, that is, are they a response to an immanent infinity? Perhaps these questions are misguided; perhaps it is unwise to make more out of these activities than they "really" are. But what really are they? And how important really are they?

This volume clarifies and deepens reflection on the importance of leisure by showing its natural connectedness to those importances that have been humanity's foundation: beauty, goodness, truth, the sacred. Particular instances of beauty, goodness, truth, and sacredness focus, but do not exhaust, the transcendence that is proper to the important. The contributions to this volume, sometimes in very different ways and sometimes in similar ways, demonstrate how leisure's finite acts can express transcendent importances. This is not conceit. This is not another example of a new or young profession *claiming* importance. These essays show that our sense of importance would be incomplete without an appreciation of leisure, as it would be incomplete without, for example, a full understanding of the place of art or religion in human experience.

One of the most interesting features of many of these essays is their critical nature. Transcendent infinitude is not a refuge. If importance is the immanence of infinitude in the finite, then we are summoned to judge, assess, and criticize how something transcendent intersects with the world. How is the actual brought to fulfillment or perfection in the light of a transcendent ideal? Must the ideal be reconstructed, deconstructed, or abandoned if it does not respond to the social, political, and economic realities of the time?

These essays demonstrate the need for leisure studies to ask questions of this kind; they also demonstrate the field's ability to provide answers characterized by depth, imagination, and sensitivity. There is something particularly satisfying about these papers, however, when judged alongside the recent, large, and increasingly redundant literature concerned with cultural and social criticism. The essays in this book explore topics and pursue lines of criticism that really are fresh. Whitehead notes that "there is a tinge of pedantry" involved in all systematic thought. Perhaps because this book *is* an assemblage and not an attempt at a system (or an application of a system), there is considerably less pedantry in it than many other attempts at affirming and criticizing what is important in our culture. Such affirmation and criticism is of great worth, even if—and maybe precisely because—the results of these activities do not lend themselves to what Whitehead calls "systematization."

To advance the ideal of leisure is important, and to criticize aspects of that ideal is important, but what is the importance of this ideal in a time when the authority of ideals is no longer taken for granted? Indeed, is there only one leisure ideal? Is there not a plurality of ideals connected with leisure, ideals which increasingly get in each other's way? Do the essays in this collection clarify the issue of importance and the authority of ideals, or do they simply suggest more candidates for the best ideals, the ethical top forty? Peter L. Berger (1979) puts the situation about as succinctly as it probably can be: *"Modernity pluralizes"* (p. 15). One profound consequence of this pluralism is that:

> In the modern situation certainty is hard to come by. It cannot be stressed enough that this fact is rooted in pretheoretical experience—that is, in ordinary, everyday social life. This experience is common to the proverbial man in the street and to the intellectual who spins out elaborate theories about the universe. The built-in uncertainty is common to both as well. This basic sociological insight is crucial for an understanding of the competition between worldviews and the resultant crisis of belief that has been characteristic of modernity. (p. 19)

The reflections on the philosophy of leisure that compose this volume do not resolve, mitigate, or vanquish the "built-in uncertainty" of our situation. Although virtually every one of the essays is concerned with clarifying some aspect of the relationship between moral consciousness and the concept (and experience) of leisure, the tone and outlook of the book is, in addition to its relative lack of pedantry, wonderfully free of moral dogmatism. That "certainty is hard to come by" of course does not mean that some things are not more reliably known and understood than other things. None of the authors of these essays wishes to contribute to the nihilist tendencies that might be found in certain areas of contemporary American life. Neither, however, do any of these authors wish to deny, I think, the risk and adventure that attends the "immanence of infinitude in the finite," that is, the risk and adventure proper to importance.

The essays in this volume go a long way toward addressing a perplexing question: Is leisure a good in itself, that is, is its importance self-contained or does its importance derive from other importances like self-realization, pleasure, challenge, serenity, skilled performance? The importance of leisure is what we do with our leisure, so the argument goes, and thus it is the importance of these activities that governs any discussion of the importance of leisure. Leisure cannot pronounce more widely on the nature of the good life than the particular instances that are its instances. Leisure is a place holder for the real importances; whatever importance leisure may have, it is a borrowed importance. If, however, Whitehead is to be believed, this view is mistaken, for all importance is a borrowing of some sort, a borrowing of infinitude by the finite. Leisure studies help to redeem the finitude of experience by keeping the ideal of leisure before us, an ideal that gives point and meaning to its exemplifications.

In asking what leisure's importance is, the essays in this volume inevitably are concerned with the meaning of the "leisure ideal." If the finite borrows from the infinite, then the infinite borrows from the ideal. Many of the essays in this book are critical, some are practical, all are, in a certain sense, "idealistic." They seek to describe those transcendent importances, those ideals, not merely embodied in finite leisure activities but celebrated in those activities. Whitehead's approach to importance is heavily indebted to Plato. My approach to the importance of leisure is certainly indebted to Plato. And in ways that perhaps not all contributors to this volume would necessarily agree, I think most of the essays in this work are indebted to Plato. John Herman Randall (1970) says of Plato:

> For him the important point is, we will *know* and *see* what life is only if we see it as more than it actually is—only if we see what is imperfect in fact as perfectible in imagination. Human life is not only tolerable, it is only *intelligible*, if we idealize it. We do not understand what it really is unless we see what it *might* be. (p. 206)

The "leisure ideal" serves to remind us what painting, dancing, singing, fixing, collecting, walking, volunteering, climbing, listening, "*might* be." Similar to aesthetic, religious, and philosophical ideals, the leisure ideal helps to fix our attention on what these finite activities borrow from infinitude, an infinitude not so wholly transcendent that at least a few of the ideals resident there cannot inspire a life.

It seems to me that the editor of this volume, Gerald S. Fain, captures the proper spirit of the work in the title of his paper, "Moral Leisure: The Promise and Wonder." Leisure is not an ultimate or final importance. There are those who do not believe that art, religion, or philosophy are final importances either, or if they are ultimate importances, only fragments of their ideals have been realized in the course of human experience. Perhaps every epoch, every generation, only approximately realizes or fulfills the promise of these forms of importance. This is no reason to become cynical about the possibility of importance in general, nor is it a good reason to become cynical about particular forms of importance. One of the mysteries harbored by importance is that though it is always threatened by extinction due to a remarkable variety of forces—social, political, economic, intellectual, practical—it does not wither away. We continue to borrow from infinitude even when the finite has nearly destroyed us.

The wonder, though, that attaches to importance is not limited to only those circumstances where the very survival of importance is at stake. We find importance and wonder in successfully installing a new stereo in one's car; in learning Spanish, or Japanese, or American sign language, because it seems like an interesting, satisfying, good thing to do; in helping to build a tot lot for neighborhood kids; in perfecting one's skills in throwing, lifting, running, swimming, passing. To fail to see the importance and wonder of a cross perfectly executed by your daughter's 12-and-under soccer team is to dull and coarsen responsiveness to what Whitehead called "that general character on which all importance depends" (p. 7). Leisure certainly is not the only source of wonder, but leisure is essential in helping us to enlarge the particular and practical so that we may see what transcends this problem, this opportunity, this worry, this moment.

Leisure returns us to an infinitude that we may not notice, even when we are deeply "enjoying" ourselves in some leisure activity. The importance of leisure may escape the person who seeks it almost as completely as the person who ignores or shuns it. We are not naturally attuned to infinitude and thus we are always liable to misplace importance, misjudge it, misunderstand it. Art, religion, literature, labor, music, science, are pathways to importance. Leisure is a pathway to importance. Whitehead says that "morality is always the aim at that union of harmony, intensity, and vividness which involves the perfection of importance for that occasion" (p. 19).

Previous scholarship in leisure studies has invited us to see leisure as an important part of the human condition. The essays in this volume demonstrate the power of leisure to embody and to illuminate the "perfection of importance." They help us to appreciate leisure as witness to the human condition.

References

Berger, P. L. (1979). *The heretical imperative: Contemporary possibilities of religious affirmation.* New York: Anchor Press.

Randall, J. H. (1970). *Plato: Dramatist of the life of reason.* New York: Columbia University Press.

Whitehead, A. N. (1938). *Modes of thought.* New York: Capricorn Books.

Moral Leisure

Gerald S. Fain

Leisure is discovered when the opportunity to freely choose how one will live, apart from work and other subsistence activities, is realized. Various forms of self-improvement, socialization, sport, and entertainment illustrate the types of choices made in the name of leisure. By reflecting on the moral meaning of these choices, we become enlightened with regard to who we are and what we value. Moreover, because reflection cannot be separated from these choices, we know that every act of leisure has moral meaning.

Choosing what to do with freedom from the necessities of work and subsistence is an act of self-discovery that has profound and predictable consequences. When leisure is thought of as only freedom from occupation or vacant time the result is often evidenced in the degradation of the culture and the human spirit. If there are no expectations beyond rest from work or the search for what is immediately pleasurable, leisure becomes demoralized. There is reason to believe that this is what is happening in present postindustrial society.

> The appearance in history of an escapist conception of "leisure" coincides with the organization of leisure as an extension of commodity production. The same forces that have organized the factory and the office have organized leisure as well, reducing it to an appendage of industry. (Lasch, 1979, p. 217)

The leisure in twentieth century popular America fails to fully actualize the meaning of leisure first articulated by Aristotle. He considered leisure as a classical ideal, to be more than simply freedom from the necessity of being occupied. It was not only liberation from occupation, it was intrinsically driven virtuous activity leading to the greatest happiness. This conception of leisure included a logic for the disciplined life and the basis for a cultivated mind. It was a state of being, in which activity performed for its own sake provided the fundamental basis for a person's whole life, along with the possibility of creating a better society. Those with the opportunity of leisure had a moral obligation to use it with great seriousness and respect.

> At first he who invented any art whatever that went beyond the common perceptions of man was naturally admired by men, not only because there were something useful in the inventions, but because he was thought wise and superior to the rest. But as more arts were invented, and some were directed to the necessities of life, others to recreation, the inventors of the latter were naturally always regarded as wiser than the inventors of the former, because their branches of knowledge did not aim at utility. Hence when all such inventions were already established, the sciences which do not aim at giving pleasure or at the necessities of life were discovered, and first in the places where men first began to have leisure. This is why the mathematical arts were founded in Egypt, for there the priestly caste was allowed to be at leisure. (Aristotle, *Metaphysics*, p. 691)

From this classical point of view, leisure took the form of contemplation about life beyond the ongoing demands associated with business, politics, and other civic affairs. It was the privilege of a few and the dream of many. This classical, though elitist, view provided hope for civilization in the way it advanced reflective thinking, generated ideas, and gave dignity to the human condition in a state of transcendence from the necessities of work and utility. It enlightened faith in the potential of the human spirit. In this sense, the classical view of leisure embraced a precise standard of moral reflection.

Today, and also in the name of leisure, masses of people for hours at a time sit in front of television sets, roam shopping malls, watch movies, and attend sporting events. Leisure, now synonymous with *any* free time activity, is understood as a form of activity, vacant time, or state of pleasing relaxation. As de Grazia explains, we have lost sight of leisure as an ideal. In the place of leisure, we have "an ideal of free time or of the good life.... The good life consists in the people's enjoyment of whatever industry produces, advertisers sell, and the government orders" (de Grazia, 1962, p. 279).

This evolution of the word "leisure" reflects the destruction of the ideal. There is today no popular image of leisure by which the perfection of this classical ideal is judged. When any freely chosen activity or experience during vacant time qualifies as leisure we find the word can be attached to most any moral meaning. From this relativistic point of view it is possible for one to claim that any activity or experience is leisure simply because it is pleasing to self. Freely chosen destructive acts cannot, from the perspective of leisure, be distinguished from freely chosen constructive acts. In the absence of consideration of values, leisure is fundamentally amoral.

Moreover, it is not possible to assume that the virtue attributed to the classical idea of leisure can be liberated from its popular conception. While it is true that a prerequisite for leisure is freedom of time, it is also true that all free time is not leisure. At some point, it cannot simultaneously be thought of as unoccupied time, recreation, relaxation, *and* the Greek ideal that found leisure in the disciplined life and cultivated mind.

Yet the contemporary need to understand and advance the notion of leisure as an act necessitating moral reflection is great. The drive of a postindustrial society for the freedom to live as one chooses must surely result in a more valued goal than simply spending ever increasing time and money in the pursuit of one's pleasures. The reflective view of leisure, as a particular ideal of freedom, gives a distinctive purpose to life not available when one is concerned merely with the basic necessities of daily living. Simply, there is no other concept that better provides this distinctive perspective on the ideal of happiness and the "good life." Leisure, from this point of view, is more than time, more than activity; it is the opportunity to choose how one "ought live."

Having stated the necessity for the consideration of the moral perspective, it is equally important to stress that such reflection does not assume a universal system of ideas or values. To suggest this would be antithetical. There must be openness for multiple pathways if in fact the essential quality of freedom is to be retained. Leisure necessitates a particular kind of freedom, and as such cannot easily be bound by a single set of values, mores, or styles that restricts the liberty of individual creativity and expression. With respect to values systems, leisure is not like politics, schooling, religion, or any other established institution. In fact, it is the way in which it varies from these institutions that makes it so valuable to the individual and culture. Knowing that leisure is neither dogma nor subjective relativism liberates the human spirit as only leisure can.

With the explicit intention of advancing the possibilities of the moral ideal as a contemporary concept, the phrase "moral leisure" has been adopted. Adding the adjective "moral" to leisure may appear redundant to those familiar with the classical meaning of leisure. However, by giving thought to the moral side of leisure, we can now transcend the classical meaning and open the possibility of discovering new contemporary freedoms and ideals.

Moral Leisure—The Happy Life

The happy life is thought to be virtuous; now a virtuous life requires exertion, and does not consist of amusement. (Aristotle, *Nicomachean Ethics*, p. 1103)

Experiencing amusement and living a happy life are not the same. In the view of Aristotle, happiness is joined with virtue. While amusement need not meet the same demands of happiness for moral excellence, a virtuous life, distinguished by moral excellence, is disciplined and can lead to happiness. As an individual matter, virtue is based upon moral beliefs that are manifest in our mores and everyday public lives. It then follows that since leisure is fundamentally concerned with happiness, it is more likely that we will find happiness from virtuous living than from a life of amusement.

Leisure is a free and personal expression of one's character. Because it is personal it is not fully knowable without understanding the human experience it manifests and reflects. This is to recognize that leisure has meaning only in relation to other personal experiences, beliefs, and abstractions. In this way the moral meaning of leisure cannot be entirely understood apart from the individual or context in which it is observed. Therefore, beyond the individual, leisure is a collective social phenomenon inseparable from culture. The leisure of twentieth century America is not the same as that of twentieth century England, or ancient Greece. The patterns and forms of leisure expression vary as a function of culture over time. In a direct way, these patterns and forms of expression reveal the character of the culture and the individual lives that shape it.

What were the conditions, related to the moral basis of leisure, that gave rise to the fall of the Roman Empire or brought about the Puritan Reformation or the Cultural Revolution in China? Were there too many or too few holidays? Was there too much or too little creative expression and personal freedom? Is there something self-destructive in the human spirit that is manifest when the opportunity for collective freedom is realized as an alternative to work-centered living? How much freedom "ought" people have and of what kinds? These are not questions of politics, economics, or education alone. They are questions of personal happiness and freedom. The study of leisure through history and across cultures is revealing and allows understandings that give insight to our own lives and times. Thinking about these historical events, we wonder what it would have been like to live at that time, what we would have done in that situation, and what lessons we can learn that might enable our own happiness.

The possibility for viewing leisure expression as moral action is based upon the understanding that leisure is a type of freedom. But freedom of any type has no meaning unless we know what we are free from and free to do. By thinking about leisure as personal and collective freedom, we are better able to know who we are and what we value, for there can be no exercise of freedom that is void of value. Every choice has moral implications. When presented with a set of vacant hours, we may choose to either feed hungry people, take a vacation, actively support public education, or work to advance world peace as a matter of civic responsibility. Choices and judgments are a reflection of values and do directly affect personal freedom. Leisure is influenced by these actions and in turn influences our views of them.

The idea of invention, a special kind of creative expression, is a way of understanding the role of leisure in a society. Inventions, as statements of values, also provide a way of understanding the character of the culture. What are the inventions of our times, what relationships do they have to leisure, and what do they tell us about the times in which we live?

Illustrations could be drawn from any domain of human affairs: the family, commerce, politics, education, recreation, or science. In a technological period, inventions in science are commonly available and often highly publicized. One highly controversial invention, which attracted sensational attention, concerns a revolutionary solution to a long-standing problem concerning energy. This is an invention claimed by two scientists.[1]

B. Stanley Pons and his British colleague Martin Fleischmann invented what they believed was cold fusion, the creation of a source of energy that could well change the world as we know it. They came up with the idea for the fusion experiment more than five years ago while drinking bourbon in Pons's kitchen. The creative thinking transcended their laboratory work and spilled into their nonwork time. We could say that because they had the freedom to think beyond the necessity of everyday existence, the cold fusion experiment was invented. No doubt, while there was freedom of thought expressed in the kitchen talks, there were also other driving forces in their lives that led them to be inventive. What they did was not mandated in the same way that one has a job to produce a particular product or deliver a particular service. Invention, as an act of freedom, is typically considered to be determined by individual dedication to an idea. Therefore we assume they chose, or at least agreed, to work on a problem that would not be easy, that would require great knowledge, skill, and dedication. Sitting at the kitchen table drinking bourbon, they could have sought to invent less difficult things, or dreamed up ways to cheat their employers, or entertained themselves with drugs, sex, and rock and roll. They could have told jokes or watched television. Instead, they chose to design an experiment they would pursue for the next five years.

In this illustration, science and leisure joined in a creative act about which we can make moral judgments. The inventors' act of choosing

---

[1]There is, at this time, considerable controversy concerning the claim of this invention. However, this illustration is useful in asking one to think about the process of invention as creative enterprise as well as raising the imagination stimulated by potentially revolutionary ideas.

to invent, for better or worse, for good or evil, is something we can each decide for ourselves. We may want to argue about the moral merits of this invention along with asking if invention, as a creative action, is a better use of leisure than any other action. Nonetheless, the point is simply that they did work on invention and we do make judgments about that decision. We think about what else they might have been doing, and we think about their invention as having utility. We know that along with the opportunity for leisure comes the hope of advancing our collective self-interest.

Aristotle's observation, that we cannot expect invention unless there is the opportunity of leisure, a chance to do what one *ought* to do, has endured as a useful idea.[2] It is also necessary to note that this invention, unlike mathematics, was touted for its utility. In this way, it does not meet Aristotle's higher standard for invention, and in this way also reveals something about ourselves and the times in which we live.

Undoubtedly, this discussion about invention would be much different had Stephen W. Hawking been the focus.[3] This inventor, a world leader in physics, has a disease that confines his mobility to a wheelchair and keeps him from speaking and writing clearly. Yet his mind and his ability to think with a skill and freedom to be admired by all have enlightened understanding of the universe. In comparison to Pons and Fleischmann, Hawking's work, or inventions, concerned with super nova, quantum mechanics, the big bang, and black holes are not directed at utility and therefore seem to provide a better parallel to the Egyptian's invention of mathematics.

Through the act of invention is evidenced the potential of leisure. When we are free to do as we please, what do we do, why do we do it, and what do our actions portend? Over time, the ideal of living a "happy life" has required the unique freedom provided by the opportunity and challenge to invent—and invention is a classic form of leisure.

Emancipating of the Moral

John Dewey in his discussion of science spoke about "emancipating of an idea from the particular context in which it originated and giving it a wider reference. . . ." (Dewey, 1916, p. 230). This observation is useful in explaining the point that moral meaning is unavoidably imbedded within leisure. At once we recognize the popular view of leisure as free

---

[2]The Latin root of leisure means "to be permitted."
[3]A good example of his contributions may be found in his book, *A Brief History of Time, From the Big Bang to Black Holes* (1988).

time as well as knowing that these freely chosen actions spring from some moral basis. By emancipating the idea of moral from the popular contemporary meaning of leisure, we give *wider reference* to what we know about our moral or ethical selves. This view of leisure, one which claims that freedom cannot be disassociated from values, broadens the possibility for study and provides a more critical view of freedom.

Leisure is characterized by freedom and moral reflection. This conception assumes that one cannot truly act freely without first having thought about what one ought to be and ought to try to become. In so conceptualizing leisure in the context of value structure, it is assumed that one is attuned to the moral consequences of one's leisure actions. Thinking about leisure in this way is to suggest that the leisure experience is an expression of the operating value structure that recognizes consequences about which judgments are made.

What leisure brings to the individual and culture matters greatly. Leisure is a form of human discretion and has enormous impact in directing the forces that shape our world. Those who study in this field inevitably make judgments about the value of "what is" and "ought be." In this sense, within a pluralistic democracy, we understand that leisure is inherently neither "good" nor "bad"—rather it is opportunity. It is opportunity to think about freedom, in respect to both the individual and the collective social order. The actions of leisure disclose and articulate the self along with the culture. If we want to know whether we live in a place and time of high or low morality, all the evidence we need to review may be found in leisure.

Emancipating the moral reminds us that leisure is thoughtful, purposeful, consequential, and more than free time. It has always been that way.

A Conceptualization for the Study of Moral Leisure

Moral leisure is a way of thinking about all we know.

How do we grow and develop and for what purposes? Do we live in a "good" or "bad" time or place? Are our thoughts and actions virtuous? What do we think and feel about the events around us? How "ought" we live and, when given choice, what do we actually do? What is the "good life" and what are our hopes for humankind?

These are complex questions involving matters of academic inquiry, social action, professional life, human potential, and personal growth. When considered from the leisure perspective, such questions are not easily understood or studied without some reduction of meanings into an organized system. Toward that end, the following conceptualization, represented by five themes, is presented as one way of illustrating the idea of moral leisure.[4]

Leisure, Ethics, and Philosophy
Moral Life and Professional Practice in Leisure Science and Service
Moral Development and Leisure Experience
Global Perspectives on Leisure
Multidisciplinary Works in Leisure and Ethics

Leisure, Ethics, and Philosophy

Since the days of Aristotle, philosophers have paid attention to leisure. To philosophers, leisure is a consideration for understanding the "good life" and the idea of happiness. Those with particular interest in ethics and moral philosophy share a fundamental curiosity with those who study leisure. To illustrate this like-mindedness, one is reminded of this union by the organization of the collection in many libraries. The friendly epistemological tie between leisure and moral philosophy is readily apparent in such collections where the referent "moral philosophy" is in close proximity to the "philosophy of leisure." On the library shelf Alasdair MacIntyre's *After Virtue: A Study in Moral Theory* (1981) may be only a few volumes from Max Kaplan's *Leisure in America: A Social Inquiry* (1960).[5] Evidently, those who structured the systems that organize many of our library collections know that leisure philosophy and moral philosophy share much in common. In point of fact, there should be little difference in the academic realm between those who study the "oughts" of life represented in moral philosophy and those who study leisure.

Seeking knowledge about happiness, or pleasure, or the nature of living a good life, inevitably brings one to seminal works in philosophy. The idea of leisure is in no way new to philosophers. In a personal way, I have yet to find a writing in philosophy that does not in some manner inform my thinking about leisure. For at the core of leisure inquiry is the notion of the liberated mind and spirit, which driven by virtue has long been considered the aim of the "good life."

This discussion of leisure, ethics, and philosophy joins the abstract and practical worlds in a unique way. As an abstraction, leisure can be

---

[4]These same five themes served as the thematic structure for the American Association for Leisure and Recreation symposium, Leisure and Ethics, Reflections on the Philosophy of Leisure.

[5]The Mugar Library, at Boston University, places *After Virtue* by MacIntyre at BJ1012. M325 and *Leisure in America* by Kaplan at BJ1498.F60.

studied as a part of any of the theoretical schools. For example, Frankena (1973) explains the study of Plato's *Crito*, revealing three principles. The first is that we ought never harm anyone, the second is that we ought to keep our promises, and the third is that we ought to obey and respect our parents and teachers. Using these principles in making judgments about leisure reveals the values at the root of our morality.

Briefly, moral philosophy provides the basis for understanding ethics. In moral philosophy one learns how to think, in logical and rational ways, about how to live a good life. Beginning with the works of Plato and Aristotle, timeless questions of "ought" become a lively background for understanding contemporary experience.

Ethics then is that aspect of philosophy that is concerned with moral problems and judgments. As a field of study, its strength is assessed when it is applied to particular problems or specialized fields of practice. We look to moral philosophy when we question human experience and want to know about "right" and "wrong." Moral philosophers will also teach that virtue, or right action, is elusive, particularized, and debatable. This does not necessarily infer a relativistic view of morality on the part of the doer, but rather than one understands one's own actions, and those of others, as having a wholeness that makes each person unique. These judgments are best informed by understanding the place of these actions in one's own human development, social and cultural heritage, and experience in the world. Children are judged differently from their parents, and the work of a lawyer demands a code of conduct differentiated from that of a police officer. Because we know that cultures, schools of philosophic thought, and ideologies differ, we can also understand that questions of virtue are by necessity particularized.

Moral philosophy, applied to practical matters of professional practice, touches issues and concerns of everyday life. Such discussions, where ethics is used to reason the conduct of professionals, serve an important role in shaping our thinking about practitioner conduct in fields like medicine, business, and law. As a practical matter, this thinking is manifest in ethical codes designed to guide professional practice. The statement of ethical principles typically gives logic and direction on how one ought to behave in respect to personal behavior and associations with colleagues, clients, and society in general. These codes and credos are especially useful in building union within the respective professions and therefore diminish in usefulness when individual practitioners adopt systems of thought based on personal experience or intuition.

Aside from a relatively few occupations, most citizens do not swear to uphold a certain set of job-related ethical principles. However, when people organize themselves into groups, there is always the need to find agreement on moral concepts. It is when we want to be part of a group that we must work toward agreement on a moral basis for our collective action. This interest in group membership and the articulation of credos was strongest in the late 1800s and early 1900s. This orientation to declaring the importance of moral standards was evidenced in our institutions of higher education of that time (Fain, 1989; Hermance, 1924; Sloan, 1980).

The recent decades may well be characterized as the time when faithfulness to moral standards was placed below matters of self-interest. The public review of cases involving improper conduct on the part of those in politics, business, and most every profession has become commonplace.

Today, inquiry concerning the relationship between leisure and philosophy remains largely unconnected in both philosophy and leisure studies. Yet, when asked questions such as "how ought one live," it is obvious that they are, in many respects, one and the same.

Moral Life and Professional Practice in Leisure Science and Service

Postindustrial society is characterized by ongoing organization of occupations into an increasing number of specializations. This is a result of a number of factors, including the increase in knowledge within fields along with the social and economic needs for "success" among those in the higher educated middle class. Having a specialized field and title is for many, more readily attainable than moving up from one social class to the next (Bledstein, 1978). In some cases, the increase of specializations within fields may simply be explained as an entrepreneurial strategy on the part of those in higher education, a way to recruit students into the promise of a new profession.

Those who practice in the fields of leisure science and service live with this same reality. For many, specialization and overspecialization have become characteristic of their work. In response to changes in the society, universities now offer specializations in many areas, including municipal recreation management, parks management, tourism and travel, commercial recreation, campus recreation, therapeutic recreation, and so on. While such increases in specialization, driven by increased knowledge within the field, seem inevitable and understandable, specialization driven solely by trends in the popular culture does little to advance professional life. For example, if a faculty created a new specialization in "Recreation Entertainment" as a means to recruit university students interested in popular culture forms of entertainment, the first question to ask is in regard to the knowledge base of this field; specifically what will be taught, by whom and toward what end? In review, one would hope to find ample evidence of new knowledge and new questions along with the promise that significant scholarship will be generated.

The identification and analysis of factors attributing to the proliferation of specializations within leisure science and service fields goes beyond the present discussion. However, recognizing the profound impact of increased specializations upon professional life is in itself important, as it offers another way of understanding the demoralization of leisure in postindustrial society.

This field, once unified by a common set of values expressed in the form of recreation services, has evolved into a series of specializations struggling to find a common mission. For those in the natural resources field, the issues of environmental protection are of primary importance while others in therapeutic recreation have become closely allied to medical models of treatment and rehabilitation. The result is evidenced in the variations of personal values and aspirations of the young people who come to the university for professional preparation. If these variations emanate from a clearly articulated set of beliefs common across specializations, then we can conclude the field is unified. However, when the belief structure across specializations is unclear, what we may see are related fields without much more in common than the history of their respective specializations.

When we ask about the moral philosophic imperatives that drive professions, we uncover the nature and virtue of the guild. We learn what makes the group of value to the society. And there is no more important task than this for each and every profession, professional school faculty, and practitioner. Without this continuing inquiry, what we have are merely fields of work, careers, or at worst, simply jobs. To those who are given to reflective practice, those who persist in asking about the values that drive and push their practice, there is no way to travel but down the road of the moral imperative.

Every profession and field of work has, for the individual practitioner, the potential for reflective practice. Many educators, for example, feel compelled to teach in schools because they know the value of the actively inquisitive mind, the role of education in shaping and advancing the individual. Individually they may also be committed to perpetuating and enriching the culture from one generation to the next. For the most part, societies are compelled to support public education and school teachers with the belief that without them the future of the culture would be lost. It makes little difference whether it is a first grade teacher or a high school science teacher, the field of education is joined in a coherent commitment to educate the young.

Most physicians feel compelled to heal the sick and strive to lessen pain and suffering. Ideally, they treat all who seek their aid and work to advance medical science. All of the areas of specialization are joined in this way. There are no fundamental moral philosophic differences between gynecologists, ophthalmologists, or psychiatrists despite the real differences in the nature of their respective practices. It was Hippocrates who stated that physicians are compelled to share their knowledge. His medical oath, for the first time in history, clearly separated medicine from the practice of religion, superstition, and magic. He understood that the nature or natural order of the field would be clearer when the boundaries of inquiry were openly revealed. The need to serve the public must be placed in front of the desire for the individual to keep a cure secret.

The universals that connect those in leisure, while available for study, are however less well defined than those associated with other fields of practice. There is little, for example, that serves to unify the diverse fields clustering under the umbrella of leisure service or science. This is not surprising after one observes that the culture has defined leisure principally in terms of recreation and amusement. For many practitioners there are no universal values, beyond the transient needs of the marketplace, to unite them as scholars, scientists, and practitioners. As a result, their moral lives are that much lonelier and disconnected from the more precisely articulated belief systems that serve as founding points for other professional groups.

I recently directed two federally funded drug education projects for the city of Boston. One project involved 18 school teachers, kindergarten to twelfth grade, and the other involved 15 police officers. Each project lasted for two years. One of my interests in both of these groups was related to understanding the nature of their respective professional ethics and reflective practice. In this regard I was specifically interested in learning more about ethical dilemmas experienced by these practitioners. What decisions do school teachers have to make when it comes to drugs and their students? What do they do when they learn that one of their second graders earns $200 a day as a lookout for a drug dealer? Or that one of their colleagues uses drugs? How do they differentiate between the use of illicit drugs and alcohol among their students?

Many teachers in today's classrooms are expected to do a great deal about drug use, but many of them work in situations where there is confusion and lack of clarity with regard to the moral imperative directing their actions as teachers. They want the children in their classrooms to be drug-free, but they do not want to assume the role of a police officer, social worker, or drug tester. The moral concern for what they *ought* to do is real. It is lively in their reflective actions, but we also know that when there is little direction from the teaching supervisors or the profession, the moral life of teachers is bound to be quite perplexing.

Teachers know that when a child is removed from the classroom for involvement with drugs, there may be little hope for the child's future. They may also know that the criminal justice and social welfare systems are often ill equipped to serve the needs of children with drug problems. In making decisions about children, teachers know that while there are rules to follow and laws to obey, it is also their responsibility to act in the best interest of the school, the child, the family, and the community. Sometimes these responsibilities are in conflict but at all times the teacher is required to act. When these teachers spoke about these dilemmas in our class, it became apparent that there was much to discuss. There were differences that could be attributed to neighborhoods, grade levels, and supervisory personnel in the school building as well differences in the belief systems of the teachers. But what unified the discussion was the institution in which they worked and the roles they assumed. They all worked in schools and they all worked as educators who accepted the role of teaching children.

In a similar sense, I know that police officers in our drug education project also experience conflicts imbedded in their jobs. They are required, by sworn oath, to enforce all of the laws across society, and at the same time, they routinely are unable to enforce all of the laws. If they did, the courts and jails would be even more overcrowded than they already are. Officers lead a difficult life in part because they are routinely responsible for mediating between different value systems with the requirement that they also represent the interests of each and every citizen. A homeless person, in a daily search for food and shelter, acts from a value structure quite different from that of an affluent citizen out for a day of shopping. However, when it comes to matters of policing, there is only one set of laws available to the officer. This means they may at one moment be giving a citation to a motorist, the next chasing a felon, and then be asked to remove a vagrant from the steps of a department store. They are also bound, in a very special way, to be loyal to their partners and follow orders. The multiplicity of roles and responsibilities across these contexts is astounding.

Imagine the responsibility in deciding to arrest someone or to let them go free. Imagine the responsibility involved in drawing a weapon and possibly killing another human being. And imagine having to make these types of judgments within fractions of a second. This is the life of many police officers.

With both the school teachers and police officers, there is also a common union which extends beyond Boston. They know that they are connected with colleagues across this country and, to a lesser degree, across the world. The act of teaching, like the act of policing, has universal meaning.

Examining leisure science and leisure service is a much different matter. While it is true that leisure service and science has universal meaning, typically manifest in public gardens and parks, recreation centers, and the wilderness, it is also fair to conclude that for many practitioners there has been little articulation of a unified moral meaning across professional life. Looking for and studying the moral meanings that drive the leisure practitioner challenges all who study leisure and all who prepare in any of the specialized careers. Despite the apparent union of a core of knowledge, it is difficult to consider these as unified fields. The working contexts are too different. Those who have the responsibility to preserve and steward the great wild lands are on a significantly different mission from those with the responsibility for improving the quality of life within our inner cities through municipal recreation departments. Those in commercial fields of service inevitably live in a world pervaded by economic determinism. The moral life of these people is often determined by the degree to which the public will pay. Using the assumption that people pay for what is "good," it therefore follows that the greater the profit, the greater the virtue. There may be no perceived merit in asking questions which probe more profound reflection. This is a standard quite different from that of a leisure scientist with the opportunity and responsibility to advance knowledge of theory and philosophy. What could the unified moral life be?

It is no wonder that these individuals find it difficult to join and support a single national association or subscribe to a single unified journal. Based upon what we do know, it is without doubt hard to imagine how to join those in therapeutic recreation, commercial recreation, municipal recreation, outdoor recreation, environmental education, natural resources management, and tourism in a common context. And just as physicians, police officers, and school teachers are compelled by unique moral imperatives, so must each of the recreation and leisure fields be compelled. Without such imperatives, publicly understood and supported tenets for professional practice, there can be no profession nor can there be coherent science.

While my intent here is not to criticize current practice in higher education, it is difficult, when viewed from this moral philosophic perspective, to comprehend the basis by which university-based leisure service professions are sanctioned. Perhaps it is regrettable that all of these fields have found shelter, or at least are offered shelter, under the unified umbrella of a single curriculum accreditation program. Is this not like considering teachers and police officers professionally joined because they both have shared commitments to drug education?

The challenge is to better understand the nature of professional life that is both unique and discrete to each of the speciality areas, thereby allowing them to unfold, telling us what they do, what they believe, and most importantly, what it is that they purport to do for society. For without socially felt need, without public understanding and sanction, reflection is limited to a personal act of introspection.

As individuals, those involved with leisure science and leisure service are no less noble or virtuous than those in other fields. However, until there is both the articulation and acceptance of a unifying moral foundation for practice, those in these fields face the loneliness which accompanies life outside of a unified moral meaning.

Moral Development and Leisure Experience

The growth from childhood into adulthood is largely unpredictable. Factors concerning genetics, family status, the environment, and luck are significant determinants. The complexities of this growth phenomenon are evidenced in each adult. Fundamental to describing who we are as individuals is the understanding that we have developed into a certain type of moral person. It does not matter whether one is rich or poor, living with a severe disability, or in optimum physical health; each person develops morally.

How does one grow into a morally sound human being? What role does leisure play in this development over the course of life? Since values manifest in leisure behavior are highly personal, how can we judge one another on a single scale or even on a number of scales? Isn't the leisure of women different from that of men, and aren't the leisure behaviors of individuals different across cultures?

Our attention to moral development is essential because it gives us the occasion to address one of the most important yet misunderstood qualifications for leisure. To me, leisure is not a state of mind, it is not an activity, and it is not time. All of those ideas are wrong minded when we come to understand moral development and moral leisure. If this assertion is not clear or sounds revolutionary, it merits repeating. Leisure as typically defined in our studies and culture is wrong minded. Any definition or conception of leisure that fails to embrace some orientation to moral development, thereby accepting the inevitability of human development as a moral concern, fails to recognize the humanity and dignity of freedom embodied in what we know to be leisure.[6]

The natural course of growth and development includes maturation from childhood into adulthood and from adulthood we grow into old age. What happens along the way makes all the difference—differences reflected in our character, our values, our aspirations, and the way we

---

[6]Without providing critical analysis concerning the problems presented by characterizations of leisure as time, activity, or as state of mind, I will instead simply note the need to do so.

live. An absence of an understanding and appreciation for some kind of developmental orientation to leisure is thoughtless. As one grows through life there is the opportunity for ongoing moral reflection. In reflection, leisure behavior is a valuable measure of our character. We can simply ask how many books were read, hours of television watched, or how active one is in civic affairs. Find out what one does in leisure and then ask, why? The answers will reveal the soul and substance of the person. You will find out where that person has been and where that person is going in life.

The absence of such questions is at the center of the ambiguities found by many students in introductory leisure studies classes and in many of the basic texts in the field. Leisure is not simply the number of hours or number of dollars spent in the pursuit of the "good life." It is not simply recreation activities, and it is not only spontaneous human experience. Leisure, from the moral perspectives, comes from us as purposeful actions upon which reflection shapes subsequent thinking and experience.

In my experience, one reason university students are often unhappy with those who define leisure for them may be similar to the reasons that John Dewey argued about basic assumptions with the philosophers of his day. In the early 1890s some believed that there was a set of universal values that applied to all people across situations. What was "right" was "right"; regardless as to who it was, or where they had come from, basic "good" values existed. All of the citizens in the upper class knew what they were. The reason the others failed to achieve equal greatness was in large part because they were morally inferior. It was not their fault, just their lot. Dewey, on the other hand, argued that these qualities were not innate, but that they could be taught and learned and that they were *developed* through reflective experience.

Imagine asking someone you know if pulling at a woman's skirt in public is morally wrong. Then point out that there might be a difference if the "puller" was a child of three or a man of thirty. In a like sense one can also understand the value of telling the truth while simultaneously realizing that telling the truth may vary from person to person and situation to situation. What do you tell a patient in a hospital who is dying of cancer? I think the truth might be different for a three-year-old and a thirty-year-old. In a slightly different way, on viewing people in community, we can ask how it is possible to tell those living in Valdez, Alaska what the truth is in regard to the environmental impact of the 11 million gallon oil spill on their water and land. How many fish, animals, and birds killed? How dirty will the land get and what will it take to get the oil off the ground? How much will all this cost and when will it be completed? Can it ever be completed? This too is a truth that cannot simply be declared. It can only be understood over time. The "truth" of this matter is that we take action, and then as we learn more from our action, we have the opportunity to know the larger truth, as it develops and becomes known to us. This is one way to know wisdom.

And so it is with leisure. It is best understood, as a matter of personal experience, within the developmental context. It is not one thing, one time, or one state of being. Leisure requires reflection, on the "ought," the active reflection in choosing one thing over another. Such action requires a level of maturation that is rarely available to children and possibly beyond the reach of many adults. If one takes, as instructive, the writings of Sebastian de Grazia, along with others who do not see the coming of a "leisure age" as quickly approaching, it is possible to conclude that to most adults in postindustrial society, leisure is an unattainable ideal. For others, of course, it is and has always been possible through the continuing act of reflective living.

Be aware of those who claim that "this is leisure" or "that is leisure." That leisure is a timeless universal with a uniform meaning. That leisure is knowable by counting the numbers of free hours or captured in a listing of activities. That leisure can be described as a particular kind of psychological state of being. No, it is not that way. Leisure does mean different things to different people, and different things to the same people over time. The realization that we become, that we develop, and that we evolve into moral beings over our lifespan assures us that purely quantitative or purely subjective measures, which are fundamentally amoral, are inadequate in revealing what we know is leisure.

Global Perspectives on Leisure

Global perspectives on leisure include worldwide considerations related to the growth and diversity of cultures, political and economic systems, value structures, and impact upon the environment. It is here that we can address the differences between rich and poor nations, between ancient cultures and the modern world, along with our interests in getting to know more about how others search for and experience the "good life." This orientation to a world community, where leisure is understood as a universal part of human experience, is liberating. Expanded meanings, ideas, experiences, and value structures provide opportunity for self-examination. Like the interests in educating the young, over time and across cultures, it is possible to see and study leisure as a distinctive part of all peoples, a distinctive yet universal part of all human experience. However, in the global context, leisure typified by postindustrial societies as mass consumption has become the most critical of concerns.

I previously referred to the 1989 oil spill in Valdez harbor. This was and is an enormous tragedy; why did it happen? Was it due to poor judgment on the part of the captain, was it a mechanical or communication problem? While finding the reason is important, as it may help in reducing the risk of future accidents, there is a more fundamental question: Why is it that we continue to draw so heavily upon our fossil fuel? What is it that we must do that requires 11 million barrels of oil? And even after we endure a spill of that size, we don't even experience the flicker of an electric light on our videotape recorder in our second home. Imagine what we are doing to our earth, and then we must ask, toward what end?

Today it is becoming clearer that we treat our natural resources as expendable and have for too long polluted our earth. In a single-minded search for what we typically regard as the good life, we are destroying the earth. How many gasoline burning cars, pharmaceuticals and beauty aids, fast foods, and synthetic fibers can we consume and do we need? Do the benefits of modern postindustrial living justify these actions against our planet?

The relationship between leisure and the quality of life, on a personal as well as a global scale, is direct. But understanding more about how we live and what we live for requires knowing about the moral meaning of our collective actions. When we all seek, without sufficient forethought, more and "better" things to continually redefine the quality of our lives, we set into motion those actions that will inevitably result in the collapse of our earthy habitat. This view is not new and has been clearly articulated by Carson (1962), Schumacher (1975), Dubos (1980), and countless others. What is not well known or popularly practiced is the role of leisure as a way of understanding the fundamental root cause of such problems. Nearly 100 years ago when Thorstein Veblen's book on the leisure class was first published, he explained that people, in mass, choose to live in these ways because through their "conspicuous consumption" they hope to let others know that they have achieved leisure (Veblen, 1979). It is also reasonable to conclude that a certain amount and diversity of material goods and services are required by people and in and of themselves are not necessarily bad. Yet, it should be clear to those who know leisure as moral action that the excessive consumption of material goods and services in the name of leisure obviates attainment of the ideal. Leisure is no more available through material possessions than wisdom is available as a function of chronological age or years in school. The ideal of leisure, like wisdom, requires rich experience gained through integrative and reflective thought.

What one does in the pursuit of happiness, or on the quest for the ideal of leisure, falls naturally in the area of "ought." It is this perspective of leisure, the moral meaning, that gives purposeful insight into the thoughtless actions taken against our environment. As the ability to

shape the world around us increases, our responsibility to protect the
environment also increases. Regrettably, historians may characterize
the world of the late 1900s by the kind of competition for individual
success and personal happiness that resulted in the neglect and disregard of long-term global impact. Consumption-oriented leisure has
little interest in the protection and promotion of living standards that
support actualization of a higher quality of life for all living things.

According to an article in *Time* magazine (Toufexis, 1988), 17 percent
of all roadside trash is clippings from our lawns and gardens, neatly
tied up in nearly indestructible plastic bags. Our landfills and oceans
would be less full if we mulched our clippings or just left them on the
lawn. And while some Americans are thinking about trash, others are
concerned with population increases and the shortages of food and
shelter. The worldwide differences between the "haves" and "have nots"
is getting bigger. There is little doubt that the world population will
increase to 6.35 billion by the year 2000. Most of the population increase
will occur in less developed countries with per capita income of about
$200 a year. The world's forests are now disappearing at a rate of 18–
20 hectares a year (an area half the size of California), with most of
the loss occurring in the humid tropical forests of Africa, Asia, and
South America. Areas of cropland and grassland approximately the size
of Maine are becoming barren wasteland each year, and the spread of
desert-like conditions is likely to accelerate (Council on Environmental
Quality and United States Department of State, 1981). And these are
not the only problems of the modern world. Each day, shown on our
televisions, we see brutal war somewhere in the world along with reports about global illegal drug networks. We now are aware of new
illnesses and afflictions, including AIDS, a deadly global communicable
disease.

To further illustrate this concept as it relates to global issues, we can
look to the oceans. The vast life-giving and life-supporting bodies of
water cover more than 70 percent of the earth. The oceans, a resource
upon which all human life is dependent, have long been used as a
dumping area for garbage and pollution of every description. Now, in
the latter part of the twentieth century, there is evidence, clear and
publicly available evidence, that oceans can no longer continue to be
abused in this way. Pesticides, agricultural runoff, industrial waste, waste
treatment water, acid rain, sludge dumping, oil spills, and runoffs from
urban centers have poisoned ocean life and scarred the majestic beauty
of these waters. For the first time, sewage two inches thick, along with
plastic tampon applicators and medical debris (needles and syringes,
vials of blood, prescription bottles, and stained bandages) washed on
to the shores of New Jersey and Long Island (Toufexis, 1988). The
evidence of abuse to the oceans is now on beaches around the world.

Some solutions to problems of ocean pollution will be found in new technology, new laws, and enforcement strategies. There is also need to articulate new ways of thinking about such issues. Businesses, as well as individuals, that violate the laws should expect greater punishment for their crime, and those in industry that develop better ways to clean the oceans and dispose of human waste and pollution should expect great rewards. However, as the world continues to industrialize, creating more products and developing urban centers in all parts of the world, the rapid increase in the amounts of garbage and pollution worldwide will likely be unabated. The degree to which solutions can catch up and then keep pace with the increased demand is unknown.

While solutions born out of improved technology and better government are fundamental, it is equally important to try to understand the human drive to have more of the "things" that generate the garbage and pollution. The paradigm is simple. As garbage and pollution increase, our quality of life diminishes. The objective is to balance our production of garbage and pollution against the quality of life we want. Is it that simple? Can the motivation for having and doing more, to consume an ever increasing number of goods and services, be slowed? Can more conservation-oriented lifestyles prevail?

The experts, as well as our children, tell us that we must take action now if we are to minimize the impact of these global problems on our lives and those to come after us. There is no hope in quick or easy solutions to these problems—only hope in long-term shifts in the way we live. These global problems are inextricably linked to some of the most perplexing and persistent problems in the world—poverty, injustice, and social conflict.

Here, in the study of global issues, what could be more important than leisure, leisure as both the prevention and the cure? Leisure that is less consumptive, given the facts as we know them, is morally right, in fact, morally unavoidable to any thinking person. Whatever actions can be taken to promote those forms of leisure experience that are kinder to the environment are in our collective self-interest, actions that require the development of more thoughtful habits along with those inspirations springing from the creative genius.

The Egyptians invented mathematics because they had leisure. If there are to be solutions, they will not come from the politicians, business leaders, or others invested in the necessities of daily living. The ideas, if they come at all, will be from those who know leisure as both personal freedom and responsibility. And it is likely that these "inventions" will take the form of radical new styles of work and leisure, forms that are less consumptive, more cooperative, and embraced by large numbers of citizens of a growing world culture—a world culture that will embrace the best ideas, inventions, and leisure values of diverse peoples who together inhabit the planet.

Multidisciplinary Works in Leisure and Ethics

If it is multidisciplinary works that we seek, we may find it necessary to give up the word leisure as it is commonly used.

To begin, there is hardly a place on any campus where leisure, either in the form of leisure studies or as a related field, isn't studied. Leisure is part of our great books and our political and social history. It is studied in law, incorporated into the care of hospital patients, and is a fascination of many colleagues in the behavioral sciences. Mathematicians design games, computer scientists have social networks, and you can find chemists and biologists walking the fields and bogs looking for specimens. Yet, despite the unwillingness on the part of some to relate what they do to leisure, the relationships do exist. Call it economics, philosophy, history, mathematics, or biological science, elements of leisure are surely present. The word "leisure" as an organizer for academic study, however, repels those in other disciplines. Probably due to the popular meaning of leisure, delimited to vacant time, many serious scholars and students ignore leisure as a field where there is possibility for productive inquiry.

Because there is no other word to describe the phenomenon, leisure is a burden to be carried principally by those in leisure science and service. This challenge is unavoidably present in the lives of students, faculty, and practitioners. However, to recognize the challenge is a different matter from doing something about it. To address this concern from an intellectual basis, those in leisure must demonstrate the connectedness of this field to publicly felt needs.

To conjecture where this caveat could lead, one could speculate on the outcome if those in leisure science and service seriously involved themselves in the critical issues of American education. The claim by some that students are not learning to read, write, and compute at levels expected by the public is of growing social concern. The public demand is that schools do a better job in teaching the young. The theory and enterprise of education is under fire and, as a result, there is a major reform movement in the country. The movement is questioning the professional preparation of teachers. Who is qualified to teach? What should be included in the curriculum? Is there sufficient quality to ensure that the graduates will be able to contribute to society upon graduation? If the graduates cannot assume the productive roles required for the perpetuation of the culture and democracy, then the schools will be cited as having failed us.

The problems and continual debates associated with American education are a public matter. The question, with respect to the fight over which group of individuals and which ideas will serve as the foundation for the education of the next generation, is designed to be at the heart of the process. In the end, it is the public that determines the values to be taught in our public schools.

In general, the mission which drives education in America is relatively clear. Children, *all* children, "ought," to have the opportunity to attend public school. As a result of schooling, our children are expected to gain the maturity of character, mind, and body essential to the perpetuation of the culture. Schooling should give the assurance that the individual will more likely be part of our search for solutions than the source of social problems. This is quite practical. Children who grow up to become scientists who search for new knowledge are more valuable to us than children who grow up to be illiterate, unemployed, and socially destructive.

When schools graduate students into "productive" careers, where the individual has the charge to build a good life, the schools and the public take pride in the accomplishment. When schools fail to do this, the futures of our children are lost. In this sense there is no blaming the victim. The children did not fail; society has little difficulty in blaming teachers and schools. However, the responsibility of schooling rests with the citizens who build the schools and monitor the curriculum. Schools mirror who we are. For schools to change, *we* must change.

Why is it that there is so little connectedness between those in leisure and those in education? There is so much in common and so much public need. It is sadly true that while many of our playgrounds are places of violence and narcotics, they could also be places for education. If it is a good life that these people hope to help build, they must be concerned with more than simply teaching our children to play games. Teaching academic skills is for most children far more important to structuring a life of leisure than any other activity. Is it morally defensible to let them "play" while one ignores the basic human needs of a child to grow into a citizen able to know and experience freedom and liberty? There is much to gain when a culture has an educated population that understands the responsibility of living a free, creative, and reflective life—life where leisure is thought of as more than pleasing relaxation or recuperation from the tedium of work.

It is from such questions that we begin to build bridges that form the substance of multidisciplinary challenge. Without an understanding of the moral imperative, supported by publicly-felt need across fields of study, there is little future for multidisciplinary works. Education is but one field of professional service to be joined with serious and sustained interest by those in leisure. As presented in this text, multidisciplinary works across professional schools, as well as the liberal arts, enlighten and expand upon what we know and seek to learn more about.

Conclusion

Aristotle believed that mathematics was invented because the Egyptians had leisure. Aristotle used mathematics in his discussion of leisure because it was an example of an invention which emanated from non-work. The discovery was not designed to solve a "problem" or provide practical benefit. Aristotle believed that the benefit of such inventions were of the highest order and virtue.

Today, the popular meaning of leisure is conceptually amoral. The characterization of leisure in this way may not, however, signal a lack of interest in the pursuit of happiness and the idea of a virtuous life. While there appears to be little general understanding that leisure, in the form of freely chosen action, carries moral meaning, reflective adults, those who are serious about living a good life, inevitably come to know that there are better things to do with freedom than the simple pursuit of entertainment or pleasure. These are the same adults who as parents wish to help their children grow into adulthood where they can find happiness and the good life. It is because leisure does make a difference to the individual and collective social order that attention to the moral meaning of leisure is valuable and worth perpetuation.

Over the last 2,300 years, the idea of leisure has evolved from an experience reserved entirely for the elite, to a reality available to most any citizen. When the moral meaning is emancipated from the popular conception of leisure, the evolution of culture is determined. Those individuals able to grow into a state of morally reflective adulthood have the precious opportunity for freedom incorporated in the classical ideal of leisure.

The most significant characteristic of this new leisure is that social class is no longer the quintessential criteria for membership. Those with high social standing and great wealth are no more likely to know leisure than individuals from any other social or economic group. Individuals in poverty, or retired from the middle class, or with severe disabilities can now join the leisure class. Imbedded in this notion is acceptance of a pluralist view of human experience, a view that is humane and respectful of individual and collective rights and responsibilities. It is also a view that rejects the thoughtless opinion that leisure is the "good" and there can be no criticism or judgment made about how freedom, in the form of leisure, is expressed. There are many things that people freely do that bring pleasure but are not necessarily elevating to the soul, virtuous, or linked to happiness.

This idea of moral leisure should be familiar to our experience. We make judgments about the quality of our leisure as a matter of daily living and we understand these judgments are important to us as a people and a culture. We also have come to understand that the more established view of leisure as simply an extension of business and commerce, without a place of its own, is outdated and no longer useful. Leisure is best understood in a developmental context that is particularized and void of the relativism that leads one to the anti-intellectual and nonproductive actions of a life absent of moral meaning. It is again through leisure that we express our moral meaning.

Leisure is more than a state of mind, it is more than activity, and it is more than time. Leisure is the freedom to choose how one "ought live."

References

Aristotle. (1968). Ethica nicomachea. In R. McKeon (Ed. and Trans.), *The basic works of Aristotle* (pp. 935–1126). New York: Random House.

Aristotle. (1968). Metaphysica. In R. McKeon (Ed. and Trans.), *The basic works of Aristotle* (pp. 689–934). New York: Random House.

Bledstein, B.J. (1978). *The culture of professionalism.* New York: W.W. Norton & Company.

Carson, R. (1962). *Silent spring.* New York: Fawcett Crest.

Council on Environmental Quality and United States Department of State. (1981). *The global 2000 report to the president.* Washington, D.C.: U.S. Government Printing Office.

de Grazia, S. (1962). *Of time, work and leisure.* New York: Anchor Books.

Dewey, J. (1916). *Democracy and education.* Toronto: Macmillan Company.

Dubos, R. (1980). *The wooing of earth.* New York: Scribner.

Fain, G.S. (1989). Ethics and the therapeutic recreation profession. In D. Compton (Ed.), *Issues in therapeutic recreation* (pp. 188–203). Champaign, Ill.: Sagamore Publishing.

Frankena, W. (1973). *Ethics.* Englewood Cliffs, NJ: Prentice-Hall, Inc.

Hawking, S.W. (1988). *A brief history of time: From the big bang to black holes.* New York: Bantam Books.

Hermance, E.L. (1924). *Codes of ethics: A handbook.* Burlington, VT: Free Press Printing.

Kaplan, M. (1960). *Leisure in America: A social inquiry.* New York: Wiley.

Lasch, C. (1979). *The culture of narcissism.* New York: Warner Books.

MacIntyre, A.C. (1981). *After virtue: A study in moral theory.* Notre Dame, Ind.: University of Notre Dame Press.

Schumacher, E.F. (1975). *Small is beautiful: Economics as if people mattered.* New York: Harper & Row.

Sloan, D. (1980). The teaching of ethics in the American undergraduate curriculum, 1896–1976. In D. Callahan & S. Bok (Eds.), *Ethics teaching in higher education* (pp. 1–57). New York: Plenum Press.

Toufexis, A. (1988, August). The dirty seas, *Time*, 44.

Veblen, T. (1979). *The theory of the leisure class.* New York: Penguin Books.

Leisure and Ethics: Connections and Judgments

Max Kaplan

This historic conference provides a climax to a quarter century of significant studies of leisure. That is a short time for systematic beginnings to a new contemporary issue. The term itself goes back to Greek times, as the political scientist Sebastian de Grazia (1962) reminds us in a philosophical work. A historian of medieval Europe, Johann Huizinga (1950), provided the classical commentary on "play." Among the shrewdest insights on leisure in relation to work, aside from our own Stanley Parker (1971), are those of a recently retired professor of social work at the Hebrew University in Jerusalem, David Macarov (1980, 1982).

Observations on leisure have come from other historians, explorers, missionaries, anthropologists, and archeologists.

Projections have entered analysis and public policy as leisure values injected themselves into labor-management negotiations, into national Socialist planning, into the industrial transformation of Japan, and more recently, into Third World thinking.

Judgments have entered our field under the guise of policy making, the process of grant-gaming, and the responses of publics to our programs.

Earlier approaches by both academics and decision makers emphasized the available data. Our studies in America began at a midpoint in this century, at the time that the social sciences were developing a virtuosity in quantitative techniques, enhanced enormously since then by technological gadgetry. It was a simplistic but a natural step to base our studies on such manageable items as expenditures in time and money, with a passing glance at more difficult issues such as objectives, goals, or meanings.

In that elementary phase, still with us in many ways, ethics hardly entered the discussion. It was simpler to tabulate the answers given by Delta passengers to the questions we prepared for them, and ethics arose only if we sold the replies to American or United.

Yet the more successful we became (as in the massive material gathered for the recent President's Commission on Americans Outdoors [1987]), and the closer we came to an influence on legislators or administrators, the greater became the need to attach qualitative judgments to our quantitative data. The public was constantly engaged in its implicit judgment as it used—or did not use—our areas of play, our community centers, parks, concert halls, museums, or even the streets; it was helped or hindered by the authors of blue laws, by parents, by peer groups, by critics of the popular culture. The larger application or imposition of "user fees" will force closer judgments by the public.

Questions of values and judgments do not make sociologists comfortable. We squirm in their presence. They take us farther from the idols of the hard sciences that are more adept at avoiding "soft" answers. Values are foreign to the bunsen burner or chemical symbols on the laboratory wall. Coming to the field of music, I had always been comfortable with truths other than those espoused by my more positivistic colleagues in sociology and their neighbors in the silent parts of academe. I was less allergic than were they to such heretics as C. Wright Mills (1959), Pitirim Sorokin (1956), and Howard Becker (1950). Even in such a great department as Illinois, it was possible to obtain the doctorate in 1951 without even one course in statistics, before Apple, software, and Fortran were heard of. If philosophical considerations entered our consciousness, as it did among the early plowmen in the field, it was soon uprooted by the seeds from Silicon Valley. Max Weber's sermon of an earlier epoch on science as a vocation (Weber, 1946) was resurrected by the new generation, not entirely aware of his less-than-quantitative "ideal construct," which Flonan Znaniecki endowed on his students (1934, 1940, 1952), together with such other pre-Fortranites as George Simmel.

I smell a new direction among our children and grandchildren in academic corridors. They will be more willing to reread the giants. They are virtuosi all in the use of gadgets, but may be more inclined with the passing years to hold them at arm's length. It may be related to the ending of a century, to dramatic social and symbolic changes, perhaps even to an older public that is increasingly critical of confusing accuracy with significance. This new scholarship, I predict, will be less likely to worship numbers-oriented hypotheses in the face of more humble propositions such as the following:

1. Leisure, either as a social phenomenon or as a base for public policy, cannot be understood except with ethical considerations.
2. This is fundamental because even the analysis of leisure, and certainly its structure and organization, is naive—indeed impossible—without implicit or explicit concern with goals, objectives, purposes.
3. These goals or purposes are external to leisure actions or interests per se, originating in the larger concerns of the society; therefore leisure is inherently tied up with the nature and sources of both values in general and ethical systems in particular.
4. The term "ethics," from either a scientific or philosophical view, needs to be broken down into types or thematic systems and applied specifically to the nature of leisure as a form of social control, social conduct, or symbolic action.
5. Similarly, leisure is also too broad a term for loose reference to ethics and must be broken down into its major approaches or subsystems.

As a caveat in even suggesting the huge task implied in this approach, especially the last two propositions, I note that an advantage of a long lifetime is a freedom from both institutional and disciplinary parameters. Now long retired, there are no deans to fear nor jobs to seek. Hence one may, with impunity and even a happy irresponsibility, venture where scholars and fools, sometimes mutually replaceable, might fear to tread.

Hence, to save us three lifetimes and endless footnotes, I shall complete the task in three short sections of this paper. With ethical systems now delineated by a miracle, another three sections will guarantee sainthood through another trinity of approaches to leisure. In only a few more pages of Ruskieite imagination calculated to enrage this august scientific community, connections will finally be drawn between the double trio. Then, God bless us all, the conference can proceed with blessed stability. I recall, during my years of happy residence in Boston, the story of three Beacon Hill dowagers who passed on about the same time and confronted St. Peter. With the graciousness that is accorded proper Bostonians, he invited them to pass down the cosmic corridors and decide for themselves where they would spend eternity. They saw a neon sign, HELL, and knew this was meant for New Yorkers. Then came a mellower, hand-painted sign, HEAVEN; here, of course, they belonged. But just before turning in, they spotted a Webster's Dictionary on an antique stand at the entrance to a corridor marked LECTURES ON HEAVEN AND HELL. Let us go with them on this path that they took; surely, both designations can be encompassed on the journeys to either ethics or leisure.

Three views of ethics will be considered: ethics as *morality, power,* and *rationality.*

Morality

There is, first, a conception that equates ethics with morality, with the good and the bad. We speak of ethics among physicians in the hospital, lawyers in the courtroom, or priests in the confessional. There can be foul-ups, such as the sociologist who went to jail for carrying a hidden taping device with him into jury duty, or the national scandal as another sociologist and a psychologist carried hidden tape recorders throughout Italy as they confessed to a variety of sexual transgressions to find out what various types of priests would say (Valentini & di Meglio, 1974). With this conception of ethics we assume, according to our cultural traditions, those transcending principles of good and bad behavior with roots in theology, law, custom, or the maxims of motherhood, manners, and manhood. Children are taught such principles in school, often through legends, folktales, nationalistic songs, holy writings, proverbs, salutes, culture heroes, and role models. One George is remembered not only for his career as our first president, but also through a cherry tree tale; a later George will some day also be judged on his career as our forty-first president, but also for a highly unethical, voodoo television campaign that brought him into office.

All societies, regardless of degree of development or ideology and economic structure, must have rules of conduct, teachings on right and wrong, even if mouthed only on holidays. All segments of behavior, including the use of discretionary time, are imbued implicitly with the resolutions of such mores and morals.

Power

Morality is the first basis for ethics. Power is the second. Its core is not the "good" or the "bad," but active or passive relationships between persons. Thus Martin Buber (1937) spoke of the "I" and the "thou" relationship. Germans equate the closeness of persons with their use of "*du*" and "*sie*." Confucianism emphasizes in its philosophy the interaction of roles: the governed and the governor, the parent and child, the teacher and student (see Bierstedt, 1957, pp. 22–23, for a commentary on "pairings" in our own society). Sociologists speak of majorities and minorities, not numerically per se, but in anticipated behavior. The ethical principle here refers to the dignity of those with the least power. Dignity for the weaker was elevated to an international level in the human rights agreement of the United Nations, brought about largely through Eleanor Roosevelt. Christianity has its Golden Rule, expressed by all major beliefs and humanism, all relying on the common good, or the moral imperative. Leisure absorbs this principle.

Rationality

A third form of ethics, based on rationality, was forwarded by the American philosopher, E. A. Jordan of Butler University. Ethics, he wrote, is concerned

> with the relation of knowledge to control, and this relation rests on the nature of man and of the world in which he lives.... But its primary purpose is not to understand the relations as they are given in fact but as they are possible between man and the world, for it is this region of possible relations that imparts the action its ethical character. (Jordan, 1949, p. 3)

In other words, when a society does not make use of the knowledge that exists for moving toward desirable objectives, an unethical relationship exists between scientists or those whom Florian Znaniecki (1940) called "men of knowledge" and the policy makers. In this sense, the responsibility of those with knowledge is to produce accurate and relevant information and to make this available in understandable form to others. Men and women of knowledge, especially of the academy, are guardians of rationality.

Thus, our brief summary speaks of ethics as morality, power relationships, and the rational use of knowledge.

Next, I propose three approaches to the study of leisure: leisure as *theory*, as *action*, and as *symbol*.

Theory

The first responsibility of the leisure theorist—no matter what disciplines are involved—is the delineation of leisure among such other interests or institutions as science, religion, education, law, family, government, or economy. This major task may call upon political science, sociology, theology, history, philosophy, demography, geography, anthropology, psychology, psychiatry, or combinations of these and other disciplines. That sociologists were among the pioneers in serious studies of leisure may be historically true, but the case can also be made that until Spencer and Comte, sociology itself was born as a hybrid.

While social science theory draws upon or even rests upon such other hybrids as logic, symbolism, and empiricism, the theorists' role—not so much in the academy as in the halls of government and in the community—is to prepare tools for the actions of others: legislators, educators, parents, counselors, prison wardens, recreational leaders, the general public, and private persons. This ethical responsibility, implicit in the theorists' historic function, assumes and demands a respect for truthfulness, completeness, innovation as well as stability, and—within the traditions of the theorist's discipline—a certain objectivity. The Greek origin of ethics is *ethos* or "character."

Character, in reference to scholarship, means that integrity is not for sale, that cultural ethnocentricity is avoided as far as possible (especially since leisure studies are increasingly international), and that in leisure there is a respect for all tastes and a simultaneous respect for accumulated wisdom and moral principle. Scholarship, in our field perhaps more than others, must avoid such academic drugs as wasteful grants or the temptations of current academic fashions.

Actions

The second approach to leisure is through actions, that is, a consideration of its unlimited activities and experiences. The theorist cannot avoid categories, and we all follow Joffre Dumazedier's list of the intellectual, social, physical, and aesthetic (e.g., 1967, 1974). My 1975 book seeks to move away from this tradition, dealing instead with categories of purposes and dynamics, such as rest-restlessness or mobility-immobility (Kaplan, 1975). Recreation leaders are primarily interested in specific typologies as guides in determining training for leadership, essential equipment, appropriate spaces and times, and the self-selection by publics.

However, we must not narrow the group of recreation leaders to those who are professionally trained in universities, belong to NRPA or WLRA, or attend conferences. Among those who are taste makers for leisure activities are sports promoters, magazine editors, drug pushers, distributors of pornographic materials, owners of legitimate book stores, employees of the local press, gun distributors, astrologers, and travel agents. Collectively, they design the facilities that the rest of us use. They influence what we see, hear, and do the thousands of hours we devote annually to our private, so-called "free" periods; where we spend our evenings, weekends, vacations; even with whom, how long, at what cost, in what sequence. These makers and shakers collectively augment, supplement, and undoubtedly surpass in power and influence the more angelic souls who play for us in the Boston Symphony, organize children's games on playgrounds, and dispense library cards. As leisure activities grow in scope, those who influence the nation's leisure will not have followed our Bostonians to those lectures on heaven and hell. Ethical considerations will be at a minimum.

Symbol

The third approach to leisure is through the commitment by the public itself to symbols, especially to the so-called "leisure ethic." By this we imply that leisure as a whole has become a major value, both a means and an end. The end is seen in various ways: as a personal reward for prior hard work; as one's right to rest or play; as an inherent part of the rhythm of life; or, in the socialist agenda, as time to be devoted to study and serve an ideology.

But by the "leisure ethic" we also imply a triumph of the human will and of the industrial enterprise over work itself, based originally on survival needs and embellished later as symbolism for heavenly reward. Currently, the Japanese government is advocating more leisure for its masses, as an economic national measure; thus Japan moves toward a major social, symbolic transformation. Our transformation accompanied the rise of our industrial and economic power, an integral part of the emergence of social values; Japan, already highly developed, seeks to use leisure as a brake, a control, a policy means. Among us, leisure as end has caught up with its function as means. Scholars of leisure will have the task in the next fifty years of comparing these cultures, and perhaps modifying Max Weber in the course of this cross-cultural study.

Within our own Western cultural frame, I have a very personal reading of the leisure ethic: a theological, at least a spiritual three-act drama. Judaism in the first act set the issues, inventing through the Sabbath what Abraham Heschel has called the "architecture of time" (1951, pp. 28–29). Christianity found these issues of time, lifestyle, and rewards central to its maturity in the later centuries as capitalism and industry evolved, and relied on heavenly stimulation to confront the oppression of the have-nots by the haves. Now came, in our lifetime, a Humanism that seeks to combine the earthly orientation of Judaism and the heavenly rewards of Christianity. The day may come when some theorist expounds on leisure itself as a new religion. This new-born George Simmel of tomorrow will perhaps note the various archetypes of leisure actions—sports, arts, etc.—as quite comparable to denominations, each subsuming types of values, attracting types of minds, requiring types of sacrifices and commitments.

Already we are aware that the arts, as a leisure form, serve to link the present with past generations, as does sports. The new physics, as it matures from the infant present stage, is already speaking of a "wormhole theory," in which a "time traveler" might theoretically be able to change events of the past as an application of Einstein's theory of relativity. Already the minds of each of us are historically and laterally compartmentalized, so that our politics may be ancient, our musical tastes baroque, our attitudes about love romantic, and our worship of the gods primitive. In our work processes as we sit before a computer terminal, we may be entirely postindustrial, yet we think, pray, speak, eat, read, dress in a multitude of time levels. What the religions do, including the anticipated religion of leisure, is provide some thread of continuity; as a Jew, I find a remarkable paradox in the adaptability and usefulness of that tradition as it served through persecutions and Diaspora, a fact that will be celebrated in 1992 in the 500th observance of the Spanish Inquisitions, and now finds itself as one unique guardian of leisure in a moment of triumph for mankind. That is the ultimate significance of the leisure ethic: a celebration, a triumph over labor, a universal and democratic reaching for self-actualization on a grand scale.

Now we have seen leisure as theory, action, and symbol.

The introduction to this paper promised that following a triactic exposition of approaches to ethics and leisure, connections would be drawn between these trinities. As the skeleton for these linkages, I offer the following hypotheses, or for the more humble among us, three propositions.

1. That those among us who are primarily theorists are responsible for the ethics that Jordan talked about: the rational use of available knowledge.
2. That those among us who are primarily the policy makers, that is, those who administer or lead leisure-recreation activities, are responsible for the ethics centering on power relationships.
3. That for those among the total population who speak of the leisure ethic there is a responsibility for the general consideration of ethics centering on morality as a general postulate.

Leisure Theorists and the Ethics of Rationality

On the whole, it is my judgment that theorists of leisure have performed this ethical responsibility effectively. Any policy maker who looks into this field for such purposes as recreation programming will by now find a wealth of data amidst careful observations. For example, a quarter century ago the federal legislation concerned with the purchase of lands for national parks launched a massive collection of 22 reports for the Outdoor Recreation Resources Review Commission (1962); this led President Kennedy to establish a Department of Outdoor Recreation. Only last year, President Reagan was handed recommendations and a massive anthology of working papers by the President's Commission on Americans Outdoors (1987). On leisure in general there have been numerous reports by private and public agencies, including Harris polls, books and innumerable articles and monographs by individual scholars, and bibliographies and studies by the research committee of the International Sociological Association and by the World Leisure and Recreation Association.

The ethical aspect of these many surveys and tabulations is probably on a par, no better and no worse, with that in other social science areas. I am as guilty in the shortcomings of our field as anyone, as unethical as anyone—if that is the judgment—in missing obvious leads and closing my eyes to obvious materials. For example, with others I have often noted the reduction in the number of hours we work now in comparison with the year 1900. Almost no attention has been paid to a more significant number, that is, the expansion in the hour's potential during intervening decades (Kaplan, 1975, p. 284). Such comparisons do exist for the value of "real" money in purchasing power. Even worse, we have no quantitative or qualitative comparisons of the meanings in potential time of a day, a weekend, and, now with many retirees, a year or a decade of so-called free time. I opened these issues with Buckminster Fuller when he was carrying on his ingenious inventories of resources, but I push him far enough. Perhaps my problem was one of omission and mental laziness, more than ethics. But I turn to a more serious omission in scholarship that touches directly on the ethics of knowledge in E. Jordan's insights.

Since its publication in 1972 a massive volume has been prominent on my shelf, *The Use of Time*, a study of time budgets in 12 nations (Szalai, 1972). Its editor, the late Alexander Szalai of Hungary, and his brilliant team came up with 525 pages of text and 300 pages of tables, based on about 30,000 interviews. Over 90 basic leisure activities were named by men and women over the age of 18 in urban and suburban areas. It is a triumph of international cooperation.

Yet as I was preparing a paper for the WLRA conference last May in Lake Louise, my thinking turned to some destructive aspects of leisure. Returning to the Szalai volume, I noted that all the activities listed by the subjects, or perhaps elicited in the interviews about a specific 24-hour period, were positive, such as radio, TV, conversation, attendance at cultural events, participation in sports, and so on. Obviously, what was obtained from television or from a book may have been negative in value, but we generally accept reading per se as a good. Strangely, not a single mention was made explicitly of gang activity aimed toward fun through violence; there was no mention of drugs or alcohol or of sex whose objective was less than procreation. The word sex came up only in connection with divisions in the work place. Yet in some nations, alcoholism is openly noted as a major social problem.

In a comprehensive study these negative aspects would almost certainly come up for empirical investigation. Why did they not? Were these simple omissions of fact, or do they in some way suggest an unwillingness or hesitation for middle-class scholars to accept leisure as anything but a good? Objectivity is an ethical as well as a scientific matter. The unethical, cacophonous notes creep in when objectivity and social values become confused. Anyone who imagines that social science departments are necessarily the rational guardians of objective knowledge is not experienced in such processes as the games played for promotion, for obtaining grants, or even with interdepartmental and cross-departmental politics. But I gladly leave this aspect of scholarly life after 43 years in it to look at our second proposition.

Leisure Policy Makers and Power

These real people, both the leaders-organizers and the public-clients, are in hospitals, workplaces, prisons, parks, concert halls, community centers, nursing homes, schools, campsites, gambling halls, movie houses, sports arenas, taverns, drug gatherings, bridge tournaments, chess matches, alleyways, alongside rivers or lakes, and on the mountains. They are in every home.

Some of the directors, leaders, planners, or promoters of this mélange of leisure pursuits and settings are trained for their jobs. If they think of themselves and are considered by others as "professional persons" they are aware of ethical codes; they come to conferences of their peers; they have come out of institutions of higher learning and have supposedly been exposed to principles of human relationships; they have been observed in practical situations before getting their degrees or certificates.

However, the great bulk of leaders or policy makers for so-called leisure, in rational or cultural settings, have little or no training or intellectual and moral perspectives; their indoctrination is in arranging trips for tourists, managing a movie house, or selling sports equipment. Ethical perspectives may be vaguely present in the recesses of their minds and not at all in those of the corporation executives who touch on such services. An example is in order.

The planners of the 1981 White House Conference on Aging subcontracted with the U.S. Department of Labor for a study of the desirable specifications for the position of recreation director in a nursing home, even though only 5 percent of our elderly live in private or public nursing homes. The issue was, what is the need for professional leadership in such situations, and how is the need being presently filled? The data became clear: that administrators in such institutions were most often ignoring the recreation profession or the guidelines laid down by gerontologists, and simply pulling in so-called recreation leaders off the street, with little or no training, at minimum wages. Those of us called in for consultation by the Department agreed that much of the fault lies at the door of the recreation profession for its lack of political savvy in obtaining licensing legislation, familiar for such workers as cosmotologists and barbers.

Permit an example of successful political action, theoretical planning, and the close cooperation of several professions. Those who joined in their efforts to transform a 4.7-mile strip of desolated and crime-ridden land of South Boston into a 55-acre park included recreationists, landscape architects, social workers, engineers, horticulturists, social workers, and engineers. According to a report in the *New York Times* of October 13, 1988, teenagers now bicycle along paths planted with trees and bushes, young men shoot baskets beside the rolling lawn of a church, and children play in a nearby sandlot.

Somehow, having known this desolated area when I lived in Boston, this transformation to me is an ethical as well as a social, physical affirmation of vision. It was surely based upon a creative, constructive relationship of power on both political and professional levels, turned to the good of the powerless residents of the inner city.

Perhaps the central issue that penetrates the second proposition—the profession and the public—focuses on social class, race, and ethnic differences. Philosophically, as noted earlier, Martin Buber (1937) conceptualized the broad dichotomy as the "I-thou." Politically, we are in UNESCO territory of the difference between the democratization of culture and cultural democracy. In vernacular terms, to what extent should leisure activities be funded and transmitted from the standards and values of this profession; to what extent is there the fundamental respect for indigenous values of the segments being served? This is an issue that concerns public educators as well. One example is the hot dispute over bilingual education. The vast array of actions that we call leisure or recreation includes the full range of elitism and mass or popular culture, from the viewpoints of de Tocqueville to William Morris.

In practical terms, this ethical issue came to a climax in the United States when we left the assimilationist values that my immigrant parents embraced at the turn of the century and moved into a pluralistic "black is beautiful" value structure of recent times. As to the relevance of leisure and recreation, I remind you that soon after the 1948 desegregation ruling by the Supreme Court, public recreation was singled out for a parallel decision.

The more direct implication of ethics to many of you in the profession arises from tighter public funding and the consequent movement of trained persons to the private sector such as theme parks and company controlled programs. I am employed, say, by IBM or 3-M, both known for their advanced employees recreation programs. I ask for a sizeable sum to hire a top recreation person, but the company is cutting budgets; I am asked to find a recent graduate. What balance do I come to, short of leaving the job? At what personal risk shall I insist that the corporation should install safer equipment?

Other fields face similar issues, as with the *Atlanta Constitution*, where an innovative editor resigned when he was chastised internally for investigative reports on the differences in bank loan policies for blacks and for whites of that city. Ronald Riggins, in the October 1988 *Journal of Physical Education, Recreation and Dance*, had advice of sorts to his profession. "Our task," he wrote, "is to balance the need to address economic exigency with a renewed commitment to the significant service mission to which our profession is called" (Riggins, 1988). I sought to find this "balance" on one occasion when I requested a larger budget for one of my projects; but before appealing to the dean I had offers for two other positions in hand.

Still without a satisfactory answer to the issue of professional security vis-à-vis ethics, I turn to the third proposition. It reads, "That for those among the total population who speak of the leisure ethic there is a responsibility for the general consideration of ethics centering on morality as a general postulate."

Leisure Publics and Morality

This, of course, is the most nebulous and important of the three propositions. It speaks to cultural values, to all segments of the population. While leisure theorists number a few hundred, recreation administrators and leaders some thousands, the consumers or participants of leisure are all of us, all 246 million.

The key phrase widely used to cover the collective desire for control over our own time is the "leisure ethic," as opposed to another popular phrase, the "work ethic." Both are vague terms, denoting leisure or work as ends, purposes, major objectives. We have no catchy word about the leisure fanatic to match "workaholic" yet there have always been and still are those whose lifestyle has focused on play. Perhaps this has been implicit historically in the category of the "upper-class," who have proverbially found others to work for them. John Galbraith has observed that to the rich the work ethic is for the poor. Bernard Shaw thought of the worker walking and the nobleman riding in his distinction of English classes as the "equestrians" and the "pedestrians." If they could express themselves thus, the milk horse and the polo horse could have their say.

Yet the dichotomy of work and leisure has, since the Industrial Revolution, become too complex, psychologically and productively, for such simplicity. The bosses too often are the workaholics; the workers are guaranteed paid vacations and retirement benefits by the government. France, long ago, had a month paid vacation for everyone by law. In much of Socialist society, the guilds or labor associations maintain their own facilities, such as those I have enjoyed on Lake Beleton in Hungary. Japan, just now, is officially encouraging new attitudes toward leisure as an economic policy. The Third World has begun to pay attention to this matter in the face of its larger proportion of elderly and the formation of ideologies about work as they modernize.

In the industrial societies, moral attitudes toward work and leisure passed through several stages: free time as a *reward*, then as a *right*, and finally as a *resolution* or *realization*. To trace this progression would take a review of labor history, religious history, the story of the middle classes, the struggle for equality of women, the emergence of industrial psychology, the fashions of therapy and psychiatry, and the gradual but difficult enlightenment of capital and industrial managers. My feeling is that while attitudes toward leisure as a reward, right, or realization will continue, no matter how many hours we work, the next stage will turn to leisure as a means of adjustments in the economy aimed at special needs and populations. I have in mind the latest concern for women in America, based on the so-called "momma's track." To assure their equal rights—which of course they still do not have in much of our management areas—it is now suggested that women fall into two categories, those with or without concerns for family needs. The answer has been known throughout Europe for some decades, but as our experience vis-à-vis the Japanese has amply illustrated, American businessmen are sometimes strangely bereft of common sense in relation to their employees. They have yet to master a fundamental fact, that people work best when they want to work. The principle of flexible work schedules has not yet penetrated here, as it has in central Europe. This principle, if applied to the entire work force wherever feasible, takes women off the hook, and enlarges life's possibilities for men as well.

But I and others have made several dollars from the stupidity of even America's largest corporations, feeding them information that we were teaching in introductory courses of sociology. Among such information is the simple fact that leisure and work attitudes and values are related, that 3-M and IBM and Phillips are not visionary but practical when they take an interest in the full life of their employees. American industry will match its competition only if it takes new directions, not only with the Japanese and their effective constellation of capital-management-workers-government but, after 1992, vis-à-vis the European Common

Market. Among the new directions must be more than the ethics that have been exposed in recent years, ethics of greed, ethics of nonconcern with the human aspects that often accompany mergers, or ethics that include enormous waste and chicanery in military contracts. American ethics for business must move into a concern for the honesty that the Iaccocos hear about on Sunday morning in their suburban pews, but more, for the concern with the total cultural, educational, and family life of their workers. The observations of O'Toole's task force (1971) on the dissatisfactions in the work place are as important to America's industrial future as the next handbook on the next computerized system for their productive network.

Without this social and ethical transformation among those who control our lives economically, there is some nebulousness in talking about the ethics of leisure and life for the millions whose lives are at the mercy of the economic forces. That we are the master of our souls, the captain of our ships, has long been a poetic sentiment worthy of romantic trash in the drugstore literature or in soap operas. Yet whatever freedoms the average person has, aside from those that can be obtained through the ballot box, through unionization, or through direct action as in civil rights struggles, will come in good part from the uses that Americans will make of the leisure facilities and experiences. That is where the personal and the social come together. That is where there are greater opportunities for choice than in the work areas of life.

I plead that this conference not get bogged down from the beginning in a concentration entirely on the individual as the actor. Yet the conference will be right to recognize that it is in private action that most of us have some voice, if at the same time it is more than isolated in its consequences, even in its conception. We will be right to ask the questions, how do I choose the uses of my freedoms, how do I apply my skills, what commitments do I make? What satisfactions do I expect or desire as I fiddle or travel, or watch, or hear, or paint, or drink, or read, or walk, or catch butterflies, or write a poem, or flirt, or drug myself, or simply sit? Each has meanings, each falls into or violates some ethical concepts that lie dormant in the back of my mind.

The study of this ethical presence in a field of human activity that has seemed to be free of responsibility is perhaps the next major stage in our leisure studies. It will be a far more difficult stage than the gathering of data, the creation of tables and models. Finally, it will take us out of the dominant purview of one discipline, and even of social science alone. Philosophy, even ideology, will again resume a rightful place in future discussions of leisure, taking us full circle to the *paidia* of the Greeks and the "architecture of time" that came from the Judaic perception of the cosmos and life.

References

Becker, H. (1950). *Through values to social interpretation.* Durham, NC: Duke University Press.

Bierstedt, R. (1957). *The social order.* New York: McGraw-Hill.

Buber, M. (1937). *I and thou* (R.G. Smith, Trans.). Edinburgh: T. Clark.

de Grazia, S. (1962). *Of time, work and leisure.* New York: Twentieth Century Fund.

Dumazedier, J. (1967). *Toward a society of leisure?* New York: Free Press.

Dumazedier, J. (1974). *The sociology of leisure.* New York, Elsevier.

Heschel, A.J. (1951). *Man is not alone: A philosophy of religion.* New York: Jewish Publication Society.

Huizinga, J. (1950). *Homo ludens: A study of the play element in culture.* Boston: Beacon.

Jordan, E.A. (1949). *The good life.* Chicago: University of Chicago Press.

Kaplan, M. (1975/1985). *Leisure: Theory and policy.* New York: John Wiley; Springfield, IL: Charles Thomas.

Macarov, D. (1980). *Work and welfare, the unholy alliance.* Beverly Hills, CA: Sage Publications.

Macarov, D. (1982). *Worker productivity.* Beverly Hills, CA: Sage Publications.

Mills, C.W. (1959). *The sociological imagination.* New York: Oxford.

O'Toole, J. (1971). *Work in America.* Report of the Special Task Force to the Secretary of Health, Education and Welfare. Cambridge, MA: MIT Press.

Outdoor Recreation Resources Review Commission. (1962). *Trends in American living and outdoor recreation.* Washington, DC: U.S. Government Printing Office.

Parker, S.R. (1971). *The future of work and leisure.* London: MacGibbon and Kee.

President's Commission on Americans Outdoors. (1987). *A literature review.* Washington, DC: U.S. Government Printing Office.

Riggins, R. (1988). Social responsibility and the public sector entrepreneur. *Journal of Physical Education, Recreation, and Dance, 59* (8).

Sorokin, P. (1956). *Fads and foibles in modern sociology.* New York: Regnery.

Szalai, A. (1972). *The use of time: Daily activities of urban and suburban populations in twelve countries.* The Hague: Mouton.

Valentini, N., & di Meglio, C. (1974). *Sex and the confessional.* London: Hutchinson and Co.

Weber, M. (1946). Science as a vocation, in H.H. Gerth & C.W. Mills (Eds.), *From Max Weber: Essays in sociology.* New York: Oxford University Press.

Znaniecki, F. (1934). *The method of sociology.* New York: Farr and Rinehart.

Znaniecki, F. (1940). *The social role of the man of knowledge.* New York: Columbia University Press.

Znaniecki, F. (1952). *Cultural sciences: Their origin and development.* Urbana: University of Illinois Press.

On Liberty and Leisure

John M. Charles

Josef Pieper leads the reader into his essay, *Leisure, the Basis of Culture* (1952), by asking why we should take time from the busy processes of the work world to reflect on the philosophy of leisure. How can we justify diverting our attention away from the mainstream of life to such a tributary as leisure? Education, like leisure, has frequently been viewed in its checkered past as an adornment to civilization, an afterthought when creating a culture. For example, King William and Queen Mary were probably perplexed at the persistent entreaties about that very subject by one of their transplanted citizens, an irascible Anglican clergyman, who they would have probably preferred to have been more preoccupied with building the religious foundation of their new colony than pestering them about education. Nevertheless, James Blair prevailed and on February 8, 1693, the College of William and Mary was granted a royal charter to provide "a certain place of universal study." Blair's vision and persistence began a tradition of educating eminent citizens, senators, judges, presidents, and the like from William and Mary and colleges country-wide who have collectively shaped the face of this nation.

Yet the impact of education is dependent upon leisure. Much as we have found leisure in order to discuss leisure, the interlude in life that constitutes higher education is a period of time away from the vicissitudes of the daily regimen of the work world. No wonder that leisure and education are linked at the semantic hip, school meaning leisure in Greek (*schole*) and Latin (*scola*). This link should not be attributed to a quirk of lexicographical evolution but to a fundamental interrelationship. Pieper (1952) is one theorist who recognizes that education and leisure share a common purpose: the honing of wholeness. He says that "education concerns the whole man" and then uses the same cri-

47

terion of "wholeness" as the basis of genuine leisure, which he describes as "a mental and spiritual attitude."

He suggests that "because wholeness is what man strives for, the power to achieve leisure is one of the fundamental powers of the human soul." In other words, both education and leisure provide what Pieper calls "a gateway to freedom." Through education, the whole man is able "to grasp the totality of existing things." Through leisure, man is freed "to grasp the world as a whole and realize his full potentialities as an entity meant to reach wholeness."

In other words, education and leisure can offer the participant the opportunity to strive for wholeness along two dimensions, those of vision and self-development. Both education and leisure provide vistas of opportunity that may lead to a more holistic world view and a fuller sense of self. To fully appreciate the potential of leisure as a gateway to such growth, it must be construed as a dynamic process, as an activity, as more than a state of mind. Baker further delineated this distinction in *The Politics of Aristotle* (1946), when he said that "leisure (*schole*) is not contrasted with activity. It is itself activity, and the highest form of activity, the activity of the part of the soul which possesses rational principle." It is furthermore an activity that is premised upon freedom, the liberty to grow, but not according to another's definition, not to reach some extrinsic goal. John Stuart Mill seems to embrace a similar perspective when he suggests in *On Liberty* (1956) that, "Human nature is not a machine to be built after a model, and set to do exactly the work prescribed for it, but a tree, which requires to grow and develop itself on all sides, according to the tendency of the inward forces which make it a living thing."

Given this symmetry of perspective, could Mill's utilitarian purpose be adapted as an ethical basis for leisure services? What repercussions would the adoption of utilitarianism have for the AALR Applied Strategic Plan (1988), the leisure professional, and leisure programing? The American Association for Leisure and Recreation has developed a mission statement, one which includes commitment "to uplifting the human spirit and all human endeavor by promoting through leisure enjoyment of life." This emphasis upon bringing about the greatest happiness of the greatest number echoes the moral purpose proposed by Jeremy Bentham and explicated by John Stuart Mill in *Utilitarianism* (1959). Not, of course, that Mill should be considered as progenitor of this moral purpose but as one in a line of philosophers basking in the reflected glow of Aristotle's often repeated message in the *Nicomachean Ethics* (1962) that happiness is the highest good, that it is an end in itself, and that the well-spring of happiness is virtue. Furthermore, in his distinction between civility (a person's ability to behave in a responsible manner) and polity (the highest calling of a civilized person),

Aristotle laid the foundation for Mill's twin emphasis upon the development of individual character and public service.

In developing this Aristotelian premise to focus the happiness principle upon a relatively modern industrialized society, Mill's perspective may be instructive when considering the value of a utilitarian ethic for leisure today. Mill was more than a theorist; he was a believer in utilitarianism, and hence his devotion to the principle of utility, which he regarded "as the ultimate appeal on all ethical questions," and his adoption of theological terminology to describe utilitarianism as "a creed," "a doctrine," and "a religion." The focal point of the creed that Mill found so persuasive is "the greatest happiness principle," which holds that "actions are right in proportion as they tend to promote happiness; wrong as they tend to produce the reverse of happiness."

Although he defined happiness as "intended pleasure and the absence of pain" and unhappiness as "pain and the privation of pleasure," he was quick to point out that he did not intend that pleasure should be understood as an ignoble ideal. Much as Huizinga (1950) sought to distinguish "noble" play from "the trivial recreation and crude sensationalism" of "puerilism" and Pieper made a distinction between leisure as a gateway to wholeness and leisure as idleness, Mill construed pleasures to be "more elevated than the animal appetites." Indeed he bridled at the criticism of his theory as being essentially Epicurean arguing that "there is no known Epicurean theory of life which does not assign to the pleasures of the intellect, of the feelings and imagination, and of the moral sentiments a much higher value as pleasures than to those of mere sensation." Thus, he established a hierarchy of pleasures. Selection between these pleasures should be based upon personal taste and should lead to the good of the larger community. Mill contends that choices should be based not only on "the agent's own greatest happiness, but the greatest amount of happiness altogether."

To help distinguish between options on a qualitative basis, Mill suggested that the public should turn to the competent judge, a role which should be assumed by the leisure professional, one who has influence over the choices and decisions of people at leisure. This leisure professional may fulfill the dual function of educator and resource. Mill suggests that until children reach maturity, competent judges can paternalistically impose their wisdom upon them in the hope that they may inculcate values and decision-making criteria that may stay with the individuals as they age. As the individuals reach maturity and are able to make informed and rational decisions, the role of the competent judge changes from teacher to resource person, available but not intrusive. Given the responsibility of providing leisure services and guiding clients through a maze of alternative pathways to recreation, how should leisure professionals be prepared for their vocation? Are graduates emerging from colleges with a degree in recreation and allied fields today ready to minister to the leisure needs of the general public?

Beyond the needs of the public for renewal, the rediscovery of potential, and the reaffirmation of worth, leisure also serves as a vehicle for play. Through the ages, play has profoundly affected the face of civilization. Two thousand years ago Plato answered the question "What then is the right way of living?" by responding in *Laws* that "Life must be lived as play." More recently Huizinga came to the conclusion that "real civilization cannot exist in the absence of a certain play-element." The guidance given by these competent judges can effect the civilizing function of play invoked by Huizinga and may mold leisure into "the preserve of freedom, of education and culture, and of that undiminished humanity which views the world as a whole" recognized by Pieper. Professional preparation that is primarily pragmatic, technical, and administrative in focus would seem inadequate to cope with such profound issues. As Goodale and Witt suggest in their critique of recreation today, "Professionalism, registration/certification, accreditation and professional preparation receive more attention than issues of 'where to, what next,' 'how do we get there from here,' and more importantly 'why?' "

A concentration emphasizing philosophy and critical cultural consciousness, combined with a variety of field experiences through which to ground the theory would better prepare the competent judge. So says Mill, who relegates vicarious theoretical knowledge to below the authority of experience. He says, "On a question which is the best worth having of two pleasures ... the judgment of those who are qualified by knowledge of both must be admitted as final." To temper the insights based on experience Mill requires competent judges to have habits of self-consciousness and self-observation. So preparation of leisure professionals in Mill's mold would blend a focus on critical sensitivity through philosophy with frequent opportunities to test those principles in actual situations.

Although I do not intend to endorse their overall position, Russell Jacoby (1987) and Allan Bloom (1987) do seem to have struck a responsive chord in contemporary educational criticism. One of their themes seems to reflect Mill's philosophy. Jacoby, in lamenting the passing of *The Last Intellectuals*, is disturbed that specialization and vested interest within universities is depriving the culture of the Renaissance scope of understanding so important to the competent judge. Similarly, in *The Closing of the American Mind*, Bloom is critical of the disintegration of higher education into discrete competitive compartments, an alienating experience for the undergraduate attempting to gain the breadth of insight that transcends departmental boundaries. This student must "navigate among a collection of carnival barkers, each trying to lure him into a particular side-show." He continues that "this undecided student is an embarrassment to most universities, because he seems to be saying I am a whole human being. Help me to form myself in my wholeness and let me develop my real potential, and he is the one to whom they have nothing to say." This problem can only be resolved by reaching beyond disciplinary boundaries and even beyond the confines of the ivory tower. If we are to accept Mill's utilitarian vision, competent judges must be furnished with more than the tools of the trade. Their preparation should be holistic in nature, encompassing moral purpose, metaphysical analysis of play, leisure and recreation, understanding of culture and of civilization, interpersonal skills ranging through teaching, counseling, and communication techniques, and a plethora of theory-based field experiences.

At this point in the argument, we have recognized the importance of leisure as "one of the foundations of western culture" and the onus which that places upon the community of scholars to focus upon the moral purpose of leisure. Mill's utilitarian "greatest happiness principle" refined through the perspective of Pieper produces an emphasis upon freedom and wholeness in leisure. Leisure professionals may help individuals to select appropriate pathways to wholeness as they pass through the gateway of freedom to the extent that they can share their dilemma of choice and have developed perspicacity. However, a major quandary faces the leisure professions: the nature and extent of guidance and restrictions that leisure professionals should exert upon the mature, rational individual at leisure. Goodale and Witt (1980) raise the spectre of paternalism when they ask whether leisure professionals, the competent judges in Mill's scenario, "can mandate what people should do according to some notion of social utility, personal well-being, wholesome involvement, human experience." How intrusive should the leisure professional be in actualizing the goals of the AALR, which are to promote "self-determination and independence, intellectual growth, creativity, positive mental health, physical fitness, self-discovery, exploration, and individual group and family well-being."

It can be argued that the extremes of authoritarian paternalism and laissez-faire anarchy should be avoided at any cost. The visions of technocentric recreation (Charles, 1979) characterized by mechanistic, reproducible, measurable programs producing stereotypical attitudes and behavior that I raised a decade ago still haunt the dusty library shelves. Equally disturbing is the other extreme, a world of leisure out of control, the play-world that Huizinga labels puerilism. He calls it "that blend of adolescence and barbarity which has been rampant all over the world for the last two or three decades." Fifty years later, Huizinga's fears of a disintegration of the world of play have not been assuaged. The leisure habits that disturbed him most are waxing still; witness the "gregariousness" of the modern day soccer fans, the "insatiable thirst for trivial recreation" exemplified in a culture of pac man and pinball, and the "crude sensationalism" of a growing cadre of cheap-thrill seekers.

Given that both of these trends are anathema to the leisure services that subscribe to the wholesome image of leisure portrayed by the AALR, what recourse should the profession have to remedy the situation? Intervention in the cycle of choice between leisure pleasures may take the form of persuasion or coercion through words and deeds. Persuasion may range from educational advice to directives, reinforced through a system of rewards and punishments given an aura of credibility by the expert status of the professional. Persuasion may also take the situational form of manipulation of the play or leisure environment, alignment of the administrative structure and organizational methodology of leisure services with a preferred ideology. Coercion may take the form of plans, rules, and regulations that must be obeyed by people at leisure.

To illustrate paternalism through statute, consider this list of laws which impinge upon leisure. They include:

1. Laws requiring motorcyclists to wear safety helmets when operating their machines, or mandating that boaters must wear flotation devices.
2. Laws forbidding persons from swimming at a public beach when lifeguards are not on duty.
3. Laws making it illegal for women, children, or other special groups to play certain sports or at certain locations.
4. Laws regulating certain kinds of sexual conduct, e.g., homosexuality among consenting adults in private.
5. Laws regulating the use of certain drugs, such as performance-enhancing steroids, which may have harmful consequences to the user, but may not lead to anti-social conduct.
6. Laws requiring a license to engage in certain professions with those not receiving a license subject to fine or jail sentence if they do engage in the practice. Although few recreation professions are as stringent as to prosecute for failure to have acquired certain certifications, an accident within a program supervised by an individual without appropriate qualifications (e.g., WSI for swimming) is grounds for a negligence suit.
7. Laws forbidding various forms of gambling (often justified on the grounds of protecting the poor who cannot afford this choice of pleasure).

In addition to laws that attach criminal or civil penalties to certain kinds of action, there are rules, regulations, and decrees that make it either difficult or impossible for people to carry out their plans and that are also justified on paternalistic grounds. Examples of this are:

1. Requiring members of certain athletic communities to submit to compulsory drug testing.
2. Tampering with or restricting the use of natural resources such as water by (a) putting fluorides in the community water supply, or (b) prohibiting recreational swimming or windsurfing in a public reservoir.
3. Restricting visitation hours and imposing a curfew on the leisure time of a student body.

Recently the College of William and Mary student newspaper, *The Flat Hat* (1989, January), took the editorial position that Boston University administrators were trying to legislate moral behavior in the leisure time of students in order "to align a student's living environment with B.U.'s academic and intellectual mission." The editorial's conclusion was "long live self-determination," which echoes the call of the AALR for self-determination and independence, yet how can these qualities be reconciled with group and family well-being when they might lead to chaos and conflict?

In *On Liberty*, Mill sides, within limits, with individual rights: "There needs protection also against the tyranny of the prevailing opinion and feeling, against the tendency of society to impose, by other means than civil penalties, its own ideas and practices as rules of conduct on those who dissent from them." The implied strategy of this perspective for the leisure profession is to create autonomous individuals through respecting their liberty rather than intervening to force clients to conform to some notion of happiness or safety. However, Mill does recognize that occasionally intervention may be justified: "There is a limit to the legitimate interference of collective opinion with individual independence; and to find that limit, and maintain it against encroachment, is as indispensable to a good condition of human affairs as protection against political despotism."

Thus Mill introduces his "one very simple principle" in which he rejects paternalism except to prevent harm to others. Paternalism may be defined absolutely as any action that infringes upon the personal liberty of an individual: the "hard" antipaternalistic approach of Richard Arneson (1979), that "paternalistic policies are restrictions on a person's liberty which are justified exclusively by consideration for that person's own good or welfare and which are carried out either against his present will or against his prior commitment." Alternately, the interpretation suggested by Joel Feinberg (1971) would allow the leisure professional more leeway to intervene in an individual's leisure choices. Within this "soft" antipaternalism, Feinberg suggests that "The state has a right to prevent self-regarding harmful conduct only when it is substantially nonvoluntary or when temporary intervention is necessary to establish whether it is voluntary or not."

What are the implications of Mill's utilitarian principle for leisure policy? To realize the AALR's goals of self-determination, independence, creativity, self-discovery, and exploration, the mature, civilized, sane individual should be accorded total liberty in self-regarding choices. In other words, the right to select a lifestyle by choosing between leisure pleasures is sacrosanct, even though it may be self-destructive and lead to unhappiness, providing these choices bear no negative ramifications for others. The leisure professional, the competent judge, must therefore allow adult clients to make their own mistakes, should counsel rather than dictate, peruse rather than police, and be a positive resource rather than an intrusive martinet. For as Mills says: "It is the privilege and proper condition of a human being, arrived at the maturity of his faculties, to use and interpret experience in his own way. It is for him to find out what part of recorded experience is properly applicable to his own circumstances and character."

However, the leisure professions do have a role in guiding the decisions of the public, for Mill considers that even self-regarding choices should be informed and rational. Thus the leisure professional, sensing that a client is not basing a choice upon all the evidence available or is acting in an irrational manner, may intercede in an effort to acquaint that individual with alternative choices including those higher in the hierarchy of pleasures. The competent judge could intervene on behalf of the individual's well-being in some predicaments. These might include lack of knowledge of a situation, such as the depth of water in a pool before diving, the perception of irrationality of an individual leading to a reduced decision-making capacity, and those situations where the subject gives expressed or tacit consent to the leisure professional to intervene.

Nevertheless, the utilitarian leisure professional would basically encourage the liberty of self-determination through leisure and allow liberty in leisure to encompass any self-regarding behavior. Mill's "harm principle" suggests a very different standard for evaluating "other-regarding" behavior. Since human beings rarely conduct their daily business in a vacuum, most leisure choices will affect people in the vicinity. Consequently, it is important to define the limits of harmful other-regarding behavior in order to define the legitimate parameters of intrusion into the leisure choices of the public.

Mill takes the position that the society should intercede "as soon as any part of a person's conduct affects prejudicially the interests of others" or when a person fails to "bear his share of the labors and sacrifices incurred for defending the society or its members from injury and molestation." Thus, to paraphrase one of Mill's examples; no person ought to be punished simply for being drunk, but a recreation center pool manager should be punished for being drunk on duty. Mill's rationale is that "whenever there is a definite damage, or a definite risk of damage, either to an individual or to the public, the case is taken out of the province of liberty and placed in that of morality or law." But until the act crosses the boundary from self-regarding to other-regarding behavior he finds quite reprehensible such infringements of personal liberty as that of the colonists in prohibiting alcoholic beverages or as that of puritans in putting down "all public and nearly all private amusements; especially music, dancing, public games, or other assemblages for purposes of diversion, and the theater."

The challenge confronting the leisure professional eager to maximize personal liberty while at the same time protecting public interest is to distinguish the boundaries of harm. Safety regulations designed to protect others from dangerous physical harm seem to be permissible within the utilitarian framework, but how offensive must a physically non-threatening act become before it warrants regulatory interdiction? Feinberg (1971) summarized the determinants of the seriousness of an offense as being the magnitude of the offense (by which he meant intensity, duration, and extent), the standard of reasonable avoidability (could it be avoided?), the Volenti maxim (was it voluntarily incurred?), and the discounting of abnormal susceptibilities. In other words, if the conduct of an individual at leisure "affects prejudicially the interests of others by, for instance, affronting their senses, disgusting and revolting them, shocking their moral, religious or patriotic sensibilities, embarrassing, frightening or humiliating them in a major, unavoidable intrusive way it may be deemed harmful behavior and thus merit paternalistic intercession."

Mill appears willing to authorize intervention in the actions of people at leisure that are "directly injurious only to the agents themselves, but which, if done publicly, are a violation of good manners and, coming thus within the category of offenses against others, may rightly be prohibited." He classifies offenses against decency as an example of this category, but declines to dwell upon what constitutes decency. While the leisure professional would rightly be concerned with protecting the sensibilities of the general public from indecency and public offense, the interpretation of this, and all fringe issues of soft paternalism, should be consistent with the spirit of utilitarianism. Because offense and decency are relative terms, varying through cultures, attitudes, and time, potentially outrageous or offensive situations such as public nudity or choice of epithets should be evaluated on an individual basis. For example, the Millian utilitarian should only impose a ban on nude windsurfing if it were known that such an activity would certainly cause offense to others in the vicinity. The concern of the utilitarian for personal liberty would preempt legal moralism: a coercive system of rules and regulations designed to legislate moral behavior.

Through this discussion, I have endeavored to suggest that in clarifying their professional ethics, the leisure professions can adopt Millian utilitarianism to their purpose. Leisure may be a painting without a purpose, music without melody, unless a unifying principle is defined and refined. Utilitarianism is largely in tune with the professed purposes of the profession. Its adoption would help in repelling the incursions of current cultural pervasive forces such as capitalism and technology.

McNeill's (1987) concerns about the direction of wellness may ripple out to all facets of leisure unless leisure professionals rally behind a common purpose: "We are pawns in the hands of industry where corporate profits dictate corporate practices, where utilitarianism appears to be essentially extinct and the phoenix of corporate existentialism has arisen from its ashes." Linked to the profit motive, competition, and the desire for progress is the incursion of technology into play and leisure practice. Huizinga laments that the play in sport is being engulfed by technology: "In the case of sport we have an activity nominally known as play but raised to such a pitch of technical organization and scientific thoroughness that the real play-spirit is threatened with extinction."

Jacques Ellul (1967) paints an even more morose picture of the impact of technology upon the autonomy of the individual in *The Technological Society:* "The human being is delivered helpless, in respect to life's most important and trivial affairs to a power (technology) which is in no sense under his control. For there can be no question today of man's controlling the milk he drinks or the bread he eats, any more than of his controlling his government."

Utilitarianism, with its emphasis upon the cultivation of both individuality and social conscientiousness, provides a basis for leisure that may, at least partially, offset the impact of such dehumanizing forces as competitive capitalism and technology. However, the adoption of this ethical position will entail certain adaptations in the nature of the professional preparation of leisure professionals and will require continuing deliberation of unresolved dilemmas revolving around the hierarchy of pleasures, the role of the competent judge, and paternalism.

Despite the problems inherent in bringing the leaders of the diverse leisure profession together, in agreeing to adopt a unified position, and in adapting a philosophy to principles of action, the correlation between the underlying principles of Millian utilitarianism and the professed purpose of the AALR warrants a concerted effort to reach a consensus of interpretation of *Utilitarianism, On Liberty,* and leisure.

References

American Association for Leisure and Recreation. (1988). *Applied strategic plan.* Reston, VA: AALR.

Aristotle. (1962). *Nicomachean ethics.* Indianapolis: Bobbs Merrill.

Arneson, R. (1979). Mill versus paternalism, *Philosophy Research Archives.*

Baker, E. (1946). *The politics of Aristotle.* London: Oxford University Press.

Bloom, A. (1987). *The closing of the American mind.* New York: Simon and Schuster.

Charles, J. (1979). Technocentric ideology in physical education. *Quest, 31,* 2.

Ellul, J. (1967). *The technological society.* New York: Vintage Books.

Feinberg, J. (1971). Legal paternalism. *Canadian Journal of Philosophy, 1,* 7–9.

Goodale, T., & Witt, P. (Eds.). (1980). *Recreation and leisure: Issues in an era of change.* State College, PA: Venture Publishing.

Jacoby, R. (1987). *The last intellectuals.* New York: Basic Books.

Huizinga, J. (1950). *Homo ludens, a study of the play-element in culture.* Boston: Beacon Press.

McNeill, A. (1987). Wellness programs and their influence on professional preparation. In J. Massengale (Ed.), *Trends toward the future in physical education.* Champaign, IL: Human Kinetics.

Mill, J. (1956). *On liberty.* Indianapolis: Bobbs Merrill.

Mill, J. (1959). *Utilitarianism.* New York: Macmillan.

Pieper, J. (1952). *Leisure, the basis of culture.* New York: Pantheon Books.

Leisure and Democracy: Incompatible Ideals?

John L. Hemingway

"There are no longer protagonists; there is only the chorus."
J. Ortega y Gasset, *The Revolt of the Masses*

Is Aristotelian leisure compatible with liberal democracy? This paper chooses an Aristotelian perspective on leisure and thus adopts a critical stance toward liberal democracy. It does so in the belief that the aspirations of Aristotelian leisure are lofty and coherent, offering a path to the elevation of human activity, community, and spirit, a path presently closed off by liberal democratic theory and practice. It is this paper's purpose to suggest how this is the case.

The argument proceeds in several stages. The first presents a reading of Aristotelian leisure significantly different from that generally received in the study of leisure, but one more in keeping with what Aristotle actually wrote and closer to contemporary Aristotelian scholarship. The need for such reinterpretation has been argued elsewhere (Hemingway, 1988); here it will suffice to outline its substance. The second stage reviews selected elements in liberal democratic theory as it has evolved since the seventeenth century. This task is made manageable by drawing on the work of political theorist C. B. Macpherson (1962, 1973, 1977), who has undertaken an ongoing critical exploration of the genesis and present state of liberal democracy. The third stage surveys the results of recent qualitative examinations of liberal democratic society in the United States. This review reinforces the conclusion, based on the preceding analysis, that Aristotelian leisure and liberal democracy are indeed incompatible. This incompatibility rests on the fundamental divergences in their conceptions of human essence and purpose, and the qualitative studies will further reveal that the liberal democratic conception has worked its way out in ways not unexpected by Aristotle himself, as well as by Macpherson and other theorists. That this affects leisure in ways antithetical to the Aristotelian conception is made clear in the concluding section.

Before proceeding, there is one item to be cleared away. A major objection to the Aristotelian conception of leisure is the inclusion in Aristotle's thinking of slavery and a narrowly circumscribed citizenry. These are, surely, towering obstacles to any complete acceptance of his thinking. Still, scholars of leisure (e.g., Dare, Welton, & Coe, 1987, p.39; Kraus, 1984, pp. 42–43; Murphy, 1981, p. 24) have been too quick to suggest that Aristotelian leisure is unrealizable in contemporary society primarily because of them. The argument here is that when we separate these objectionable features out of Aristotle, there remains within liberal democracy and its concrete working out an impetus against Aristotelian leisure, and further that this, rather than any peculiarly Greek conditions (absent slavery and restricted citizenship), prevents the realization of Aristotelian leisure. Thus it is possible to stipulate at the outset an absolute rejection of slavery and imposed elitism, to go on to argue for the widest spread of Aristotelian leisure, and yet to conclude that the onus for its ultimate impossibility rests on liberal democratic theory and practice.

The Aristotelian Conception of Leisure

The prevailing interpretations of Aristotle on leisure are not satisfactory.[1] These couple a rejection of his endorsement of slavery and elitism with the observation that they are intended to provide the opportunity for an elite to undertake philosophical contemplation, which is regarded as the highest form of leisure activity (see the citations immediately above). Without the leisure created by the labor of slaves and the presence of noncitizens to carry out daily tasks, there could be no opportunity for an elite to devote itself to the pleasures of contemplation. Were contemplation indeed the content of Aristotelian leisure, this approach would be irrefutable, so that the impossibility of achieving Aristotelian leisure under modern conditions would lie within that conception of leisure itself.

Such contemplation is not, however, the content of Aristotelian leisure, or, alternatively, it is but a part of a much broader concept. Scholars of leisure have been misled by an uncritical acceptance of Pieper's

---

[1]Material included in this section appeared originally in my "Leisure and Civility: Reflections on a Greek Ideal," *Leisure Sciences, 10* (1988), pp. 179–191 (Taylor & Francis, Publishers). Permission to extract it here is gratefully acknowledged.

(1952) eloquent argument, influenced as it is by a Thomist reading of Aristotle, and by an unreflective approach to secondary sources. What follows is a summary presentation of a competing reading of the Aristotelian conception of leisure. It takes its spirit from de Grazia's (1964) call to an "ideal of leisure" (p. 402; cf. Goodale, 1985) based on the search for truth in action and the strength of character necessary for that search.

Civility

To Aristotle, and to the Greeks generally, leisure was an arena for the development of the individual as a member of the community. As Tinder (1964) notes, "Leisure was conceived [by the Greeks] as an opportunity for the cultivation of personal excellence. But this excellence was to be achieved through participation" (p. 78). The participation in question here was in the community, in the affairs of the all-embracing *polis*, the Greek city-state celebrated by Aristotle. What makes such participation possible is the development of a character defined by civility. With Tinder (1976, pp. 182–183), we may identify four virtues embedded in the concept of tolerance, which he suggests shapes the "contours of civility." These are attentiveness to people, openness to truth, veracity as a bond among human beings, and responsibility for the preservation of this bond. This "general definition of civility" (pp. 182–183) can also be summarized as "the capacity for sharing existence" with those among whom one finds oneself (p. 9).

The focus of civility is on the character represented in this "sharing of existence" rather than on the results of any specific action. This emphasis on character, so different from the modern preoccupation with results, is a theme in Greek thinking from Homer on. To the Greeks, as Kitto (1957) comments, "the quality of a man matters more than his achievement" (p. 64). Civility is the quality of a person, the sum of the virtues expressed in one's actions, or, as Tinder (1980) puts it, "the primary question of civility" is "How shall I bear myself" (p. 186). Without action, there can be no expression of virtues, hence no character. The "problem of civility," then, becomes what Tinder (1980) aptly calls the search for the means to "exemplary action" founded on individual character and aimed at serving "as a statement of principle" about one's virtues, one's character (pp. 180–181). Such exemplary action occurred in leisure, for this was the arena in which the Greeks pursued the development of character. Civility can be regarded, in this context, as a continuing process of public education, through which the development of character occurs in public view with the purpose of continuing public discourse about right conduct. Leisure, then, far from being withdrawal into a detached contemplative state, was a major arena for

activity "undertaken with the serious purpose of cultivating and realizing the self" (Tinder, 1964, p. 328).

"Theoria" and "Praxis"

There are several issues of textual reconstruction and interpretation
that bear on this reading of Aristotle, many of them relating to Book
10 of his *Ethics*, in which *theoria* (contemplation) and the associated
virtue of *sophia* (wisdom) are taken as the highest good, the best life,
and hence as the content of leisure. Nonetheless, Book 10 and its relation
to the remainder of the *Ethics* is at the least problematic, and the
contradictions between it and the bulk of the work are significant. It
seems quite possible that Book 10 is a fragment attached at a later date
in Aristotle's career, or possibly still later by an uncritical editor.

In any event, among these contradictions is one important to us, that
between *theoria* and *sophia*, on the one hand, and *praxis* (practical
knowledge) and its virtue *phronesis* (moral wisdom) on the other. It is
the case that most of the *Ethics* takes the latter, that is, good action,
as the best life (Ackrill, 1974, p. 3; Stocks, 1939, pp. 159–160). The
contradiction with Book 10 cannot be resolved by the commonplace,
though accurate, observation that for Aristotle, contemplation is a form
of action. Aristotle himself sharpens the issue by writing that in matters
of practical knowledge, "the end is *not* to study and attain knowledge
of particular things to be done, but rather *to do them*" (E 1179a-b; see
note on sources; emphasis added).

In reference to leisure, the avenue to resolving the contradiction
passes through the fundamental similarity between *theoria* and *praxis*.
This similarity is that both demand rigorous intellectual effort and both
pursue truth, creating equally high esteemed virtues, namely *sophia* and
phronesis, in those who make this effort (Bernstein, 1983, p. 149). The
distinction between *theoria* and *praxis* is the mutability of what they
study so that the contrast is one "within knowledge" (Gadamer, 1981,
p. 89) rather than between knowledge and something else. *Theoria*
studies first principles, the eternal and the unchanging, mathematics,
logic, and metaphysics. *Praxis* studies the transitory and the changing,
including the activities of human beings as they seek to organize and
to conduct themselves, that is, politics and ethics. This is in keeping
with Aristotle's doctrine (E 1094b) that one may legitimately seek from
an object only that intellectual precision the object is capable of supporting.

Another approach to this issue is to ask whether human beings are
themselves capable of achieving knowledge of the eternal and unchanging. Although all human activity aims at some good and those goods
can be ranked according to the degree they approach the true good

(E 1094a), part of the eternal and unchanging, Aristotle argues human beings themselves are transitory and changing, thus making the life of *theoria*, of pure contemplation of the cosmos, in its perfection too high a mark for human ambition (E 1177b). In keeping with the doctrine of *Ethics* 1094b, human aspirations must match human capacity, and so it is that Aristotle, perhaps somewhat reluctantly, concludes the best *human* life is in pursuit of *praxis* and *phronesis*. In the end, as Ackrill (1974, p. 20) points out, Aristotle is unable to proclaim the irrevocable superiority of *theoria* because a life of *theoria* is beyond human achievement.

"Telos" and "Eudaimonia"

Aristotle's conception of the universe is teleological (from *telos*, or characteristic end). This is the source of his complex doctrine of cause and his hierarchical ordering of nature. We must never neglect the systematic structure of Aristotle's thought, with every element having an *ergon*, a specific function. Not only does each object have its own characteristic end, but these function to bring about the *telos* of nature as a whole, which is to achieve a full development and perfect ordering of its parts. Thus the *telos* of each part is, in a sense, to excel (to achieve *arete*, excellence) in the performance of its *ergon*. In the *Metaphysics* (1075a) Aristotle writes that "all things are ordered together somehow, but not all alike. . . ; and the world is not such that one thing has nothing to do with another, but they are connected."

Sabine (1961) explicates this idea: "Nature is at bottom a system of capacities or forces of growth directed by their inherent natures towards characteristic ends. They require for their unfolding what may be called broadly material conditions, which do not produce the ends at which growth is directed but may aid or hinder growth according as they are favorable or the reverse" (p. 121; see generally pp. 119–122; cf. Ackrill, 1981).

We may say that each object contains within itself the possibility of full development and is endowed to greater or lesser extent with capacities to achieve full development. In purely natural objects this is a reasonably straightforward process. A flower grows and blossoms according to the form inherent in it, according to whether it is tulip or hyacinth. It has no particular choice in the matter, cannot become puzzled over whether it wants to be a tulip or a hyacinth, or over whether it is better to be one rather than the other. Human beings share this teleological nature, but they may reflect on it, posit it to themselves as one of their characteristics. They are beings who have a particular *nisus*, an impulse toward development of a particular kind. This is the attainment of the good, and of a good expressing their highest capacities in their fullest development. Given the limitations of their transitory and changing natures, human beings must search out from among competing goods those most appropriate to them, and they may err by striking too low or too high. Considering this, the good at which Aristotle believes it most reasonable for human beings to aim is *eudaimonia*, or felicity (on the difficulty of finding an English equivalent for *eudaimonia*, see Ackrill, 1974, pp. 12–13).

Eudaimonia is the result of continued application of oneself to the question of how one ought to live one's life and of the continued attempt to carry this into exemplary action (E 1079b). It is important to recognize the active element in this concept. It represents a character able not only to reflect on the content of a virtuous life, but also to carry this reflection over into action. Such a character is inherent in the very nature of human beings and they own the raw materials able to carry them forward in its development. This character is best described in terms of civility as outlined earlier. The hallmark of civility is its engagement in open and public discussion of the sort of life one ought to lead, discussion according to the virtues embedded in civility (i.e., attentiveness, openness, veracity, and responsibility). Aristotle does not regard a life as virtuous if it remains content only with mere knowledge of virtues. It becomes virtuous only when the virtues are developed, when they are carried from reflection over into action (E 1177a). To achieve *eudaimonia*, to become felicitous, a life must be active.

Leisure

The existence of many lesser goods is a threat to achieving *eudaimonia*, which is possible only through pursuit of the highest goods within human achievement. Human attention can be diverted from these highest goods, and human passions can become hindrances in pursuit of both the highest and lesser goods. For *eudaimonia* to be achieved, an arena must be opened for it within human activity, in which the virtues of civility may be activated, in which practical wisdom may be achieved and displayed. *Phronesis* (moral wisdom) can indeed be seen as a name for the collective virtues of civility. These virtues are necessary to prevent human passions and self-interest from interfering with attaining *eudaimonia*. Such an arena must therefore be separated from involvement with the passions and self-interest, must be set aside from lower order activities (e.g., from the need for daily labor: E 1099a, P 1273a). For Aristotle, leisure is this arena.

In leisure we find the unity of reflection and activity underlying civility. Leisure is one of the essential "material conditions" for civility and thus for *eudaimonia*. In leisure, politics and ethics, in the broadly inclusive sense Aristotle and the Greeks apply to these terms, form part of the same reflection and the same action (E 1094a-b, 1181b). It is necessary to keep in mind the organic nature of Greek life in the *polis*, at least as it was taken by Aristotle to have been intended if not realized. Modern thought and life tend to hold separate the many spheres that were conjoined in the *polis*, in which the political, religious, economic, cultural, and social were all bound up together. This intertwining of human activities marked the superiority of the Greeks over the "barbarians," who were simply non-Greeks. This at least was Aristotle's view, for he could not conceive it possible for a human being to live well, to live a full life that achieved *eudaimonia*, outside the *polis* (P 1252b, 1280b). The depth of loyalty to the idea of the *polis* is a major feature of Greek thinking (cf. de Burgh, 1961, pp. 101–102; Kitto, 1957, chaps. 5, 9).

Aristotle makes three major statements that hold together his study of human beings: that they "by nature desire to know" (M 980a), that all their activity aims at some good (E 1094a), and that "man is by nature an animal intended to live in a *polis*" (P 1253a). Note that these are statements about the nature of human beings and that they reflect Aristotle's teleological thinking, for these are human beings' most characteristic attributes, their ultimate ends. It is the latter, the political, that assumes the most importance in this context because the *polis* not only represents the highest refinement of human association, but also provides the arena in which knowing and good actions become at all possible. The "main concern of politics is to engender a certain character in the citizens and to make them good and disposed to perform noble actions" (E 1099b).

Leisure is the arena in which this civil character was cultivated and displayed. Leisure must be present in any "well organized state" (P 1269a) and the *polis* must share "in the qualities required for the use of leisure" (P 1334a). Leisure was sufficiently important that the founding legislator was to create "the right laws" (E 1178b) to provide "training for the proper use of leisure" (P 1333a).

This is not, however, something imposed from the outside on to recalcitrant human nature. It was meant to correspond to and release a natural human capacity and thus express a fundamental teleological principle in Aristotle's thinking. He argues that "Our very nature has a tendency ... to seek of itself for ways and means which will enable us to use leisure rightly" (P 1337b), and this is in fact "the end of politics." The *polis* and its organic activities are the setting in which the character necessary for the right use of leisure is formed (P 1338a), in which this teleological development becomes possible. This contributed to the release of the full range of human excellences, for "it is the power to use leisure rightly ... which is the basis for all our life" (P 1337b). Thus the search for *eudaimonia*, for the full life of virtue, flowered in the *polis*, and most brightly in leisure. Leisure, in stark contrast to the modern world, was the arena in which the drives to know, to become virtuous, and to express virtue came together in the organic activities of the individual and the community. This can be summarized by saying that the *ergon* of leisure is the unfolding of *phronesis*, that its *telos* is the felicitous life of virtue, and that its *arete* is that of the citizen whose character reflects civility in the active life of the *polis*.

Liberal Democratic Theory: The Rationality of Acquisition and Possession

The preceding interpretatin of Aristotle focuses on his developmental view of human activity, intended to produce excellence in character and activity, and the display of these in the public arena created by leisure. The grounding assumption in Aristotle's approach is that human beings have an innate drive to achieve excellence, and that this excellence was a character marked by civility rather than material wealth and labor to attain it. In this section our attention will turn to features of liberal democratic theory that have been prominent in its development and that are strikingly at odds with Aristotelian conceptions. The result will be a clear schism suggestng an impoverishment of human nature and a narrowing range of human activities.

The Ascendancy of the Market

The Aristotelian view remained dominant, though certainly not without significant alterations, until into the fifteenth and sixteenth centuries. In the next two hundred years or so there was a "sea change" in views of human beings, a transformation integrally connected to the transformation in society then accelerating. A new interpretation emerged in western Europe, taking human beings not as pursuers of excellence in character and action, but as seekers of security and wealth. The focus of human activity shifted from communal to individual, from character to acquisition. If the Greeks, as de Grazia (1964, p. 332) has suggested, understood themselves as standing closest to the pinnacle of human achievement during leisure, the transformed view elevated labor and taught that leisure was the devil's playground. To apply present language, human beings were seen as maximizers of individual utilities, and these themselves came more and more to be seen as economic utilities.

The communal arena faded while the market ascended. As excellence became measured by wealth and character by gain, the arena that concentrated human activity was the market. Where the *polis* had been the forum for exemplary action, modernizing government was itself conceived in the images of market activity. No longer concerned with providing leisure for its citizens, government was now intended to minimize interferences in the competitive, acquisitive activities of individuals. Indeed, the market is one of the dominant metaphors in modern social and political thought (cf. Lindblom, 1977). Its application to wider and wider realms of human activity completes the transition from the Aristotelian developmental view to the modern notion of the human being as "essentially a consumer of utilities" (Macpherson, 1973, p. 79).

It is necessary to explore briefly the development of western liberal democratic theory, for this is the origin of the justifying ideas reflected in contemporary practice. We find in this development a series of contradictions working their way out, many of which occur along the axes of what Sabine (1952) calls "the two democratic traditions," liberty and equality. Despite Sabine's claims, these two "traditions" are not equal partners in the development of liberal democratic thought. Liberty is the earlier concept, emphasizing the inviolability of the individual and protection of property; equality is a later addition, asserting the equal worth of all individuals even in the face of unequal economic outcomes of liberty (cf. Hobhouse, 1964; de Ruggiero, 1959). The earlier articulation of liberty, particularly in its protection of property rights, meant that its economic orientation was well established prior to the infusion of egalitarian thought that was to yield liberal democracy. Using Macpherson's work, we will see more clearly the shift from the Aristotelian conception of human activity to one that, although acknowledging the rational, purposeful nature of this activity, also held "the essence of rational behaviour . . . to lie in unlimited individual appropriation" (1973, p. 5).

Possessive Individualism

Macpherson (1962) argues that the possessive element in liberal democratic theory "is found in its conception of the individual as essentially the proprietor of his own person or capacities, owing nothing to society for them. The individual was seen neither as a moral whole, nor as part of a larger social whole, but as owner of himself" (p. 3). The conception of ownership of person and capacities became increasingly important, to the point that freedom was founded on the idea of ownership. The more individuals are proprietors of their capacities, and hence independent of others, the freer they are. This is not entirely dissimilar to the Greek requirement that citizens be freed of the need for daily labor. The difference is, however, that while the Greeks saw this as a liberation from economic concern to attend to higher matters, liberal theory glorified acquisition and possession as such. In doing so, it came to regard society as a collection of individuals related one to the other "as proprietors of their own capacities and of what they have acquired by their exercise [i.e., of these capacities]" (p. 3).

In possessive market society, there is no longer any authoritative allocation either of work or of rewards, in contrast to traditional societies where custom and status controlled allocation. As Macpherson (1962, p. 48) goes on to point out, there is a difference, too, between this society and one in which "independent producers" exchange only the products of their own labor. In possessive market society, there is a market for labor capacities as well as products. Macpherson makes this the "single criterion of the possessive market society," that "man's labor is a commodity, i.e., that man's labor and skill are his own, yet are regarded not as integral parts of his personality, but as possessions" that can be bought and sold on the labor market. Since human labor is regarded here as an essential human capacity, this transaction may be interpreted as the alienation of a fundamental defining feature of what it is to be human.

From the foregoing it is an easy step to an insistence on the rationality of unlimited desire. It is this that is decisively new in liberal thought after the seventeenth century (Macpherson, 1973, p. 27). In the absence of any external allocation of labor and reward, the individual's own capacities to labor, acquire, and consume guide individual actions. Under market conditions this was assumed to create an "endless increase in productivity" (p. 17) leading to further acquisition. Indeed, one of the principal value assumptions in developing liberal thought was "the rationality and naturalness of unlimited desire" to acquire and consume (p. 18). This is a radical shift. If human desires are rationally and naturally limitless, then people are no longer beings intended to achieve knowledge and practical wisdom and to live in community with others. They are now, as Macpherson points out, infinite consumers (p. 31) competing with each other in an infinite market. Nor is this restricted to an effort to overcome the enduring scarcity of goods, for what is now scarce is satisfaction itself, made unachievable by the new conception of human beings as infinitely desirous and consuming.

This development may be traced in the writings of the most eminent early liberal theorists, Hobbes and Locke, with such later writers as Hume accepting the possessive view of human beings even when they discard other long-standing components of liberal thought.

Hobbes (1955) makes an individual's power, and the desire to acquire more, the centerpiece of human psychology: "So that in the first place, I put for a general inclination of all mankind, a perpetual and restless desire of power after power, that ceaseth only in death" (p. 64). Such power is not calculated along any absolute scale since one does not exist. There is no teleological purpose unfolding in and through nature.

Here virtue has changed from something valued for its own sake, as in Aristotle, to what enhances the individual's power in comparison to that of others. "Virtue generally, in all sorts of subjects," writes Hobbes, "is somewhat that is valued for eminence; and consisteth in eminence. For if all things were equal in all men, nothing would be prized" (p. 42). It is not a thing's being worth desiring in itself that lends it value, but that others desire it, too. The more one acquires of what is mutually desired, the greater one's virtue (for which read: power; cf. Macpherson, 1962, p. 35).

The individual can never rest from this acquisitiveness. By their natures, the desires of human beings are never at an end. In the absence of some ultimate goal, they must continue to strive against each other. Power is relational, comparative. Thus, if one rests a moment, one's competitors press ahead, putting the individual at a comparative disadvantage. It is not that there are no higher pleasures to be sought or that human beings are unwilling to be content, but simply that by their natures they must constantly measure themselves against each other. The general insecurity of life means an individual "cannot assure the power and means to live well, which he hath present," Hobbes argues, and so the individual is compelled "to the acquisition of more power" (1955, p. 64). In the absence of a "greatest good" (p. 63), human beings are left to strive after power, and with greater power to live "a more contented life thereby" (p. 109). Such contentment is not marked, however, by a cessation of desire or any ultimate state of achievement. To Hobbes, the lack of desire is equivalent to death. Contrasting sharply and deliberately with Aristotle, Hobbes proclaims that "Felicity is a continual progress of the desire, from one object to another; the attaining of the former, being still but the way to the latter" (p. 63).

From Hobbes to Locke might seem a journey of some distance, Hobbes the proponent of absolute state sovereignty before a human nature conceived as incessantly competitive and intermittently violent, Locke the defender of individual rights against encroachments by an authoritarian government. Yet the distance is not so very great when one considers the psychologies they propose, their mutual emphasis on acquisitiveness and possession as characteristics of human activity. If Locke is the defender of individual rights, it is a very narrow defense, resting on his argument that "government has no other end but the preservation of property" (1970, sec. 94, 124). Whatever else might be done, it is this task that must remain paramount.

Locke begins by noting that all people are "able to dispose of their Possessions, and Persons as they think fit" (sec. 4; see also sec. 123). This is most particularly true with the individual's capacity to labor, for it is out of this labor that property arises (sec. 27). Since the individual's person and possessions, of which the capacity to labor is considered part, are inviolate, it follows that the products of this capacity, that is, property, are also inviolate. We find in Locke two justifications of property, the right to preserve one's life and the right to the products of one's labor (sec. 28; cf. Macpherson, 1962, p. 201), which Locke regularly collapses into a single proposition: "And the Condition of Humane Life, which requires Labour and Materials to work on, necessarily introduces *private Possessions*" (sec. 35; emphasis in original). These are limited initially by the law of nature to only what the individual can utilize before it spoils (sec. 23), which works against accumulation of wealth. With the introduction of money as a form of property that does not spoil, but can be stored up, it becomes possible for individuals to acquire property far beyond the limits of their immediate needs (secs. 47, 48).

This is a continuation of the Hobbesian theme of unlimited desire. Indeed, Locke wished for his own political purposes to insist that unlimited desire and acquisitiveness define rationality itself. He begins his argument by asserting that the earth has been given in common to human beings so they may by their labor "make use of it [i.e., the earth] to the best advantage of life and convenience" (sec. 26). The introduction of money reinforced the "different degrees of industry" that "were apt to give Men Possessions in different Proportions" (sec. 48). Money, in other words, allowed greater accumulation than had been possible before. Locke also holds, however, that although "God gave the World to Men in Common ... for their benefit, and the greatest Convenience of Life they were capable to draw from it," God did not mean for the world to remain "common and uncultivated," but rather intended it for human industry. Locke maintains God gave the earth "to the use of the Industrious and Rational (and *Labour* was to be *his Title to it*)" (sec. 34; emphasis in original). Thus the capability to exploit the earth for "the greatest Convenience of Life" represents rationality in conformity to God's will, and this rationality is conceived as greater the more the individual's acquisitiveness increases. To accumulate is to respond to God's will (sec. 35), and what could be more rational than this? Those left with lesser holdings were simply less rational, and from this Locke went on to defend a two tier society, the implications of which are far less than democratic, for he assigns political power on the basis of rationality, which is limited to the propertied class (cf. Macpherson, 1962, pp. 220–221). To become fully realized as a human being, then, requires acquisitive, possessive behavior.

The assumptions of Hobbes and Locke about the acquisitive nature of human beings became commonplace in liberal thought. Hume, otherwise a debunker of liberal mythology (e.g., 1955) and a general skeptic, argued that human beings are stamped by the "numberless wants and necessities with which she [nature] has loaded" them (1948, p. 55; this is at the opening of III.2.2). Reviewing the available means to overcome these wants and necessities, Hume notes that although society and government permit human beings to achieve prosperity to some degree, they also cause a further multiplication of wants and necessities, drawing human beings into a constant search to satisfy ever greater acquisitive desires. Macpherson (1973, p. 17) suggests Hume's acceptance of these liberal themes illustrates the degree to which they were embedded in liberalism generally. He goes on to argue that later modifications in liberal thought (e.g., by J. S. Mill, T. H. Green, A. D. Lindsay, E. Barker, J. Rawls, and others) were attempts to mitigate the undemocratic, inegalitarian consequences of possessive individualism, but did not escape the underlying emphasis on economic maximization.

Summary

Macpherson's analysis allows us to do two things. The starkness with which it illustrates the centrality of acquisitive behavior in liberalism offers a clear contrast to the Aristotelian rejection of economic activity as a route to the *eudaimonia* achieved in the arena opened by leisure. Surely Aristotelian leisure is incompatible with a culture that defines rationality by the degree of economic acquisitiveness people display. At the same time, Macpherson offers us an angle of approach to our own society by which we may test whether the possessive and acquisitive implications of liberalism have worked their way out and how. The next section surveys two assessments of contemporary U.S. society, reinforced by the observations of de Tocqueville and Ortega y Gasset. Anticipating the outcome of this effort, we will find that individual acquisition characterizes this society and that acquisition extends to leisure activity as well, a point to be developed in the concluding section.[2]

Possessive Individualism and Contemporary Society

The rise of possessive individualism, with its emphasis on the market, competition, and the rationality of unlimited desire, redefined human

---

[2]Although sympathetic to Macpherson's (1973) claim that "Western democracy is a market society, through and through" (p. 25) and that in it democracy is therefore "reduced from humanist aspiration to a market equilibrium system" (pp. 78–79), this paper does not take up his argument in detail. It should be noted, however, that a prominent theme in recent discussions of democracy has been to distill democratic theory into a calculus based on principles of economic choice, and that these attempts have enjoyed considerable vogue. Among others, see Dahl (1956), Downs (1957), and Schumpeter (1950). Even Rawls (1971), seeking to resuscitate the ethical dimension in liberal democracy, falls back on utilitarian decision making models. Davis (1964), although ultimately at odds with Macpherson's diagnosis and remedy, makes an eloquent statement on the losses entailed in such market-oriented approaches to democracy.

nature in terms of economic powers. The differences between these ideas and those entailed by Aristotelian leisure could scarcely be more marked. Still, we have yet to ask how liberal ideas are manifested in contemporary society and whether they have shaped leisure as well. The point here is not to find absolute identity, but rather to look for something along the line of "family resemblances," to use Wittgenstein's phrase. Have these liberal ideas led to the commodious and contented living foreseen by Hobbes, Locke, Hume, and others? Have they opened up the way for an expansion of human capacities? Or, following Macpherson's critical account, has there been in fact a narrowing of these capacities? The discussion in this section will draw from two qualitative assessments of contemporary society, one a superbly executed and detailed sociological exploration of the structure of values and character in the United States (Bellah et al., 1985), the other an articulate historical analysis of the derivation of contemporary attitudes toward the good life (Baritz, 1988). The different perspectives taken by the authors should allow a reasonable exploration of the questions raised here, for if Macpherson's critique is accurate, we can expect to find economic images and concerns dominating individual aspirations and thus shaping human interactions.

Isolation and the Market

This is indeed what Bellah et al. (1985) find: "Americans define success in terms of free competition among individuals in an open market" (p. 198). Although willing to acknowledge assistance received from others, people cannot believe in their own success unless they have been self-reliant competitors. Baritz (1988) suggests those who are successful "adhere to a crippling rationalism" (pp. 305–306) that may be interpreted essentially as market oriented. It is a crippling, isolating rationalism because the competitors "concentrate on themselves" at the expense of forcing family, personal, and other noneconomic relationships into market form. Bellah et al. call this a "giving-getting" model (p. 133). They find a "utilitarian contractualism" prevalent in both public and private relationships, in which the aim is mutual benefit along market lines, with each person standing alone possessing individual powers and capacities as tokens for exchange.

The price of possessive individualism is thus the isolation of the individual in a matrix of market oriented relationships. Reduced to economic terms, determined to succeed in this competition among utilitarian personalities, the individual is left nonetheless uncertain, in the absence of all but relative scales, what exactly is to be pursued. Baritz calls the contemporary American "radically alone" (p. 290) because the emphasis on process leaves a "sense of impermanence" that offers no means of organizing the world and one's experience of it. Despite the importance of open market competition as a cultural icon, it becomes "at the same time a source of deepening anxiety."

We may note here that de Tocqueville (1969, p. 444) recognized this isolating tendency early in U.S. history. With only their own subjective ideas to guide them, absent permanent or traditional standards, the limitless (so de Tocqueville) independence people achieve in democracy becomes not liberating, but frightening. The response to such conditions is to isolate the individual ever more firmly: "Each man is forever thrown back on himself alone, and there is danger that he may be shut up in the solitude of his own heart" (p. 508). This is in fact the final effect of the market-based utilitarian contractualism that Bellah et al. find dominating American character: "American cultural traditions define personality, achievement, and the purpose of human life in ways that leave the individual suspended in glorious, but terrifying, isolation" (p. 6).

Work and Acquisition as Therapy

Clearly, some means of coming to grips with this isolation is necessary if individuals are not to collapse under its weight. Such a means cannot, however, challenge the fundamental validity of the competitive, possessive values underlying society. These values must be themselves translated into standards, no matter how empty of substance, by which people may anchor themselves in society. Successful competition in the market of competing individuals has become the controlling standard, and success is measured economically (Baritz, p. 317; Bellah et al., p. 22). De Tocqueville, again, observed this a century ago, noticing that "the taste for well-being is the most striking and unalterable characteristic of democratic ages" (p. 448).

There is a further, possibly more significant meaning in the attempt to reduce isolation through work and economic success. As we have seen, the roots of liberal psychology lie in the conception of the individual as laborer and infinite desirer. When the search for material well-being is added to this as the standard of success, the result is that work and acquisition become confirmations of personal identity. One is not only represented by one's economic achievements, one *is* those achievements. In Baritz's words, the only hierarchies that matter are "those based on personal wealth" (p. 307). Work and gain offer an opportunity to measure ourselves against others. They become a test of who one is and what one is fundamentally worth, a worth that can quite literally be measured in coin of the realm. The issue is not simply a "work ethic," although this is an important legitimating concept, but the way in which work links, or fails to link, individuals to each other. Work and acquisition become therapy for the isolation imposed on the individual by the economic conception of personality and the market conception of relations among people. The nature of our work and its economic rewards declare who and what we are. By immersing ourselves in our work, we are able to become ourselves more completely: "however we define work, it is very close to our sense of self. What we 'do' often translates to what we 'are'" (Bellah et al., p. 66).

The danger is that as therapy, work attempts to overcome the effects of defining human nature in economic terms, the very incentives underlying work. Doubling back on itself, work consumes us, becomes the dominant feature of our lives. We work to work, and not, as Aristotle observed, to have leisure. Work and acquisition place us directly in the Hobbesian dilemma discussed earlier. Having once committed ourselves, we can never rest or we fall behind. Work and acquisition are a shifting scale, based on comparisons between ourselves and others. If we stop, the basis of comparison shifts to our disadvantage as others press on. Having invested so much of our identity and self-esteem in work, this result is disquieting if not unacceptable. We become less, even though our material conditions have not changed. There can be no standing still; there can only be pressing on or falling back. One can never rest content with one's position, and hence with oneself. There must be constant movement and hence, as Lakoff (1964, p. 167) notes, there is also a state of perpetual discontent.

The Eclipse of the Communal

Devotion to one thing above others restricts our horizon, excludes other ways of seeing. A single definition of success, based on an external criterion like material wealth, narrows the range of one's attention and energy. When personal identity and value are tied so closely to a single criterion, any distraction from it is threatening not just to success but also to self. The result of such narrowed range is to dismiss or to avoid anything outside it, creating "a profound ignorance and usually a distrust of those aspects of the world that [seem] not to relate to the ownership of wealth" (Baritz, p. 316). Here is confirmation of Aristotle's teaching that freedom from the need to labor, a need that may be defined not only in terms of physical subsistence but also psychologically, is prerequisite to the development of character during leisure. As liberal psychology has manifested itself in society, however, everything unrelated to acquisition and to a self defined in economic, market terms is pushed aside in favor of the demands of work and gain. Once again de Tocqueville has preceded us: "A breathless cupidity distracts the mind of man from the pleasures of the imagination and the labors of the intellect and urges it on to nothing but the pursuit of wealth" (p. 455).

Ortega y Gasset's (1957) trenchant criticism of "mass man" suggests another angle of approach to the narrowing of focus in contemporary society: "Human life, by its very nature, has to be dedicated to something, an enterprise glorious or humble, a destiny illustrious or trivial" (p. 141). What a particular instance of "human life," whether a person, society, or an age, chooses to be dedicated to reveals its inner character. The message in both Bellah et al. and Baritz is that Americans are engaged in a search for the "good life." This is in itself unremarkable, but the distinctly economic content given to the "good life" and the notion of human nature accompanying it distinguish the modern liberal conception of the good life from others. The narrowing focus on work as the definition of self requires a withdrawal from involvement elsewhere. Most particularly, work is no longer seen as contributing to wider purposes; it does not reach out to others except as they become participants in the net of market relations established by the individual. Work, and little else, becomes the vehicle for the individual's interactions in society, and other models fall away, including that of the citizen: "The individual's need to be successful becomes the enemy of the need to find the meaning of one's work in service to others. . . . Work does not integrate one into the public household but estranges one from it. It becomes hard to do good work and be a good citizen at the same time" (Bellah et al., p. 197; cf. Baritz, p. 317).

Life in contemporary society is split essentially into two cultures, and these become progressively more antagonistic to each other. Baritz states this proposition in harsh terms: "American life has become two hostile cultures: shared and private; static and fluid; acquiescent and critical; local and cosmopolitan; ascetic and therapeutic; faithful and agnostic" (p. 303). Somewhat more dispassionately, Bellah et al. find the split into "a number of functional sectors" to be the "most distinctive aspect of twentieth-century American society" (p. 43). They summarize it as a division between the public utilitarian sphere and the private expressive sphere (pp. 45–46). The public utilitarian sphere is, as we have seen, dominated by work and acquisition. What of the private expressive sphere? If the communal has been eclipsed in the one, can it appear in the other?

The dominance of the market as the model for human interaction is such that it enters even people's expressive activities. Indeed, these private activities may be seen as an extension of the search for self grounded on relative, comparative, rather than enduring, scales. Even the commitments one makes in the private expressive sphere are thought of "as enhancements of the sense of individual well-being rather than as moral imperatives" (Bellah et al., p. 47). This search for well-being is carried out by "withholding commitment" rather than by engaging in a wider whole (Baritz, pp. 307–308; cf. Bellah et al., p. 50). Communal involvement is limited to those associations and issues affecting the individual's own small life space.

The privatism characteristic of contemporary individual "self-enhancement" is extended even into what was once regarded as the sphere of communal activity. This is encountered only in a negative context, when the need arises to protect the individual's life space from encroachment by outside, alien forces. There is no shared basis, nor any shared arena such as was once found in the Aristotelian conception of leisure, on which to establish public institutions fostering some measure of civil understanding among the heterogeneous private spheres that experience each other as opposed, as foreign, as other.

Given the conception of human nature and well-being governing this society, with its economic and competitive elements, this could hardly be otherwise. The result is that even the civic participation that does occur is aimed at settling claims based not on right or wrong, but by creating "neutral technical solutions that are beyond debate" (Bellah et al., p. 187), that is, by creating some form of market mechanism (cf. Lowi, 1979). This dynamic is aimed, in its central tendency, at a "permanent disestablishment of any deeply internalized moral demands"; it is emphatically "not in the name of any new order of communal value" (Rieff, 1966, pp. 239–240).

The Devolution of Leisure: Lifestyle and the Narcissism of Similarity

What has become of leisure in this contemporary society shaped by possessive individualism? We began with an interpretation of Aristotelian leisure that stressed its active communal focus, the development and display of character in a public arena. Having explored the roots of liberal democratic thought, with attention to the psychology underlying human interactions, and having sketched their manifestations in our own day, what shape does leisure take and what role does it play? Here, in answering this question, we see quite starkly our utter remoteness from Aristotle, and we understand how it is that the ideals of Aristotelian leisure can sound but faint echoes in the present.

De Tocqueville, viewing emergent democracy, finding the search for gain, but the absence of leisure, asked a similar question: "In the midst of this universal tumult, this incessant conflict of jarring interests, this endless chase for wealth, where is one to find the calm for the profound researches of the intellect?" (p. 460). Where can one find the public expression of these researches if leisure becomes a retreat to private confirmation of self?

Bellah et al. (p. 72) introduce a concept that goes to the heart of the matter. This is the "lifestyle enclave," which they define as "linked most closely to leisure and consumption and . . . usually unrelated to the world of work. It brings together those who are socially, economically, or culturally similar, and one of its chief aims is the enjoyment of being with those who 'share one's lifestyle.' " This is a rich concept and deserves more attention than it has received. Consider, for example, the following three propositions that emerge from it: leisure is linked with consumption; leisure is privatist, cutting the individual off from the public arena; and leisure is a search for reinforcement derived from being with those who are much like oneself.

The first point suggests it is inaccurate to separate leisure and work completely, for contemporary leisure depends on one's ability to consume, which is in turn an economic ability dependent on material gain through work. Leisure thus becomes the expression of oneself and its value, the confirmation of the search for identity through work, as discussed in the preceding section. What one is able to consume is who one is, and leisure is an important arena for this consumption. Leisure thus confirms the economic grounding of the self and fosters the rationality of unlimited desire in the determination of this self.

The private nature of leisure reinforces the withdrawal from commitment. It is the extension of the search for the enhancement of self, an affirmation of self by negation of all that is not self. This point may be extended by pointing out that contemporary leisure is increasingly passive and focused on consumption in the home, as one extensive analysis of trends in the United States found (Oxford Analytica, 1986, p. 99). Television watching, for example, was the only "leisure activity" (here this phrase seems oxymoronic) showing an increase in participation across all social classes. A corollary to this privatism is that it accelerates the consumption orientation of leisure. There is an expanding need to acquire "a mass of complicated domestic technology" (p. 100) to be utilized during leisure (cf. Linder, 1970). Possession in the privacy of one's home confirms one's sense of self-identity and self-worth, but essentially to an audience of one.

Finally, the leisure lifestyle enclave is structured deliberately to prevent challenges to the individual's cultivated image of self. Exposure to difference, to challenge, to contradiction is avoided as people seek out others who are essentially likenesses of themselves, economically, socially, and culturally. Since consumption drives leisure, it is a determining factor in filtering out dissimilar others. Thus although leisure might bring similar people together, it also helps them separate from those who are different. It denies the communal element in Aristotelian leisure; indeed, it denies community altogether: "Whereas community attempts to be an inclusive whole, celebrating the interdependence of public and private life and of the different callings of all, lifestyle is

fundamentally segmented and celebrates the narcissism of similarity"
(Bellah et al., p. 72).

It becomes, on this account, impossible to identify through contemporary leisure the content of the good life or to see its extension into the public sphere, in other than the most personal terms, matters of preference enabled by access to various patterns of personal consumption. It need hardly be said that this is far from Aristotelian leisure, but does this distance matter? It matters profoundly if we value the ideals embodied in Aristotelian leisure. There is little meaning to any talk of recovering these ideals in a societal milieu so antithetical to them.

The discussion of liberal thought and its manifestation in contemporary society suggests, to my mind, that our loss here has been fundamental, going to the heart of our conceptions of human purpose and interaction. It might remain true that happiness is the end of life (Bellah et al., p. 6), but the contemporary notion of happiness is not at all what Aristotle understood by *eudaimonia*. Rather than clearly defined cultural standards that guide conduct and anchor the individual in society, happiness is now reduced to a matter of personal preference, a utilitarian calculation that can be changed whenever convenient for the individual. Happiness as the aim of leisure is, for the privatist expressive self, simply a "purely subjective grounding of the self" (Bellah et al., p. 46). Leisure thus has no extension beyond the individual, leaving the individual still adrift among the multitudes of other similarly subjectively defined selves.

The liberal democratic aspiration has always been founded on the liberating effects of competition, most particularly competition in pursuit of wealth. In its working out, however, it has become apparent, as Macpherson (1973) notes, that "the income and leisure resulting from extractive power are not automatically conductive to the development of essentially human capacities. The presumption . . . is to the contrary" (p. 72). The failure of liberal democracy stems from the essentially possessive, market orientation it imposes on human activity, legitimated by the assumption of the rationality of infinite human desire.

But if indeed human desires are infinite, there is never a point at which sufficiency is achieved, at which the turn can be made to the development of human capacities beyond the economic. It is not that there is a complete ignorance of other standards, other values, but that these are seen as simply irrelevant to possessive, acquisitive society. Noneconomic human capacities become peripheral, cultivated when the serious business of life permits. But this serious business seldom permits because it is justified by postulating infinite desire and acquisition. The possessive self is grounded in subjective terms on a scale whose measurement is always shifting, always relative. The individual can never stop because this threatens the fragile construction of the acquisitive self. Capacities other than the economic simply have no place in this construction, and alternative conceptions of the self are regarded merely as archaic.

Commenting on this, Baritz makes specific reference to Greece: "The middle class simply substituted its pecuniary standards for the culture of what it considered an irrelevant civilization." Among the elements of this "irrelevant civilization" Baritz believes to have been discarded are "intellectual curiosity, the ability to understand each other, the necessity of beauty, and a deep sense of proportion" (p. 317). All these, of course, were present in leisure as conceived by Aristotle and practiced, to some degree at least, by the Greeks.

Ortega (1957) observes that "If you want to make use of the advantages of civilisation, but are not prepared to concern yourself with the upholding of civilisation—you are done" (p. 88). What engaged the citizen of the Greek *polis* during leisure was exactly this, upholding civilization as the Greeks conceived it, with all the difficult questions and choices this entailed. This is not a romanticized image, for though we know there were many instances in which the Greek ideal was violated, by men such as Alcibiades, for example, we know also that their actions were recognized as violations and it was understood what had been violated. But what engages the individual today if not the cultivation and confirmation of self, in leisure as elsewhere? What standards can this individual be said to uphold or to violate? When and where are such standards articulated and examined critically?

De Tocqueville described the effects of the absence of leisure in liberal democratic society as a decrease in intellectually rigorous activity: "Men living in times of equality have much curiosity and little leisure. Life is so practical, complicated, agitated and active that they have little time for thinking. So democratic man likes generalizations because they save him the trouble of studying particular cases" (p. 440). The particular case they seem to have most difficulty studying is their own. The grounding of the self in subjective terms only makes it exceedingly difficult to step outside the "narcissism of similarity" to achieve an alternative angle of vision, nor, in their self-certitude, are individuals likely to see the need or find the means to do so.

As Aristotle notes, "a time of the enjoyment of prosperity, and leisure accompanied by peace, is more apt to make men overbearing" (P 1334a). Not conceiving an end, *telos*, to leisure, it is a simple matter to misuse it, to neglect the character it both calls for and builds. The absence of this character had unfortunate, perhaps tragic, consequences in other ages (cf. P 1271b). If we are prevented from recapturing the ideals of Greek leisure, we can at least reflect on the reasons why this is the case and prepare to meet the consequences of our failure with the necessary understanding and, perhaps, character.

References

Note: In the text, reference to Aristotle's works are denoted by E for the *Ethics*, by M for the *Metaphysics*, and by P for the *Politics*.

Ackrill, J. L. (1974). *Aristotle on "eudaimonia.* " The British Academy 1974 Dawes Hicks Lecture on Philosophy. London: Oxford University Press.

Ackrill, J. L. (1981). *Aristotle the philosopher.* Oxford: Clarendon Press.

Aristotle. (1941). *Metaphysics.* In R. McKeon (Ed.), *The basic works of Aristotle* (pp. 682–926) (W. Ross, Trans.). New York: Random House.

Aristotle. (1946). *Politics* (E. Barker, Trans.). London: Oxford University Press.

Aristotle. (1962). *Nichomachean ethics* (M. Ostwald, Trans.). Indianapolis: Bobbs-Merrill.

Baritz, L. (1988). *The good life: The meaning of success for the American middle class.* New York: Alfred A. Knopf.

Bellah, R. N., Madsen, R., Sullivan, W. M., Swidler, A., & Tipton, S. M. (1985). *Habits of the heart: Individualism and commitment in American life.* Berkeley: University of California Press.

Bernstein, R. J. (1983). *Beyond objectivism and relativism: Science, hermeneutics, and praxis.* Philadelphia: University of Pennsylvania Press.

Dahl, R. A. (1956). *A preface to democratic theory.* Chicago: University of Chicago Press.

Dare, B., Welton, G., & Coe, W. (1987). *Concepts of leisure in Western thought: A critical and historical analysis.* Dubuque, IA: Kendall/Hunt.

Davis, L. (1964). The cost of realism: Contemporary restatements of democracy. *Western Political Quarterly, 17,* 37–46.

De Burgh, W. G. (1961). *The legacy of the ancient world* (rev. ed.). Baltimore: Penguin Books.

De Grazia, S. (1964). *Of time, work, and leisure.* New York: Twentieth Century Fund/Anchor Books.

De Ruggiero, G. (1959). *The history of European liberalism* (R. G. Collingwood, Trans.). Boston: Beacon Press.

De Tocqueville, A. (1969). *Democracy in America* (J. P. Mayer, Ed. ; G. Lawrence, Trans.). Garden City, NJ: Doubleday/Anchor Books.

Downs, A. (1957). *An economic theory of democracy.* New York: Harper & Row.

Gadamer, H. G. (1981). *Reason in the age of science* (F. G. Lawrence, Trans.). Cambridge: MIT Press.

Goodale, T. L. (1985). If leisure is to matter. In T. L. Goodale & P. A. Witt (Eds.), *Recreation and leisure: Issues in an era of change* (pp. 44–55), (rev. ed.). State College, PA: Venture Publishing.

Hemingway, J. L. (1988). Leisure and civility: Reflections on a Greek ideal. *Leisure Sciences, 10,* 179–191.

Hobbes, T. (1955). In M. Oakshott (Ed.), *Leviathan, or the matter, forme and power of a commonwealth ecclesiastical and civil.* Oxford: Basil Blackwell.

Hobhouse, L. T. (1964). *Liberalism.* New York: Oxford University Press.

Hume, D. (1948). A treatise of human nature. In H. D. Aiken (Ed.), *Hume's moral and political philosophy* (pp. 3–169). New York: Hafner Publishing Co.

Hume, D. (1955). Of the original contract. In C. W. Hendel (Ed.), *Political essays* (pp. 43–63). Indianapolis: Bobbs-Merrill.

Kitto, H. D. F. (1957). *The Greeks.* Harmondsworth, UK: Penguin Books.

Kraus, R. (1984). *Recreation and leisure in modern society* (3rd ed.). Glenview, IL: Scott, Foresman, & Co.

Lakoff, S. A. (1964). *Equality in political theory.* Boston: Beacon Press.

Lindblom, C. E. (1977). *Politics and markets.* New York: Basic Books.

Linder, S. (1970). *The harried leisure class.* New York: Columbia University Press.

Locke, J. (1970). *Two treatises of government* (P. Laslett, Ed.). Cambridge: Cambridge University Press.

Lowi, T. J. (1979). *The end of liberalism: The second republic of the United States* (2nd ed.). New York: W. W. Norton.

Macpherson, C. B. (1962). *The political theory of possessive individualism, Hobbes to Locke.* London: Oxford University Press.

Macpherson, C. B. (1973). *Democratic theory: Essays in retrieval.* Oxford: Oxford University Press.

Macpherson, C. B. (1977). *The life and times of liberal democracy.* Oxford: Oxford University Press.

Murphy, J. F. (1981). *Concepts of leisure* (2nd ed.). Englewood Cliffs, NJ: Prentice-Hall.

Ortega y Gasset, J. (1957). *The revolt of the masses* (Anon. trans.). New York: W. W. Norton.

Oxford Analytica. (1986). *America in perspective.* Boston: Houghton Mifflin.

Pieper, J. (1952). *Leisure, the basis of culture* (A. Dru, Trans.). New York: Pantheon Books.

Rawls, J. (1971). *A theory of justice.* Cambridge: Belknap Press of Harvard University Press.

Rieff, P. (1966). *The triumph of the therapeutic: The uses of faith after Freud.* New York: Harper Torchbooks.

Sabine, G. H. (1952). The two democratic traditions. *The Philosophical Review, 61*, 451–474.

Sabine, G. H. (1961). *A history of political theory* (3rd ed.). New York: Holt, Rinehart, & Winston.

Schumpeter, J. A. (1950). *Capitalism, socialism, and democracy* (3rd ed.). New York: Harper Torchbooks.

Stocks, J. L. (1939). Leisure. In D. M. Emmet (Ed.), *Reason and intuition, and other essays* (pp. 152–171). London: Oxford University Press.

Tinder, G. E. (1964). *The crisis of political imagination.* New York: Charles Scribners' Sons.

Tinder, G. E. (1976). *Tolerance: Toward a new civility.* Amherst, MA: University of Massachusetts Press.

Tinder, G. E. (1980). *Community: Reflections on a tragic ideal.* Baton Rouge, LA: Louisiana State University Press.

Ideals and Reality: Classical Leisure and Historical Change

Byron Dare

Several years ago I was offered the opportunity to teach courses on the history and philosophy of leisure. My first observation of the students in the Department of Leisure Studies and Recreation at California State University, Northridge, included their apologetic responses to fellow students and relatives, who openly questioned the significance and rigor of their discipline. If I left them with anything, I hope it is the ability to turn the tables on their detractors through the recognition that to study leisure is to open the door to questions about human nature, ethics, our species' potential, and ultimately, the quality of life on the planet.

As I came to know the students better, I detected a widespread attitude that reflects our society's open denial of the significance of history. "The Greeks had leisure, we have recreation," seemed to be the consensus—with the obvious implication that studying the Greeks and their leisure was passé. Finally, an outspoken student provided me with the opportunity I was waiting for when he noted that the Golden Age of Athens lasted less than a century and suggested that "their leisure didn't get them very far." My response provides the point of departure for this paper: The Athenians did not engage in classical leisure. They engaged in greed and imperialism. They enslaved and killed fellow-Greeks under the auspices of a protective foreign policy. They used their institutions of representative government to legitimize their violent factional disputes. While paying lip service to their ancient ideals of moderation, reason, and balance, their actions promoted war, plague, and ultimately, their own bankruptcy and destruction.

But from this debacle an ideal developed, an ideal that has served as a model to prompt hope through some of the most tumultuous periods of western history. The power of this ideal—the ideal of classical leisure—becomes clear as we identify its continual resurgence in the tension between human aspirations for a more ethical life and the darker sides of the history of western civilization.

The dialectical interaction between ideals and reality is a well developed concept in post-Kantian thought. But as early as the fourth century BC, Plato stressed the distinctions between the world of ideas and the world of our observations:

> But people seem to forget that some things have sensible images, which are readily known and can be easily pointed out ... ; whereas the greatest and highest truths have no outward image of themselves visible to man ... ; for immaterial things, which are the noblest and greatest, are shown only in thought and idea, and in no other way ...." (Jowett, 1937, p. 313)

This quote from the *Statesman* echoes the argument developed in the *Republic*. But in the *Statesman*, Plato has opened the door to grappling with the empirical world, and his earlier work is "relegated to its place as a 'model fixed in the heavens' for human imitation but not for attainment" (Sabine, 1961, p. 74). The world of eternal truth is now viewed as interactive with "the differences of men and actions, and the endless irregular movements of human things" (Jowett, 1937, p. 322).

Plato's *Statesman* and *Laws* provide the bridge between his earlier, and better known, works and Aristotle. And while Plato's former student consciously attempted to focus on the empirical world, remnants of utopianism (especially by twentieth-century standards) remain in his thought; most notable is his argument of an established potential, toward which actuality is moving.

Ethics presents a standard of proper, or right, behavior. Hence it necessarily begins by focusing on the individual, though most of the pivotal figures in western thought have extended this initial focus into discussions of proper social behavior as well. To determine right behavior, the classical philosophers began by establishing the parameters of what we have to work with, that is, human nature. To one who considers human beings to be basically evil, an ethical imperative may seem childishly simplistic or, at best, a mechanism to minimize this evil as much as possible. To someone who considers us to be basically good, ethics provides reinforcement for what we are naturally inclined to do.

If we were to classify western thought on such a continuum, I would place Calvin toward one extreme and Kropotkin toward the other. Such a classification would encourage us to identify significant similarities and differences in western thought. For instance, both Hegel and Marx argued that individuals are molded by their culture and controlled by their state. To Hegel this is positive because culture and the state are mechanisms of coercion to limit the innately destructive tendencies of human beings. Marx's critique of bourgeois culture and the nation state is predicated on his assumption of innate human creativity and sociability; hence, culture and the state are impediments to the flowering of the human potential. Attitudes toward leisure time are equally as revealing, with those placed toward the negative extreme denying the significance of leisure because any lack of regimentation, coercion, and fear, that is, totally free time, would allow the evil inclinations of our species to flourish. Those who celebrate the human potential and condemn regimentation, coercion, and fear as constraints on our true nature view leisure in a positive manner. Obviously, most thinkers fit somewhere in between the extremes; but note that this approach has already suggested an interesting parallel, at least in attitudes toward leisure, in the thought of Aristotle and Marx—two thinkers who are not generally considered as having much in common. The tension between actuality and potentiality provides the basis for both systems of thought.

While both Plato and Aristotle drew heavily from the pre-Socratic intellectual legacy of ancient Greece, the decline of Athens provided the catalyst for their work. Plato's dichotomy between the true world of eternal ideas and the world of empirical illusion can be viewed as merely an attempt to escape from the tragedies he experienced. But his grappling with these tragedies provided the foundation of western philosophy. Reason, that quality which Homer had reserved for the gods, was offered as a human capacity to dominate our lower drives of passion and desire. Plato was certainly an elitist, arguing that those who are capable of truly rational thought and action will always be a small minority. But his challenge to transcend the illusions of the cave and subordinate the lower drives to our rational capacity serves as a wellspring for personal ethics and as the cornerstone of classical leisure.

In the *Republic* Plato extends personal ethics into a social system by arguing that the few who are capable of rationality should control the entire society. Hence, leisure as the active contemplation of eternal truth becomes the key to the good society—a society that would not succumb to the whims of desire or the blindness of passion, as the Athenians had.

Aristotle integrated Greek natural science with Plato's ethical and social concerns by arguing that nature encompasses both the actual material manifestations of a thing and the potential form that the thing will become. Hence, each thing in nature is potentially something more than it actually appears to be. The hierarchy of nature, then, is established by the degree to which a thing consciously participates in the actualization of its potential. Human beings are at the top of the hierarchy because we have "active reason"—the unique ability to contemplate and generalize about our lives, society, history, and our future. The essence of animals is to satisfy their material needs. The essence of human beings is to understand the world around us. Hence, classical leisure is our goal in life, and we participate in our own actualization by pursuing our essence as rational beings. And while Aristotle's elitism is not as rigid as Plato's, he allows that slaves shall be necessary to produce the material needs of a society while others devote their time and energy to active reason.

The Athenian ideal of classical leisure is based on the assumption that we are something more than we appear to be; both Plato and Aristotle argued that there is more to being human than the history of Athens suggests:

> We must view ourselves as very special beings, with an essence that transcends the satisfaction of animal needs and physical desires. In short we must view our lives as the opportunity to know truth and practice goodness. Everything we do—our time and our energy—should take this uniqueness into account and our priorities must begin with the discovery and pursuit of this uniqueness. (Dare, Welton, & Coe, 1987, p. 44)

But the Greek city-state was the only environment familiar to the Athenian philosophers, and their ink had barely dried when it faded into oblivion.

The tension between the Athenian ideal and reality became acute as the Roman Empire entered its cycle of imperialist expansion, internal corruption, and decay. Philosophy came to focus on personal ethics and social withdrawal—a tendency that is also detectable in the early Christian movement. The transcendent message of Christianity meshed easily with Plato's world view: the inevitably disappointing and chaotic empirical world can be transcended, through the soul, into a higher realm of being. Saint Paul replaced reason with faith and, finally, Saint Augustine synthesized Plato and Christianity: oneness with the eternal God through faith, as opposed to oneness with eternal ideas through reason, became the object of contemplation.

Aristotle's views were echoed by the Stoics, with nature viewed as the deity providing the guidelines for an ethical life. Again, the values of classical leisure emerged as a stark counterpoint to the realities of Rome:

> ... it is beneath man's dignity to begin and to end where the irrational creatures do: he must rather begin where they do and end where nature has ended in forming us; and nature ends in contem-

plation and understanding and a way of life in harmony with nature.
(Oates, 1940, p. 23)

As the Empire crumbled, the organized Church asserted its authority
and moved to fill the institutional void. From the beginning, there was
tension between the Church's attempt to maintain a universal community tied to Rome and the interests of local political elites. A second
area of potential conflict can be recognized as the result of the elimi-
nation of reason from Plato's metaphysics and the Stoics' deification
of nature; with the Greek unity shattered, the door was open for a
massive struggle between religion and science. In addition, charges of
corruption and impiety were leveled against the Church as its power
and wealth increased. By the thirteenth century the assault on the Church
(spearheaded by the reemergence of Aristotelian science and reason)
had reached crisis proportions, and while the Inquisition was terrorizing
Europe, Thomas Aquinas was summoned to defend the papacy in a
more peaceful manner.

Aquinas synthesized the Aristotelian tradition with Roman Catholi-
cism by making God the creator of nature. Hence, the conflict between
religion and science was eased by viewing nature as a divinely-inspired
system to be understood by man. God also gave us active reason as a
capacity to rise above sin and improve our society. And while ultimate
actualization can occur only in the spiritual afterlife, relative actualization, and our highest human capacity, can be achieved through the
contemplation of God's perfection. Again, classical leisure is the purest
form of truly human activity, and God has given us the capacity, and
the responsibility, to actualize our unique humanity.

Despite the Inquisition and Aquinas, the attacks on the papacy grew,
and a tide of secular humanism swept Europe during the Renaissance.
By the sixteenth century, the market economy emerged as still another
challenge to the medieval status quo, Henry VIII expelled Roman Ca-
tholicism from England, and Luther's attempt to reform the Church
erupted into the Reformation.

In stark contrast to the optimism of the Renaissance, the Reformation
offered a particularly dismal view of the human condition. Sin and evil
pervade the earth, reason is an illusion, and rigid authority over secular
matters must be maintained at all costs. Luther's obsession with sin
and the carnal dimensions of the physical world led him to dismiss
reason as human folly, and Calvin cemented the argument: "We take
nothing from the womb but pure filth . . . all human works, if judged
according to their own worth, are nothing but filth and defilement"
(Bouwsma, 1988, p. 36). If nothing else, Calvin was consistent, as he
extended this view of human nature to attack any rational human potential: "For even if God wills to manifest his fatherly favor to us in
many ways, yet we cannot, by contemplating the universe, infer that he

is father. . . . Dullness and ingratitude follow, for our minds, as they have been blinded, do not perceive what is true . . . all our senses have been perverted" (Bouwsma, 1988, pp. 139–140).

In such an inhospitable world, it is not surprising that Calvin's followers chose to overcome their anxiety through work. One's vocation became viewed as God's calling, and the Calvinist work ethic provided the cutting edge for the development of modern capitalism in western Europe; virtually every aspect of classical philosophy, including leisure, was denied.

The unlikely link between Protestant theology and empiricist philosophy was forged in the seventeenth century by John Locke, who secularized the calling into the labor theory of value (Dunn, 1982, p. 219). Locke argued that all value is the direct result of human labor and that reason is secondary to desire. His fellow-empiricist David Hume argued that reason is a "slave" of the passions. In 1776, Adam Smith published his economic history of the species that glorified the productive efficiency of the assembly line in a pin factory as the culmination of the human potential. Almost incidentally, and in his matter-of-fact style, Smith notes that "A shepherd has a great deal of leisure; a husbandman . . . has some; an artificer or manufacturer has none at all" (Smith, 1937, p. 659).

It is difficult to imagine how any observer of reality in the industrial cities of England in the early nineteenth century could have imagined that the classical ideal of leisure would survive. Ten-year-old children commonly worked 16 hour shifts and were whipped when they fell asleep. The wealth of the nation was growing, but at what cost? At a hearing held by the Sadler Committee of Parliament in 1833, a physician summarized the impact of these conditions on both children and adults: "The reflecting or spiritual mind gradually becomes debased . . . the being is necessarily ruined, both for the present and for the future life" (Knoles & Snyder, 1954, p. 586). But how could the physician know that in only two years a German student would enroll at the University of Bonn, move on to Berlin, write his dissertation on Athenian science and philosophy, and challenge the world to rediscover its creative essence through classical leisure. That student, of course, was Karl Marx.

When Marx entered the University of Berlin in 1836, the institution was steeped in Hegelian thought. Like Adam Smith, Hegel meshed the "egotistical laborer" definition of humanity with progress. But the German theologian placed this argument in a sweeping metaphysical perspective that presented human labor as a tool of divine rationality. Every event and idea in history, then, became a significant part of the divine rational plan. Human beings are crucial actors in this plan, but are merely laborers to actualize the goals established by nonhuman rationality.

Marx's contribution to the ideal of classical leisure lies in his insistence on reintegrating actuality and potentiality as human qualities. Like the Athenian philosophers, Marx argued that reason and potentiality are human attributes. And to him, the goal of the historical process has been to unite human thought and action. He attacked his fellow economists for assuming that, just because we have acted like egotistical animals, we are innately egotistical economic animals. Until the development of capitalism, biological necessity forced us to act in this manner to guarantee our existence. But with advanced capitalist production, machines will increasingly perform the productive tasks and allow our species to grapple with our essence of rational freedom, creativity, and sociability.

The Marxian synthesis of western thought is staggering—especially in its treatment of leisure. Historically, the need to survive has denied us the opportunity to practice the ideal. But the future holds the chance to actually engage in classical leisure, as economic abundance replaces scarcity and essence can emerge from our preoccupation with existence.

Marx's ideal of a communal future challenges us to transcend ethical norms based on animal existence and become truly human through rational contemplation of our reality and our potentiality and through conscious action moving us toward the latter. But while his thought is based on this Athenian view, Marx radically democratized the ideal by arguing that all people could participate in actualizing the human potential, as advanced machinery replaced the slave in modern industrial society.

There is evidence that the material reality of postindustrial society has provided us today with such an opportunity. And if we are to progress toward a more ethical world, it is safe to assume that the ideal of classical leisure will play a role.

References

Bouwsma, W. J. (1988). *John Calvin: A sixteenth-century portrait.* New York: Oxford University Press.

Dare, B., Welton, G., & Coe, W. (1987). *Concepts of leisure in Western thought: A critical and historical analysis.* Dubuque, IA: Kendall/Hunt Publishing Company.

Dunn, J. (1982). *The political thought of John Locke.* Cambridge: Cambridge University Press.

Jowett, B. (Trans.) (1937). *The dialogues of Plato,* vol. II. New York: Random House.

Knoles, G. H., & Snyder, R. K. (1954). *Readings in Western civilization.* Chicago: J. B. Lippincott.

Oates, W. J. (Ed.). (1940). *The Stoic and Epicurean philosophers.* New York: Modern Library.

Sabine, G. H. (1961). *A history of political theory* (3rd ed.). New York: Holt, Rinehart and Winston.

Smith, A. (1937). *An inquiry into the causes and consequences of the wealth of nations.* New York: Random House.

Leisure, Transcendence, and the Good Life: From the Greeks to the Existentialists

William Coe

In a report titled "Humanities in America," Lynne Cheney, chairman of the National Endowment for the Humanities, quoted the philosopher Charles Frankel, who suggested that when we ask about the place of the humanities in America we are really asking "what images of human possibility will American society put before its members? What standards will it suggest to them as befitting the dignity of the human spirit? What decent balance among human employments will it exhibit? Will it speak to them only of success and celebrity and the quick fix that makes them happy, or will it find a place for grace, elegance, nobility, and a sense of connection with the human adventure?" (Cheney, 1988, p. 3). I submit that these are the sorts of questions which we should also be asking when we consider the nature and place of leisure in our lives. These are questions which force us to consider the nature of the good life and, most fundamentally, what it means to be human.

Leisure has been said to be that part of life which is valued for its own sake. It is the intrinsically valuable part of life—that part for the sake of which we live and to which our other activities are subordinate. It is certainly, then, to be cherished rather than squandered or wasted, and it should be the object of our reflective concern. In almost three thousand years of recorded speculation about good, evil, and ourselves, however, we seem to have reached no consensus about the nature of the good or, therefore, about the meaning of leisure in our lives.

Most of us identify leisure with spare time, and the good life with freedom. We live for the weekend. Unless we are among the few fortunate enough to find our work fulfilling, we value what we do with our discretionary, or "free," time more than we value our work. If our leisure is to be part of the adventure of life, however, we must understand freedom as more than spare time and the absence of coercion. To understand freedom as what Jean-Paul Sartre called the transcendence of consciousness is to understand leisure as even more important than it was for the Greeks.

Until recently there has been no ontology of freedom and therefore no adequate basis for understanding leisure and the nature of the good life. It is the existential thinkers of the late nineteenth and the twentieth centuries who have most directly challenged the assumption behind both the classical Greek and the Judeo-Christian views of human nature and the good life and hence of most western thinking about ourselves. They have challenged the assumption that there is such a thing as human nature, which is tied up with the notion that human beings are objects that can be known and understood in essentially the same way other things are known and understood. In the eighteenth century Immanuel Kant first clearly formulated the idea that to be a subject, or knower of knowledge, was to be something radically different from being an object, or what is known. The consequence has been a reevaluation of the nature of knowledge and of what it means to be human. To be human has come to mean to be the sort of being who can never be adequately understood as an object of knowledge. Human subjects are very different from objects. Because objects are objects only in relation to knowing subjects, they and the world which they compose are necessarily permeated with subjectivity. There is no pure objectivity anywhere. Subjectivity, or consciousness, then, cannot be reduced to any kind of objectivity, but must be understood to transcend the world that is its object.

Before Kant it was not possible to conceive a universal leisure and freedom for everyone. For the Greeks, for example, the universe was a hierarchy in which some were naturally free and others were naturally slaves. But the objective properties that made one a natural master or natural slave are properties of persons considered as objects. For the Kantian tradition we are all equal members of the community of intrinsically valuable beings precisely because we are not fundamentally objects. It is our transcendental subjectivity that was for Kant the foundation of our freedom, dignity, and humanity. Continental philosophy since Kant has been a working out of the idea of transcendental subjectivity and therefore has been the antithesis of the classical view that to be human is to be part of the natural order. It has become clear that we, as conscious subjects, are not *in* the natural world, and that the natural world must not be understood as a reality independent of the minds that know it. During the nineteenth century, thinkers like Nietzsche were beginning to understand that our knowledge of the world, and therefore the world itself, is formed or structured by the concepts we use, by the subject-object structure of our language and thought, and by the assumptions, presuppositions, and prejudices we bring to experience. The world as it is known reflects the mind that does the knowing.

But natural science and the technology it feeds still command enormous respect. From the scientific point of view, human beings are objects to be studied and brought under the same purview as other natural things. Maurice Merleau-Ponty (1962) has written that "we must begin by reawakening the basic experience of the world of which science is a second-order expression. . . . Scientific points of view, according to which my existence is a moment of the world's, are always both naive and at the same time dishonest, because they take for granted, without explicitly mentioning it, the other point of view, namely that of consciousness, through which from the outset a world forms itself around me and begins to exist for me" (p. ix). It is this other point of view, that of consciousness, which we must understand if we are adequately to understand the adventure of life.

Without conscious beings the world would not be a *world*; it would not be that meaningful arena within which we make choices and live our lives. To the question whether the world would still be here if all conscious beings were to die, the answer is that it would still be here in the same sense that the works of Shakespeare—the printed pages— could still be said to exist if there would never again be anyone able to read them. What would be missing, would be the significance (cf. Warnock, 1970, p. 36). There is a fundamental truth about ourselves that is prior to all objective truths. It is the truth that at the most primordial level what we normally call objective truth is dependent on our subjectivity—on our commitments to certain world views and their presuppositions, on the values we have embraced, and on choices we make to take certain evidence seriously or to ignore it. To be human is to be a transcendental subject who is actively creative in formulating the meaning of the world.

For the classical mind and, indeed, for most of our tradition, meanings are derived from absolute and objective truths such as the Platonic Forms, God's existence, or our human nature. It is considered our business to discover and live by those truths. For Merleau-Ponty and Sartre, however, it is through human, conscious being that meaning and truth enter the world. They point out that the world, or any collection of facts, is ambiguous until confronted by consciousness. Sartre (1956) writes that an obstacle is not intrinsically an obstacle. It is an obstacle for me only if I have chosen a goal which lies beyond it, and that such choices are fundamentally free (p. 488). They can never be conditioned

by facts alone. Whatever choice I make is one by which I transcend
what is given. To understand an action is to understand it in terms of
its end, which is not a fact because it is not yet realized. What is the
case is never sufficient to explain human purpose. Life is an adventure
because we are creators of truth, not mere discoverers—because we
are free, not acting out a drama the script of which, although imperfectly
known, has already been written.

Since Kant, then, there has been an important philosophical tradition
that denies the adequacy of any understanding of ourselves as objects.
Sartre (1956) describes the person as "a being which is what it is not,
and is not what it is" (p. 58). An object, on the other hand, is what it
is. It is not problematic, as is a conscious subject, and it does not have
the dignity and ultimate worth of a human being. To see others as
students, as workers, or as consumers is to see them as objects and to
overlook the subjectivity that is the foundation of their humanity. We
are aware of our subjectivity and that of others, but still we too frequently do see ourselves and each other as objects. To understand
oneself most adequately, however, is to know one's own freedom. It is
to encounter one's responsibility for what one is at the same time that
one realizes that one transcends what one is because one might have
chosen differently and been a different person.

The picture painted by the early Sartre was a picture of the human
condition which was as ahistorical as that of the Greeks. But, as Merleau-
Ponty knew and Sartre came to realize, it was a caricature of the human
situation. We are social and historical beings through and through. Our
consciousness may be, as Sartre insists, spontaneous, but it is all the
same conditioned by its social context. It was in the philosophy of the
early Karl Marx that Sartre discovered a social philosophy which, once
he had replaced its materialist metaphysics with existentialism's ontology of consciousness, would give us a way of talking meaningfully
of the human situation. The nature of consciousness, Sartre had always
argued, was to be absolutely free, but now he could talk about how we
exercise this absolute freedom within limits which are historical and
often very narrow. All knowledge is situated, positional, and historical.
Nature in itself has no inherent meaning. Whatever meaning it has, we
give it. "History, on the other hand, as the record of human actions as
well as the context within which human choices are made, is meaningful.
To understand history is to understand human actions, which means
to understand the projects and values which make them meaningful"
(Dare, Welton, & Coe, 1987, p. 241).

To understand history is to understand the purposes and values underlying choices, and it is to see how the economic and political situations
at any moment are not only the result of free choices people have earlier
made in response to their situations but also the determinants of the

conditions within which the next generation must make its choices. History is dialectical. In judging the past and my situation, and then choosing, I transcend them toward a future of my choosing. As long as one has any meaningful choice at all, one's freedom, no matter how restricted, is absolute. Although there can never be any proof that I am making the right choice, whatever choice I make is one by which I transcend what is given.

Marx had recognized that men make history, although in the context of conditions which they have not chosen. To understand history, Sartre realized, is impossible without understanding freedom and consciousness because history is the product of human creativity in the face of circumstance. It is the result of free choices which might have been different and not, as orthodox Marxists insist, a steady and inevitable march toward a predictable and foreordained outcome. Those orthodox Marxists who embrace such a determinism while living their own freedom, Sartre accused of bad faith (1968, p. 48).

For Sartre, then, the best life is the life in which one acknowledges one's own freedom and assumes responsibility for what one has made of oneself. Refusing to hide behind deterministic excuses, we should live as much as possible in good faith. We should accept responsibility for what we do and who we are. We live for the future in terms of projects and values which transcend any facts. Such values, as Martin Heidegger says, are chosen in meditation. Yet Sartre goes beyond Heidegger to give an account of how the projects we adopt in contemplation or meditation can, in concert with the projects of others, be successfully realized. It is clear that the good life is no longer simply the authentic life as it can be considered in isolation. It is also the active and creative participation with others in the dialectic of situation, thought, and action. Community is important, for it enhances one's freedom and therefore one's humanity. Exercising one's freedom in concert with the freedom of others with the same values and goals, one makes connection with the human adventure. Leisure must reinforce this connection.

According to Sartre we are what we do. It is by knowing a person as he acts—as he transcends what he has been toward the person that he will be—that we come to know him best. Likewise, I suggest, it is by knowing a community or culture as it transcends the past toward the society it will be that we know it best. Just as one can find individuals to be in bad faith because they flee from recognizing the transcendence which is the core of their humanity, so can we talk of whole cultures in bad faith. Any culture, for example, which insists on regarding human beings to be essentially consumers so that those who consume more or with more expertise are considered superior could be said to be in bad faith.

Of course, there are many other recent expressions of the critique of objectivism begun by Kant. Consider Jacques Derrida, a contemporary thinker who is continuing the criticism of western tradition. Directing his attention to texts, and recognizing that the aim of language as traditionally understood is to bring the mind into the presence of the real, he denies that any text can put us in touch with reality.

Derrida calls the notion that Being is present to thought "the myth of presence." Western thought supposes that reality, or Being, is present to the mind and that language names that presence. Deconstructing the tradition, Derrida insists, reveals that it is wrong because Being is never present as the myth of presence claims it is. Nothing is ever simply present. Anything which I might propose as present is constituted in part by relationships to, and differences from, things which are not present. It is impossible to give an account of what is present without referring, at least implicitly, to what is absent. Reality is inhabited by absence. Being is haunted by nonpresence. Derrida points out that the explication of any text is always another text, either spoken or written. It is never a metaphysical presence. As long as we accept the myth of presence we shall search the endless empty corridors of language for revelation and enlightenment—for the voice of Being. And language will fail us. In language there is no presence, but only absence.

So, just as the existentialists reject the traditional dualism of mind and world, insisting that the world reflects the mind, Derrida has rejected the traditional western dualism of text and world. "There is nothing outside the text" (Derrida, 1976, p. 158). Now where are we? Where does Derrida leave us? The problem is that he wants us to get out from under the tradition, but, as Richard Rorty has argued, any attempt to do that is bound to "fail, because every statement of the attempt will be in terms that the tradition has created for us" (Rorty, 1977, p. 677). So Derrida's message cannot be stated directly. And if he could so state it, we could not understand it, for we are all captives of the tradition. The conclusion seems to be that there is no salvation, since there is no ultimate text and no direct revelation of Being. Our words represent nothing but themselves. There is no divine revelation. We are left to our own devices. Then why bother to deconstruct western thought at all? Because, it seems to me, if we can't find salvation by coming into the presence of Being, we can at least settle for the adventure of life, with all of its unsettling but exhilarating uncertainties and paradoxes. Derrida's mission is to save us from wanting to be saved. The core of his deconstructionism "is a sustained argument against the possibility of anything pure and simple which can serve as the foundation for the meaning of [what we say and write]" (Garver, 1972, p. xxii).

I am proposing a humanistic reading of Derrida, although he rejects humanism and talks of texts as if they write themselves. When Derrida talks of "the deconstruction of consciousness" (1976, p. 70) and writes that "writing is the becoming-absent and the becoming-unconscious of the self," (p. 69) he is signaling the dissolution of the subject and therefore the death of the idea of transcendental subjectivity. On the other hand, he denies that there is any original meaning against which my reading of his text can be judged and so has authorized whatever reading I propose. Derrida has revealed the open-ended indefiniteness not only of textuality and language, but also of the world and of being human. My texts are my creations, and so is the meaning of my life. If we could realize the goal of presence, if language and consciousness were innocent and transparent and our inner lives therefore direct encounters with Being, that would be total death. Without that lack of presence Derrida calls *différance*, we would not be lost and disoriented, but neither would we be alive and free. We would be safe in the bosom of Being, at home, immobile, no longer alienated, but with nowhere to go and nothing to dream of or work for. Our salvation is the fact that there is no salvation. The meaning of life is in the adventure of living.

So it seems to me that other current thinking in my discipline continues to lend credence to the existentialist idea that to know who we are is to know ourselves as free, creative, transcending beings. As the originators of meaning—of texts, if you will—we transcend them. Our very lives are texts, and we are continually rewriting our lives and the world as we transcend our pasts and our situations. We need not submit to the texts of Madison Avenue and Hollywood—those images, entertainments, and amusements which treat us as predictable consumers of goods and pleasures. They encourage us to forget our humanity by treating symptoms such as boredom and restlessness rather than the condition, which is the failure to have a sense of who one is and what are one's purposes in life—what is generally called alienation. They therefore direct our attention away from the need to make our lives meaningful in a sense more fundamental than that understood by the gospel of consumerism.

Today we are constantly assaulted by social, governmental, and entrepreneurial forces which influence our concepts of how we should live those parts of our lives we describe as recreation and leisure. We allow advertising images to influence our very concepts of ourselves and of the meaning of life. Leisure activities have become commodities in an increasingly confused marketplace. Alienation was once located primarily in labor. Now it has invaded even our leisure. We have turned everything, including ourselves, into commodities. It is critically important to the good life that we not submit to notions of how we should live our leisure that trivialize our lives, and to avoid such submission we must understand ourselves not as consumers and spectators, but as free, creative, and transcendent beings. Socrates said that the unexamined life is not worth living and Aristotle maintained that the good life was the self-actualized, and therefore the contemplative life.

It is not true that philosophers have failed to achieve any consensus. The message common to the ancients and the moderns seems to be that the good life is that life in which we are most in touch with our humanity and that leisure must be self-actualizing and therefore must be reflective as well as active. It must be a life of the mind as well as of the body; it must involve reflection and self-understanding rather than escape from thinking. This is an old message as well as a new one, and it is one we ignore at our peril.

But the humanistic vision born of Marxism and existentialism has other profound implications for our conceptions of ourselves and, therefore, for our understanding of all human activities, especially of leisure. Its message is that to be human is precisely to be free, to have to choose, to have no necessary essence, and always to transcend one's situation. This implies not only that to be most fully human is to be actively contemplative, but that it is to be responsible, creative, and always to transcend what one has been toward what one chooses to become. So the authentic contemplation that is essential to any truly significant leisure is only in part a return to the classical ideal of the contemplative life. There is a significant difference between contemplation as conceived by the Greeks and authentic reflection as the existentialists understand it. For the ancients, contemplation put one in touch with eternal verities such as the nature of man, the universe, God, and the good life. These essences were thought to exist independently of our contemplation of them.

The contemporary humanist vision, on the other hand, sees that what we make of ourselves will establish not only the meaning of our own lives, but that of the world. This vision must be that what is essential to the good life is the honest and authentic engagement with our human condition, which demands the acknowledgment of the fundamental truth that the meaning of life is not foreordained but is up to each of us. Just as we have outgrown the notion that there are gods who direct our destinies and determine the meaning of life, we have transcended the belief that it is the essences which are its objects that make contemplation important. Our destiny is in our own hands, and how we understand and live our leisure is both a symptom and a determinant of what we make of ourselves and of the world.

References

Cheney, L. V. (1988). *Humanities in America: A report to the President, the Congress, and the American people.* Washington, DC: National Endowment for the Humanities.

Dare, B., Welton, G., & Coe, W. (1987). *Concepts of leisure in Western thought.* Dubuque, IA: Kendall/Hunt Publishing Company.

Derrida, J. (1976). *Of grammatology* (Gayatri Chakravorty Spivak, Trans.). Baltimore & London: Johns Hopkins University Press.

Garver, N. (1972). Preface to Derrida, *Speech and phenomenon and other essays in Husserl's Theory of Signs* (David B. Allison, Trans.). Evanston, IL: Northwestern University Press.

Merleau-Ponty, M. (1962). *The phenomenology of perception.* London: Routledge & Kegan Paul.

Rorty, R. (1977). Derrida on language, being, and abnormal philosophy. *Journal of Philosophy, 74* (11), 673–681.

Sartre, J. (1956). *Being and nothingness.* New York: Philosophical Library.

Sartre, J. (1968). *Search for a method.* New York: Vintage Books.

Warnock, M. (1970). *Existentialism.* New York: Oxford University Press.

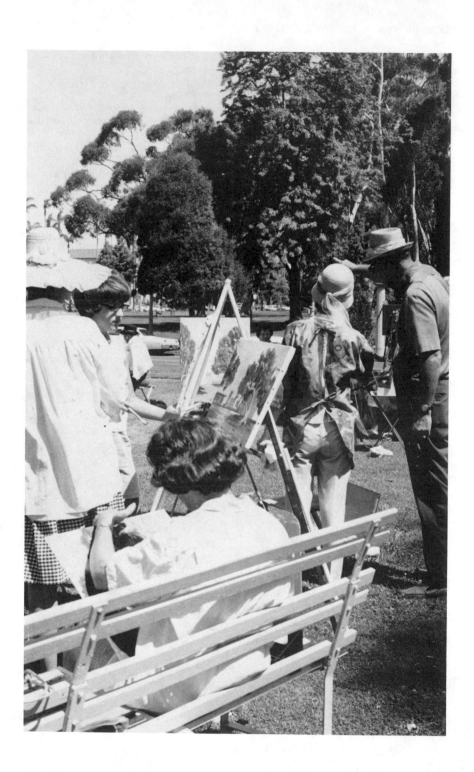

Leisure: A Moral Imperative

John R. Wilcox

It was bound to happen. The ethics squad has finally reached the playing fields of leisure, having investigated the world of work and the activities of the professions. Is there nothing sacred, nothing beyond the purview of academe's cottage industry: applied and professional ethics? Leisure is, after all, relaxation time. How introspective should we be about that? Upon some reflection, all would probably agree that we need to evaluate what is moral, what is right and wrong in all dimensions of our lives, even when we are having fun. But that is not the issue here.

Accountability and Accessibility

Is leisure just a change of pace from work? What is the relationship between work and leisure in these rapidly changing times? These queries give some indication of tone and direction in this paper. The primary issue that one must address with regard to leisure in these times is one that underlies these questions: we must decide whether leisure itself is a moral imperative.

In response to the question about anything being sacred, the only possible response is no; in this age there does not seem to be anything sacred in itself. But this is not due to philosophers in need of work. The accountability to standards demanded from individuals and institutions, whether they be an Ivan Boesky, Oliver North, and Jimmy Valvano or the savings and loan industry, the executive branch of the federal government, and North Carolina State, is a demand arising from society itself.

Accountability to standards and the assessment of a leisure imperative are related to each other and are both aspects of a larger concern about the moral quality of life in a rapidly changing society. This concern is, to a large extent, an American phenomenon, as distinctive of our late-twentieth century culture as was the volunteerism that Alexis de Tocqueville described in *Democracy in America*. Thus, we must approach leisure in conjunction with an evaluation of the current interest in accountability in a rapidly changing world.

Accountability has arisen in large part because of accessibility: immediacy of information—what might be called the "bottom line" of the telecommunications age. The news is quite literally in the air. Who doesn't know about John Tower's drinking, Jim and Tammy Baker's fortune, Joel Steinberg's abuse, or Dan Quayle's career? It is not only the broadcast waves from transmission towers on earth and satellites in space; radio and television waves bombarding the continent seem to communicate "the news" even if you don't have your Walkman or Watchman on. In fact accountability and accessibility symbolize the cultural upheaval in contemporary American society.

Accessibility or immediacy of information is the pervasive indicator of how technology has shaped our society and has initiated changes as complex and far-reaching as the ones brought about by the printing press in the Renaissance and the steam engine in the Industrial Age. Just as the age of the printing press and that of the steam engine were characterized by freedom of conscience and democracy respectively, accountability characterizes our media age of accessibility.

In fact, accountability itself may be interpreted as a search for values in the face of rapid change. Thus, we ask here: what is the value of leisure as we approach the third millenium? "The very rapidity of technological change contrasts with the slower changes in human values and attitudes. People can tolerate rapid change in some areas of their lives if there is stability in other areas; but technological change alters nearly every area of modern life" (Barbour, 1980, p. 43). It was the social upheaval, for instance, both during and after World War I that prompted William Butler Yeats to observe in "The Second Coming":

> Things fall apart; the center cannot hold;
> Mere anarchy is loosed upon the world,
> The blood-dimmed tide is loosed, and everywhere
> The ceremony of innocence is drowned;
> The best lack all conviction, while the worst
> Are full of passionate intensity.

Access brings to the fore two aspects of accountability: the demand that both the media itself and those subject to media attention be accountable. Immediacy of information is itself a stunning technological revolution. Because of the rapid change induced by this revolution we search for norms and values to guide us in our use of the media.

This is no easy task. For example, the latest political or economic crisis of the morning is the subject of the global conference call on Nightline in the evening. But we ask: Is television simply the conduit for informed conversation brought to our living rooms in ways scarcely dreamed of 50 years ago? Or is the media the creator of the information we receive in ways that are qualitatively different from print media? We ponder such questions as: Is the presidential candidate's message what he believes in his heart or is it what he believes we want to hear? Or worse, is the candidate a product of anchorpersons' proclivities or prejudices? How do we even begin to develop norms and assess the values inherent in the Age of Telecommunications?

On the one hand, we flail at the media because it has few sexual inhibitions. We bemoan the lack of aesthetics in family television. We boycott program sponsors in an attempt to assert viewer control. Above all, we worry about the way in which the media, in all its manifestations, is shaping the next generation, our children.

On the other hand, it is access to information that is an important catalyst stimulating the accountability demanded of the geneticist experimenting with fetal transplants, the stockbroker trading on Wall Street, or the candidate for Secretary of Defense. Not only is the media itself a cause for moral concern, it informs and sensitizes us to the value conflicts that pervade virtually all areas of life. Moreover, some of these conflicts are caused by new technologies themselves, as in the case of fetal experimentation. Other conflicts exemplify an ethical tradition regarding use of privileged information or avoiding conflicts of interest in one's work. In any case, the rapidity of change in the society impels us to seek accountability from those who are now visible in ways never before possible.

In our society, the ever-present TV is both source of access and catalyst for accountability. Television symbolizes telecommunications in all its complexity—from the computer to the satellite dish. TV is, moreover, virtually synonymous with leisure. But for those who think seriously about American society this is a poor equation and raises the question of what exactly constitutes or defines leisure. Such definition is central to any discussion of leisure and ethics. Before one is offered, however, the analysis of the telecommunications revolution is necessary, especially in relation to what many consider the very antithesis of leisure—work.

Work

It is conjectured that in a fully automated society, only 2 percent of the population would be needed to supply the food and manufactured goods for the entire population (Barbour, 1980, p. 38). This does not mean the other 98 percent are at leisure. That which would reduce the farming and manufacturing sector to miniscule numbers has already spawned new industries and millions of jobs in the service sector. Why so? Essential to automation is the silicon chip. The chip is also the source of modern telecommunications, which includes sophisticated computers, complex programming, television, and audio linkage, as well as high-speed global transmission. Thus the chip is the progenitor of the contemporary information-based industries including finance, education, and the media among others in the service society. On this point see "Employment by Selected Industry, 1970 to 1986, and Projections, 2000" (*Statistical Abstract of the United States, 1988*, p. 380).

In discussing work in this essay, the primary emphasis will be given to career and professional aspirations. The contemporary discussion of work as career or profession is very much related to the pursuit of work by means of a college education (*Wall Street Journal*, 1988). The annual surveys of entering college freshmen are instructive on this point (Astin, 1988). They have been conducted for the last 22 years by the American Council on Education and the Higher Education Research Institute at the University of California, Los Angeles. "A record 72.6 percent [of the incoming freshmen surveyed in the Astin study] indicated 'making more money' was a very important factor in the decision to attend college" (*New York Times*, 1989, p. 1). Being very well off financially was deemed essential or very important by over 75 percent in the 1987 Astin survey, while developing a meaningful philosophy of life continued to decline from over 80 percent in 1967 to 39 percent in 1987 (*New York Times*, 1988; *Chronicle of Higher Education*, 1989a). College today is not so much an opportunity to learn for its own sake or to develop a meaningful philosophy of life as it is an apprenticeship for the new union card of management or marketing expertise. Furthermore, while many aspire to be a "professional" in pursuit of the bachelor of science in business, one is impelled to ask how many are willing to embrace the central demand of the classic professions: concern for the public good.

The proliferation of service industries and the pursuit of undergraduate education as the foundation of economic security go hand in hand. Upward mobility in those industries depends on the rationality and expertise provided by higher education. Here access—the information revolution—again raises questions of accountability, but in a more subtle way. Earlier on in this essay, access to information was seen as the stimulus to greater accountability not only because of knowledge possessed, but also because of the dissolution of normative criteria in such a rapidly changing society. Now we must ask what accountability means to the new professionals in the burgeoning service sectors. To whom is one accountable and for what? The answer to this question will set the stage for an evaluation of leisure.

Accountability in the workplace may be determined by an organizational chart. But there are other perspectives, aside from such a rational model. To a great extent, accountability is dependent upon the subjective understanding of to whom one is accountable. A manager may hold the view that he or she is accountable to higher management, other employees, shareholders, the local community, and other stakeholders including the government and society at large—to any and all of these or to no one but oneself and the work itself. However, the quality of that accountability, the moral tone, is a function of one's personal relationship with the work itself. William K. Frankena (1976) is perceptive on this point. Work is not simply a job. It is a vocation.

For Frankena, there is a paradigm case of vocation: "Usually, it is thought of as including an occupation, not just in the sense of something that occupies one's time, but in the sense of some activity or service which fills much of one's time and for which one is paid by someone else in such an amount as to enable one to live" (p. 396). He also defines a "true" vocation as "the vocation one should have or have had, which is not necessarily the vocation one is actually pursuing. It is one's ideal vocation, however this is to be determined" (p. 397). Moreover, "most actual vocations certainly are not so all-inclusive, and even when we think a person has found his or her true vocation, we would usually think that it does not exhaust either the good or the moral life for that person" (p. 404).

Work is not the person, as all-encompassing as work might seem. "One's vocation does not include all of one's roles or social contributions, anymore than it includes one's avocations, hobbies, leisure activities, or recreation" (Frankena, 1976, p. 396). In fact, Frankena distinguishes between one's supervocations, defined as "serving God, promoting social well-being, living the good life, or realizing oneself—some 'high calling' shared with all other persons or perhaps with all Christians" (p. 397), and one's vocation or "earthly employment." Frankena distinguishes between the supervocation eliciting "morality and its requirements" and the supervocation calling for "the pursuit of the good life." One need not include the supervocations in any discussion of this employment, but Frankena affirms that employment or vocation is an important means of fulfilling the moral supervocation, which is the promotion of the general well-being, justly distributed (p. 401).

Thus, "there are good moral reasons why one should have a vocation. At least for most people, having one is necessary for making a living, for not being dependent on, or a burden to, others, for having the means needed to do what one morally ought to do, or for doing one's fair share of the work needed by society" (Frankena, 1976, p. 403). One's vocation becomes the means for applying the principle of beneficence or equal treatment. "We need something," he says, "besides the basic principles of morality, aretaic or deontic, to tell us who is responsible for what— some station that helps to determine our duties and our rights because it brings them to us when we take it" (p. 403).

However, Frankena cannot "conceive of a vocation that is such as to include all of one's moral activities and/or all of the best life one is capable of—such as to determine all of one's moral duties and/or all of what is good for one" (p. 404). Beneficence toward others and the pursuit of the good life for oneself are not to be swallowed up in work, though it is in and through work that social well-being and the good life are achieved.

Frankena's concluding remarks are significant. He discusses the role of liberal education and prepares us for an analysis of leisure. Education, he contends, must be, to a large extent, vocational, though not entirely so. Education must prepare us not only for the moral life but also for the good life. Because these two are so closely connected, education must be liberal: "if a vocational education is necessary to prepare us to pursue the vocation of our choice, a liberal education is even more necessary to prepare us for making that choice freely and wisely" (p. 408).

Freedom and wisdom in vocational choice means that one sees much more in life than vocation. And, as we shall see, that "more" certainly includes leisure. Furthermore, if vocation or employment is crucial to fulfillment of the moral demands of the supervocation, then vocation is not limited to the pursuit of economic security for oneself or one's family, but is much more in line with the classic understanding of the professions as enhancing public welfare or the common good (Hatch, 1988; Kultgen, 1988; Martin & Schinzinger, 1983; Reeck, 1982; Shaffer, 1987; Wilcox, 1989).

Important as goals are to personal fulfillment, work is wanting as the goal in life. It is not sufficiently transcendent in meaning and value. The primary reason for this critique is that economic security is, in the final analysis, a means to an end no matter how much it appears to be an end in itself. We can always inquire: for what purpose is economic security? (Baum, 1982; John Paul II, 1981; National Conference of Catholic Bishops, 1986). That question pushes us toward a more overarching or transcendent purpose in our employment.

Transcendence, however, does not diminish the significance of work. In the Roman Catholic tradition, "work is a fundamental dimension of man's existence on earth (John Paul II, 1981, p. 11), a conviction the Pope believes is reenforced by anthropology, palaeontology, and other sciences. That work is so significant is a matter of mathematical calculation. The best part of our lives is spent working: 40 years times

48–50 weeks a year, times 40 hours a week (at the very least). The majority of our days and the best part of these days are at work. How could they not sculpt our personhood in the most nuanced of ways? We already begin to see why leisure can be viewed as a moral imperative, given the weighty role work plays in our lives.

At the core of Jewish and Christian theology is the belief that the person is made in the image of God. John Paul II affirms that this image is seen "partly through the mandate received from his [sic] Creator to subdue, to dominate, the earth" (1981, p. 12). It is work that provides the person with specific dignity (p. 8), "the mark of the person operating within a community of persons" (p. 5). But as Gregory Baum asserts, "because labor is the axis of human self-making, it is also by labor that people are most vulnerable to wounds and distortions" (1982, p. 10). Or, as the Pope says: "work contains the unceasing measure of human toil and suffering, and also of the harm and injustice which penetrate deeply into social life within individual nations and on the international level" (1981, p. 6).

As with Frankena, so with the Pope: the moral supervocation is enhanced through work, for herein social well-being is achieved. But the totality of one's life is not achieved solely through work. The good-life supervocation is the complement of the moral supervocation in Frankena's analysis of vocation. Both must be kept in tandem. In a sense, the Pope says the same. Work so closely defines the person that it may be wrongly conflated with the person and actually become the total meaning of the person: "however true it may be that man is destined for work and called to it, in the first place work is 'for man' and not man 'for work'" (1981, p. 17).

At the same time, the Pope asserts that work is not a punishment or resultant of our first parents' original sin. The mandate in Genesis, "Be fruitful, multiply, fill the earth and conquer it," [Genesis 1:28] is given before the fall, not after it (1981, p. 11–12). Given the fact that work does so clearly identify the person and thus may itself be the source of "our wounds and distortions," could it not be that the original sin was in fact our parents' aspiring to take on God's role as Creator or The Worker par excellence? This is not the place to follow such speculation. That needs to be done elsewhere. I raise this issue primarily as a way to highlight the limitations on work, important though work is to human meaning.

In their discussion of work, Robert Bellah et al. (1985) make distinctions among job (a way of making money), career (achievement and advancement in an occupation through life, encompassing social standing, prestige, power, competency, self-esteem), and calling (a person's work is morally inseparable from his/her life and making a contribution to the common good) (p. 66).

Calling is for the authors of *Habits of the Heart* a "practical ideal of activity and character" (Bellah et al., 1985, p. 66). Although it is frequently identified with the classic professions of medicine, law, ministry, and education, it may well serve as a "practical ideal" for all who work. Certainly so, if we link calling to Frankena's philosophy of vocation. Bellah et al. observe that "it [calling] has become harder and harder to understand as our society has become more complex and utilitarian and expressive individualism more dominant" (p. 66). Work is seen more as a "segmental, self-interested activity." Serious problems arise when the job or the career level off and the challenges of each day diminish. "The possibility fades of a self that can use work and its rewards to provide the matrix of its own transcendent identity" (p. 69). Bellah et al. conclude: "The absence of a sense of calling means an absence of a sense of moral meaning" (p. 71). Meaning is then sought through the lifestyle enclave of expressive individualism, a category closely bound up with leisure.

Leisure and the Lifestyle Enclave

This essay has argued that work and moral meaning are closely tied. Social well-being, justly distributed through one's vocation, goes far toward fulfilling Frankena's moral supervocation. He cautions that work does not provide the totality of meaning or the fullness of the supervocation. John Paul II indicates that work is a two-edged sword: it is crucial to identity but the source of great suffering and injustice. Thus, obsession with work may prevent the fullness of the good life by work becoming an end in itself. Work is a transcendent activity, one which has overarching meaning when it is understood as a "calling." "In a calling ... one gives oneself to learning and practicing activities that in turn define the self and enter into the shape of its character. Committing one's self to becoming a 'good' carpenter, craftsman, doctor, scientist, or artist anchors the self within a community practicing carpentry, medicine, or art. It connects the self to those who teach, exemplify, and judge these skills. It ties us to still others whom they serve" (Bellah et al., 1985, p. 69). Calling is not easily understood in American society because we have lapsed into excessive individualism and thus the lifestyle enclave.

Frankena's affirmation that the supervocations involve work as an aspect of the moral life brings us to the role of leisure in relation to both the moral life (which comprises more than work) and the good life. Furthermore, Bellah et al.'s critique of the lifestyle enclave offers an important insight into American leisure.

Leisure and the "lifestyle enclave" are closely connected. *Habits* defines the lifestyle enclave as a group of people sharing some feature of private life: appearance, consumption, and leisure activities. These people "are not interdependent, do not act together politically, and do not share a history" (Bellah et al., 1985, p. 335). They are not a community.

In describing such groups, Bellah et al. point to the example of a retirement community where very few of the men regret leaving work. Work had no intrinsic meaning for them. "Yet what leisurely pursuits do these freedom- and privacy-loving individuals most enjoy?" *Habits* asks. "Golf and bridge, games for sociable problem solvers who love rules as much as competition, who want 'security within a fixed social order' ..." (p. 72). Lifestyle is private, emphasizing consumption and leisure, celebrating "the narcissism of similarity." At the same time, it might well be "the necessary social form of private life in a society such as ours" (p. 73).

When serious commitments carry individuals beyond these enclaves into public endeavors, the lifestyle enclave is transcended and a genuine community is possible. However, Bellah et al. see the distinction between community and lifestyle as "more analytic than concrete." In fact, they believe these elements are probably mixed in most groups. They conclude on quite a pessimistic note, however: "In a period when work is seldom a calling and few of us find a sense of who we are in public participation as citizens, the lifestyle enclave, fragile and shallow though it often is, fulfills that function for us all" (p. 75).

This analysis raises a number of questions. If, as the authors of *Habits* contend, work is seldom a calling, can leisure be other than the goal of work, a much sought after relief from jobs or careers tied to economic security or personal esteem? If one does not have a stake in work-as-calling, and thus one is not related to the public good or the fulfillment of Frankena's moral supervocation, what meaning can leisure have? Furthermore, if Bellah et al. are correct, what happens to Frankena's individual who "retires" after spending many years in a "vocation" (equals employment or what *Habits* describes as "calling"), where he or she largely fulfilled the moral supervocation both in and through the vocation?

Bellah et al. have offered a critique of our society, one in which they see the long-standing American tension between individualism and community being lost in favor of a dominant expressive individualism in which the uniqueness of the person takes precedence over interdependence. It is a society where community is used loosely, not necessarily in the strong sense adopted by Bellah et al.: "A community is a group of people who are socially interdependent, who participate together in discussion and decision making, and who share certain practices ... that both define the community and are nurtured by it" (p. 333).

Leisure—A Moral Imperative

What does leisure mean in a rapidly changing society where there is a loss of community? And has not television itself, as both a medium and as a creator of "values," abetted the destruction of community through its programs? (The rapid change discussed in the first part of this paper comes back once more for our consideration.) Can leisure in any way be assessed without a prior discussion of the various and conflicting worldviews, the interpretive mechanism whereby we give meaning to leisure? If work, for instance, is viewed solely as a job or a prison, such an interpretation will assuredly shape the meaning of leisure.

Once we are aware of the presuppositions we bring to bear on leisure, the concept will be easier to understand. "Vocation" in Frankena, "calling" in Bellah et al., and "work" in Pope John Paul II are all closely connected to a sense of community, in fact they build the community. When work is sundered from one's moral supervocation, when job and career impel one toward expressive individualism, when the person exists for work and not the reverse, there is no sense of calling nor the challenge of community building because the presuppositional worldview excludes the transcendent goal of the moral supervocation.

What then can be the meaning of leisure and in what sense can it be considered a moral imperative? If work is perceived as a career and centers on lifelong achievement and esteem, leisure may have several meanings: a retirement fantasy in the lifestyle enclave, but not something enjoyed in the present. Or leisure may be the present enjoyment of a "yuppie" lifestyle enclave such as the health club, the "in disco," country club, exclusive neighborhood, or weekend retreat. Without the glitz, leisure may be as simple as time with the family, a card game, attendance at church or synagogue—in a word all those activities not associated with work. As *Habits* indicates in the assessment of lifestyle enclaves, these may be all the things one can reasonably hope for in a society such as ours. It may well also be that leisure time is envisioned as the only time available for the building of a true community in Bellah et al.'s terms.

We have also discussed work as "job," understood primarily as a source of personal or familial economic security, without much personal meaning or fulfillment. The emotional toll taken and the alienation developed by such work may well lead to the use of leisure time for building of true community or, unfortunately, it may engender "couch potato" leisure.

In either the career or the job, work is not a calling. Of course, we are speaking of ideal types whereby we assess career, job, calling. In practice we will find all sorts of variations and combinations. It is also evident in what has been said thus far that there is a wide range of latitude in describing what constitutes leisure activity and the meaning it may have for individuals or groups. One person's work is another person's pleasure. And for some, work or leisure may be so compulsive that each virtually excludes the other from the individual's life.

The danger for a society such as ours, one which is experiencing rapid change and thus a loss of consensus about values and norms, is that we too easily accept a relativistic approach to values: "you do your thing and I do my thing, if we both happen to do the same thing, great. (As long as we don't annoy each other.)" We are thus hard put to give leisure a substantive meaning and place it in a normative context. It is more comfortable to describe different types of leisure activities from apple dunking to zen meditation. Can we say more?

While the forms leisure takes are many and diverse, there is a fundamental moral imperative that compels us to take leisure very seriously. In order to do so, however, attention must be paid to the distinguishing characteristics of leisure. When 8:00 a.m. crowds stampede the elevator bank at the World Trade Center in New York or in the John Hancock building in Boston we are fairly certain they are on their way to work. But take the case of two individuals watching a film. For one it is a leisure activity, for another it is work as a film critic. One artist paints for fun, the second for profit. In many instances we can determine fairly easily what is work, what is leisure, but this is not always the case. One might be inclined to say that the tip off would be whether the person gets paid for what is done, whether it be a job, a career, or a calling. However, as the Special Task Force on Work in America (1973) notes, it is all too easy to equate work with "paid employment." Such a definition "utterly ignores its profound personal and social aspects and often leads to a distorted view of society." The Task Force offers a multidimensional definition: "an activity that produces something of value for other people" (p. 3). But, as we shall see, even this definition needs analysis.

Regardless of the three categorizations of job, career, calling, or the transcendent goals one may aspire to through work, work is not the sum total of the person. While this is clear in both Bellah et al. and Pope John Paul II (as well as the distinctively American application of the Pope's insights to be found in the American bishops' pastoral on the economy (National Conference of Catholic Bishops, 1986), it is Frankena who is particularly helpful here.

Frankena distinguishes two transcendent vocations, what he calls supervocations: the moral supervocation and the good life supervocation. He affirms the centrality of work for fulfillment of the moral supervocation, but work and moral supervocation are not equated, no more than work and the good life supervocation are synonymous.

It simply is difficult to conceive of a vocation that is such as to include all of one's moral activities and/or all of the best life one is capable of—such as to determine all of one's moral duties and/ or all of what is good for one. Even if there are some vocations of which this is true, there are surely many of which it is not.... Most actual vocations certainly are not so all-inclusive, and, even when we think a person has found his or her true vocation, we would usually think that it does not exhaust either the good or the moral life for that person. (1976, p. 404)

In a time of rapid technological and social change with consequent moral confusion about norms, relativism easily becomes the regnant philosophy. Individualism in self-understanding, heterogeneity in population, pluralism in worldviews, as well as a pervasive secularism marching arm-in-arm with a panoply of religious sects, denominations, and churches of conservative, moderate, and liberal hues, do much to reenforce this relativism. An appeal to vocational insight goes against this trend. It is interesting to note that Alexander Astin concludes that we must do more than passively watch the trends of the younger generation. We must encourage other values. The category of supervocations transcends the individualism of today's morals (*Chronicle of Higher Education*, 1989b) and offers a path out of the morass of the dominant self.

Vocational choice is an effective means of fulfilling the demands of the moral life supervocation as well as the good life supervocation. Furthermore, Frankena is "inclined to think that the Good Life supervocation has a certain priority over the Moral Life supervocation in the determination of one's vocation" (1976, p. 406). Vocation must not only be moral, it must be conducive to the happiness of the person. "The Good Life supervocation also has priority in theory, at least if it must be the basis for any answer to the question, 'Why should I be moral?' " (p. 406).

In assessing Frankena's theory of vocation, one can view it as a justification for leisure though he is not about that in his essay. He is clear in limiting the demands of work, careful not to equate vocation with the fulfillment of the moral life supervocation. There is more to doing good than the social welfare effected through a calling, sublime as it might seem. And while Frankena would probably agree with the Task Force on Work in America that work is "an activity that produces something of value for other people," he would be quick to add that many of those things of value which we "produce" for others are not the result of work: an intimate relationship, good feeling (e.g., those all-important but intangible qualities of life: intimacy, good feeling, acceptance). It is all too easy to receive applause for unlimited hard work that may benefit many people. At times it is necessary and for some the times may be frequent and prolonged. However, the fullness of the moral life supervocation is not reached by work alone. Leisure, pursued as an end in itself, may also be seen as a path to fulfillment of the moral life supervocation. This is not to be made into the equation of work done as leisure or work that is enjoyed as much as leisure. No monetary compensation is involved in leisure and it is not pro bono work. The leisure of family life enjoyed at table, in a game, watching a movie, conversing together, walking in the woods—the affirmation of love and acceptance that comes through such leisure is surely a discharge of the moral life supervocation. (The numerous household tasks and errands, the things one must do to maintain family life, even though compensation is not involved, should be excluded from the umbrella of leisure.) Finally, the pursuit of solitude is a further enrichment of this life (Storr, 1988).

Whether it is solitude or the leisure of interpersonal relations, there is much more to leisure than attainment of the moral life. For no matter how internalized the moral life may be for any person, each of us is impelled to look beyond morality to the completeness envisioned in the good life supervocation in which we find our "highest happiness and well-being." Not that morality is a burden to or a point of comparison with the good life. On the contrary, morality is essential to that life.

While the good life supervocation subsumes vocation and other paths to moral fulfillment, such as the leisure accompanying family and personal life, the vision of the good life supervocation transcends the limitation that comes with the concreteness of work and the particularity of the family and the self. The good life supervocation has an elusiveness about it, an open-endedness that is as alluring as it is refreshing and fulfilling. Could we not say that it is primarily through leisure spent with others and in the enjoyment of our own solitude that we experience this good life? While deeply felt and profoundly enjoyed, the good life has a utopian dimension that foreshadows or promises an even greater fullness.

Leisure: A Theological Interpretation

While the fullness of the good life can always be meaningfully discussed through rational discourse, Christianity affirms that the good life is a prolepsis, the breaking in of God to our lives, the foretaste of a fullness in human life reached only in the transcendence of mortality. "We see now through a glass, darkly, but then face to face" [1 Corinthians 13: 12]. Would it be too bold to speak of leisure as the eighth sacrament, alongside the seven of the Roman Catholic tradition, as a sign of God's presence in the world and a source of life in God? In a world where leisure is identified with consumption and much sought after, do we not need a transcendent understanding of leisure and the attainment of the good life on this earth, and for those religious believers so persuaded, a foretaste of things to come?

In a perceptive book, *A Rumor of Angels: Modern Society and the Rediscovery of the Supernatural*, Peter L. Berger discusses an argument for the supernatural based on "signals of transcendence" found in human experience. He defines such signals as "phenomena that are to be found within the domain of our 'natural' reality but that appear to point beyond that reality" (1969, p. 53). By transcendence he means "the transcending of the normal, everyday world" and he equates it with the notion of the "supernatural."

Berger argues for the supernatural from the experience of play and in so doing gives further religious insight into the meaning of leisure. (He is also indebted to Johan Huizinga's work *Homo Ludens—A Study of the Play Elements in Culture*.) While play is an integral part of all human societies, an essential mark of culture, it also represents a suspension of ordinary time (e.g., first inning, third quarter, 18th hole). It is an "enclave" in the serious world and is, moreover, generally joyous. The realization of joy in play has the further quality of eternity. And while the sense of eternity probably pervades all intense joy, "this intention [creating the quality of eternity] is, however, particularly patent in the joy experienced in play, precisely because the playful universe has a temporal dimension that is more than momentary and that can be perceived as a distinct structure" (p. 58).

The "eternity" of joyful play creates a sense of liberation and peace, especially in the face of suffering or death, says Berger. That one makes jokes on the scaffold or plays games on death row is part of our nature, not simply bravado. In sum, play is "an affirmation of the ultimate triumph of all human gestures of creative beauty over the gestures of destruction, and even over the ugliness of war and death" (p. 60).

In the ordinariness of everyday life, play signals transcendence, pointing beyond to a "supernatural" justification. Such justification is not "provable," but only understood in an act of faith, an inductive faith resting on common experience. "All men [sic] have experienced the deathlessness of childhood and we may assume that, even if only once or twice, all men have experienced transcendent joy in adulthood. Under the aspect of inductive faith, religion is the final vindication of childhood and of joy, and of all gestures that replicate these" (p. 60).

The ascendency of applied and professional ethics in present-day discussions of moral values in American society has been due largely to the initiative of philosophers. Thus, much of the argumentation about values, whether it be clarification of what is right and wrong or the resolution of moral dilemmas, has been developed within frameworks such as teleology with an emphasis on consequences or utility, deontology with emphasis on duty or rights, and responsibility with an emphasis on personalism or the fitting (Niebuhr, 1963). As a result, our ethical reflection on the moral problems arising in this rapidly changing world has been enhanced with a consequent widespread societal awareness of the moral challenge facing us.

However secular our society may be and however congenial philosophical analysis is to public discussion in a pluralistic population, a purely philosophical analysis of personal and social life must be found wanting. This is so because of the Jewish and Christian traditions upon which our society is built. While it is certainly true that these traditions themselves are viewed by many as causative of a secular society, the religious worldviews of these traditions cannot be neglected. The majority in our society have a religious worldview. When those who reflect on personal and social life neglect that weltanschauung, they do not address the experience of and questions asked by so many Americans. Do we regard leisure only from the point of view of the greatest good for the greatest number? Must we only analyze procedural rights which will assure sufficient time for leisure? Or do we focus on the obligations of employers toward employees and the consequent impact on leisure? Critiquing these questions does not belittle the answers arrived at. The difficulty is that they do not go far enough because they are not the only questions people ask themselves.

What are my moral obligations toward others and, more broadly, what constitutes the good life for me? One might object that these are clearly philosophical questions classically discussed by Aristotle. True enough, but history tells us that this discussion has been found wanting. Religious faith has clearly provided more satisfying and enduring answers, although we are also aware of the brutal fanaticisms espoused by individuals just off their knees. As we have seen in the case of leisure, both philosophy and the religious traditions opt for establishing a "leisure imperative." Of course, one must be inside a philosophical or religious circle of faith for that imperative to make sense.

The fullness of the moral life and the good life, what Frankena called the supervocations, cannot be achieved solely through work. Leisure alone provides a transcendent time for reaching a fullness in our relations with others. It is leisure which allows time to appreciate "God's Grandeur," what Gerard Manley Hopkins called "the dearest, freshness deep down things," the good life, the fullness of the self experienced now. For those within the circle of religious faith, fullness in our relations with others and the self-actualization of the good life are signals of transcendence, a foretaste of things to come and a justification for the religious tradition itself and the God who is the foundation of that tradition.

References

Astin, A. W. (1988). *The American freshman: National norms for fall 1988.* Los Angeles: American Council on Education and the University of California at Los Angeles.

Barbour, I. G. (1980). *Technology, environment, and human values.* New York: Praeger.

Baum, G. (1982). *The priority of labor.* New York: Paulist.

Bellah, R. N., Madsen, R., Sullivan, W. M., Swidler, A., & Tipton, S. M. (1985). *Habits of the heart: Individualism and commitment in American life.* New York: Harper and Row.

Berger, P. L. (1969). *A rumor of angels: Modern society and the rediscovery of the supernatural.* New York: Doubleday Anchor.

Chronicle of Higher Education. (1989a). Fact file: Attitude and characteristics of this year's freshmen. January 22, p. A34.

Chronicle of Higher Education. (1989b). Survey of freshmen finds a growing level of stress caused by anxieties about money and status. January 11, p. A32.

de Tocqueville, A. (1969). *Democracy in America.* New York: Doubleday, Anchor Books.

Frankena, W. K. (1976). The philosophy of vocation. *Thought, 51* (203), December.

Hatch, N. O. (Ed.). (1988). *The professions in American history.* Notre Dame: University of Notre Dame Press.

Huizinga, J. (1955). *Homo ludens—A study of the play elements in culture.* Boston: Beacon Press.

John Paul II. (1981). *On human work.* Boston: Daughters of St. Paul.

Kultgen, J. (1988). *Ethics and professionalism.* Philadelphia: University of Pennsylvania Press.

Martin, M., & Schinzinger, R. (1983). *Ethics in engineering.* New York: McGraw Hill.

National Conference of Catholic Bishops. (1986). *Economic justice for all: Catholic social teaching and the U.S. economy.* Washington: United States Catholic Conference.

New York Times. (1988). Freshmen found stressing wealth. January 14, p. A14.

New York Times. (1989). New college freshmen show shifts in attitudes. January 9, p. 1.

Niebuhr, H. R. (1963). *The responsible self.* New York: Harper and Row.

Reeck, D. (1982). *Ethics for the professions: A Christian perspective.* Minneapolis: Augusburg.

Shaffer, T. L. (1987). *Faith and the professions.* Albany: State University of New York Press.

Special Task Force on Work in America. (1973). Cambridge: MIT Press.

Statistical Abstract of the United States, 1988 (108th ed.). (1987). Washington, DC: United States Department of Commerce.

Storr, A. (1988). *Solitude: A return to the self.* New York: Free Press.

Wall Street Journal. (1988). Benefit of the B.A. is greater than ever: Latest data show college degree greatly increases earnings power. August 17, p. 23.

Wilcox, J. R. (1989). Professional Ethics, in *New Catholic Encyclopedia,* Vol. 18, supplement, pp. 396–398. Palatine, IL: Jack Heraty and Associates.

New Work, Leisure, and Decadence

Richard Gull

> To forget the primacy of work is the perpetual idiocy of the independent consciousness. It undid the master and his servant and it comes to shake "natural man" profoundly.
> —Judith Shklar, *Freedom and Independence: A Study of Hegel's 'Phenomenology of Mind'*

> The Americans would suddenly find themselves "rescued" from the physical necessity and social pressure which alone, perhaps, had been driving them to their habitual satisfactions. They might soon come to regard commercial pleasures as flat and unpalatable, but they would not suddenly thereby find any others. They would be like the little girl in the progressive school, longing for the security of having her decisions made by the grown-ups, who asks, "Teacher, today again do we have to do what we want to do?"
> —Paul Goodman, *Communitas*

> To be in a situation, as we see it, is *to choose oneself* in a situation, and men differ from one another in their situations and also in the choices they themselves make of themselves. What men have in common is not a "nature" but a condition, that is, an ensemble of limits and restrictions: the inevitability of death, *the necessity of working for a living* [italics added], of living in a world already inhabited by other men.
> —Jean-Paul Sartre, *Anti-Semite and Jew*

Introduction: What Is New Work?

The Copernican Revolution displaced mankind from the center of the universe and engendered a crisis of purposelessness. The industrial and postindustrial revolutions, by threatening to displace mankind's central occupation, work, from its central importance in human life, has similarly brought with it a crisis. It concerns not only the ends of human life, but also how to rearrange the means to carry it on. The so-called liberation from work seems closer than ever before. Yet if we are increasingly freed from the burdens of laboring to produce the necessities and superfluities, then what will fill the ever expanding spaces created by this advance? We shall either have to fill them with old or new forms of leisure practices, or we shall have to have *new* work to do.

But the concept of new work seems paradoxical: What will work be like after the liberation from work? Hannah Arendt (1958) has accused Marx of falling into this paradox and leaving it unresolved. She writes:

> The revolution, according to Marx, has not the task of emancipating the laboring classes but of emancipating man from labor; only when labor is abolished can the "realm of freedom" supplant the "realm of necessity." For "the realm of freedom" begins only where labor determined through want and external utility ceases, where "the rule of immediate physical needs ends."

But

> The fact remains that in all stages of his [Marx's] work he defines man as an *animal laborans* and then leads him into a society in which this greatest and most human power is no longer necessary. We are left with the rather distressing alternative between productive slavery and unproductive freedom. (pp. 104–105)

Thus the frustration in capitalist society of the basic need for unalienated labor is not abated in communist society if the most salient feature of communism is the liberation from work.

The paradox can be given a different formulation independent of Marx's vision of communist society, as a problem of the distribution of income in capitalist society. Consider this much quoted passage from Wassily Leontief (1982):

> Sooner or later, and quite probably sooner, the increasingly mechanized society must face another problem: the problem of income distribution. Adam and Eve enjoyed, before they were expelled from Paradise, a high standard of living without working. After their expulsion they and their successors were condemned to eke out a miserable existence, working from dawn to dusk. The history of technological progress over the past 200 years is essentially the story of the human species working its way slowly and steadily back into Paradise. What would happen, however, if we suddenly found ourselves in it? With all the goods and services provided without work, no one would be gainfully employed. Being unemployed means receiving no wages. As a result until appropriate new

> income policies were formulated to fit the changed economic con-
> ditions everyone would starve in Paradise. (p. 103)

Marx's famous formula—"From each according to his abilities, to each according to his needs"—does not help here. It is not clear what abilities would be developed in any serious way after the liberation from work, and with most needs satisfied with little or no work, the need for work itself might become more intense. Abilities that fulfill needs would deteriorate because opportunities to employ them would have vanished. Of course Leontief's fictitious workless paradise is difficult to imagine because there must always be some work. The future (and often the present) is now described as "postindustrial" society, which is not work-free. Its "new work" is creating and running the new technology, working in the vastly expanded knowledge and communications sectors. But its high paying old manufacturing work greatly decreases, while many more have inane service jobs at poverty wages. The sphere of leisure expands. In fact, in an earlier prediction of what postindustrialism would mean, Clark Kerr and his associates in 1973 touted as one of its more alluring features the opportunity for a new leisure to flourish—"a new bohemianism" as they called it—in which the full talents of individuals could be developed (Kerr et al., 1973, discussed in Rojek, 1985, pp. 101–102). But with the collapse of economic expansion since 1973, the dream of a "new bohemianism" has faded. It has come to look even more ethnocentric and decadent than it did when it was first proposed. New work is what is called for. But what would that be? Is it inventing solutions to the problems engendered by industrialism (inequalities, meaningless affluence, ecological imbalances, etc.) and postindustrialism (same as above, but much more joblessness)? "Man no longer struggles with nature, but with the side effects of man's conquest of nature" (Gellner, 1987, p. 121).

The current array of political agendas from conservative to radical might agree with this diagnosis, but their prescriptions are not new work solutions. We need a new work ethic (conservatives), more compassion (liberals), a change in property arrangements (radicals), and improved education and less decadent leisure (all three). There are anticonsumerist and antimaterialist movements. A few drop out completely from modern society, attempting to recapture the virtues of old agricultural work done by hand and with animals instead of with machines.

John Maynard Keynes, speculating in 1930 on the economic possibilities for our grandchildren, saw the end of what he called mankind's economic problem—the need to expend most of the energy of life acquiring the means of life. When this occurs, thought Keynes, the avarice that was a pseudo-virtue of the capitalism which generated the accumulation necessary for solving the economic problem could then be replaced by a return to premodern virtues. "We shall be able to rid ourselves of many of the pseudo-moral principles which have hagridden us for two hundred years, by which we have exalted some of the most distasteful human qualities into the position of the highest virtues. [And] we shall once more value ends above means and prefer the good to the useful," (Keynes, 1951) but what then would new work be, if it is not simply old virtues, old work under new conditions, expanded leisure, or paradoxical?

First, I will critically examine Andre Gorz's conception of new work in postindustrial society. Upon closer examination of what he calls "autonomous" activities, the postindustrial utopia he envisages is based on a dubious interpretation of domestic life. Second, I speculate that Gorz's proposed utopia may have a dark psychological underside, a speculation based on my general point that, like Marx and some other theorists, he has not succeeded in clearly delineating *new* work. Third, I will sketch an idea of new work as appropriately professionalized and collectivized, and of a corresponding sense of leisure as a property of performances of work and, in a wider sense, as a category of aesthetic and ethical judgment. In contrast to what I will call the "private," "liberal" sense of leisure, the performances of work are themselves appropriately leisured, which allows them to be judged and experienced as episodes of self-realization or autonomy. A society that values the private sense of leisure to the detriment of the public one is decadent.

(Without a new work arrangement, proposals for the future will only have going for them exhortations to old virtues or appeals to better leisure. In the background is the assumption that as such these proposals will not be realized. Moral exhortations are ineffective and hypocritical. Mere appeals to higher leisure will be resented by those disenfranchized by advancing technology. They will also provide even more rhetoric for those who control wealth and have the attitude that sharing some of it to solve the problems of postindustrialism is just another form of welfare, both for the rich and for the poor.)

The "Autonomous" Work of Andre Gorz

According to Andre Gorz, the introduction of ever more technology by capital has not led to a collective worker consciousness capable of transforming history (Gorz, 1980). Indeed, he asserts that from the beginning Marx's "myth of collective appropriation" was destined to remain an abstraction outside the reality experienced by the individual worker. Gorz's point is that if the labor movement takes as its primary goal control over the machinery of production, such an enormous change in the power relations of the economy will bring little change to the lives of individual workers. That is because the nature of work itself as it has evolved in industrial society is the root of oppression, not the system or apparatus (capitalist or socialist) in which it is carried on. Even if workers would wrest control of the means of production from managers and capitalists, without a change in the character of work itself, the workers in control would similarly oppress other workers (p. 33).

From Gorz's perspective, the working class seeks neither control of work nor its transformation into something higher or better. Gorz's argument is that if control does not bring transformation, then control has little value. Furthermore, Marxism from Marx himself to the present in most of its forms concentrates on control, but has lacked a vision of transformation, a vision or concept, as I have expressed it, of *new* work.

For Gorz, this deeper alienation from what the working class could aspire to, a different life, a different society less oppressed by work, amounts to an alienation from a human need that lies dormant and suppressed in contemporary society, but nonetheless exists. Gorz believes that we have lost sight of this *specifically existential* (his italics) "demand" or "need" for autonomy (p. 36). This buried need for autonomy is not satisfied in modern industrial society either in work or outside of work. The mechanization of work has increased its fragmentation and its now "indeterminate" nature has fostered an "attitude of indifference" toward it. Gorz agrees with Marx that waged labor, no matter how much it is hoked up, will always remain alienated or "heteronomous" (Gorz's term). Outside of work, consumerist needs predominate, "needs to buy," "needs for money." This is the inevitable outcome of the logic of a society where, as Gorz succinctly puts it: "No one produces what they consume or consumes what they produce" (p. 41).

Therefore, we face at present the unpalatable combination of alienated work and consumption, both of which leave our need for autonomy buried and unrealized. Controlling the apparatus of production would not automatically create a means of realizing our potential for autonomy. We must instead (1) liberate ourselves from work by minimizing heteronomous work through the efficient use of technology, (2) provide a minimum income for all in return for a greatly reduced amount of necessary labor time, and (3) create an alternative to mere passive consumption outside of work.

The potential for this transformation is the buried desire for autonomy, which lies just below the surface of modern society as latent content of its consumerism and emphasis on private life. The subject of this transformation will be, not a working class, but a "nonclass of nonworkers" (p. 72) which is coming into being. What is meant by this nonclass? It is the conceptual inversion of Marx's notion of the working class. Just as industrialization brought with it the formation of a class of workers, increasing automation has created not only a growing number of unemployed but, more fundamentally, a reduction of necessary labor time. With the accelerated automation of work, the labor-time necessary to produce, not just this society, but also a much more viable one, rapidly declines. As a result people sense that much of the employment that does exist is superfluous. "Work in general comes to be tainted with the suspicion that it is but a useless compulsion devised to mask the fact of each individual's redundancy" (pp. 72–73). Therefore the "nonclass of nonworkers" includes not just those who are literally unemployed, but those whose jobs fall into a vaguer category of excess work, not strictly necessary labor because the needs it fulfills could be meet by newer technological means (e.g., in auto manufacturing) or the "needs" generating the employment are judged to be artificial (e.g., manipulated by large-scale false corporate advertising).

Gorz's concept of "nonclass of nonworkers" conveys as well as this vagueness an element of Sartrean bad faith-work as a mask of redundancy. The working class consciousness of the working class has diminished in inverse proportion to mechanization; the working class is less than ever an autonomous political subject. Thus the working class and the unemployed are a fragmented "nonclass," unable to discern their common interest in transforming society. But therein lies a serious problem. How is the supposed latent desire for autonomy to become an active political demand with a program for creating postindustrial, postwork society? Is it not more likely, as more pessimistic writers impressed by the false consciousness of modern capitalism have asserted, that the current decadence of consumerism and private life will become even more extreme? Will we not continue to remain Neros in our private lives, fiddling away while the society outside the confines of our narrow little private sphere goes up in flames?

For Gorz, hope lies in "cultural mutation" toward the attitude that "real life begins outside of work" (p. 81). But this attitude, insofar as it exists, is an ambiguous and possibly self-deceptive one. Does this mutation announce, as he claims, "the transition to postindustrial society?" (p. 81). Cultural mutation is one thing, a realistic political alternative is another. The cultural mutations of the sixties—rock music, long hair, anti-authoritarian postures—were in part a cultural rebellion against the work ethic. But no viable political agenda issued from them.[1]

---

[1]Todd Gitlin, in his recent *The Sixties*, however, elegantly captures a certain spirit of the times and its attitude about what Clark Kerr referred to as "the new bohemian" leisure in the following passage: "Against the corporate-military-professional future for which the university was training ground, perhaps what was developing was the embryo of a

Even when seemingly viable alternatives to the present organization of work have been seriously studied and proposed as in the well-known and cogent *Work in America* report in 1973 by the U.S. Department of Health, Education, and Welfare (Special Task Force, 1973), the all too rare attention that this problem has received from government has led to nothing. As David Braybrooke, writing in 1982, assessed the situation:

> [The report] recommended a comprehensive Workers Self-Renewel Program, which would in effect provide sabbatical leaves for every-body in the work force and enable them to acquire periodically new, higher skills. The cost, estimated (in 1973 prices) to be on the order of $22 billion, a very modest fraction of the United States Gross National Product, would have been paid for in part by funds transferred from training programs already carried on by govern-ment and industry, and in part recovered through increases in em-ployment and productivity. Nothing, so far as I know, has been done to establish such a program. (pp. 336–337)

At present this situation is the same or worse. No such systematic programs for retraining or for greater freedom from work in such forms as shorter work weeks have been serious political agendas. On the contrary, the lack of a coherent politics of work has perhaps never been more evident. There is no consensus, for example, whether mothers with children and incomes below the poverty line should be forced to seek jobs.

Where, then, are we to locate the source of, the impetus for, change? Gorz thinks that the women's movement is the vanguard of change. The women's movement will

> become a dynamic component of the post-industrial revolution [but] only *insofar as the* women's movement [asserts the] centrality of non-economic values and autonomous activities.... Its main con-cern can no longer be that of liberating women from housework but of extending the non-economic rationality of these activities beyond the home. It has to win over men both inside and outside the home; to subvert the traditional sexual division of labour; and to abolish ... the hegemony of the ... values of virility, both in relations between the sexes and in society at large. (p. 85)

Winning men over inside the home means, I take it, that men and

___

postindustrial, postscarcity society, in which work would be undertaken not for the extrinsic reward of the paycheck but for its social good and intrinsic satisfactions. To the hip radicals and the radically hip, dropouts and runaways were the vanguard of the leisure class, and the South Campus area along Telegraph Avenue—with its cafes, rep-ertory cinema, funky shops, dope dealers, wide sidewalks, leaflet-plastered telephone poles, sojourning blacks and bikers, and some of the best bookstores in America—seemed to prefigure a society in which the arts and crafts would flourish, and people would sip cappuccino in the morning, criticize in the afternoon, smoke dope and make love at night." (Gitlin, 1986, p. 354) women should share housework. But all of the empirical studies show that men do relatively little housework, in spite of many other changes resulting from the women's movement. Therefore, for most men, housework would indeed constitute *new* work. Joking aside, proposals for shared housework are not only ineffective, but tend to put solutions off for at least a generation. Nor do they envision any essential transformations of domestic work corresponding to drastic reductions in employment. Gorz's picture of women's domestic work as *autonomous* activity in his sense is a piece of socialist gender conservatism, in spite of his radical agenda for changing waged labor. He considers the domestic activities of women *autonomous* because they constitute a "noneconomic" base of a market economy in that women's labor produces and reproduces the labor force without receiving wages in return. For Gorz, women's unpaid domestic labor is an assertion of noneconomic values like love and caring in contrast to waged, *heteronomous* work, which is tainted by economic rationality.

It will no doubt strike some as odd in the extreme to argue, as Gorz does, for the preservation and extension of housework (indeed, to take it as a model for autonomy), rather than for its transformation as many feminist writers have done. Four critical points are relevant here. First, the prevalence of divorce and the generally changed configuration of family life have weakened the sense in which private life is a sphere of autonomy. It is a fallacy to conclude from domestic work not being waged or not being included in the GNP that it therefore constitutes a "noneconomic" sphere of autonomy. Such an argument fails to notice the degree to which women's work is conditioned by numbers of factors including such exogenous variables as advances in technology that influence decisions women make about how to allocate their time. Economist Barbara Bergmann (1986) expresses this type of economic determinism as follows:

> How can we rate the importance of the factors encouraging women's liberation from compulsory and exclusive domesticity? The "social" factors—fewer births per woman, less stable marriages, better education for women, the rise of an ideology of equality—must have been important. They have supported and furthered that liberation and indeed have been indispensable to it. However, the most important source of that liberation is elsewhere—in advancing technology, which has been the source of the long, upward trend in the real reward for human beings' time. (pp. 60–61)

This passage suggests that the motivations for women's choices about their lives in the "private" domestic sphere are mixed—economic and noneconomic—and that economic rationality exerts a centrifugal pull out of the household into the labor market. This line of reasoning calls into question the view that domestic decisions about work are more autonomous because less conditioned by economic factors.

Second, Jon Elster (1986) has recently discussed the sense in which the domestic sphere is not a sphere of autonomy as follows:

> The critical assessment of other people is needed to tell me whether I am performing well or not. For this purpose, it is crucial that the assessment could be—and sometimes is—negative.... Family members and friends cannot easily perform this function, since spontaneous interpersonal relations do not go well with this coolly evaluative attitude. Cooking for strangers is more satisfactory.... Even if cooking is drudgery rather than self-realization, one might prefer to cook for strangers. Doing or producing something that others are willing to pay for is a source of self-esteem even when the work itself is not challenging or interesting. This may be among the reasons why women often feel the need to escape the close and sometimes suffocatingly ambiguous atmosphere of the family. (p. 120)

In other words, autonomy understood as a form of self-realization requiring criteria of evaluation more objective than those provided by family members may best be found in heteronomous work.

Third, the supposed sense of autonomy in domestic over waged work is further weakened by the degree to which the nature of the former has been conditioned by the nature of the latter. The twentieth century has brought a massive "commodification" of housework requiring the use of an array of household technologies. These commodities were manufactured, of course, by waged workers in mass production industries. The strikingly small degree to which these so-called "labor saving" devices have actually reduced the time and energy spent in housework has been known for some time. But to look only at time spent in isolation from other factors is to miss the larger significance of the transformation of housework: One bought a certain conception of domesticity along with the appliances. Dolores Hayden (1984) concludes that the operation of these external forces, both technological and ideological, negatively affected the autonomy of women in the domestic sphere.

> The first to modify the house as haven were manufacturers who introduced industrially produced appliances and products into the home. These were profitable extensions of the market economy justified as aids to the hardworking homemaker. What is astonishing is that these inventions eroded the *autonomy* [my italics] of women at least as much as they contributed to saving women's labor. (pp. 75–76)

Therefore, in addition to the centrifugal pull away from domesticity exerted by the revaluation of her time by technology outside the home, the labors of housework and nurturance were transformed in an arguably degrading manner by the new technologies for use inside the home (for example, in the use of television as an automated baby-sitting machine).

Fourth, in addition to economic and technological factors which undermine the alleged autonomy of work in the private sphere, there is a psychological devaluation which is the other side of the coin of the already noted overvaluation of waged work. Gorz's distinction between autonomous domesticity and heteronomous waged labor unjustifiably leaves the former pristinely untouched by this sort of bad faith. But to cite a paradigm case: A high paid executive creates false and manipulative advertising promoting household products aimed at women. His work is self-deceptively overvalued, the women's work, at which the advertising is directed, is not perceived as work at all. Putting the point another way, why does Gorz's "nonclass of nonworkers" not include women's work in the private sphere? Because to do so would be to extend the disaffection from work to the domestic sphere at least as it is now generally constituted. And that would be to confine the transformation of work to waged work. Which indeed Gorz does. His argument is therefore a variant of the idea advanced by many socialists that the achievement of socialism in the public sphere will resolve the problems of the domestic sphere. He writes of "extending the noneconomic rationality of the domestic sphere beyond the home" as though this kind of rationality survives the forces of economic rationality from the public sphere. The enchantment of the domestic sphere is magically thought to survive the disenchantment of the world. Jessica Benjamin (1988) expresses this psychological romanticizing of the public/private distinction as follows:

> The public world is conceived as a place in which direct recognition of and care for others' needs is impossible—and this is tolerable as long as the private world "cooperates." The public sphere, an arrangement of atomized selves, cannot serve as the space between self and other, as an intersubjective space; in order to protect the *autonomy* [italics added] of the individual, social life forfeits the recognition between self and other. This public rationality necessitates that women's different voice be split off and institutionalized in the private sphere. . . . A strain of social criticism has arisen (right and left, feminist and antifeminist) that celebrates the private sphere of female nurturance and criticizes social rationality. (p. 335)

In short, gender conservatism of the left and right fantasizes an enchanted, organic private realm in the midst of an atomized society operating by the mechanical laws of economic necessity.

In spite of these criticisms of Gorz, however, there is an important partial truth in his intuition that autonomy belongs in the private sphere, that is, that it is a necessary condition for autonomous work that it fulfill *needs* and that nurturance and other skills typically developed in this sphere have a close and obvious connection with *needs*. The mistake is to take this necessary condition for autonomy as sufficient. Recent writing by philosophers on the nature of autonomous work has explored the connection between autonomy and meeting needs. One central thesis, which I shall defend with one qualification in more detail in the next section, is that work as an idealized profession is the basis of autonomy.

Autonomy requires a connection with needs, but meeting needs does not itself create autonomy. Autonomists argue that new work in postindustrial society should be professionalized and subsidized, abolishing to the greatest possible degree work as waged labor, as a commodity. By contrast, pessimistic utilitarians like Braybrooke (1982) argue that the ideal of the autonomists' work-oriented society, though desirable as a focal point for social policies concerning the future of work, will be unrealizable because advancing technology will bring the fulfillment of needs with less work. This will be the case, so the argument goes, even if we factor in such new needs created by technology or those arising from increases in the minimum standards of provision. By this line of reasoning, then, the outlook for finding *new* work is bleak. We will out of necessity become a more leisure-oriented society. But this liberation from work may turn out to have been a mixed blessing. As Braybrooke ponders the attitudes of people in the leisure-oriented society looking back on the work-oriented societies of their ancestors, he wonders whether their need for work itself will cause them to experience a sense of moral loss.

> What will have been lost, with the loss of opportunities to help other people in urgent, morally primary matters, will have been so many opportunities to demonstrate sympathy, compassion, gratitude. A large part of the field of application for moral sentiments and ethics will have gone. One may anticipate, even if despair and boredom are avoided, an impoverishment of sentiments, a growth of egoism, a certain moral emptiness. (p. 335)

May we not legitimately wonder whether Gorz's postindustrial society will have a dark side of boredom and egoism such as described here? And even if work becomes increasingly professionalized, as the proponent of autonomy advocates, it is legitimate to ask whether a large segment of the population will still be doing unprofessionalized work, for Braybrooke says: "It is an illusion to suppose that the esteem which these activities now obtain for their most successful practitioners can be transposed to their practice by anything like the entire population" (p. 333).

Is the transposition of work into professions here thought to be limited only because it is anticipated that less work of all kinds will be

needed to fulfill needs? But for the autonomist, the expansion of professionalism is not only a function of needs. It is a function of applying
the concept of leisure as an ethical and aesthetic category for assessing
work, rather than as time and activity separate from work. Thus leisure
is to be understood adjectivally. As an adjective, it can be used to judge
a performance of professionalized work "as appropriately leisured," and
a virtue or attitude of character. Therefore it is possible to conceive of
professionalized work expanding indefinitely because, first, the need to
work can be developed as a function of this improvement or "perfection" of work and, second, to a large degree the products of self-realized
work will create new needs—in more economic terms: "Supply will
create its own demand" (cf. Piore & Sabel, 1984).[2] The details of this
account will be given below in the section on the professionalization
of work.

Leisure as Self-Expression

What concrete image of work in postindustrial society does Gorz
offer? The resulting free time will not be filled with "empty leisure," by
which he means the "programmed distractions of the media and the
oblivion merchants" and the like. Gorz describes his vision of new work
as follows:

> More than free time, the expansion of the sphere of autonomy
> depends upon a freely available supply of convivial tools that allow
> individuals to do or make anything whose aesthetic or use-value is
> enhanced by doing it oneself. Repair and do-it-yourself workshops
> in blocks of flats, neighborhood centres or rural communities should
> enable everyone to make or invent things as they wish. Similarly,
> libraries, places to make music or movies, "free" radio and televi-
> sion stations, open spaces for communication, circulation and ex-
> change. (p. 87)

But are these *autonomous* activities in the do-it-yourself workshops
of this postindustrial utopia leisure practices or work? Not that there
is an absolute, unambiguous line between work and leisure; perhaps
they belong strictly to neither category. Yet they are thought of here as
activities motivated not by economic considerations but as being the
activities of a society liberated from work. We begin to understand this
by first noticing that Gorz has defined leisure too narrowly, as passive

---

[2]While Michael Piore and Charles Sabel defend this idea in economic terms, they use the
notion of reskilling manufacturing work rather than professionalizing work. The logic of
their arguments, however, is the same.

consumption. Most people regard active hobbies in workshops, or even remodeling and building houses, if it is not done for a living, as leisure. Add to this that Gorz envisions a utopia in which at least basic needs are taken care of by a guaranteed income so that, strictly speaking, these autonomous activities are not done for an income even though, as in our present society, one might receive incidental income from selling the product or service resulting from one's hobby.

Nor is Gorz's utopia one in which people have been made independent of the need for a wage or salary by self-providing, autonomous activities like building one's own house and growing one's own vegetables. This may happen, of course but in the society Gorz envisions self-sufficiency is only incidental; it is not an economic necessity. Thus his idea of do-it-yourself is to be understood as *self-expression* rather than self-sufficiency. In fact, Gorz warns about the dangers of social claustraphobia in small self-sufficient communities or households. Besides, village societies inevitably lack the technology sophisticated enough to give us much greater space for autonomy.

But there are deeper, more philosophical reasons for regarding Gorz's autonomous activities as leisure. Gorz imagines, as we have seen, that there is an underlying desire for autonomy, what he calls at one point "free subjectivity." But this is to imagine, as Nietzsche expresses it, that "a doer (a 'subject') was slipped under all that happened" (Nietzsche, 1954, p. 495). Gorz thinks that the work ethic of productivist capitalism submerged this subject or self, that collectivist socialism refused to recognize it, and that postindustrial society now brings with it the possibility for this autonomy to express itself. This explains why he says so little about how the cultural mutation toward the personal and private is to become a political movement advocating the transformation of work. He thinks that the multiplicity of private doers (to paraphrase Nietzsche) have less and less work to do; they will eventually realize, helped along by the women's movement, that freedom from work is superior to control of work. No new work is needed, only substitutes for passive leisure. So the do-it-yourself workshops of Gorz's postindustrial utopia are places where our autonomy can now emerge in self-expression.

There is nothing wrong with self-expressive leisure activities in themselves. We may in fact judge a life filled with this sort of self-expression superior to a life filled with mere passive consumption. That is because we judge writing, collecting, or building as active, and hence higher, forms of leisure than, say, habitual passive television watching. The latter is not self-expression at all. If someone were so self-deceived as to claim that such passivity is a form of self-expression—someone might say: "Well, that's just what I am, a couch potato"—they would only be making a desperate attempt to have some kind of identity, to be positively defined (cf. Dostoyevsky, 1960, for a classic discussion of this form of self-deception).[3] But to greatly enlarge the sphere of leisure as a utopian vision is quite another matter. In such a utopia, what people did as leisure sidelines would become their primary activity. It is at least reasonable to suspect that people would begin to wonder in such a utopia what they *are*, which might result in depression instead of liberation. In industrial, work-oriented societies, people tend to define themselves by their contributory station or role in society, by their work or profession. People have, so some have argued, a *need* to do this. Gorz may be arguing, however, that since such a need is historically conditioned and relatively recent, it is at most a *false* need, not deeply rooted in human nature.

A recent critic of Gorz has countered that simply because the need for work is historically conditioned does not render it "artificial" or "false." On the contrary, "it [the need for work] is a real and ineliminable feature of contemporary psychology" (Sayers, 1988, p. 736).

Whether or not the need for work is thus "ineliminable" is, however, far from self-evident. If the basis of the need is grounded in a Marxian view of human nature as *animals laborans*, as this claim is, that view is not itself obvious. At least it is no more obvious than Gorz's more Sartrean "free subjectivity" which could, presumably, adjust more readily than *animal laborans* to a greatly reduced work schedule. One less metaphysically burdened middle ground between Marx's man the worker-by-nature and Gorz's indefinitely malleable free subjectivity is Braybrooke's:

> There are no grounds for denying that activities apart from work—play—will be a source, too, indeed an increasing source of satisfactions; or that the satisfactions found there will in large part be the same as those of work—challenges to strength, ingenuity, and responsibility surmounted by elegant demonstrations of masterly skill. Yet many people—most people, as they are now constituted in our society and may be expected to be constituted for some generations to come—would find the fullest measure of these satisfactions in work, if the work were commensurately challenging. (1987, p. 250)

We therefore sense that the dark psychological underside of a leisure utopia such as the one proposed by Gorz would be that people would become confused about who and what they *are*. It is as if all Gorz has done in proposing that we rearrange society in order to reap the benefits

---

[3]Note, for example, the following quotation from *The Notes from Underground and The Grand Inquisitor:* "Question: Who is he? Answer: A loafer. After all, it would have been pleasant to hear that about oneself! It would mean that I was positively defined, it would mean that there was something to be said about me. 'Loafer'—why, after all, it is a calling and an appointment, it is a career, gentlemen" (p. 17).

of advanced technology is to propose that society in general take an early retirement. In this early retirement we would live off a guaranteed minimum income and center our lives on what he calls "autonomous" activities. But upon examining these activities we find that they are merely self-expressive leisure, not new work. As such, they do not adequately replace old work, even if the old work is what some call alienated labor.

It is well known that people in present society often suffer a tremendous loss of meaning in their life in retirement even after three, four, or five decades of relatively uninspiring work, even if they have cultivated active leisure pastimes like gardening or collecting outside their paid labor. To merely rearrange the timing and importance of these aspects of life, which would require enormous alterations in production and the state to put them into effect, would not in the end result in much change. Such alterations may only exacerbate certain features already evident at present due to the accelerating disappearance of work. A much larger portion of life devoted to self-expression may bring an ever greater emphasis on the private side of life in a way which deepens present tendencies toward decadence, by which I mean the loss of the sense of one's contributory station.

Gorz's conception of a postindustrial utopia suffers the same defect that many critics find in Marx's description of postwork communist society in *The German Ideology*. Marx (1986) writes:

> For as soon as the distribution of labour comes into being, each man has a particular, exclusive sphere of activity, which is forced upon him and from which he cannot escape. He is a hunter, a fisherman, a shepherd, or a critical critic, and must remain so if he does not want to lose his means of livelihood; while in communist society, where nobody has one exclusive sphere of activity but each can become accomplished in any branch he wishes, society regulates the general production and thus makes it possible for me to do one thing today and another tomorrow, to hunt in the morning, fish in the afternoon, rear cattle in the evening, criticise after dinner, just as I have a mind, without ever becoming hunter, fisherman, shepherd, or critic. (p. 53)

As many interpreters of this passage, including Arendt, have pointed out, since work has been eliminated in the postwork society Marx envisages, these activities would be done as leisure, or hobbies, or self-expression. But this is not only paradoxical, given the man-as-worker metaphysic, but even on a more liberal interpretation of that doctrine the suspicion still remains that we will be unable to make a transition to a leisure-oriented society without a crisis of meaninglessness. Could we live in a society in which we could not become what we do?

A similar paradox of the end of work leading to a vision of a future society with no work, but only self-expressive doings, is found in Frithjof Bergmann's *On Being Free* (1976). Rejecting what he takes to be Marx's idea of work, he writes:

> For Marx accepted not only the necessity of work, which we reject, but made work the axle around which his own thinking and the society he projected turned. The future will bring a society of *workers*. Socially they would be the only class, and individually their work would give them their primary self-definition. The Calvanistic sanctity of the vocation was secularized and enveloped manual labor in its mystique. Yet if the natural and normal place of work through most of human history was marginal then this drives an aberration to extremes.
>
> Only the reduction of obstacles which stunt the self, undermine the possibility of its expression, and extinguish the "whisper of subjectivity" furthers freedom. The termination of the struggle for mere sustenance would finally bring down these hindrances. More crucial still, under this new dispensation the time and energy now spent on one's job would be given to the one activity each individual preferred to all others. This large portion of the life of many would thus become a form of *self-expression* [my italics]. (pp. 229–230)

Bergmann here represents Marx's vision of the future as *more of the same* kind of work, a socialist workers' utopia. As we have just seen, this is but one Marxian vision, the other being the communist utopia, which, as far as work is concerned, has *none of the same* after the liberation from work. But in delineating a future society in which the struggle for mere sustenance has ended, Bergmann places in opposition to the socialists' *more of the same* a society with little of the old work and an enormously enlarged sphere of self-expressive activities. In doing so, the society he envisages encounters the reservations we have just expressed concerning the futures sketched by Gorz and the communist Marx of *The German Ideology*. A society where people mostly engage in self-expressive pursuits would be largely work-free. But we must wonder whether people can so easily give up their attachments to the work-oriented society to which they have become accustomed. It will not be a society in which there is *new* work to do. We already have expressed misgivings about such nearly work-free lives, that they might be too much like early retirements, prone to meaninglessness and depression. This is because these self-expressive activities, insofar as they are not work or leisure that involves self-objectifying standards by which one obtains self-realization, the same standards by which one escapes the domestic morass of subjectivity, will not be new work. Such autonomy can be obtained, so the autonomist maintains, only by professionalizing work.

The Professionalization of Work

The idea of new work offered by the autonomist is that work should be professionalized (cf. Haworth, 1977, 1986). This definition of a profession is idealized and stipulative. Occupations as they are now actually practiced only approximate the ideal. They are distorted and corrupted away from the ideal by materialism, bureaucracy, and other factors. These distortions have given the word "profession" negative connotations that should not be associated with the ideal sense. (To avoid these associations "worker collective" might be substituted for "profession," and "pursuit" for having a profession.) The virtue of professionalizing work is autonomy. The autonomist wishes to argue for the superiority of a work-oriented over a leisure-oriented society on utilitarian as well as other grounds. The adjectival conception of leisure as a property of professional performances and of traits of character is essential to the autonomist's vision. Leisure is not time away from work but an ethical and aesthetic category by which performances are to be judged and experienced.

Work in the old sense of what one is paid for doing is fundamentally different from a purified profession. In the old sense, work has as its primary objective producing some product or service that fulfills a need or has some utility. What is done is done not primarily because the work as an activity in itself is worth doing. The worth of the work itself is subordinate to the success or failure of what is produced to make a profit or make a wage, salary, or living. Success or failure of the result to please people and therefore sell is the ultimate test of how much the performance of the work is worth. Since work in this sense is not worth doing in itself, there must be something extraneous to the activity of working itself which answers the question: How much is it worth? There is the pervasive attitude toward work that since it involves some inherent pain, incentives must be offered to people to get them to do it. The incentives might be negative ones like the fear of being unemployed. Sometimes, as in quality of work life programs in factories, work might be hoked up to make it less distasteful.

A profession in the ideal sense is different from work. A profession involves a performance of an activity that is fundamentally worth doing in itself. Typically a profession is seen as worthy of doing for its own sake and in its results. Its performance and the standards are fixed relative to the valuations put on the product of the profession, whether the product is an object or a service. People engaged in professions need to be particularly qualified to carry them on. Ideally the professional performance should not be distorted simply to please those who might purchase the result nor to give satisfaction to the performer of the activity.

For example, film makers who are more concerned with the size of their box office than with the artistic integrity of their films are distorting the ideal of a profession. We expect someone with authentic standards to be *uncompromising* in the struggle to achieve them. The pleasure of the audience or the consumer of the product of a professional activity is not the objective of the activity. This pleasure or success is related to the integrity of the performance, of course, but in the sense that success or failure is confirming or disconfirming instances of the competence of the performer. The surgeon may consider her particular performance on a patient who subsequently died as impeccable. A chef may feel a particular creation is not up to his usual high standards and be contemptuous of the compliments he receives from those he regards as knowing nothing about the relevant standards. The movie director John Sayles is subsidized so that he can make movies that have more inherent integrity than movies whose essential objective is commercial success. I am told by the Yugoslav philosopher Mihalo Markovic that a system of grants supporting that country's film industry has been a reason for the industry's international success.

A small business owner may be in business not for profit as such but to make just enough money to allow the business to continue. The business person may in fact be an idealist, motivated by the noneconomic goods that the business contributes to the community. This is often recognized by members of the community who sometimes pay more to subsidize a business which has the characteristics of a pursuit.

Ideally the payment one receives for a purified professional performance is not a payment for what is done. It is a subsidy or grant that is taken in the spirit that the reward is given to allow or enable one to continue doing what one is doing. Taking the reward in this spirit is to be given respect by society because it is recognition that your performances and their immediate results are worth continuing. The payment is not a valuation of the activity itself; it is an estimate of what is needed to allow one to keep carrying it on. By contrast, the value of work is dependent on what the result brings in the market. So work in this sense has no value in itself that is recognized. Its value is therefore accidental in a sense in which the value of a profession is not. The reason people are said to be alienated from work is that they intuit that the value placed on what they do is arbitrarily and capriciously determined by extraneous factors like the market. They do not identify with work because it would be foolish to do so. People therefore tend to get their respect worthiness outside of work.

Professionalizing work might be thought of as a different social critique than many liberal philosophers like John Rawls offer. They propose ways and criteria for society becoming more just. But insofar as they advocate equal valuations of work, they reenforce the idea that work creates a right to certain rewards. Their motives are high and understandable, but they presuppose what Marx might call the fetish that work creates the right to rewards and that therefore it is not inherently valuable.

Leisure can now be thought of not as free time separate from work but as a complement to professionalized work. As Haworth explains it:

> The Greeks, less committed to relating all of their fundamental ideas with the sphere of work, had a more promising conception of leisure than that which identifies it with free time, and one that complements professionalism. With them, "leisure" often had a primarily adverbial use. In this use, to act leisurely is to take a distinctively aesthetic stance. The significance of one's activity is then seen to be intrinsic to it, the present is savoured for its own sake, and one is not busy working for some future result in such a way that the value of present activity is deferred and made dependent on the activity's contribution to that result. (1977, pp. 55–56)

The leisured dimension of professional performances is described as follows:

> Professional activity not only may be leisured but in the best circumstances will be. Distinctively professional activity expresses a specialized competence that uniquely fits the person for performing a characteristic task. Assured possession of the competence is shown in activity that has a leisurely pace. It neither drags nor is rushed but moves at the rate the unfolding events themselves require.... By not forcing events, the person who has the competence does not put himself in the position of willing the result he seeks, of imposing it. Rather he co-operates with a process already underway and perceived as independent of himself, making a contribution that may induce the process to yield up the desired result. (p. 57)

The leisure of a leisured performance is thus a property of the performance that can be evaluated and experienced by both the performer and others. The experience of the performance is the source of satisfaction derived from achieving from work a degree of autonomy or self-realization. Arguably this is one meaning of the Marxian conception of the good life as work-oriented rather than leisure- or consumption-oriented. (Paradoxically, as we have seen, Marx's own vision of postindustrial society is too leisure-oriented.) So conceived, the work-oriented society is to be preferred even on utilitarian grounds because the satisfaction derived from self-realizing work is much greater than that derived from consumption, once the initial period of disutility associated with self-realization (its "start-up" costs) has been gotten through. Consumption has greater initial utility, but over time with repeated episodes the satisfaction derived falls (cf. Elster, 1986).[4] From this perspective the problem with moving toward new work is not that we are running out of it because needs can be met more easily with technology, but because of myopia and risk-aversion regarding the benefits of self-realization through work. It is not, as we have seen Braybrooke claim, that we are turning toward a leisure-oriented society because we sense that no work-oriented alternative is available. Rather we are resisting the greater utility of a work-oriented society because in the short run at least we are attracted by the greater satisfaction of consumption.

According to Martha Nussbaum (1980), Aristotle used what I have been calling the adjectival concept of leisure when facing the difficult issue of inequality of self-realization through work. She writes:

> In any city there is labor to be done, and not all of it can be done by animals or natural slaves. But the men who perform this labor will necessarily lack the leisure required, in Aristotle's view, for full intellectual and moral development.... We are making some men who are capable of virtue and self-respect do this work so that other naturally similar men may have a good life. This is a dark spot in Aristotle's political theory—a point concerning which he himself is evidently insecure and unhappy.... Some liberal theorists tend to skate rapidly over this problem, assuming that to give men political rights and opportunities is to give them all they need to exercise them well, that the man on the assembly line can have as rich and satisfying a moral/political life as the executive, the professor, or the writer. (pp. 420–421)

Perhaps it is not that liberal theorists "skate over" this problem but rather hold to a different conception of leisure and hence of society. The liberal society so conceived is a leisure-oriented society. Its fundamental ethical category is that of rights and freedoms. Government serves primarily as an umpire to see that these rights are respected. The focal point of self-realization is the self-directedness of the individual which is a condition best achieved when the individual is protected by a sphere of rights. That which results from such leisured self-directedness is good. In contrast to the work-oriented society described, there is no essential connection between self-realization and work. As Haworth expresses it:

> If we contemplate a society that satisfies Mill's principle the image we get is of a collection of individuals caught up in predominately private affairs that have no essential impact on the society at large, each enjoying his rights and pursuing his own good. Exercising our

---

[4]J. Elster presents a utilitarian defense of the superiority of self-realization over consumption. I follow Elster in believing that the Marxian notion of self-realizing work should be expanded to include substantive political pursuits.

rights involves making frequent choices, employing our distinctive capabilities in the act of choosing, following out the implications of those choices on our own initiative, and learning even from our mistakes. The object throughout is individual growth and development, and the principle stress is on the indispensability of self-directedness as a condition of growth.... It would be difficult to find a more natural basis for the ideal of a leisure-oriented society. (1977, p. 81)

On this leisure-oriented conception of self-realization, whatever is true and good is what flows from the lives of those with sufficient leisure to be self-directed.

Richard Rorty (1989) has recently defended such a view of liberalism and leisure as follows:

All that matters for liberal politics is the widely shared conviction that ... we shall call "true" and "good" whatever is the outcome of free discussion—that if we take care of political freedom, truth and goodness will take care of themselves.

"Free discussion" here does not mean "free from ideology," but simply the sort which goes on when the press, the judiciary, the elections, and the universities, are free, social mobility is frequent and rapid, literacy is universal, higher education is common, and peace and wealth have made possible the *leisure* [my italics] necessary to listen to lots of different people and think about what they say.

The social glue holding together the ideal liberal society ... consists in little more than a consensus that the point of social organization is to let everybody have a chance at self-creation to the best of his or her abilities, and that the goal requires, besides peace and wealth, the standard "bourgeois freedoms." (p. 84)

Liberalism so understood does not take work as a source of autonomy the way in which Aristotle, Marx, and other philosophers have done. Autonomy is achieved through leisure, quite independently of the contributory station one occupies in relation to the society as a whole. The liberal notion of leisure is private; by contrast the autonomist's is public. The self in the self-creation of the liberal utopia is a private self. One might say that it is a form of consciousness. The self in the self-realization of the autonomist's work-oriented society is public. One senses one's autonomy in performances of work. Self-realization in this sense involves self-objectification. By objectification is meant experiencing oneself in relation to larger wholes like one's profession or workers' collective, society, history. The complementary sense of leisure, that is, as it occurs outside of work, for example in experiencing the arts such as theatre, is similarly an exercise in objectification. In leisure one practices the aesthetic attitude which draws one out of oneself so that one sees oneself in the present, appreciating things in themselves and not exploitively as means to something else. (If I am an entrepreneur and go to theaters primarily with an eye toward buying them or the plays, I am not sufficiently leisured.)

Liberal leisure consciousness is by contrast private and by definition self-directed. Its paradigm arts are novels, especially those of writers like Nabokov because he so self-consciously seeks to avoid the "topical trash" of writers who relate one to large political themes like Orwell (cf. Rorty's discussions of Nabokov and Orwell). Nevertheless, Orwell is also classified in this topology with writers of private liberal consciousness because he warned of forces that he thought could triumph over it and destroy it. *1984* asks if liberal leisured consciousness can survive totalitarian and technological manipulations.

The question is even more urgent if one sees that liberal private consciousness has no essential connection to self-objectification. Otherwise it would not be sufficiently leisured. It is possible then to have a more or less self-directed society that does not take self-realization through work as its focal point. Haworth calls such a society "decadent." A totalitarian society would not experience leisured performances of work, nor would societies constantly at war because work itself is then perpetually subordinated to extraneous purposes.

The autonomist's sense of a "leisured performance" of work is of work free from undue pressure from, for example, bureaucratic or material considerations. The ideal of liberal leisure is that all choices and consciousness are self-directed. The corresponding autonomist's sense of leisure is that work is self-directed. But this work-oriented sense of being self-directed involves unforced cooperating and negotiating with larger processes. A professional in the ideal sense autonomously applies the methodology or practice of the profession. Such applications are necessary for the continued evolution of the methodology. A practice that is continuously distorted by business or ideological pressures tends not to be leisured or self-developing, even if the results are desirable in the short run.

References

Arendt, H. (1958). *The human condition.* Chicago: University of Chicago Press.
Benjamin, J. (1988). *The bonds of love.* New York: Pantheon Books.
Bergmann, B. (1986). *The economic emergence of women.* New York. Basic Books.
Bergmann, F. (1976). *On being free.* South Bend, IN: Notre Dame University Press.
Braybrooke, D. (1982). Work: A cultural ideal ever more in jeopardy. *Midwest Studies in Philosophy, 7,* 336–337.
Braybrooke, D. (1987). *Meeting needs.* Princeton, NJ: Princeton University Press.

Dostoyevsky, F. (1960). *The notes from underground and the grand inquisitor.* New York: E. P. Dutton & Co.

Elster, J. (1986). Self-realization in work and politics: The Marxist conception of the good life. *Social Philosophy and Policy,* 3 (2), p. 120.

Gellner, E. (1987). *Culture, identity, and politics.* Cambridge: Cambridge University Press.

Gitlin, T. (1986). *The sixties.* New York: Bantam Books.

Goodman, P. (1960). *Communitas.* New York: Vintage Books.

Gorz, A. (1980). *Farewell to the working class.* New York: South End Press.

Haworth, L. (1986). *Decadence & objectivity: Ideals for work in the post-consumer society.* Toronto: University of Toronto Press.

Haworth, L. (1986). *Autonomy.* New Haven, CT: Yale University Press.

Hayden, D. (1984). *Redesigning the American dream: The future of housing, work, and family life.* New York: W. W. Norton & Company.

Kerr, C., Dunlop, J. T., Harbison, F. H., & Myers, C. A. (1973). *Industrialism and industrial man.* Harmondsworth: Penguin in association with Heinemann Educational Books.

Keynes, J. M. (1951). Economic possibilities for our grandchildren (1930), in *Essays in persuasion.* New York: W. W. Norton & Company.

Leontief, W. (1982). The distribution of work and income, in *The mechanization of work.* San Francisco: W. H. Freeman and Company.

Marx, K. (1986). *The German ideology.* New York: International Publishers, Inc.

Nietzsche, F. (1954). Twilight of the idols, in W. Kaufmann (Trans.), *The portable Nietzsche.* New York: Viking Press.

Nussbaum, M. (1980). Shame, separateness, and political unity, in *Essays on Aristotle's ethics.* Berkeley: University of California Press.

Piore, M. S., & Sabel, C. (1984). *The second industrial divide: Possibilities for prosperity.* New York: Basic Books.

Rojek, C. (1985). *Capitalism & leisure theory.* London: Tavistock Publications.

Rorty, R. (1989). *Contingency, irony, and solidarity.* Cambridge: Cambridge University Press.

Sartre, J.-P. (1948). *Anti-Seminite and Jew.* New York: Shocken Books, Inc.

Sayers, S. (1988). The need to work. In R. E. Pahl (Ed.), *On work.* Oxford: Basil Blackwell, Inc.

Shklar, J. (1976). *Freedom and independence: A study of Hegel's Phenomenology of Mind.* Cambridge: Cambridge University Press.

Special Task Force. (1973). *Work in America: Report of a Special Task Force of the Secretary of Health, Education, and Welfare.* Cambridge: MIT Press.

Understanding Leisure Experiences: The Contribution of Feminist Communitarian Ethics

Debra Shogan

Feminist contributions to traditional disciplines have evolved through three broadly defined phases. The first phase has consisted of a critique of the absence of women's experiences from records of human culture. The second phase is an active attempt to alter this omission by documenting women's experiences so this deletion does not continue. The third, more ambitious and intellectually challenging phase of feminist scholarship is the recognition that the dynamics of gender are pervasive in all of what we do, including the social construction of experience. Consequently, the third phase of feminist scholarship consists of a transformation of the ways in which we understand disciplines, practices, and institutions and ultimately a change in the ways in which these are experienced.

Valuable work is being done in leisure studies in each of these three phases (e.g., Deem, 1986; Wimbush & Talbot, 1988; Bella, 1989). These studies contribute to our understanding of women's experiences of leisure and consequently to how these experiences might inform either a more inclusive conceptualization of leisure or an abandonment of the concept altogether when it cannot accommodate the experiences of women. This scholarship also helps us see that asymmetrical experiences of leisure, like other asymmetrical experiences women and men have in a society, contribute to the maintenance of gender hierarchy.

Gender is a relational concept that describes the relation of women

141

to men in a society. Research about gender and leisure pays attention to contexts in which this relation manifests itself. These contexts are often families, neighborhoods, and communities of various sizes. It is this link to communities that interests me in this paper. An ethics that focuses on community and the social relationships to be found there can help us understand experiences of its members, including leisure experiences.

Although I believe that an ethics of community can provide important insights about social relationships, I also argue that communitarian ethics must notice that gender is not a neutral category in a community of women and men. I call a communitarian ethics that does recognize gender as a pervasive organizing principle in our lives a feminist communitarian ethics. I attempt to locate some recent efforts to account for gendered experience of leisure within what has been called the "new communitarianism" (Gutmann, 1985, pp. 308–322) and within what I see in addition as the correctives of feminist communitarian ethics.

Communitarian Ethics

Communitarian ethics is often contrasted to contract ethics, the dominant ethic in contemporary western society. One of the major differences between communitarian ethics and contract ethics is the view of self or personhood in each. On the contractarian view:

> People are viewed as social and moral atoms, armed with rights and reason, and actually or potentially in competition and conflict with one another.... If any attention is given to relationships on the rights view, it is assumed that they exist on a contractual or quasi-contractual basis and that the moral requirements arising from them are limited to rights and obligations. (Whitbeck, 1984, p. 79)

Communitarian ethics, on the other hand, emphasizes relation of self to others in communities. "Persons," writes Annette Baier, "are essentially successors, heirs to other persons who formed and cared for them...." (1985, p. 85).

> One becomes a person in and through relationships with other people; being a person requires that one have a history of relationships with other people and the realization of self can be achieved only in and through relationships and practices. (Whitbeck, 1984, p. 82)

Central to communitarian ethics, then, is the notion of a social self.[1] Related to this is the notion of the continuity of a life in community. As Alasdair MacIntyre writes:

> The story of my life is always embedded in the story of those communities from which I derive my identity. I am born with a past; and to try to cut myself off from that past, in the individualist mode, is to deform my present relationships. (1981, p. 205)

An implication of experiencing oneself as separate from communities in which one lives, according to MacIntyre, is that one's life is experienced in segments. "So work is divided from leisure, private life from public, the corporate from the personal" (MacIntyre, 1981, p. 190). When one regards one's experiences as both separate from others and separated into discrete experiential activities, one looks to these segmented activities, which are usually conceptualized as either work activities or leisure activities, for meaning. Communitarians argue, however, that segmentation of one's life and separation of oneself from others often mitigates against finding meaning in one's experiences. Many leisure scholars are making similar claims. As Thomas Goodale writes:

> One appeal of the suburbs, for many at least, is that they are not close to work. The space, and the time needed to traverse it, provides insulation between home and work, leisure and work, living and working. We are not supposed to take our work home; what goes on at the plant or office is supposed to be left at the plant or office. We can and do work at home, but that is a different matter. It is more imperative that one does not take home to work in the sense that one's activities and affairs outside are not to influence work at the plant or office. So half our lives, for a period of 40 years or more, is supposed to be unrelated to the other half. (Goodale, 1985, pp. 50–51)

Goodale's comment is helpful here because it exemplifies how an attempt to account for the ways in which lives are segmented can nevertheless miss the experiences of a still significant part of the North American population—in this case the experiences of those whose

---

[1]Although there are emphases to communitarian ethics which are not central, and perhaps inimical to contract ethics, most notably the view of self, it is important to be wary of setting up a false dichotomy between them. As Amy Gutmann writes, setting up an opposition between contract ethics and communitarian ethics leads to choosing between one of the following sets of alternatives: "either our identities are independent of our ends, leaving us totally free to choose our life plans, or they are constituted by community, leaving us totally encumbered by socially given ends ..." (1985, pp. 317–318). Such an either/or proposition rules out the possibility of relationship and the impact of social factors on the one hand while ruling out agentic action on the other hand.

work is in the home. These people are most often women. A conceptual framework is required that allows us to recognize that some people *do* attempt to live their lives in the artificially segmented way described by Goodale and to also recognize that experiences of some are often not seen at all when they do not fit into these artificial segments.

For these reasons, Leslie Bella advocates abandoning the notion of leisure because, she argues, leisure can only be understood in a dualistic relation to work, thus segmenting human lives in the way described by MacIntyre and Goodale. Leisure, Bella writes, does not "tell us about people's lives, about the meaning of those lives" (1986, p. 4). Instead she suggests that we assume the concept of "relationality"[2] as a way to understand activities as experienced by the human beings engaged in them.

> The meaning of the activity is in one's relationship to those with whom one is doing the activity. The meaning lies not in the activity itself—whether it is washing dishes, playing squash or reading aloud—but in the context of relationship and responsibility. (Bella, 1986, p. 40)

Bella argues that the notion of relationality is a helpful principle when attempting to identify meaning in women's experiences, which are often even less neatly divided into work activities and leisure activities. The claim that relationality is central to women's experiences is supported by the well-known empirical work of Carol Gilligan (1982), which shows that women tend to identify relation and connection to others as central to their decision making.

Feminist Communitarian Ethics and the Understanding of Leisure

The view of self as social is helpful to understanding life experiences in community. However, promoting any and all social relations or promoting community, for the sake of community, cannot form the basis of a communitarian *ethics.* An appeal to community without specifying the features of that community obscures the fact that

> 'community' . . . can take on radically different meanings, depending upon the perspective and strategies of those making the appeal. . . . Communities can be open, evolving, and changing—or static, parochial, defensive, and rigid. They can encourage new roles for those traditionally marginalized or powerless within their midst or they can reinforce traditional patterns of patriarchy, racial bigotry, homophobia, and exclusivity. A people may see itself as one people

---

[2]Bella credits Jeri Wine (1982) for introducing the notion of relationality.

among many, part of a great mosaic of peoples coexisting in potential harmony. Or it may see itself as a people against and opposed
to others, its very existence threatened by any admission of others'
similar rights to a sense of peoplehood. (Boyte & Evans, 1984, p.
84)

A communitarian ethics which does not critique those communities
which are organized to maintain the power of some over others is, as
Marilyn Friedman cautions, "a perilous ally for feminist theory" (Friedman, 1989, p. 277). In what follows, I identify some concerns of a feminist
communitarian ethics that are important to understanding leisure experiences in community.

Feminist ethics, new communitarian ethics, and some leisure scholarship share an understanding of the self as social. A communitarian
ethics that is informed by gender as a social organizing principle takes
notice of the ways in which lives *are* social. This includes seeing that
there is asymmetrical power in communities of men and women and
that this asymmetry is supported by communities which, while promoting "gender difference," attempt to undermine other types of differences among its members. Both of these serve to keep the hierarchy
that is gender in place.

Gender and the Celebration of Differences

Gender, as a social organizing principle, is foremost a principle that
establishes a hierarchal relationship between men and women. This
hierarchy is maintained in two central ways. One way is through the
construction of social differences between biological females and males.
Dominance of one group over another cannot occur if the groups cannot
be differentiated from each other. The other way is by obscuring, re-
pressing, and censoring intergroup similarities and intragroup differences. The maintenance of gender hierarchy depends not only on creating differences between women and men but on not noticing that
there are differences among women and similarities between women
and men. To notice differences among women and similarities between
women and men is also to blur the boundaries between women and
men and to make it difficult to keep hierarchy in place.

Recognition and celebration of difference in a community is at odds
with many prominent views of communitarian ethics that posit community as necessarily dependent upon commonality. Benjamin Barber,
for example, writes that a community "owes the character of its existence to what its constituent members have in common" (1984, p. 232).
When, however, commonality is a goal of community, in which

some groups are privileged while others are oppressed, insisting

that as citizens persons should leave behind their particular affili-
ations and experiences to adopt a general point of view, serves
only to reinforce that privilege; for the perspectives and interests
of the privileged will tend to dominate this unified public, margin-
alizing or silencing those of other groups. (Young, 1989, p. 257)

It is the acceptance of communities as we find them that prompts
Marilyn Friedman to caution against communitarian ethics. Any valor-
ization of community that "appears to support the hegemony of such
communities, and which appears to restore them to a position of un-
questioned moral authority must be viewed," writes Friedman, "with
grave suspicion" (1989, p. 281).

Central to the project of celebrating differences among people is
avoiding essentialistic portrayals of women's experiences. Leslie Bella's
paper on "The Production and Reproduction of Leisure: The Invisible
Work of Christmas" in which she indicates that today's women's experience of Christmas is manifested in a "Christmas imperative [that]
is embedded within women's consciousness as personal conflict" (1989,
p. 73) must be read as an account of only some women's experience
and only some women's consciousness and not as an essential experience that women have. To do otherwise is to marginalize some wom-
en's experience (in this case, non-Christian women, women without
children or husbands) and support "an important bulwark for sexist
oppression"—the claim that there is a monolithic women's experience
"to which we must all adhere lest we be deemed inferior or not 'true'
women" (Alcoff, 1988, p. 414). There is no monolithic woman's experience. To think that there is is as much a false universalism as accounts
that assume that some men's experiences account for all human experiences.

Gender and Social Selves

The enthusiasm generated by Carol Gilligan's (1982) documentation
of women's accounts of their moral lives has been tempered somewhat,
at least in the writing of some feminist ethicists. Gilligan's work describes moral life of women as nurturing, connecting, and caring—
characteristics thought to be important to a self in relation to others in
community. Since nurturing, connecting, and caring are most often responsibilities of women in communities, some questions need to be
asked about characteristics which women have developed in communities organized by gender. For example, are these characteristics ones
which women have developed as survival skills in communities in which
women have little power? Do these characteristics contribute to wom-
en's oppression?

Relation of self to others through nurturing and caring is limiting as a requirement for social self in communities in which women are both subordinate in their relations to men and nonreciprocated nurturers and providers of care. As Barbara Houston says in a paper titled "Rescuing Womanly Virtues: Some Dangers of Moral Reclamation," women's distinctive morality is self-defeating when exercised with those more powerful or "when exercised in conditions in which the social structures are likely to deform our caring or disguise it as a form of consent to the status quo" (Houston, 1987, p. 252). Moreover, as Houston points out, recognition must be given to the fact that, because women have been devalued and subordinate, women are "susceptible to a pathological use of the ethics which may further entrench their subordination" (1987, p. 253).

Paying attention to gender allows an analysis of the ways in which selves are social in community. Since selves *are* social, we must notice how gender asymmetrically affects the ways in which we are able to experience our social selves. Leslie Bella's call for "relationality" as a means to understand experiences is helpful in that it allows us to see that meaning in experience is affected by social relations. However, as Bella recognizes, we must ask the further question about whether relationality is a good principle for women in a nonreciprocal community in which women are considered to be responsible for relations and in which such responsibility often contributes to women's oppression. Gender, after all, is also about relationality but the power differential implicit in the relationality of gender is not the sort of relationality which contributes to a womah's life in community. Not all relations, not all connections, are indication of an *ethical* community. Some very profound connections to others can occur in submissive, powerless, and dependent relationships (Morgan, 1987, p. 264–289). This caution must be noted by those who wish to account for women's experiences of leisure in community.

Accounts of women's experiences of leisure that do not question the asymmetrical ways in which women experience community will also not notice that women and men have asymmetrical experiences of leisure. It is not sufficient to detail differences between women's and men's experiences of leisure in a community. Attention must be given to how men's experiences of community profoundly affect the ways in which women are able to access community. For example, it must be noticed that

> women do not feel comfortable or safe on the streets if they are alone there after dark. They cannot therefore come and go as they please, but have to make careful choices about where they spend their leisure time, and about who they spend it with. (Green et al., in Deem, 1986, p. 46)

To valorize traditional community ties, without examining whether those ties make it possible for some to maintain a hierarchal relation with others in the community, is to valorize the status quo.

I have drawn attention to both valuable and problematic features of communitarian ethics. The valuable features are those which emphasize the social nature of selves both with respect to the interconnection of self to others and the continuity of life's experiences. Understanding leisure experiences in the context of communitarian ethics allows us to see life experiences as contiguous with others in community. A principle like relationality is helpful in recognizing the importance of others to our experiences and as a way of understanding meaning in life experiences. Communitarian ethics is problematic when it is not noticed that social selves are gendered and that this asymmetrically affects the ways in which women and men experience their lives in a community.

Understanding differences in leisure experiences depends upon seeing that leisure experiences are also gendered. This requires not only noticing that women and men often have different experiences of leisure but that the nature of these experiences often reinforces the difference in power between women and men. What is distinctive about a feminist contribution to understanding leisure experiences in the context of communitarian ethics is the insistence that if anything is to be declared ethical, that is, "good, right, or just, it [must be] demonstrably good, right, or just for women" (Houston, 1987, p. 261).

Author's Note

I am grateful to Catherine Bray for her helpful comments as I wrote this paper.

References

Alcoff, L. (1988). Cultural feminism versus post structuralism: The identity crisis in feminist theory. *Signs, 13*, 405–436.

Baier, A. (1985). *Postures of the mind: Essays on mind and morals.* Minneapolis: University of Minnesota Press.

Barber, B. (1984). *Strong democracy.* Berkeley: University of California Press.

Bella, L. (1986, November). *Androcentrism and the sociology of leisure.* Paper presented to the Canadian Research Institute for the Advancement of Women. Moncton, New Brunswick.

Bella, L. (1989). The production and reproduction of leisure: The invisible work of Christmas. In D. H. Currie (Ed.), *From margins to centre: Essays in women's studies research* (pp. 52–74). Saskatoon: Women's Studies Research Unit, University of Saskatchewan.

Boyte, H., & Evans, S. (1984). Strategies in search of America: Cultural radicalism, populism, and democratic culture. *Socialist Review, 84*, 73–100.

Deem, R. (1986). *All work and no play?: The sociology of women and leisure.* Philadelphia: Open University Press.

Friedman, M. (1989). Feminism and modern friendship: Dislocating the community. *Ethics, 99,* 275–290.

Gilligan, C. (1982). *In a different voice: Psychological theory and women's development.* Cambridge, MA and London: Harvard University Press.

Green, E., Hepbron, S., & Woodward, D. (1985). Leisure and gender: Women's opportunities, perceptions and constraints. Unpublished report to ESRC/Sports Council Steering Group. Reported by R. Deem, in *All work and no play?* (p. 46).

Goodale, T. (1985). If leisure is to matter. In T. Goodale & P. Witt (Eds.), *Recreation and leisure: Issues in an era of change* (pp. 50–51). State College, PA: Venture Publishing.

Gutmann, A. (1985). Communitarian critics of liberalism. *Philosophy and Public Affairs, 14,* 308–322.

Houston, B. (1987). Rescuing womanly virtues: Some dangers of moral reclamation. In M. Hanen & K. Nielsen (Eds.), Science, morality and feminist theory, *Canadian Journal of Philosophy,* Suppl. 13, 237–262.

MacIntyre, A. (1981). *After virtue.* Notre Dame, IN: University of Notre Dame Press.

Morgan, K. (1987). Romantic love, altruism, and self-respect. In Greta Hoffman Nemiroff (Ed.), *Women and men: Interdisciplinary readings on gender* (pp. 264–289). Toronto: Fitzhenry and Whiteside.

Whitbeck, C. (1984). A different reality: Feminist ontology. In C. Gould (Ed.), *Beyond domination: New perspectives on women and philosophy.* Totowa, NJ: Rowman and Allanheld.

Wimbush, E., & Talbot, M. (Eds.). (1988). *Relative freedoms: Women and leisure.* Philadelphia: Open University Press.

Wine, J. (1982). Gynocentric values and feminist psychology. In A. Miles & G. Finn (Eds.), *Feminism in Canada: From pressure to politics* (pp. 67–88). Buffalo, NY: Black Rose.

Young, I. (1989). Polity and group difference: A critique of the ideal of universal citizenship. *Ethics, 99,* 250–274.

A Theological Perspective on the Ethics of Leisure

Margaret Trunfio

The most basic of all moral issues is the quest for the good life. In the *Nichomachean Ethics*, Aristotle related the good life to pleasure, happiness, leisure, and virtue. Virtue (or excellence of the soul) in itself is the source of true pleasure, happiness, and leisure because it is the fulfillment of divine purpose. Leisure, as conceived by Aristotle, was different from our contemporary notion of free time. The ancient Greek meaning for leisure was more than freedom from the necessity of being occupied. It was a state of being, characterized by an intrinsic peace, freedom, joy, and contemplation. According to Aristotle, it is the essence of this meaning of leisure that leads to virtuous choices.

The idea of leisure as a virtue is somewhat foreign to our contemporary meaning of leisure. A long-standing virtue which has been accepted in our society is work. The inferences of the work ethic are: Work is utilitarian; leisure is nonutilitarian. Work involves social concern; leisure is egoistic. Work is a virtue; leisure (by reason) is a vice. It is this dualistic notion of work and leisure which contributes to the demise of leisure.

A utilitarian ethic which embraces work has deprived us of a meaning of leisure as being an experience which is worthy in itself. Although leisure is occasionally viewed as being an enemy of work, the most common justification of leisure is that it has a functional purpose to work, that is, restoration, respite, or reward. The problem with a functional meaning of leisure is that leisure is subordinate to the meaning of work. A problem which faces leisure philosophers today is the ethical justification that both work *and* leisure are good. It is my intent to show that Christian theology provides the foundation for this argument that leisure is good.

151

Traditionally, the Protestant Church has been attributed with a strong commitment to work, achievement, and success. On the other hand, the appreciation of leisure as a worthy end in itself has had little regard. In this paper, I will draw from a research project which I conducted with Protestant theologians, as well as reexamine the theology and lifestyle of the early Puritans to suggest a Christian framework for viewing leisure as a moral virtue.

The integration of a leisure ethic and theology is not a new concept, but one which needs to be revisited. In his book, *Leisure, The Basis of Culture*, Josef Pieper (1964) argued that in society's changing concept of the nature of man, it is critical that the understanding of leisure be based in a theological meaning of human existence.

In a similar tone, Robert Lee stated in his book, *Religion and Leisure in America*, "The problem of leisure is, of course, the problem of life. Leisure finds its significance in the total context of a meaningful life. Leisure is a part of man's ultimate concern. It is a crucial part of the very search for meaning in life.... Increasingly it is in our leisure time that either the meaningfulness or pointlessness of life will be revealed" (1964, p. 25–26).

According to Lee, the lack of ethical systems in the understanding of leisure is largely due to a silence on the part of religious institutions. Perhaps it is not so much that Christian leaders today teach against leisure; rather, the Church has basically ignored a theological interpretation of leisure as a nonutilitarian virtue. Although the integration of religion and the ethics of leisure has been recognized by leisure philosophers (Pieper, 1964; de Grazia, 1962; Kaplan, 1960) for several years, it is a curiosity that theologians have not delved into the leisure phenomenon.

In a recent research project, I interviewed theologians at an evangelical Protestant seminary on their perception of the integration of Christian faith and leisure. These theologians agreed with Lee's accusation. Several of the interviewees stated that they had not given much previous thought to the ethics of leisure, and that there is little education on leisure within the Church.

I was particularly interested in whether these theologians perceived leisure from a holistic perspective, or from a dualistic perspective. The holistic perspective, which is aligned with an Aristotelian ideal of leisure, describes leisure as a state of being free. It is holistic in that this state of being integrates all of life with a spiritual meaning and thereby is worthy in itself. The dualistic perspective, on the other hand, defines leisure in a role that is dichotomized from work. With the dualistic perspective, leisure derives its meaning from its utilitarian function to work and is, therefore, not an end in itself. This dualistic concept of leisure as nonwork time or nonwork activity is perhaps the predominant view of contemporary Americans.

The findings of this study revealed multiple perceptions, definitions, and experiences of leisure. There was not evidence of a strong differentiation of values between work and leisure, that is, work and leisure were not in total dichotomy. However, most of the theologians acknowledged that leisure for them took on somewhat of a utilitarian role, but not always in regard to their work. The functions of leisure which surfaced frequently were: change of activity, family obligations, exercise, and reward.

This group of Christian theologians felt that they placed an acceptable level of importance on leisure. The priority of leisure for many of them meant that they found it necessary to schedule in time for leisure along with their many other activities. They responded that if they did not schedule it in, leisure would escape them. These responses tended to reveal leisure in a more dualistic role to work.

The question of the direct influence of faith on their leisure experience brought out a variety of responses. In various ways, each of these theologians stated that the purpose of life is to glorify God through all experiences. Several of the individuals pointed to scriptural principles which they felt influenced their experience of leisure. The two most common principles were those of rest and stewardship. They expressed an obligation to not use leisure just for self-gratification, but also for altruistic purposes.

In summary of this research project, these individuals profess that faith is the integrating factor in their lives and that it is their "calling" which contributes to a sense of holism. For most of them, leisure is not experienced as an ideal state of being or as an end in itself. Primarily, the good of leisure is in its utilitarian value.

The Puritan Influence

To better understand why evangelical Protestants tend to endorse this utilitarian spirit toward leisure, it would be helpful for us to reexamine their Puritan heritage. It is widely accepted that our society's embracement of the work ethic originated from the theology of the early Puritans. Accepting the exposé of Max Weber's *The Protestant Ethic and the Spirit of Capitalism* (1958), we have assumed that the Puritan Protestant theology gave little consideration for the good of leisure. According to Weber, at the heart of the Protestant ethic was a moral code which emphasized austerity, ascetic self-denial, self-discipline, frugality, utilitarianism, rational thought, delayed gratification, and success in one's work. Scholars (Green, 1959; Hyma, 1937; Ryken, 1986), however, have revealed the inadequacy of Weber's thesis.

To blame the ills of our misguided work ethic on the original Protestant movement in this country reveals a misconception of the theology and lifestyle of the early Puritans. Our general historical interpretations of the Puritans tend to exaggerate their preoccupation with work and their distrust of leisure or pleasurable activities.

The Puritan concept of a work ethic was much different from the workaholic syndrome of our present society. Their values of hard work, thrift, and personal restraint were due more to the survival basis of their setting than to their theology. They praised diligence in work because God appointed work as a means of providing human needs, not because it was inherently virtuous.

Their theology, however, did give them the basis of the sanctity of all legitimate types of work. To the Puritan, it was not that work in itself was good and to be idolized, but that their ideal was "obedience to God, service to humanity, and reliance on God's grace"(Ryken, 1986, p. 33). The rewards of work were to be spiritual and moral because work glorified God and benefited society rather than gratifying selfish ambitions. Self-interest, however, was not totally denied because they believed that glorifying God and benefiting society in one's calling led to contentment and satisfaction of the soul. One's calling was not only their vocation, but it encompassed their whole range of tasks and duties. It was this concept of calling which was a vital link in giving their lives a sense of purpose, satisfaction, and balance—all for the glory of God.

In their attempt to seek balance in their lives, they rigorously kept Sunday as a day of rest and worship. Sunday observance was considered necessary to protect the workers from the danger of corruption due to worldly devotion to work and wealth. They also would frequently hold days of thanksgiving and celebration.

According to Leland Ryken in his book, *Work and Leisure in Christian Perspective* (1987), the Puritans have been falsely charged with values which would be in opposition to leisure. For example, charges such as: "the Puritans were opposed to fun" is untrue because they believed that God desired more joy than sorrow in life. The charge that "Puritans did not allow sports or recreation" is false because they enjoyed hunting, fishing, bowling, reading, music, swimming, skating, and archery, and were to be thankful for these freedoms. Whereas the Puritans rejected some sports on moral grounds, they were taught to seek healthful, recreational activities which would refresh both mind and body.

The Puritans were realists and recognized that some refreshment was an integral part of their human needs. Benjamin Coleman wrote in 1707: "We daily need some respite and diversion, without which we dull our

Powers; a little intermission sharpens 'em again" (Miller & Johnson, 1965, p. 392).

In the Puritan's pursuit to be Christian in all aspects of life, leisure was not exempt from moral consideration. They had high ideals and attempted to live out those ideals. It was not recreational activities or amusements which the Puritans condemned, but the immoral consequences of overindulgence. For example, the Puritans strongly objected to drunkenness, but had no qualms about drinking in moderation.

In general, leisure was not perceived as a diversion to life, but contributed to the quality of life. As long as their earthly pleasures contributed to their service and obedience to God, that concept of leisure was approved. The early Puritans encouraged creative uses of leisure and the educational value of leisure. Perhaps it was their intrinsic appreciation for classical culture and education that best represents the Puritan value of leisure. Their purpose of education was largely for religious and moral purposes as well as scholarship which expressed the truths and beauty of God's world.

In summary, the accusations which portray the Puritans as overly rigid, work-driven, and self-abased people are exaggerations. Although they disdained idleness, they engaged in moderate forms of healthy leisure activities. Their intrinsic appreciation for classical culture and education is also an indication that they did not reject leisure in theory. A positive contribution which we can learn from the Puritans is that their spiritual leaders did not exempt leisure from moral and spiritual considerations (Ryken, 1986). Whether we totally agree with all of their moral guidelines or not, we can at least commend their consideration of the implications of leisure behavior.

I do not want to describe the Puritans as the perfect model for a Christian leisure ethic. Although their perspective toward leisure was perhaps more holistic than we find in our contemporary society, the Puritans essentially made their defense of leisure on utilitarian grounds. In a cultural context, it is this utilitarian ethic of leisure which the Protestant Church has inherited. There is a need for theologians to step beyond this cultural heritage and investigate a Christian theology of leisure based on Biblical doctrines.

Christian Doctrines and Leisure Ethics

Are there Scriptural principles which establish a nonutilitarian value of leisure? I suggest that the doctrines of creation, rest, worship and celebration, freedom, grace, and calling provide that theological foundation. These doctrines are not conclusive, but provide a general rationale for the potential of leisure being a Christian virtue.

Creation

According to Scripture, everything which God created has a purpose. Why did God create mankind? He created us for the pure joy of it, and then acknowledged His creation as being "very good." God created us in His image; therefore, He has given us creative gifts for His and for our delight. He desires that we enjoy the life and world around us. This also leads to enjoyment and responsibility with nature and the appreciation of the order and beauty which He created. Understanding the doctrine of creation can guide us toward enjoying our creative gifts and appreciating God's created world in our leisure. Leisure which leads a person to a deeper appreciation of God's love for truth, beauty, and holiness is the highest ideal.

Rest

When God rested on the seventh day, it was not in a state of exhaustion, nor as recreation to go back to work. It was to delight in what He had created. In the same way He gives us the Sabbath "for our pleasure," not for pure selfish pursuits, but in honoring the Sabbath as the Lord's holy day (Is. 58:13–14). The purpose of the Sabbath, according to Abraham Joshua Heschel in his book *The Sabbath*, is not for the sake of the weekday routines and obligations, but rather, weekdays are for the purpose of the Sabbath. "It is not an interlude but the climax of living" (1951, p. 14).

When we understand that all of life is not work, but rather God desires for us to rest just as He rested, we can begin to appreciate leisure as an end in itself. God's rest allows us to experience leisure and relaxation without guilt. Leisure's rest is a vital aspect of a balanced life. Instead of frantically carrying our work attitude of competition, compulsion, achievement, and hurry into our leisure activities, we have the freedom to change our pace.

Worship and Celebration

Josef Pieper (1952), one of the most often quoted classic leisure theorists, stated that leisure is rooted in divine worship and involves the celebration of life. Worship is the freedom to allow our minds and spirits to realize the ultimate concerns in life and establish our personal meaning and relationship with God. This concept of leisure is supported in Scripture. In the twenty-third chapter of the book of Leviticus, God appointed many feasts and festivals for the Israelites. These were to be days without work, and the people were to worship God and celebrate the life He had given them. Although for the most part, the Christian Church does not carry out these holy days, there is a principle here which can guide one's leisure attitude and experience. God desires for His people to be thankful for life and to enjoy His goodness. Worship is a state of being which is enhanced by a leisurely (freedom) attitude. Worship also influences all aspects of one's life; therefore, even in choosing leisure activities, the believer can consider which experiences will elevate his/her relationship to God.

Freedom

The root word for leisure is the Latin word "licere," which means to be free. The freedom of leisure can be expressed in several ways: freedom to choose, freedom from work, freedom of the usage of time, and freedom from inward constraints and outward obligations. For the Christian, freedom is at the foundation of the faith: "You will know the truth and truth will set you free.... If the Son sets you free, you will be free indeed" (John 8:32, 36). The Christian therefore possesses the potential for truly experiencing the freedom of leisure. It is in the experience of leisure that we express the divine truth that we do not have to justify ourselves or our existence. The Christian believer accepts God's free provision. Leisure, then, is a vital expression of the truth of Christ's supreme act of love.

Obviously, Scripture also outlines duties and responsibilities, but duty and responsibility can be lived out in an attitude of freedom. It is this perspective that can provide a balance for the Christian in the leisure experience. There is freedom which is found in discipline. Overindulgence in any leisure endeavor can lead to self-bondage rather than freedom. Knowing one's priorities and limits can also give one the freedom to experience leisure in the fullest way.

Grace

The doctrine of freedom is closely associated with the doctrine of grace. Grace is the idea that a person cannot earn eternal presence with God through good works alone. It is the belief that God Himself has done everything which is necessary to ensure a relationship with Him. Neither our salvation nor the justification of our lives is dependent upon what we do. This is a doctrine which is difficult to grasp, and yet it has particular relevance for the leisure experience. As the Christian believer does not have to work feverishly to earn eternal salvation, there is freedom to experience leisure as a gift. Leisure does not have to take on the meaning of reward to one's work. It can be experienced as a good thing in itself.

Calling

The doctrine of calling is frequently misinterpreted in the Christian Church today because it is implied as being one's career. A more accurate description of calling, however, is that it is our unique contribution to the purpose of God's kingdom. One's work would be considered as being part of one's calling, but not synonymous with it. Instead of centering our lives on our work, the biblical perspective is to focus on our callings.

When one embraces a total life calling, leisure then takes on new meaning. Leisure is not viewed in a functional role to work, but is viewed as a vital aspect of one's calling or purpose of being. Through the gift of leisure, we realize that our life is not our own, but is a gift to be offered back to God. There is freedom to experience the fullness of leisure as one chooses leisure experiences which are viewed as good in light of one's calling.

The doctrines of creation, rest, worship and celebration, freedom, grace, and calling are theologically foundational in establishing leisure as a virtue. Although leisure may appear to have elements of selfish indulgence, it must first be seen as being an act of obedience to God. C. S. Lewis (1965) once wrote: "Unselfishness is not the highest virtue, but rather love" (p. 1).

In his book, *Desiring God: Meditations of a Christian Hedonist*, John Piper (1986) states: "To the extent we try to abandon the pursuit of our own pleasure, we fail to honor God and love people. Or, to put it positively: the pursuit of pleasure is a necessary part of all worship and virtue. That is, 'the chief end of man is to glorify God by enjoying him forever'" (p. 19).

Leisure is a time to let go of one's urge to control and produce. It is a receptive time and is evaluated in terms of the quality of its events. With leisure, the pressure to conform to schedules, routines, compulsions, and urgency is exchanged for rest and relinquishment of one's worldly status and desire to acquire.

When leisure is perceived as a virtue, there are moral guidelines which guide that experience. A Christian commitment to excellence in leisure results in the fulfillment of God's divine purpose with self as well as others.

To desire excellence in leisure is a moral virtue. Leisure means freedom, and therefore, we are presented with a wide range of opportunities. In our leisure, we can either choose mere distractions and egocentric "time filling" experiences; *or* we can choose experiences which enlighten us, restore peace and satisfaction, instill intrinsic joy, maintain health, and encourage our spiritual, familial, and community relationships.

References

de Grazia, S. (1962). *Of time, work, and leisure.* Garden City, NY: Anchor Books, Doubleday.

Green, R. W. (Ed.). (1959). *Protestantism and capitalism: The Weber thesis and its critics.* Boston: D.C. Heath.

Heschel, A. J. (1951). *The Sabbath.* New York: Farrar, Straus, and Giroux.

Hyma, A. (1937). *Christianity, capitalism, and communism: A historical analysis.* Ann Arbor: George Wahr.

Kaplan, M. (1960). *Leisure in America: A social inquiry.* New York: John Wiley and Sons.

Lee, R. (1964). *Religion and leisure in America.* New York: Abingdon Press.

Lewis, C. S. (1965). *The weight of glory and other addresses.* Grand Rapids: Eerdmans.

Miller, P., & Johnson, T. H. (1965). *The Puritans* (rev. ed.), 2 vols. New York: Harper and Row.

Pieper, J. (1952). *Leisure, the basis of culture.* New York: Pantheon.

Piper, J. (1986). *Desiring God: Meditations of a Christian hedonist.* Portland, OR: Multnomah Press.

Ryken, L. (1986). *Worldly saints: The Puritans as they really were.* Grand Rapids: Academie Books.

Ryken, L. (1987). *Work and leisure in Christian perspective.* Portland, OR: Multnomah Press.

Weber, M. (1958). *The Protestant ethic and the spirit of capitalism* (Talcott Parsons, Trans.). New York: Scribner.

Of Managers and Therapists: A Deconstruction of Leisure Discourses

David Whitson

This paper addresses the implications, for moral life and for professional practice, of current developments in recreation and leisure studies. Drawing on the work of Michel Foucault, Alisdair MacIntyre, and Jurgen Habermas, it argues that the discourses of management and therapy, which have achieved an increasing presence in our scholarly journals and conferences as well as our professional training programs, have the effect of constructing the profession along lines that signal a retreat from moral engagement and public service.

The paper begins with a brief examination of deconstructionism, which raises the significance of language in constructing the ways in which we define problems and go about solving them, as a profession and as a society. It comments on historical changes in the discourses that have constituted recreation as a field, with particular reference to MacIntyre's argument (1981) that the contemporary ascendancy of the discourses of management and therapy in our culture and of the manager and the therapist as representative social "characters," both illustrates and reinforces the triumph of utilitarian worldviews. Each of these discourses, MacIntyre suggests, reinforces the legitimacy of reformulating political and ethical issues as questions of organizational or interpersonal effectiveness. Both represent, in their own spheres, a withdrawal from questions of morality and public philosophy, a withdrawal which has a dehumanizing effect on our understanding of leisure needs, and especially the "needs of strangers" (Ignatieff, 1986). The paper concludes that the marginalization of moral and political issues

161

from professional discourse in recreation not only reflects but further consolidates a withdrawal from our historical tradition of advocacy for social reform, for public parks, for community development. If we care about this legacy, it is suggested, it will be necessary to transcend utilitarian language and to reconnect our project with the languages of needs, of membership, and of mutual and collective obligation.

Deconstruction and Discourse Analysis

To talk about discourse is to insist on the significance of language, of the words we use to speak and write about the world, in giving form to our perceptions and our thoughts. It is not only that language is necessary to represent perceptions and experiences, and to communicate them. It is also that our languages—the languages of science, of politics, of love, and of leisure—offer us the categories of thought and feeling, and of comparison and contrast, which we use to make sense of these aspects of human life. Few may fully accept Foucault's contention (1970) that we can only think the thoughts that the language of our time and place makes available to us. However, more might agree that a rich and nuanced language affords to those who are at home with it, thoughts and feelings and insights which are simply not available to those who aren't. We might also agree that developing new concepts and new understandings of the world generally requires the development of new words and ultimately new discourses, which gradually become diffused as people are familiarized with them.

"Deconstructionism" and "discourse analysis" are today terms loosely used to refer to a wide variety of critical intellectual practices. However, all of them start from the position that language does not represent "reality" in any neutral or objective way (Culler, 1982). Rather the orthodox language of any field or subject area actively constitutes a particular perspective on the "reality" in question, organizing our perception of it in very particular ways. Even scientific language, it has been suggested, constructs a particular way of looking at the world, producing certain kinds of "truth" at the same time that other "truths" and other ways of understanding the natural and social worlds are devalued (Habermas, 1971). Moreover, the very claim to objectivity, and the privileging of "objective" explanations, together serve to obscure the social interests and relationships which have historically surrounded the production and dissemination of scientific knowledge.

The task of discourse analysis in these circumstances is to deconstruct particular academic discourses and to understand them (like we would literary texts) as linguistic and sociohistorical constructs which foreground certain meanings and obscure or devalue others (Thompson,

1987). In this process, it is often revealed that taken-for-granted ways of thinking are neither natural nor necessary, but rather socially constructed and contingent. It thus becomes possible to challenge received meanings and definitions and engage in a process of reconstruction, a project feminists have undertaken with respect to the established discourse of many scholarly disciplines (Benhabib & Cornell, 1987). It is beyond the scope of this paper to give even a brief overview of the debates which have been generated by these contentious propositions. What we wish to take from deconstructionism for our analysis of recreation discourse, though, are two main ideas.

First, "disciplines," and perhaps especially new disciplines, need to be "read" as discourses which actively attempt to "define the situation" for us, or at least define fields of intellectual endeavor, in ways that are not disinterested. Habermas and Foucault have each argued that the new sciences of human behavior, in particular, define what is "normal" in successive areas of life, and then treat all departures from these norms as proper objects of research, management, counseling, or therapy. For those who master these discourses, moreover, and who enter into any of these lines of work, words are part of action, an integral component of their professional practice.

Thus psychology, economics, management, and leisure studies (to name only a few examples) need to be approached not as authoritative guarantors of truth, but rather as intellectual and sociohistorical projects, which construct particular kinds of problems and particular ways of solving them. To deconstruct a discipline, then, is to uncover the assumptions and interests which underlie its central problem definitions, and to understand how intellectual communities have established a social role for themselves and how that role is articulated and sustained (Bender, 1984).

Second, and intimately connected with the above, is the recognition that language is an integral part of history. At first glance the point is obvious. We all know that some terms pass into and out of common usage, and that with many others the dominant meanings or connotations change over time. What is less often remarked upon, though, are the causes and effects of these changes. In the first instance we need to recognize the effects of social structures, which mean that particular definitions of the situation are widely amplified—in the education system, in academic and professional journals, and in the popular media— while others find it difficult to get a hearing (Thompson, 1987). This is what is referred to when we say that some meanings are "privileged" and that meaning is not simply a matter of definition, but something which different social forces actively attempt to establish and sustain (Williams, 1976).

What makes the contesting of meaning so important, moreover, is

precisely that the accomplishment of changes in meaning and conno-
tation (for example, with respect to "professional") is often an integral
dimension of real social change. The history of "recreation," I shall
suggest, is one which was made possible by a language of human need
which legitimized the notion that we need green space and opportunities
for cultural and sporting experience. And the history of our language
of "needs" is, as Ignatieff (1986) points out, one of ongoing struggle
between minimal definitions (that is, what we need in order to survive)
and more generous ones which encompass what we might need in order
to flourish. His point is that the discourses of needs and rights (a concept
just as historically contested) which prevail in a given society have
profound effects on political discourse and therefore on the likely scope
of government, but beyond this on our understanding of collective obligation (see also Bellah, Madsen, Sullivan, Swidler, & Tipton, 1985).

Discourses of Recreation: Historical and Contemporary

Together these insights—into the contingent nature of disciplines
and into the interconnections between language and history—provide
a foundation for an examination of professional discourse in recreation
and leisure. Brown (1986) is among those who have pointed to the role
of language in the establishment of professional "authority," and she
suggests that in these endeavors, "discourses that succeed" typically
articulate an aspirant profession's projects with the aspirations of important sectors of the community. Subsequent changes in a profession's
knowledge structures and "dominant problem definitions," she goes on
to suggest, cannot be detached from the jockeying that goes on as
different interest groups (within a profession and outside it) vie to define
a profession's "mission" (see also Lawson, 1985). Therefore any analysis
of changes in the discourse surrounding recreation will need to relate
these changes to contests within the profession and changes in the
political context which surrounds its practice.

Godbey (1989) has observed that the recreation movement, and ultimately the recreation profession, came out of social reform movements whose discourse was about public needs: for play opportunities,
accessible green space, etc. And it was the vigorous advocacy of these
early leaders—Jane Addams, Luther Gulick, John Muir—who all made
the public case that these needs constituted human rights that paved
way for public recreation and parks in the United States (see also
Stormann, 1988). Godbey comments that all these individuals were also
active in other reform movements (urban reform, educational reform,
conservation) and that recreation and leisure were not ends in them-

selves, but means to improving things for disadvantaged families and improving society. Similar analyses have been made of the "rational recreation" movement in England (Cunningham, 1981), and indeed it was the emphases on social needs and human rights in all of these discourses that make it meaningful to talk of movements at all (Stormann, 1988).

Critics of these movements have pointed to the ways in which the offer of recreational participation was tied to moral instruction and "character" training. This did mean the imposition of the values of the WASP middle class on immigrant and working class children (Hardy, 1982; Cavallo, 1981), and undoubtedly the discourses of the rational recreation and playground movements were paternalistic in ways that would be unacceptable today. However, they also—and this is the point that is understated by some critics—legitimated the idea that young people of all social origins had rights to opportunities for cultural and physical development, the idea that the mission of public recreation was to provide such opportunities, and the idea that working in recreation was a *calling* (Stormann, 1988).

What I want to address in the remainder of this paper are changes in the discourses that surround recreation today. These changes, captured in the growth of recreation management and recreation therapy (incorporating "lifestyle counseling") as career specialisms, and in the corresponding distancing of the recreation literature from the "community" literature, are changes which mean that moral language, and especially the language in which the idea of communal obligation is given voice, is rendered increasingly peripheral. At the same time, our discourse of professionalism has become increasingly distanced from the meanings of "calling," and more and more integrated with those of "career" (see Bellah et al., 1985, pp. 119–120). The following discussions will attempt a deconstruction of current professional discourse in recreation. They will focus on how the languages of recreation therapy and recreation management, in particular, involve reformulating moral relationships and ethical and political issues as matters of interpersonal effectiveness and economic efficiency.

Therapy

The critique of therapy as a language which models, and thereby subtly constructs, our understanding of helping relationships is, in part, that it reduces human relationships to "people skills" (MacIntyre, 1981; Bellah et al., 1985). The therapeutic relationship may be intimate and often intense, but it is intended to be transitory, and it is typically self-interested (on both sides) and professional, grounded in expertise rather than in any disinterested notion of caring or obligation. Most importantly, perhaps, the relationship is *instrumental* and is constructed by *techniques* for making the other feel confirmed, for helping them to grow and ultimately to take responsibility for their own growth. In therapeutic discourse, what are very valuable ideals are taught and learned as technique and become means as well as ends. "Recognizing the uniqueness of each individual appears here as an expressive end in itself *and* as a method of putting people to more efficient use as human resources" (Bellah et al., 1985, pp. 124–125, emphasis in original). The authors also comment that therapy's emphasis on the individual—whether on self-actualization or (from the therapist's viewpoint) on treating the individual—can often underwrite a retreat from politics, a view of personal growth and caring work alike as tasks quite divorced from participation in public life.

Not all of this critique is appropriate to therapeutic recreation, but two issues remain worth raising. First, recreation therapy is constituted as a public service profession and a caring profession, but it is one which in America often finds practitioners required to pursue their careers within commercial health care operations. The discourse of cost-effective caring and the very real pressures on care-givers which this produces are by no means confined to the private sector, or indeed to recreation therapy (see, for example, Henry & Leclair, 1987, with respect to nursing). However, to the extent that these workplace pressures reconstruct what is meant by "professionalism" in our field, and reconstruct what is taught in professional preparation courses, the older ideals of compassion and service described above are likely to be supplanted by an emphasis on technique and on "contractualism" (Bellah et al., 1985).

Stemming from this, if recreation therapy manifests what Bellah and others describe as the spread of therapeutic language and assumptions in the broader culture (and this is clearly the issue that concerns them), does this reframing of the language of compassion into a language of effective intervention constitute a further impoverishment not just of our language, but of our very capacity to feel identifications and commitments which have passed out of public language? Paraphrasing Ignatieff's observations on needs, it can be suggested that our feelings toward strangers and our sense of obligation toward them are constituted by words; "they come to us in speech, and they can die for lack of expression" (1986, p. 142).

Management

Thompson (1987) has suggested that one of the ways in which language is routinely used to obscure structured relations of domination is when the passive voice is employed to take the real people out of events, thereby representing contested social processes as "system needs." This is exemplified, it can be suggested, in Peter Drucker's influential account of "management" as a set of abstract principles and processes, defined by the mission of making work more productive and the worker more achieving (1974, pp. 40–42). What is noteworthy about this formulation is first that the mission of increasing productivity is simply taken for granted. The personal and social costs of a system in which other possible objectives are subordinated to a calculus of cost effectiveness are never seriously examined.

However, we can also see here what Williams describes as the growth of a discourse in which the demands of real individuals (managers, employers) are portrayed as the objective (and hence impersonal) requirements of a system (1976, p. 191). Deconstruction allows us to view "management" as a discourse which has clearly served the interests of a rising and changing business class. This discourse constructs performance norms for a new kind of corporate manager, at the same time that other aspects of the labor process are subjected to analyses which "enmesh the individual in a new calculus of expectations" (Miller & O'Leary, 1987, p. 262).

The association of management with science, moreover, in the construct of "management science," has had the effect of depoliticizing a series of issues which are ultimately political and ethical (Offe, 1984). MacIntyre has proposed that this portrayal of management as a science is an ideological construction, a "cultural fiction" which helps to naturalize a particular set of social arrangements and a particular (production-oriented) culture (1981, pp. 71–75). The particularly insidious thing about the contemporary spread of management discourse in MacIntyre's view is that it diffuses the assumptions and idioms of business (e.g., "results orientation," "the bottom line") into many institutions that are not, at least in their original purposes, business.

This is clearly visible in recreation. Stormann (1988) has described how most of our journals and conferences today contain little discussion of needs and rights, but a plethora of papers related to revenue generation, cost control, etc. He also remarks upon the growth of courses and indeed whole programs in "commercial recreation." This interest in management techniques is not confined to the private sector, moreover; indeed the transformation of many public sector and voluntary agencies so that they are run on frankly commercial lines (cf. Whitson, 1987, as well as Stormann) is arguably a pointed instance of just the diffusion MacIntyre prefigured.

What MacIntyre is also criticizing here, however, is the representation of management as technique, as a distinctive discipline the content of which is constituted by analytical and operational techniques that are valid for any kind of organization. This is the position popularized by

Drucker (1974) among others, and this is the assumption behind the uncritical rush of many kinds of public sector and voluntary organizations into management training. This is not the only possible understanding of management, and indeed Peters (1988) is today promoting a counterview that the portrayal of management as a set of techniques that can be separated from questions of organizational purpose has been erroneous. Taking issue with the Drucker position, Peters proposes that we should never manage anything we don't passionately believe in. This position makes possible the reconnection of management discourse with moral discourse, and it has important implications for recreation management, especially in the public sector (Godbey, 1989).

Unfortunately, however, Drucker's view remains the hegemonic one, perhaps especially so in courses in "something-management," where management-as-technique is often presented in a simplistic and uncritical way (Hardy, 1987). In leisure or recreation management, we typically find a utilitarian language of technique (for revenue generation and cost control, for the manipulation of human and material resources) which constructs the view of their jobs (and of the nature of their specialist knowledge) that is held by many recreation managers in the public and private sectors alike (Bacon, 1988; Coalter, Long, & Duffield, 1985). It is important, of course, that public sector managers seek cost-effective means of service delivery. Yet Allison suggests that although "The demand for higher performance from public managers is both realistic and right, ... the hope that the focal issues of public management can be resolved by direct transfer of private management practices and skills is misguided" (1984, p. 234). It is necessary to insist that the public services embody meanings and values and social purposes which are different from those of corporations, and which cannot automatically be subordinated to the discourse of the "bottom line."

Conclusions

I have argued that a deconstruction of two of the dominant discourses in recreation today, therapy and management, reveals an increasingly utilitarian emphasis in which an older language of commitment is supplanted by one of technique. This transformation of human questions into technical ones has undoubtedly contributed to an exponential increase in our technical knowledge, but following Habermas, it can be suggested that the increasing hegemony of technical reasoning, in more and more areas of life, represents "not so much the sundering of an ethical situation as the repression of ethics itself as a category of life" (1971, p. 56).

In recreation, Stormann (1988) suggests that the contemporary ascendancy of management discourse, in particular, constitutes an abdication of a tradition, rooted in the various social movements which coalesced into the recreation movement, in which compassion was the moving force in our profession and human needs and rights were in the forefront of our talk. He cites Galen Cranz's proposal that in replacing a discourse of community needs and public service with a discourse of demand, parks and recreation professionals have "put themselves on a par with commercial producers of entertainment commodities" (1982). This has led to a preoccupation with financial performance, and hence with technical and bureaucratic efficiency. However, it has also led to a loss of interest in the original social purposes of the recreation movements, a mindset manifest in Bacon's description (1988) of many managers' impatience with questions like "what are the purposes of public recreation?"

Some indeed regard such questions as a waste of time, in the context of financial limits. Goodale, however, reminds us that:

> No doubt there is an economic limit to the total amount of goods and services that can be produced. But within that limit, social and political values determine what is produced and who gets it. A budget, therefore, is an allocation based not on dollars but on values. . . . By using the economy as a scapegoat, we avoid the central question of human purpose. (1985, p. 198)

My argument has been that the discourses which today construct our profession have marginalized discussion of such questions. In our preoccupation with technique and with the bottom line, we have stopped talking in a serious way about human needs, and especially about that collective caring about the needs of strangers that allows us to call ourselves a community. It is urgent that we begin to remake the connections between resources and human purposes, before we have lost the language which makes civic belonging meaningful. This is because needs and obligations "which lack a language adequate to their expression do not simply pass out of speech; they may cease to be felt . . . and their end arrives when the words for their expression begin to ring hollow in our ears" (Ignatieff, 1986, p. 138).

I am urging, following Ignatieff, that any decent society requires a public discourse about the needs of the human person, and that it is part of the tradition of our profession that we contribute to this discourse and articulate our own work within it. When this discussion becomes an afterthought or empty rhetoric, or when it becomes transformed into a discussion of something else, we become strangers to our better selves.

References

Allison, G. (1984). Public and private administrative leadership: Are they fundamentally alike in all unimportant respects? In T. Sergiovanni & J. Corbally (Eds.), *Leadership and organizational culture* (pp. 214–239). Urbana: University of Illinois Press.

Bacon, W. (1988, July). The professionalisation of leisure management. Paper presented at Leisure Studies Association, Second International Congress, Brighton, England.

Bellah, R. N., Madsen, R., Sullivan, W. M., Swidler, A., & Tipton, S. M. (1985). *Habits of the heart.* New York: Harper and Row.

Bender, T. (1984). The erosion of public culture: Cities, discourses, and professional disciplines. In T. Haskell (Ed.), *The authority of experts: Studies in history and theory* (pp. 84–102). Bloomington: University of Indiana Press.

Benhabib, S., & Cornell, D. (Eds.). (1987). *Feminism as critique.* Minneapolis: University of Minnesota Press.

Brown, J. (1986). Professional language: Words that succeed. *Radical History Review, 34,* 33–51.

Cavallo, D. (1981). *Muscles and morals: Organized playgrounds and urban reform, 1880–1920.* Philadelphia: University of Pennsylvania Press.

Coalter, F., Long, J., & Duffield, B. (1985). *Rationale for public sector investment in leisure.* London: Sports Council and Economic and Social Research Council.

Cranz, G. (1982). *The politics of park design: A history of urban parks in America.* Cambridge, MA: MIT Press.

Culler, J. (1982). *On deconstructionism: Theory and criticism after structuralism.* Ithaca, NY: Cornell University Press.

Cunningham, H. (1981). *Leisure in the industrial revolution.* London: Croom Helm.

Drucker, P. (1974). *Management: Tasks, responsibilities, practices.* New York: Harper & Row.

Foucault, M. (1970). *The archeology of knowledge.* London: Allen Lane.

Godbey, G. (1989, March). Future directions in leisure studies. Address to faculty of physical education and recreation, University of Alberta, Edmonton.

Goodale, T. (1985). Prevailing winds and bending mandates. In T. Goodale & P. Witt (Eds.), *Recreation and leisure: Issues in an era of change* (pp. 195–207). State College, PA: Venture.

Habermas, J. (1971). *Towards a rational society.* London: Heinemann.

Hardy, S. (1982). *How Boston played: Sport, recreation, and community.* Boston: Northeastern University Press.

Hardy, S. (1987). Graduate curriculums in sport management: The need for a business orientation. *Quest, 39,* 207–216.

Henry, B., & LeClair, H. (1987). Language, leadership, and power. *Journal of Nursing Administration, 17* (3).

Ignatieff, M. (1986). *The needs of strangers.* London: Penguin.

Lawson, H. (1985). Knowledge for work in the physical education profession. *Sociology of Sport Journal, 2,* 9–24.

MacIntyre, A. (1981). *After virtue.* Notre Dame, IN: Notre Dame University Press.

Miller, P., & O'Leary, T. (1987). Accounting and the construction of the governable person. *Accounting, Organizations & Society, 8,* 341–356.

Offe, C. (1984). *Contradictions of the welfare state.* London: Hutchinson.

Peters, T. (1988). *Thriving on chaos: A handbook for a revolution in management.* New York: Harper and Row.
Stormann, W. (1988, July). The ahistorical nature of the present day American recreation and park movement. Paper presented at Leisure Studies Association, Second International Congress, Brighton, England.
✓Thompson, J. (1987). Language and ideology: A framework for analysis. *Sociological Review, 35,* 516–536.
Whitson, D. (1987). Leisure and collective consumption: Some issues for professionals. *World Leisure and Recreation, 28* (3), 17–20.
Williams, R. (1976). *Keywords.* London: Fontana.

Large-Scale Leisure Enterprises as Moral Contexts

Gerald S. Kenyon

> The wisdom of a learned man cometh by opportunity of leisure;
> and he that hath little business shall become wise.
> —*Ecclesiasticus 33:24*

This paper suggests that one way of examining the link between leisure and morality is to consider the nature and societal significance of recent institutionalized large-scale leisure enterprises. My approach is based upon the premise that our value systems, and hence our ethical and moral systems, are socially constructed, and as such have no a priori standing. As social constructs, they tend to serve certain understandable and consequential social ends.

The thesis which I advance is as follows: That the trend toward increasing social and cultural homogenization poses a threat to the continued evolution of human civilization; and more particularly, much of contemporary leisure, especially in its dominant form, namely, the large-scale enterprise, reenforces that threat.

Insofar as we regard contemporary societies as still imperfect, and insofar as we regard the enhancing of our present social arrangements possible and desirable, the ethical imperative here is the obligation of both leisure theorists and leisure practitioners to examine and to understand the nature of large-scale phenomena. To do so is to ask such questions as, "In whose interests are such developments?" "To what extent do they depart from some system of 'right' or 'good?'" and, if

173

departures are found to be unacceptable, "What are the prospects for intervention?"

Human civilization has reached a stage of evolution that in at least one respect is decidedly paradoxical. At once we enjoy an unprecedented capacity for diversity in human social affairs, while we pursue and have realized an unprecedented degree of homogeneity in this sphere. A variety of explanations have been offered, including such phenomena as "modernization" (Moore, 1979) and the "civilizing" (Elias, 1939/1978) and "hegemonic" (Gramsci, 1971; Wallerstein, 1974) processes.

However, the "desirability" of this turn of events can only be decided on ideological grounds, and as such has substantial implications for ethics and morality, both in general and in the context of leisure practice. For example, if we superimpose various value or ideological systems on the phenomenon of social and cultural homogenization, we can judge its merits. To illustrate, if we happen to subscribe to principles of equality, certain aspects of social homogenization may be applauded. On the other hand, if one takes the position that it is possible for humankind to evolve further and to achieve a form superior to anything previously known, then it might be argued that social homogenization is detrimental to the pursuit of such goals. Just as it is argued that biological diversity is an essential prerequisite to the survival and enhancement of life forms, so too, it can be argued that cultural diversity is an essential prerequisite to continued social evolution or survival. Since leisure time and leisure contexts are often purported to be the prerequisites to invention, such issues need to be considered within a leisure context, among others.

Upon examining the principal features of contemporary social institutions, we discover an increasing degree of homogenization both within and between them. The explanation for this can be had by examining the dominate forces in society. Through the legitimizing effects of professionalization we can account for much of the internal homogeneity. That the distinction among institutions has been blurring is explained to a large extent by the dominance of our economic institutions over all others. Leisure has not escaped this process; its distinctiveness is also waning. For example, where leisure was once regarded as the antithesis of work (the overt manifestation of the economy), the separation of the two becomes increasingly artificial (Parker, 1983). Rather than work as toil, enjoying it has been acceptable for some time; even workaholism is no longer a disease but a "lifestyle." Moreover, in an ideological sense, assumptions about the "autonomy" of leisure are increasingly challenged (Clarke & Critcher, 1985). Thus, the linkages between leisure today and the forces of the economy are legion. Their origin lies in the nature of the larger society.

As a starting point, we are dealing with social "reality," which boils down to some form of human interaction. In macrosociological terms, the dominant global social force which has come to impinge upon virtually all societies today—east or west, north or south, developed or developing—is the monopolistic capitalism that is now world scale (including the socialist countries, which, long before *peristroika*, became inescapably part of the world economic order). As Robert Heilbroner (1989) recently observed, capitalism has essentially won the contest with competing systems; despite its being flawed, for the moment it seems to be "good enough." Among its central features are the principles of division of interest, individual competition, and ideology of acquisition, all of which are both reinforced and undermined by leisure forms (Rojek, 1985, p. 7).

In microsociological terms—at least in developed and therefore dominating countries—social interaction occurs for the most part in either the workplace or the "play place," both of which have become highly institutionalized, with all that has come to mean. But, in leisure terms, our microworld has become heavily shaped by forces emanating from our macroworld. Thus, our play places and what goes on within them are essentially controlled by our globalized economic institutions. As students of leisure, we are aware of this, of course. Some have lamented this fact, others have embraced it. Of importance here however, is understanding where this trend is taking us, and appreciating the consequences for leisure in general and its place in our survival over the long term.

We can begin to obtain some answers through a closer examination of the juxtaposition of contemporary world capitalism with contemporary leisure forms. Admittedly, worrying about the impact of the private sector upon our leisure institutions, and some do, is hardly news. Veblen (1899/1953) gave us a good start almost a century ago, while later, the Frankfurt School and others gave us the "mass culture critique" (e.g., see Adorno, 1962/1976; Rosenberg & White, 1957). Although the arguments were later countered as naive and at odds with "reality" (Gans, 1974), more sophisticated analyses emerged later showing a substantial linkage between culture and socioeconomic structure (Bourdieu, 1979/1984; Dimaggio, 1987).

So where is the linkage going from here? Part of the answer comes from observing the growth of so-called large-scale enterprises. Today, in a climate of mergers and takeovers, surviving corporations have become both large and multinational. As a result, they have acquired unprecedented capacity to pursue a variety of megaprojects, from resource extraction to manufacturing. What we may overlook, however, is the extent to which such projects are also emerging in the leisure domain. In recent years, a number of large-magnitude ventures have emerged, in the form of vacation destinations, super shopping malls, retirement villages, international festivals and celebrations, "block buster" art exhibitions and cultural performances, theme parks, and home electronic entertainment systems.

Upon analysis, it can be seen that each large-scale leisure enterprise takes on characteristics germane to the thesis of this paper. In general, all exemplify the high art of marketing and commodification. In the process of bringing the "product" to the "customer" the consequences are several, including control over the allocation of available resources, control over user options, an emphasis on "nonserious" leisure forms (Stebbins, 1982), and a substantial rise in professionalization. Taken together, the major fallout has been an enormous **homogenization** of both product and customer, or "pacification," as Rojek (1985, p. 21–22), drawing upon the work of Elias and Dunning (1986), has called it. In other words, rather than diversity being augmented, it is being systematically diminished.

As part of the homogenization process, various messages are constructed and disseminated that legitimize the enterprise in question. If successful, consumers learn not only to want the product but also to justify their pursuit of it from some "moral" position. Just as we have seen "moral entrepreneurs" in the electronic church, so too do they exist in the large-scale leisure market place. A closer analysis of prevailing or emerging large-scale leisure enterprises will serve to illustrate these points.

In **the arts**, multimillion dollar special events are being staged with increasing frequency, such as "blockbuster" art exhibitions (e.g., "Tutankhamen") and grand opera in the football stadium (e.g., "Aida," complete with live snakes, lions, and elephants). Over and above these phenomena is the now well-established pop culture industry that, when married to technology, brings the same performance to millions, often simultaneously (e.g., Bob Geldof's "Live Aid"). Through the magic of "show business" it looks like we finally have the masses exposed to "high art." However, the manner in which such events are merchandized precludes little else except a "one-shot" encounter with the arts, which by the limiting circumstances of their presentation prevents much in the way of expanding one's awareness of the nature of art in general, or of the nature of contemporary art and its social significance in particular. More often than not, mere attendance becomes the objective, for promoter and ticket purchaser alike. Of course, people have always been prepared to queue for a good show, whether it be a public hanging or a Prince concert, and no one would deny that the art blockbusters have been well staged. The real danger lies in the potential for deception. For example, it is hard to believe that we achieve much in the way of advancing our understanding of either historical or contemporary art, or coming to grips with the socially constructed conventional wisdoms distinguishing between "good" and "bad" art. In the end we have another triumph of form over substance.

Similar observations can be made of **theme parks**, where we see the likes of the Disney installations becoming present-day "wonders of the world." Highly sophisticated exhibits are presented, often employing the very latest electronic technology. The subject matter, however, is seldom controversial, sometimes propagandistic, but never offensive. Increasingly, partly, no doubt in an attempt to meet the competition, major public galleries and museums have adopted similar "marketing" approaches. More importantly, if history is presented, then whose history is it? Solidarity, yes; critical appraisal, hardly. Again, the sheer magnitude of such facilities, together with their direct and indirect economic significance, virtually guarantees the homogenization of message content.

Shopping as popular culture was legitimized long ago (Campbell, 1987). However, today it has become focused into a truly large-scale enterprise in the form of the **super shopping mall**—the cult of consumerism carried to ends unimaginable only a few years back. The paradox, of course, is that the economies of scale achieved with greater size have brought not greater diversity, but less. Franchising and corporate mergers have guaranteed a sameness, not only among the centers themselves, but also among the products they offer. Moreover, malls function as considerably more than sites for merchandising. In many respects, they have become modern-day equivalents of the community center. In addition, some have become major tourist destinations in themselves, e.g., the West Edmonton Mall in Alberta. The existence of malls has an impact upon our lives far beyond our consumption of products.

Among the most rapidly growing institutionalized forms of leisure time use is that of **tourism**, now about to become, if not already, the world's largest industry. Its internationalization (and thus homogenization) has become substantial, whether in the form of global travel agencies, transportation companies, hotel chains, or destination facilities. Moreover, its promotion is regarded as being in the best interests of local, national, and multinational economies. Governments at all levels routinely invest in the tourism sector, often heavily. Recently, however, we have seen a shift from direct support (the creation of government owned and operated facilities and services) to indirect support, driven by the swing to the ethos of deregularization and privatization. Lately, however, there has arisen some concern in this domain. For instance, in the context of urban renewal, residents are beginning to ask, "Renewal for whom?" We see similar responses to proposals calling for the transfer to the private sector of the management of public forests.

As an offshoot of tourism, we have seen the creation of large-scale

vacation destinations. In the process of marketing the hedonism "you deserve," among other effects, we see not only the legitimation of stress, but also the more important and paradoxical reinforcement of the necessity of work. In the category of opportunities lost, many destinations have come to provide leisure experiences in a cultural and social vacuum. One can spend a week or two in a "fully self-contained resort," experiencing "the complete escape—secluded, seductive, sybaritic," usually in a third world country, and without ever having to be exposed to the indigenous culture, which is likely to be vastly different from one's own. Moreover, the presence of the resort itself can have widespread implications for the host country or region, economically, environmentally, and socially (Cohen, 1984). In the developed countries we see large-scale investments in creating self-contained, all-season artificial environments such as the "Center Parcs" in Europe, accessible on weekends as well as longer term, and obviating the cost and uncertainties of travel to more distant locations.

Similarly, with the development of large-scale **retirement communities**, we see added to social insulation and local social impact, the phenomenon of age, ethnic, and class homogenization. Although the better managed facilities report considerable user satisfaction, long-term societal implications are not yet clear.

Large-scale **electronic media systems** have made the home the dominant site for the use of leisure time. For over three decades we have been recipients of critiques of television and related technologies. Despite their being represented as a "vast wasteland," or our watching regarded as "effortless, meaningless consumption," we have come to take such phenomena for granted. Moreover, their technical sophistication continues to grow. Of course it can be argued that technology per se is neither good nor bad. But, "nor is it neutral" (Freudenburg, 1986, p. 452). The implications for leisure warrant our examination, since the fact remains that vast amounts of leisure time are occupied receiving "texts" (i.e., the continuous presentation of messages legitimating products, lifestyles, and social values) through both commercials and the program material in between.

In the case of computers, now rapidly entering homes in the developed world, we have long been warned of their "vulgarizing" effects. For example, Roszak (1969) suggested twenty years ago that information was taking the place of ideas, that video graphics are equated with art, and that manipulation of data passes for thinking. But perhaps of greater significance is the emergence of interactive television through videotext technology. The success of the government supported Minitel system in France is now spreading to North America. Apparently, among its more popular (and therefore lucrative) program options is that featuring electronic interactive sex. As Kroker and Cook (1986) put it, increasingly we are living "virtual" lives. From the perspective of leisure, whether the services be teleshopping (a threat to the super mall?) or sexual titillation, our construction of social reality necessarily undergoes still another revision.

Finally, the commodification of **major world festivals and celebrations** from world fairs, expositions, and Carnival, to the World Cup, the Super Bowl, and the Olympic Games, requires analysis. By definition, each is characterized by the suspension of "reality" and the embracing of selected values, often departing from those subscribed to during nonfestival periods (MacAloon, 1984). The good feeling and "solidarity" that ensues has both short- and long-term social consequences. Business and industry thrive in such climates, as do governments and political institutions. Not surprisingly, the competition for hosting and sponsoring of major events has reached remarkable heights. With such large and captive audiences, one cannot help but wonder to what extent such extravaganzas serve primarily as vehicles to reenforce ideologies, dominant and otherwise.

The impact of contemporary societal forces upon leisure forms and practices, while profound, is, nevertheless, reciprocal. As Bourdieu (1979/ 1984), Dimaggio (1987), Zuzanek (1988), and others have been recently reporting, the "cultural capital" acquired through the choice of leisure pursuits seems to have much to do with one's position in society in general. More particularly, it is argued that it is cultural capital which tends to preserve existing social structures and dominant ideologies. The cultural capital Bourdieu has in mind is the powerful effects of family origin, education, and a certain comfortableness in the midst of various forms of high culture. In other words, as society determines leisure, leisure determines society. In the context of large-scale leisure enterprises then, they deliver messages suggesting access to the world of the elite, while in reality, they serve to preserve and reenforce the hegemony of the dominant class.

Summarizing to this point, we have seen that much of the use of leisure time, at least in developed countries, occurs within the context of large-scale enterprises. As multinational initiatives, they are often beyond the influence of public control. Whether anything sinister is going on is to be determined by the beholder, of course. What seems to be clear, however, is that leisure messages are several, likely to be powerful, and not always those which seem apparent, or indeed, those which were intended. For example, where the work ethic might have once been regarded as the antithesis of leisure (de Grazia, 1962), we find, at least in sociological terms, a mutual and reciprocating relationship. Or, as Campbell (1987, p. 223) suggests, romantics and puritans are essentially one and the same, in his terms, a "purito-romantic" personality system.

So, for the survival of some form of human social life, if the odds are increased by maintaining greater diversity of thought and action, then contemporary leisure, particularly in its large-scale contexts, would seem to mitigate against the achieving of such an end. Despite capitalism's principle of promoting the individual, and the concomitant role of leisure as a major context for "self-development," "self-realization," and "self-actualization," we may have reached the point where we are achieving precisely the opposite, through the process of "individuation" (Rojek, 1985, p. 19–21). In Lukacs' words, "the bourgeoisie endowed the individual with unprecedented importance, but at the same time that individuality was annihilated by the economic considerations to which it was subjected" (Rojek, 1985, p. 176).

In the context of ethics, particularly from the perspective of what "ought" to be, it could, of course, be argued that leisure was never intended to be a setting for forces which have anything to do with world survival. This I would reject on the grounds that leisure does not and cannot enjoy any appreciable social or cultural autonomy. Rather, it has become so central to the dominant sociopolitical and economic order that today's play place has taken on a social significance at least as great as that of the workplace.

Returning to my thesis, I have suggested that our continued social existence depends upon, among other factors, the maintenance of intellectual, ideological, and experiential diversity. However, the pursuit of such objectives is not possible in a moral vacuum. Particularly where leisure is the subject matter, one is tempted to adopt a hedonistic view and take a Benthamic approach on the grounds that, after all, we have achieved widespread consumer satisfaction with most manifestations of large-scale leisure enterprises. But, I prefer going for the high ground, and take the proposition that civilization is worth having and, therefore, worth perpetuating, as axiomatic. In turn, of course, this necessitates some reference to what it would require.

My answer is hardly novel nor, I expect, particularly controversial. First, based upon what we think we know, surely we will need to attend to certain physical threats, which left unchecked, will wreak havoc. These include the familiar and interrelated perils of population growth, environmental deterioration, and large-scale famine. Second, from a social perspective, the control of these, together with the prevention of our mutual destruction through the inadvertent or advertent use of contemporary weapons technology, will require some further advancements in human understanding and goodwill. But, in addition, emerging from the research and scholarship in a variety of disciplines is the necessity or preserving diversity, though often the very diversity which precipitates sometimes devastating consequences. Just as biologists have made the case for keeping our genetic and species options open, I believe the same is true when we come to consider our social options, at least until such time as we can agree that we have found the ideal set of social relations and, consequently, a universally recognized perfect society. In the meantime, and albeit difficult, it follows that we will need to continue to entertain, if not promote, some form of cultural relativism.

Following from the foregoing, the ethical imperative is clear: leisure specialists are obliged to make special efforts, first, to broaden their own understanding (together with that of producers, distributors, and consumers) of leisure-society mutualities and, second, to intervene where it may be possible to reverse some present trends.

With regard to improving our understanding of what is going on, education and research invariably come to mind, but in forms which reflect the premise that information is an end as well as a means—both of which being socially potent. For example, when it comes to the preparation of leisure specialists, it will be necessary to abandon those ideologies that represent leisure as an independent and autonomous social phenomenon or, in their normative form, leisure as an autonomous social force. The social significance of large-scale leisure enterprises could serve as a powerful frame of reference for such endeavors.

In terms of specific acts of intervention, a variety of measures come to mind. By way of an example in the context of large-scale leisure enterprises, advocating a much greater degree of assessment of their social impact would be in order. Impact assessment is hardly new in the field of recreation—particularly outdoor recreation—but social impact studies remain relatively rare (Freudenburg, 1986), certainly in contrast to the extent to which environmental or economic impact studies, or for that matter, archeological assessment, have achieved acceptance. Worse, perhaps, is the fact that assessment of any kind hardly exists in lesser developed countries—the very sites of so many large-scale enterprises.

Finally, a word about the prospects for heightening ethical considerations in leisure domains. Ethical behavior is usually considered at the level of individual action, but individual actions are largely precipitated by values and beliefs which are situationally determined. Today, as a consequence of modernization in general, and its socioeconomic features in particular, we have a paradox on our hands. Namely, we may have already reached the point where those who are intellectually and professionally nearest to leisure—that is, those who have acquired substantial amounts of cultural capital from the emerging arrangements—turn out to be least equipped to intervene. In Weber's terms, they have developed central life interests and styles of life which represent symbolic expressions of power, and as such are not easily forfeited (Rojek, 1985, p. 73).

As to what will actually unfold with respect to large-scale leisure enterprises, it does not require a futurist to imagine at least two scenarios. Either they continue to contribute to the further commodification and homogenization of society—the spirit of capitalism in its present form—and all that implies (and are likely to be embraced by "us" so long as "they" adopt our worldview, for example, our self-righteous response to recent events in the socialist world). Or capitalism once more will make a "good enough" course correction to keep social life in general, and leisure in particular, alive, or at least in modest health a little while longer.

References

Adorno, T. W. (1962/1976). *Introduction to the sociology of music.* New York: Seabury Press.

Bourdieu, P. (1979/1984). *Distinction: A social critique of the judgement of taste.* Cambridge: Harvard University Press.

Campbell, C. (1987). *The romantic ethic and the spirit of modern consumerism.* Oxford: Basil Blackwell.

Clarke, J., & Critcher, C. (1985). *The devil makes work: Leisure in capitalist Britain.* London: Macmillan.

Cohen, E. (1984). The sociology of tourism: Approaches, issues and findings. *Annual Review of Sociology, 10*: 373–392.

de Grazia, S. (1962). *Of time, work, and leisure.* Garden City, NY: Anchor Books, Doubleday.

Dimaggio, P. (1987). Classification in art. *American Sociological Review, 52*, 440–455.

Elias, N. (1939/1978). *The civilizing process.* London: Blackwell.

Elias, N., & Dunning, E. (1986). *Quest for excitement.* Oxford: Blackwell.

Freudenburg, W. R. (1986). Social impact assessment. *Annual Review of Sociology, 12*, 451–478.

Gans, H. J. (1974). *Popular culture and high culture: An analysis and evaluation of taste.* New York: Basic Books.

Gramsci, A. (1971). *Selections from the Prison Notebooks.* London: Lawrence and Wishart.

Heilbroner, R. (1989). The triumph of capitalism. *The New Yorker, 64*, 98–109 (January 23, 1989).

Kroker, A., & Cook, D. (1986). *The postmodern scene: Excremental culture and hyper-aesthetics.* New York: St. Martin's Press.

MacAloon, J. J. (1984). Olympic Games and the theory of modern spectacles, in J. J. MacAloon (Ed.), *Rite, drama, festival, spectacle* (pp. 241–280). Philadelphia: Institute for the Study of Human Issues.

Moore, W. E. (1979). *World modernization: The limits of convergence.* New York: Elsevier.

Parker, S. (1983). *Leisure and work.* London: George Allen & Unwin.

Rojek, C. (1985). *Capitalism and leisure theory.* London: Tavistock.

Rosenberg, B., & White, D. M. (Eds.). (1957). *Mass culture: The popular arts in America.* New York: Free Press.

Roszak, T. (1969). *The making of a counter-culture: Reflections on the tech-*

nocratic society and its youthful opposition. New York: Doubleday. Cited by I. Robertson (1987), *Sociology* (p. 606). New York: Worth Publishers.

Stebbins, R. (1982). Serious leisure: A conceptual statement. *Pacific Sociological Review, 25*(2), 251–260.

Veblen, T. (1899/1953). *The theory of the leisure class: An economic study of institutions.* New York: New American Library.

Wallerstein, I. (1974). *The modern world system.* New York: Academic Press.

Zuzanek, J. (1988). Semantic images of high and popular culture: Opera vs. soap opera? *Loisir et Societe/ Society and Leisure, 11*, 351–364.

Environmental Ethics: Strengths and Dualisms of Six Dominant Themes

Karen M. Fox and Leo H. McAvoy

Ethics is one of the more fashionable topics in academic and popular literature these days. It seems that everyone is interested in ethics of all types—biomedical ethics, leisure ethics, work ethics, business ethics, therapist ethics. For the leisure professional, ethical concerns are not new. The leisure field's beginnings are grounded in concern for freedom, self-expression, self-esteem, and quality of life. Typically a discussion of leisure ethics revolves around individual rights, social issues, business ethics, and professional standards. Occasionally the concept of environmental ethics appears. In many cases, someone will ask "Why should we be concerned? Isn't that better discussed in other groups such as the Sierra Club?" We would like to argue that environmental ethics is a concern of equal importance to the leisure professional.

In a world that is becoming ever smaller and more interdependent, it is difficult to make a decision or take an action that does not have an environmental implication or side effect. The leisure profession's choices of activities, programs, equipment purchased and operated, and leisure style all have impacts upon the environment and reflect an unconscious environmental ethic. One of the stated purposes of leisure with an outdoor component is to increase the participant's awareness and appreciation of the natural world. Increased awareness and appreciation is oftentimes accompanied by a deeper commitment to environmental quality (Hill, 1983). Leisure professionals are in a unique position to foster, support, and influence the discussions and behavioral patterns related to environmental ethics. As leisure professionals examine their own ethics and standards, environmental ethics should be of equal priority. If and only if leisure professionals know what they believe and the underlying assumptions about environmental concerns will they begin to know how to act, how to shape responsibly their private lives, and how to influence public policies.

This paper presents a brief look at the framework of ethical philosophy and the environment, enumerates six of the more prevalent themes in environmental ethics, and sketches a possible overlay to use as each of us struggles to define our own environmental ethics. The ultimate goal of this paper is to challenge, provoke, and move the reader to contemplate his or her own beliefs, to familiarize herself/himself with the writings of prominent authors in the field of environmental ethics, and finally, to formulate a personal environmental ethic that leads to commitment and action.

Environmental Ethics and Philosophical Schools of Thought

Traditionally, the primary focus of ethics is on the limits of human beings' actions or aggressions primarily toward other human beings or society at large. Ethics originally concentrated on the parameters of relationships between individuals, most notably free men. Later, ethics described the relation between an individual (primarily men again) and society. Eventually, the definition was expanded to include women, children, and other "minority" groups as well as white, free men. In traditional Western methods, an ethic is evaluated in terms of a universal principle that considers the good of everyone alike and is applicable to all moral individuals in all times.

Recently, scholars have attempted to expand the scope of ethical polemics to include animals, species, plants/trees, wilderness areas, and the earth in general. From one perspective, the endeavor is an attempt to answer the question: "Who speaks for the biosphere?" From another perspective, it is an attempt to redefine the human relationship with other living entities.

From an evolutionary perspective, environmental ethics has two major branches or themes: the dominant, majority, Western tradition and the minority tradition. The majority tradition seeks to build upon existing philosophical frameworks to include animals, plants, species, inanimate objects, and the environment in general. The dominant theories are based on the concept of objective, rational investigation where emotions and subjectivity have no place.

The minority tradition encompasses such ideas as ecofeminism, Na-

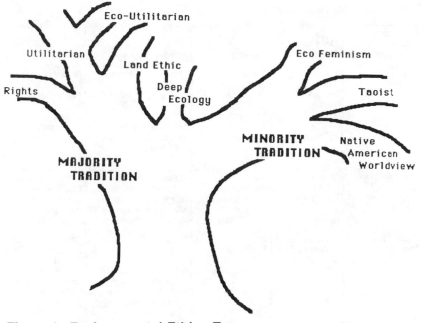

Figure 1. Environmental Ethics Tree

tive American perspectives, and Eastern religions and challenges the very assumptions of Western ethical philosophy. The authors of the minority tradition struggle to define a new framework within which to define ethics in general and environmental ethics in particular that includes recognizing the value of interconnection and caring.

Figure 1 represents the two branches of environmental ethics. The major philosophical divisions within the dominant, Western tradition are rights theory, utilitarian or eco-utilitarian, and land ethic. The position of deep ecology is controversial and is placed at the junction between the two traditions. Ecofeminism, Taoist, and Native American worldview are within the minority tradition. A review of contemporary Western environmental ethics-related literature reveals six primary philosophical lines of thought and includes all the areas in Figure 1 except Taoist and Native American worldview. (Taoist and Native American worldview are not discussed in this paper because their theoretical foundations are so different from the Western philosophical tradition.)

The matrix in Figure 2 lists those six schools of thought, the primary authors in those areas, keywords, issues, and criticisms. This matrix is presented in the hope of helping the reader better differentiate between and among the theories. The following discussion describes each of the schools of thought and then relates environmental ethics to the mission of the leisure service professional.

Figure 2. The Environmental Ethics Matrix

Philosophical School of Thought	Major Authors	Keywords	Primary Issues	Criticisms
Rights	Kant Regan Stone Taylor	Moral Agent Rights Obligations Sentient Interests Intrinsic Rational	Definition of Moral Agent Interspecies Justice Rights of Inanimate Objects Rights of Nonhumans Resolution of Conflict Between Rights Holders	Dualism Hierarchical Patriarchal Implies Conflict Atomistic Anthropocentric
Eco-Utilitarian	Singer Bentham Mill	Pleasure Community Instrumental Value Cost/Benefit Preference	Determining the "Good" Integrity of Individual Minority Position Assessing Preference	Anthropocentric Quantitative Hierarchical Patriarchal
Land Ethic	Leopold Callicott Katz	Biotic Community Land Organism Complexity	Human/Nature Separation Maintenance of Diversity Extension of Moral Consideration to Nature	Patriarchal Dualistic Simplistic Lack of Social Concern
Deep Ecology	Naess Duvall Sessions	Biocentric Diversity Egalitarianism	No Interference with Nature Economic & Idealogical Change Necessary Appreciate Life	Hierarchical Deprives Individual of Value No Criteria for Assessment
Ecofeminism	Salleh Kheel Warren Cheney	Emotions Gift Economy Web of Life Relations	Male Domination of Nature & Women Subject/Object Alienation Relationship Oriented Validity of Emotions Connections Between All Forms of Oppression Context of Issue	Dualities Denial of Responsibility "Scapegoating" Men
Synthesis/ Integrative	McDaniel Scherer Rolston Zimmerman Dustin McAvoy	Consensus Transformative Attachment Compassion Participatory	Transcending Dualities Illusion of Objective Observer Articulation of Processes and Relatedness as Central Value Avoidance of Relativism Cultural Understanding	

Rights Theory

From a rights perspective, traditional morality is associated with the
concept that there is a certain natural and morally defensible hierarchy

of beings. Ingredients from Greek and Judeo-Christian traditions state that human beings are at the top of the hierarchy because they are intrinsically valuable and alone possess an immortal soul. Immanuel Kant (1979) argued that *persons* are the sorts of beings that have "rights." Kant defined persons as rational, autonomous beings capable of formulating and pursuing different conceptions of the good. He argued that animals lack moral standing because animals are not rational. Under Kant's interpretation, humans are prohibited from abusing animals *only* because such practices may encourage humans to abuse each other. In strict Kantian terms, trees and streams have no rights or standing because they lack rational capacity, interests of their own, and a sense of caring about how one is treated (VanDeVeer & Pierce, 1986; Zimmerman, 1987).

The challenge for the environmental ethicist adhering to the rights school (Stone, 1987; Taylor, 1986) is extending inherent or intrinsic value and rights to nonrational beings, inanimate objects, and entities such as species and ecosystems. Such writers focus on what sorts of things have moral standing and defending particular criteria and on defining acceptable principles to invoke for decisions where the lives or welfare of beings that possess moral standing are in conflict.

Some animal liberationists (Regan, 1981; Singer, 1975) argue that the basis for rights should be the entity's capacity to suffer (sentience). The argument states that if a being suffers, then there can be no moral justification for refusing to take that suffering into consideration. If sentience is the standard, then criteria for ascertaining if an entity suffers is the next step. It may be relatively easy to decide if a dog or gorilla is suffering but how do we know when a lobster, oyster, spider, or bacterium is suffering?

Another variation is taken by Paul Taylor (1986) who builds upon the criteria of sentience and divides moral entities into moral agents and moral subjects. This is obviously arbitrary but demonstrates the process to extend rights. A moral agent is any being that possesses those capacities to act morally or immorally; those capacities include ability to form judgments about right and wrong, ability to engage in moral deliberations, ability to hold oneself answerable to others for failing to carry out duties, and ability to take another's view. A moral subject, on the other hand, has none of the capacities of a moral agent but is an entity toward whom or which a moral agent has duties, responsibilities, and obligations. In this framework, humans have an obligation to prevent the suffering of animals. However, Taylor does not extend his ethical system to ecosystems or inanimate objects. Inanimate objects (stones, grains of sand, puddles of water) are not themselves moral subjects. They do not have a good of their own (intrinsic value) and so cannot be treated rightly or wrongly, benevolently or malevolently.

Therefore, a river may not be a moral subject but moral agents *may* have an obligation to treat the river in a particular way in order to fulfill their duties to a moral subject (e.g., protect endangered species living near the river). Thus, the fact that inanimate objects in the natural environment can be modified, destroyed, or preserved by moral agents is a significant ethical consideration.

If a definition of moral standing can be established, the next challenge is resolving conflict between rights holders. Real life examples include the baby orangutan that was sacrificed in the attempt to save a human baby's life (VanDeVeer & Pierce, 1986) or grizzly bear/human conflicts in U.S. National Parks. When such conflicts occur, under the rights theory, a hierarchy of values is necessary to resolve the issue. The scabrous issue is if animals are always lower than human rights in the hierarchy, what is the value of animal rights? If sentience is the standard then there may not be a justification for the claim that human interests and consideration of suffering outweigh nonhuman interests and suffering simply because they are human (i.e., specism) especially if the only requirement for a right is the capacity for suffering and enjoyment (VanDeVeer & Pierce, 1986).

In summary, the rights theory emphasizes the value of the individual entity and the relationship between individual entities. The rights theory has been criticized by many over the years and so too the environmental ethicists who have built upon rights theory. The criticisms concentrate on the failure to take seriously the relevant criteria for the various rights, the emphasis on atomistic units and dualistic reasoning (good/bad; men/women; humans/nature), the hierarchical structure of values, the inherent mode of conflict, and the primacy of rationality.

Utilitarian/Eco-Utilitarian Theories

The theory of utilitarianism purports that what is right is to act so as to bring about the greatest possible balance of good consequences over bad consequences for all concerned. Evaluative criteria for moral acts are now vested in the group or whole, not in individual, atomistic units. Further, the evaluative criteria can theoretically be quantified to ensure a rational decision based on calculation of the good.

In Western history, John Stuart Mill (1979) defined good as equal to happiness and pleasure. Jeremy Bentham (1823) further expounded on the utilitarian theme by defining utility in a hedonistic manner. Hedonism, as technically understood in moral philosophy, is the view that pleasure and pleasure alone is intrinsically good. Although Mill and Bentham were not in complete agreement, pleasure, happiness, good, and utility are oftentimes used interchangeably in Western utilitarianism.

Utilitarianism emphasizes the good of the whole or the community; rights emphasizes the value of the individual. Under utilitarianism, rights do not override the concern or the good of the community. The "good" is established by identifying the positive and negative consequences of each alternative and choosing the alternative that furthers the most good. From an eco-utilitarian perspective, the health and functioning of the ecosystem or the biosphere becomes the ultimate good.

A major issue within the utilitarian theory is the concept of maximizing two variables at the same time. In some circles, this has led to the separation of the two variables: (a) most good or utility element and (b) the distribution element. So economics becomes the issue of maximizing the most good as interpreted by consumer preferences, and the issue of distribution is the question of policy and justice.

Mark Sagoff (1981) maintains consumer preferences and moral choices are two different entities. An individual may have a personal (consumer) preference for certain items or actions (e.g., consumptive recreational activities) that are detrimental to the environment; the same individual may vote to restrict those activities or objects as a responsible citizen. A human acts as a consumer to get what she or he wants individually; humans act as citizens to achieve something good and right for the community. Hence, implying moral choices from consumer preferences is erroneous.

Another possible scenario within the utilitarian framework, especially if preferences are indicators of moral choices, is that the greatest happiness may be engendered by destructive institutions or processes. This is not an implausible suggestion and may be why institutions such as racism, sexism, and prostitution have continued to flourish. If the benefits are great enough for enough people, maximization of utility may require certain kinds of destruction. If the value of the environment depends on what our preferences are or what we want, what objection can be made to a world of pizza parlors, pinball arcades, and plastic trees (VanDeVeer & Pierce, 1986)? Furthermore, who or what would voice the preferences of the animals or natural world?

Such reasoning also opens the door for an interesting twist. If a thing is valued for its role in maintaining the good of the whole, who judges this benefit and can we remove or "substitute" things? How does one define ethical modes of actions for the following: (a) "a hypothetical wilderness experience without bug bites would be more pleasurable and just as (spiritually) enriching as the wilderness experience as it actually is today ..." (Katz, 1987) and (b) human technology can substitute nonnatural for natural species (e.g., gene splicing, clones, human-controlled breeding programs, and so forth) with little or no damage to the natural system; is this morally or environmentally desired (Katz, 1987)?

Armstrong-Buck (1986) is wary of the eco-utilitarian emphasis on the *interdependence* of the members of the biotic community to the extent of depriving individuals of any value except insofar as they contribute to the system. This utilitarian emphasis accords no value to rationality, moral agency, self-consciousness, and creativity except as contributions to the community. She argues that the utilitarian emphasis seems to go against what humans intuitively know about human development and emergent characteristics. Again, who decides what is in the best interests of the community?

The Land Ethic

Aldo Leopold's land ethic was set forth in *Sand County Almanac* (Leopold, 1966). Within this concise book, Leopold describes not only the ecological and biological basis for his philosophical thoughts but also the tenets for an environmental ethic. Authors and philosophers since his death have continued to use this work as a foundation for environmental ethics and "fill in" the appropriate logic or rationale to support Leopold's original writings. We refer the reader to J. Baird Callicott's *A Companion to Sand County Almanac* (1987) and *In Defense of the Land Ethic: Essays in Environmental Philosophy* (1989) for a detailed interpretation and commentary.

Aldo Leopold's writings have a basis in evolutionary theory, ecology, and natural history. Darwin and Lecky undermined dualistic philosophies by implying a kinship with nonhumans and a natural history of morals in which our feelings are unfolded. If there is kinship with nonhuman beings, an extension of moral concern becomes a logical next step. Ecology illuminated the complexity of the "land organism" and its myriad ecosystems by studying the relationships of organisms to one another and to the elemental environment. Leopold infers from ecological principles that the interconnected, natural system or biotic pyramid is the necessary psychosocial condition to developing an ecological conscience (Leopold, 1966).

Leopold's ethic rests upon the premise that the individual is a member of a community of interdependent parts. The boundaries of this community include soils, waters, plants, and animals, or, collectively, the land (Callicott, 1987). As a member of the community, an action or thing is judged against Leopold's most frequently quoted maxim: "A thing is right when it tends to preserve the integrity, stability, and beauty of the biotic community. It is wrong when it tends otherwise" (Leopold, 1966, p. 262). This simple, yet profound statement interconnects all living things and life systems morally *and* provides a standard against which to make judgments. This is not a hard-and-fast set of timeless standards but Leopold's attempt to influence a broad base of human perceptions about the environment (Meine, 1987).

In some respects, this tenet is an outgrowth of utilitarian thinking—the most good for the most entities. Leopold extends this thinking in several ways. First, the most good is not defined in terms of pain and pleasure but in terms of the stability, integrity, and beauty of the ecosystem. Second, the land ethic demands that moral consideration be given to plants as well as animals and yet permits animals to be killed and trees felled. The decisive factor in the determination of the ethical quality of actions is the effect upon ecological systems. Therefore, it is conceivable under this framework that some bacteria may be of greater value to the health or economy of nature than dogs or people and thus command more respect.

The framework of the land ethic demands an extension of the boundaries of community to include plants, mammals, bacteria, rocks—the totality of the land. The challenge calls for a complete restructuring of basic American priorities and behavior, and a radical redefinition of progress. America's westward march was powered for three centuries by the conquest and exploitation of the environment. Leopold wanted to replace this with an ideal of cooperation and coexistence. Literally, Leopold's philosophy abruptly puts an end to the accustomed Americans' freedom to deal with nature in any fashion that suits them. The relationship with the land is no longer to be master-slave; now, the land has rights too (Nash, 1987).

One critique of the land ethic is its focus on the whole to the lack of inclusion of individual rights, human rationality, and social concerns. From another perspective, the land ethic is an extension of traditional, Western philosophical thought and does not address such tensions as the individual versus the community, the hierarchical value system within human ethical relationships, and the conflicting nature of resolving differences in needs.

Deep Ecology: Majority or Minority Tradition?

Deep ecology (Devall & Sessions, 1985) challenges the anthropocentric focus of liberal and reformist concepts of environmental ethics. From this perspective, deep ecology is sometimes classified under the minority tradition by dominant, Western tradition thinkers and the authors of deep ecology. On the other hand, some minority schools of thought such as ecofeminism classify deep ecology under dominant tradition because it does not address the patriarchal structure and the premise of rationality within philosophy.

The authors of deep ecology theories suggest that the dominant world view is characterized by a belief in opportunity for social advancement, comfort, and convenience. The greatest "good" is material progress and technological innovation. The natural world only has value by providing material to meet human, purposeful goals. In essence, there is no value to the natural world outside of human progress and purposes. Deep ecology authors want to establish a biocentric standard designed to accommodate humans within a totality of flora and fauna. The primary precepts of deep ecology are:

1. Biocentric egalitarianism, which states that humans are only a part of the ecosystem (and not necessarily more important than any other part) and that nonhuman nature should only be used by humans for *vital* needs; and
2. Self-realization must include a larger self than human population. Self-realization must identify with nature.

Deep ecology theorists hold that Western society is still locked into a search for a unique identity of self as an isolated ego striving primarily for hedonistic gratification. This belief continues in spite of the discoveries in physics that destroy the concept of the world as "sitting out there," with the observer safely separated from it by a 20-centimeter slab of glass. What is observed is not nature itself, but nature exposed to the method of questioning. Natural science does not simply describe and explain nature; it is part of the interplay between nature and human beings (Wheeler, 1973; Heisenberg, 1971). In fact, there may not be a "reality" out there separated from our knowing it. If that is the case, a biocentric equality is essential for maintaining the survival of all living things. When humans harm nature, they harm themselves by diminishing the diversity and knowledge of the totality. Human beings must begin to look at a minimum rather than maximum impact.

Deep ecology proposes that human actions be evaluated in terms of *vital needs.* Vital needs include food, water, shelter, love, play, creative expression, spiritual growth, and intimate relationships with land, humans, and nonhumans. Satisfying vital needs (in opposition to wants and desires) allows for all living beings, especially nonhumans, an equal right to live and reach their own form of unfolding and self-realization within the realm of a larger self-realization.

The tenets of deep ecology are focused on the intrinsic value of the nonhuman world, maintenance of diversity of life, a reduction of human population and consumption for nonvital needs, ideological changes, and environmental action. In a sense, this is a "hands off" attitude toward environmental management.

Deep ecology theories have been criticized by various authors (Bokchin, 1987; Sallah, 1984; Zimmerman, 1987). The main criticisms include:

strategies for decentralization without the corresponding social ethics tend to lead to racism and xenophobism; deep ecology is against humans and human progress; deep ecology solutions for complex environmental problems are simplistic; and the structure of deep ecology still supports dualistic and patriarchal thinking.

Ecofeministic Theory: A Minority Position

Weston (1985) wonders whether, at the deepest level, it may simply be impossible to have a nonanthropocentric environmental ethic within the inherited framework. The ecofeminist philosopher would agree and posits a different worldview than the prominent, male, rationalistic perspective. Ecofeminists question the assumptions and criteria of traditional philosophies including ethical theories. Historically, the feminine, women, and nature have been connected and oftentimes oppressed. According to ecofeminists, *any* ethic which fails to take seriously the interconnected system of domination of women and nature is simply inadequate (Warren, 1989).

The ecofeminist argues that all moral theories have a conceptual framework. A conceptual framework is a set of beliefs, values, attitudes, and assumptions that describes, shapes, and reflects how one views oneself and the world. The ecofeminist maintains that an environmental ethic based on traditional moral theory has a conceptual framework that includes hierarchical thinking, patriarchal values, oppression of minority groups, supreme value accorded to rationalistic thinking, and dualistic categories.

Ecofeminist theory claims to be gender inclusive but not gender neutral. In other words, it is important to identify gender because the current world is not genderless or comprised of just humans. Some are black women; some are Chicano men; some are wolves and grizzly bears. The identification is necessary because it defines a different reality and position within society and the world.

The conceptual framework of ecofeminism includes contextualism, humans-in-relations, and opposition to any form of oppression. Contextualism allows for the identification of gender, individual and local differences, and cultural perspectives. Traditional ethics highlights similarities over differences by looking for a standard that applies to all beings in all times. The ecofeminist wants to highlight the differences because it may be in the differences that solutions are found. The ecofeminist is striving for a theory that supports solidarity through diversity and empowers the minority position. It might be morally correct for Native Americans with their rituals of respect to kill an animal for food but not for the "transmogrification" of animals by "mechanicochemical" means by mainstream agricultural process (Callicott, 1980).

An ecofeminist also concentrates on *humans-in-relations* rather than what the being is or what value the being has. This perspective makes visible the conceptual and practical interconnections between sexism, racism, classism, and naturism as defining relationships. As an alternative, ecofeminist Cheney (1987) describes a "web of relationships" where relationships with others are central to ethical decision-making and expand the alternatives for action. If existence, individually and communally, is based on giving away what one has to give or what is needed by another the "gift" becomes a way to sustain and pass on life. The gift must be consumed; it cannot be allowed to pile up like capital in the hands of the recipient. The gift must be passed on and the gift increases and confers its benefits on the community and individuals only by being passed on. Cheney (1987) states: "In the case of food, literally, and in the case of much else, metaphorically, we die into one another's lives and live one another's deaths."

The writings of ecofeminists are relatively new phenomena in professional journals and the critiques have been few. Recent critiques of ecofeminism have included the charge of dualistic thinking by continuing gender distinction, denial of responsibility for environmental destruction by women because they are oppressed, and scapegoating men for environmental problems (Fox, 1989).

Synthesis or Integrative Approach to Environmental Ethics

It may be impossible and not even desirable to develop one environmental ethic for all. It may be desirable to create flexible and dynamic frameworks from the current positions to guide our decisions. New developments within the world of physics are revolutionizing scientific and philosophical thought. Quantum physics has challenged the long-held belief that the observer is distinct and separate from the observed; the detached observer is an illusion; the real observer participates in the reality observed (McDaniel, 1983). "Judgments about what *is* (mass, space, color) have proved observer dependent and indistinguishable from judgments about what *is good* (pleasure, beauty, grandeur)" (Rolston, 1982). Hence, if you alter the relationships, you alter the thing, since it does not exist apart from the relationships. "Humanity, too, is an aspect of the fabric of life on Earth; we are not apart ... the emergence of self-conscious human beings [may] be interpreted as an event by which nature can observe and evaluate itself" (Zimmerman, 1981). Within this context, we need to consider differences, patterns of oppression, and patterns of respect and honor for all beings and cultural frameworks.

These new observations should lead us to be methodologically humble (Narayan, 1988) as we strive toward an environmental ethic. Methodological humility means to sincerely act under the assumption that, when interacting with other human beings or species, we might miss something and that what appears to be a "mistake" on the part of the other may make more sense if we had a fuller understanding of the context. There is much we do not understand of the natural, social, and cultural world. As we develop an environmental ethic we need to always keep in mind our own conceptual framework and maintain a methodological humility so we can learn from other cultures, animals, plants, or rocks. They may hold the secrets that will add, modify, or deny the very framework we have developed.

In addition, it may be that only those who feel their connection to all of nature will be able to take an interest in its continuation. It then follows that even to begin to talk about environmental ethical issues implies that the participants must care (or feel something). The emphasis on feeling and emotion does not imply the exclusion of reasoning; feelings, to be effective, must take shape as thought, and thoughts, to be effective, must be powered by suitable feelings (Kheel, 1985). So, logic, rationale, observation, caring, conceptual frameworks, and attention to relationships must be interconnected and taken into account in the development of a new environmental ethic. To be involved and committed to the challenge of developing an environmental ethic, humans must care about the biosphere and all its inhabitants. To care about something means to "know," "understand," and "appreciate" it. To know, understand, and appreciate the biosphere, an individual must be exposed to its wonders. To be exposed to its wonders creates caring and awe and desire to know more (Kheel, 1985).

A Leisure Environmental Ethic—A Look to the Future

When one describes a lake by looking down at it from above, or by only skimming across its surface, one gets a limited and partial view of the nature of the lake. It is only when one dives deep and looks at the lake from the bottom up that one sees the diversity and richness of the various life forms and processes that constitute the lake. (Warren, 1987)

The preceding sections begin to scratch the surface of the complicated issues involved in developing an understandable and practical environmental ethic. We do believe that each has something to offer and there are many avenues for the leisure professional to explore in terms of personal philosophy, management policy, and program ideas. In the absence of some well-defined environmental ethic against which

Figure 3. Implementing an Environmental Ethic for Leisure Services

FORMULATE A CODE OF ENVIROMENTAL ETHICS
- Protection and Preservation
- Respect All Elements in Nature
- Differentiate Activities by Moral Goodness

EDUCATE OTHERS
- Moral Goodness of Recreation Pursuits
  Why Some Morally Better
  Implications to Living Community
- Understanding of and Identification with Natural Environment, Awareness, and Sensitivity
- Responsibility of Stewardship

DETERMINE AMOUNT OF CARE NEEDED
- Understanding Natural Processes
- Indepth Environmental Assessments
- Environmental Practice Guidelines

PROCURE GENERAL ACCEPTANCE OF ETHIC
- Education and Public Relations
- Indirect and Direct Intervention
- Social Approbation and Social Disapproval
- Political Advocacy for Ethical Tenets

NURTURE DREAMS OF A BETTER FUTURE
- Capture Imagination
- Inspire Action

all other decisions would be assessed, the leisure professional must choose among a variety of paths that are suggestive of certain ends.

We, as leisure professionals, have an excellent opportunity to work with the development of a new environmental ethic based on the premise that it gives us an opportunity to demonstrate our care for others and the earth. McAvoy (1988) proposed a process to demonstrate the leisure field's commitment to the earth's survival (see Figure 3).

First, this environmental ethic should insist on environmental protection and preservation. The ethic should engender a deep respect for all members of the natural community.

This environmental ethic should also differentiate between the higher and lower order morally good recreation pursuits and activities. A moral goodness standard would consider activities as good when they add to the health and well-being of the individual, the society, and the environment (Dustin 1988). For instance, the leisure profession may want to look at ways to purchase equipment that is environmentally sound, to recycle more, or to give more support to environmentally sound activities over activities that engender destruction and lack of respect for the environment.

The next step is to educate others about their responsibilities and obligations toward others and the earth through leisure. To educate others requires the leisure professional to understand environmental ethics in general and her or his own environmental ethic in particular. For a successful education effort, the leisure professional must have a genuine respect for the diversity of life and a methodological humility toward others with differing conceptual frameworks.

Many times an environmental ethic is viewed as a restriction of activities or desires. This seems to run contrary to the very definition of leisure, which includes freedom and choice. Yet, if the environmental ethic includes a description of how to demonstrate our care and respect for the environment and recreational areas, the leisure professional has a whole range of positive educational avenues. Further, it becomes a powerful rationale to support recreational pursuits that contribute to the health and well-being of humans as well as the environment.

Finally, the leisure professional contributes to general acceptance of the environmental ethic tenets by nurturing dreams of a better future. We must give professionals in our field as well as the people we serve a vision of a future that will be better than today; a vision of living more in harmony with a clean, beautiful natural environment full of clean air and water, quiet and tranquility, full of the majesty and grace of nature; a vision of how healthy, caring leisure styles promote the experiences we are looking for in our leisure pursuits.

In conclusion, we suggest the analogy of a whitewater kayaker to the leisure professional in a world of change. The leisure professional, like a kayaker, must learn certain principles and skills to remain upright. These principles and skills allow both to dance upon the waves of change and uncertainty. However, the principles and skills are only guides and must be used with finesse and flexibility because each wave and each situation is different. The leisure professional, like the kayaker, maintains balance by constant motion, attention, and learning about the surrounding world. The leisure professional maintains balance by knowing the frameworks of environmental ethics positions, understanding conceptual frameworks—our own and others, and using methodological humility as she or he faces each challenge. Ethics, whether leisure or environmental, is not static or a framework that doesn't flex and move, but a process, a dance upon the waters. We encourage everyone to learn the skills to perform elegantly and gracefully.

References

Armstrong-Buck, S. (1986). Whitehead's metaphysical system as a foundation for environmental ethics. *Environmental Ethics, 8*, 241–259.

Bentham, J. (1823). *An introduction to the principles of morals and legislation.* London: W. Pickering.

Bokchin, M. (1987). Social ecology versus 'Deep Ecology.' *Green Perspectives: Newsletter of the Green Program Project,* Summer.

Callicott, J. B. (1980). Animal liberation: A triangular affair. *Environmental Ethics, 2,* 311–338.

Callicott, J. B. (Ed.). (1987). *A companion to Sand County Almanac: Interpretive & critical essays.* Madison, WI: University of Wisconsin Press.

Callicott, J. B. (1989). *In defense of the land ethic: Essays in environmental philosophy.* Albany, NY: University of State of New York Press.

Cheney, J. (1987). Eco-feminism and deep ecology. *Environmental Ethics, 9,* 115–145.

Devall, B., & Sessions, G. (1985). *Deep ecology: Living as if nature mattered.* Salt Lake City, Utah: Peregrine Smith Books.

Dustin, D. (1988). Recreation rightly understood. Paper presented at the Congress of the National Recreation and Park Association, Indianapolis, IN.

Fox, W. (1989). The deep ecology-ecofeminism debate and its parallels. *Environmental Ethics, 11,* 5–25.

Heisenberg, W. (1971). *Physics and beyond.* New York: Harper and Row.

Hill, Jr., T. E. (1983). Ideals of human excellence and preserving natural environments. *Environmental ethics, 5.*

Kant, I. (1979). *Lectures on ethics* (Louis Infield, Trans.). Indianapolis: Hackett Publishing Company.

Katz, E. (1987). Searching for intrinsic value. *Environmental Ethics, 9,* 231–241.

Kheel, M. (1985). The liberation of nature: A circular affair. *Environmental Ethics, 7,* 135–149.

Leopold, A. (1966). *Sand County almanac.* New York: Ballantine Books.

McAvoy, L. (1988). An environmental ethic for recreation and parks. Paper presented at the Congress of the National Recreation and Park Association, Indianapolis, IN.

McDaniel, J. (1983). Physical matter as creative and sentient. *Environmental Ethics, 5,* 291–317.

Meine, C. (1987). Aldo Leopold's early years. In J. B. Callicott (Ed.), *A companion to Sand County Almanac* (pp. 17–39). Madison: University of Wisconsin.

Mill, J. S. (1979). In G. Sher (Ed.), *Utilitarianism.* Indianapolis: Hackett Publishing Company.

Narayan, U. (1988). Working together across difference: Some considerations on emotions and political practice. *Hypatia, 3,* 31–47.

Nash, R. (1987). Aldo Leopold's intellectual heritage. In J. B. Callicott (Ed.), *A companion to Sand County Almanac* (pp. 63–90). Madison: University of Wisconsin.

Regan, T. (1981). The nature and possibility of an environmental ethic. *Environmental Ethics, 3,* 19–34.

Rolston, III, H. (1982). Are values in nature subjective or objective? *Environmental Ethics, 4,* 125–151.

Sagoff, M. (1981). At the shrine of Our Lady of Fatima, or why political questions are not all economic. *Arizona Law Review, 23.*

Salleh, A. K. (1984). Deeper than deep ecology: The eco-feminist connection. *Environmental Ethics, 6,* 339–345.

Singer, P. (1975). *Animal liberation.* New York: A New York Review Book (Random House).

Stone, C. D. (1974). *Should trees have standing? Toward legal rights for natural objects.* Los Altos, CA: William Kaufmann, Inc.

Taylor, P. W. (1986). *Respect for nature: A theory of environmental ethics.* Princeton, NJ: Princeton University Press.

VanDeVeer, D., & Pierce, C. (Eds.). (1986). *People, penguins, and plastic trees: Basic issues in environmental ethics.* Belmont, CA.: Wadsworth Publishing Company.

Warren, K. (1987). Feminism and ecology: Making connections. *Environmental Ethics, 9,* 3–20.

Warren, K. J. (1989). Toward an ecofeminist ethic. Manuscript submitted for publication.

Weston, A. (1985). Beyond intrinsic value: Pragmatism in environmental ethics. *Environmental Ethics, 7,* 321–339.

Zimmerman, M. E. (1987). Feminism, deep ecology, and environmental ethics. *Environmental Ethics, 9,* 21–44.

Author Notes

We are deeply grateful to Karen Warren of Macalester College for her discussions and comments during the development of this paper. We also thank Jay Sorenson of the University of New Mexico and Wayne Ouderkirk of Empire State College for their comments on a near final draft and Kathleen Munger for the graphics support.

Leisure and Islam

Hilmi Ibrahim

Not all Arabs are Muslims. Most Muslims are not Arabs. Yet the Arabs are responsible for bringing Islam to the fore. Estimates of Muslims in today's world vary from about 600 to 800 million persons, spreading across each continent, distributed as follows: Africa, 153,220,400; Asia, 378,100,100; Europe, 20,200,400; North America, 1,580,900; Oceania, 87,000; South America, 405,000.

There are close to 60 countries with 15 percent or more of their populations who are Muslims. However, Muslim countries are ethnically different. For instance, the Nigerians are black and their country has 37,900,000 Muslims (45 percent), as compared to the Chinese, who claim 40 million Muslims. The Muslims, then, are an ethnic mix, who owe their Islamic faith to an ethnic group called the Arabs. It was through the Arab armies, Arab trade, and Arab culture that the world today has 600 to 800 million Muslims.

The word "Arab" refers to residents of some 22 nations who speak the Arabic language and share Arabic history and culture, despite the fact that some of them are not Muslims. Today, Egyptians, Syrians, Iraqis, Saudis, and Moroccans share Arabism, but the original Arab who gave them this commonality came from a desolate place which at one point was called Arabia, and from a particular city in Arabia, Mecca.

The Genesis

In the year 570 of the Common Era (CE), Mohammed was born in Mecca. Little is known about his boyhood and youth, except for the

---

This paper includes parts from Chapter 6, Leisure and the Intermediate Societies, *Leisure and Society*, H. Ibrahim (Dubuque, IA: Wm. C. Brown, 1991).

trips he took with his merchant uncle to Damascus and Jerusalem. At the age of 40, Mohammed managed the affairs of a wealthy widow whom he later married. He used to spend his leisure hours contemplating in a cave outside the city. One night he heard a voice, which he assumed to be the archangel Gabriel, calling him to recite. Mohammed recited, after the angel, what was to become the first chapter, *Sura*, of what was to become Islam's holy book, the *Kor'an*. The message conveyed through the *Kor'an* attracted a small group of followers who were headed by Mohammed. This group remained a small sect in polytheistic Mecca. Later, they began to preach rather boldly. Mohammed's message brought about strong opposition from local leaders and guardians of the local sanctuary of Mecca's megalithic idols, and he and his followers were forced to flee to nearby Yathrib (today's Medina). This signaled the beginning of the Islamic calendar, some 1,410 lunar years ago, on September 27, 622.

The Message: The basic message is not simply the existence of a single deity, but that his character is all-important. The conception of Allah is that of a stark, absolute, transcendent power. He is separated by an impassible chasm and the whole duty of his subjects is Islam (submission). Thus, they are called Muslim (submissive).

The Book: *Kor'an* (that which is read or recited) contains those utterances Mohammed made when he was under the influence of direct revelation. The *Kor'an* was supplemented by Mohammed's *Hadith*, his guidelines for Muslims.

The Creed: A real Muslim is one who follows five articles of faith: (1) belief in one God, (2) belief in His angels, (3) belief in His revered books, (4) belief in His prophet Mohammed, and (5) belief in the Day of Judgment.

The faithful should also practice the five pillars of Islam: (1) reciting the profession of faith, (2) performing the five daily prayers which are preceded by ablutions, (3) paying *zakat*, the obligatory tax collected for the needy, (4) fasting during the month of *Ramadan*, from sunrise to sunset, and (5) visiting Mecca, *Haj*, whenever affordable.

The Nation

Mohammed was able to convert a few of the original residents of Yathrib, and along with enough of his own Arab compatriots who came with him to Yathrib, he formed a small army for a holy war, or *jihad*, and regained Mecca. His first task was to rid the shrine of Abraham (today's Kaaba) of idols, making it the center of monotheistic Islam. Now the faithful could face, bow, and kneel toward the Kaaba. It must be pointed out that Mohammed became both the spiritual and secular leader of the early Muslims, setting a principle in motion. No separation between "church and state" existed. In fact, Islam became a much more dominant force in the lives of the people who adopted it. It became a way of life, as Islam permeated not only the spiritual and political aspects of the society, but also the social, economical, and relational aspects of the Muslim's life.

Upon Mohammed's death, a successor, *caliph*, was selected by consensus, a process which lasted for no more than three *caliphs*. Disagreement over the value of this consensus process split the nation into two camps. The *Sunnis*, the majority of early Muslims, favored selection by consensus, while the *Shiites* advocated succession within Mohammed's family. Despite the chasm, which has lasted to this day, Islam spread through assimilation, coercion, or invasion. But a totally united nation of Islam was never fully realized. Even in this disjointed state, the Islamic empire was one of the greatest in history, combining Greek ideas with Persian knowledge. Yet the power remained with the Arabs who spoke the language of the *Kor'an*. The other non-Arab Muslims who lived within, but mostly on the periphery of the empire, the Turks, Africans, Iranians, Pakistanis, Indians, and Indonesians, recited their prayers in Arabic, the only language of the *Kor'an*, making Arabic a universal language, an official language of the twentieth century United Nations.

Lifestyle of Early and Medieval Muslims

There were many capitals and dynasties of the empire, beginning with Damascus, then to Baghdad with an independent state in Cordova in 750 CE, followed by another one in Cairo in 969 CE. The last of the dynasties was a non-Arab one, when the Ottomans took over Constantinople as their capital around 1500 CE, lasting until World War I.

A perusal of Islamic literature in both Arabic and English reveals that the Western world's definition and conception of leisure does not have a comparable term (Ibrahim, 1982a, 1982b). Yet other words, such as play, free time, recreation, sport, art, music, drama, and literature, exist. The main concept can be equated to that of the Roman *otium*; despite the fact that the influence of the ancient Greeks on Arabs and Muslims was much greater than that of the Romans, their *schole* was not adopted. Aristotle described *schole* as having three forms: contemplative, recreative, and amusive. The Muslim view was closer to the Roman, with emphasis on the recreative and the amusive. Greek and Roman influence on Muslim took place after the death of Mohammed and during the Islamic expansion into Egypt and North Africa. By that time, the Muslims had already learned Mohammed's philosophy of "leisure" in two of his *hadiths*, or sayings (Ibrahim, 1988a):

> *Recreate your hearts hour after hour, for the tired hearts go blind.*

> *Teach your children swimming, shooting and horseback riding.*

Here we see that the nucleus of the Islamic attitude toward recreation is undoubtedly different from that of Judaism and Christianity. Accordingly, leisure, in its truncated form, as basically recreative-amusive, flourished among the newly established lords and their entourages. There, as in aristocratic Athens, autocratic medieval Japan, and cavalier medieval Europe, a leisure class emerged.

Leisure and the First Caliphs: The first set of caliphs who ruled from Mecca were quite ascetic and it was not until the second dynasty (known as the Ummayyids), when the capital was moved to Damascus, that a revival of some pre-Islamic practices came back under their patronage.

Mohammed had frowned upon, but did not prohibit, many of the "play" activities of polytheistic Mecca, particularly music and poetry. In the annual fair of Ukaz, a sort of literary congress took place, before Islam. The winning poet was awarded handsomely, and his place in the community was enhanced drastically. All that ended with the coming of Islam in 630 CE. But poetry, as a pastime for the listener, was to come back to Damascus around 750 CE.

> The evenings of the Caliphs were set apart for entertainment and social intercourse. Muawiyah (the first Ummayyid Caliph) was particularly fond of listening to historical narratives and anecdotes, preferably, South Arabian and poetical recitation. To satisfy this desire, he imported from Al Yaman, a storyteller. (Hitti, 1970, p. 227)

Muawiyah's son Yazid was the first confirmed drunkard among the caliphs of Damascus (circa 661–750 CE). One of his pranks was the training of a pet monkey to participate in his drinking bouts. It is said that another caliph in that dynasty went swimming habitually in a pool of wine, which he would gulp enough of to lower the surface appreciably (Hitti, 1970). But other pastimes included hunting, horse racing, and dicing. The chase was a sport developed earlier in Arabia in which a Saluki dog (originally from Saluq of Yemen) was used initially to fetch the game. Later, cheetahs were used. One of the caliphs of that dynasty had just completed arrangements for a national competition in horse racing, when he unexpectedly died, and the race did not take place (Hitti, 1970).

The dynasty subsequent to the Ummayyids was the Abbasids, who built a new capital, the city of Baghdad. There, new forms of pastimes for the wealthy took place, for according to Stewart (1967), they were able to have a near-duplicate of paradise on earth. In accordance with the words of the *Kor'an*, paradise for the faithful is envisioned as a verdant garden where the chosen recline on beautiful carpets, delight in the aroma of flowers and the ripple of running water (chapter 37, versus 42–50). The Abbasid caliphs created lush gardens, with pavilions, pools, and fountains. Gardens played an important role in the daily life of the wealthy, where they spent hours relaxing, entertaining friends, and playing chess.

At night, the entertainment came from the personnel of the palace, both male and female, dancing until dawn (Hitti, 1970). During the reign of Haroun Al-Rashid, Baghdad became the center of a galaxy of musical stars. Salaried musicians accompanied by slave singers of both sexes furnished the anecdotes, immortalized in the pages of *Arabian Nights*.

It was during that time that the Persians were converted to Islam. A number of pastimes (which later found their way to Europe) including polo, backgammon, and chess were introduced to the wealthy Muslims. Was it the lifestyle of the wealthy that led the great Arab scholar, Ibn Khaldun (circa 1337–1408 CE), to include leisure in his masterpiece, *The Prolegomenon*?

Leisure, Idleness, and Ibn Khaldun

Ibn Khaldun was a prolific writer whose early writings were summaries of previous works. But he will always be remembered for his *Kitab al Ibar*, a collection of origins and information concerning the historical development of many societies. The *Kitab al Ibar* is divided into three parts: (a) *al Muqaddama (The Prolegomenon)*, a philosophical introduction; (b) a history of the Arabs and other Semites, such as Jews, Copts, and Persians, along with a history of the Greeks, Romans, Turks, and Franks; and (c) a history of the Berbers and the Muslim dynasties of North Africa.

Ibn Khaldun suggested a new science, the purpose of which is to examine the nature and causes of human society and to reveal the internal aspects of the external events of history (Mahdi, 1964). The relationship between the new science and history is described in three ways: (a) in sequence through which the mind achieves knowledge where the new science comes after history, (b) in the art of the historian, where history and the new science should be combined, and (c) in the order of being where the object of the science of culture comes before the object of history. According to Mahdi (1964), Ibn Khaldun felt that culture is not an independent substance, but a property of another substance, man. In essence, he suggested "sociology," although he had called it *ilm-al-umran*, the science of citification.

Human Desires and Leisure

Ibn Khaldun believed that human desires are capable of infinite variation, from the simplest instinctive urge to the most intricate, complex, and specialized desire, and that they are developed in a highly specialized social order. He classified human desires as follows (Mahdi, 1964):

1. Bodily appetites, to satisfy hunger and thirst, and the needs for warmth and coolness, as well as for sex and reproduction. These desires are necessary for existence, and vary little in time and place.
2. The desire for safety, prosperity, and calm comes next. In general, humans seek the absence of serious causes of alarm, which allows for confidence and hope. Otherwise, they may be struck with fear of anger and desire vengeance.
3. The desire for affiliation with others, who are either related or resemble one; humans tend to want to live together in companionship and fellowship.

These are the basic desires which lead to the formation of human society and help to sustain it. The basic mechanism for this formation is a strong group feeling of solidarity, which Ibn Khaldun called *assabiyya* (esprit de corps).

4. After the formation of human associations and organizations as modes of relations within society, the fourth types of desires are fulfilled. Among these are the desire to be victorious and superior, as well as the desire for wealth. These desires may be the source of conflict and war. But something positive may come out of them, for example, the feeling of pity and the lending of assistance.

Finally, humans seek to fulfill three sets of desires associated with leisure. The first set includes the desire for amusement, relaxation, and laughter. The second set includes the desire for rhythmic tunes and the desire to experience objects of hearing, tasting, touching, smelling, or seeing, which leads to delight and delectation. The last set includes the desire to wonder, to learn, and to gain knowledge.

Leisure and the State

When the community of necessity that provides food and safety is established, it generates the forces that could lead to its destruction.

Men cooperated to feed themselves; that cooperation and the division of labor among them lead to opulence, which transforms the community of necessity to a community of luxury. Men begin to transgress the property of others. The injured party, driven by anger, would react, resulting in conflict and confusion, and social existence is threatened once more. The most able among the group would restrain and reconcile the community, forcing it to follow his directives. The result is a kingship (sultan) and the state is established. The state is natural and necessary because society, which is also natural and necessary, cannot exist without the state.

Once the state comes into being, it follows the natural laws of growth, maturity, and decline, for it passes through five distinct stages (Mahdi, 1964; Rosenthal, 1958).

1. A period of establishment, when *assabiyya*, based on kinship and religion, preserves the state.
2. The ruler succeeds in monopolizing power and becomes an absolute master. As any well disposed body, the state should consist of a hierarchy of powers. Solidarity is replaced by a paid army and a bureaucracy.
3. A stage of leisure and tranquility is next. Crafts, fine arts, and science are encouraged and flourish.
4. Having reached its zenith, a period of contentment pervades the society. Ruler and ruled believe that their luxury and the advantages of civilization have always existed, and that it will exist forever.
5. The habits of comfort and luxury generate physical weakness and vice. People no longer make long-range plans and birth rate drops. The entire population lives in large crowded cities, becoming subject to disease and plagues. Prodigality and waste set in. The state has reached old age and is doomed to a slow or violent death, like a wick dying out of a lamp whose oil has gone.

Leisure and Islamic Tradition

In a manner not dissimilar to what may have occurred in most societies, Islamic traditions and rituals affected both leisure behavior and leisure occasions of the commoners. The impact comes from the Sabbath and the holy day, among other things. Most of these traditions, with their rituals, continue to exist in today's Islamic world and are gradually being supplanted by modern occasions, for example, Mohammed's birthday coupled with Nasser's Revolution day in Egypt (which is not dissimilar to Christmas and Washington's birthday as leisure occasions in the United States).

The Sabbath: In the Muslim world, Friday is the Sabbath day. Yet time is not treated in Islam as it is in the Judeo-Christian theology, where the Bible is more concerned with time than is the *Kor'an*. Accordingly, Islamic Friday is a much more relaxed Sabbath than either the Jewish Saturday or the Christian Sunday, at least originally. The only requirement is a community prayer at noon in the mosque, which lasts only about an hour. The rest of the day is spent as each individual pleases.

Public Festivals: One of the best descriptions of traditional, public, religious festivals in Islam came from Edward William Lane (1973), whose account of the manners and customs of the modern Egyptians became an early Victorian best-seller in 1836. He lived in Cairo for six years and spoke Arabic fluently. According to Lane, the Festival of the Prophet, celebrating Mohammed's birthday, took place where several large tents were erected around a dry bed of an overflow lake. The tents were to be used by the Darweeshens to perform *Zikr*. A *Zikr* is a ritual performed by holy men while standing in a circle or an oblong ring or in two rows facing each other. They exclaim or chant, "There is no deity but God" over and over until they become exhausted. They were often accompanied by one or more flute players or a stringed instrument and a tambourine. In the middle of the dry lake around which the tents were erected were four masts, set in a line a few yards apart, with numerous ropes stretching across them for lanterns. The festival lasted 12 days and 11 nights. During the day, people were amused by Sha'ers, or reciters of glory, and sometimes by rope dancers. On the side streets, a few swings and whirligigs were erected. Numerous stalls were built for vendors, who sold chiefly sweetmeats. The aforementioned *Zikr* took place at night.

Another public festival was the birthday of Hussein, Mohammed's grandson, who is revered more among the Shiites than the Sunnis. Yet Sunni Egypt had two evenings of celebration in a fashion similar to Mohammed's day, except that this took place around Hussein's mosque, where the streets in the vicinity were thronged with persons lounging about or listening to musicians, singers, and reciters of romances. Every night a procession of Darweeshens passed through the streets to the mosque preceded by two drummers, men with cymbals, and bearers of torches.

Holy Days: Ramadan is the name of the lunar month when Muslims are required to fast. Islam fasting requires that the person refrain, totally, from ingesting anything—drink, food, or smoke—from dawn to sundown. The faithful usually have two meals, one immediately before dawn and one immediately after sundown. This created a lifestyle that is uniquely Muslim. The faithful sleep a little longer during the day. He or she usually takes a long nap for two hours in the afternoon. At sunset, real leisure sets in. From 8:00 p.m. on, the Muslim is free from all restriction, other than not drinking alcohol, and may pursue any activity. Coffee houses were crowded, and still are today, with organized social gatherings of men, for the Islamic society is sex segregated. Little children roam the streets of the old city carrying lanterns and singing religious songs. Muslims do not fall asleep until a field gun or a street crier signifies that it is *suhour* (time for the late meal).

Eid al-Fitr: A three-day feast celebrates the end of Ramadan and the breaking of the fast. This is when young people get their new wardrobe for the year. On the first day, it is customary to visit relatives and friends when cake is served. Some visit the graves of loved ones.

Eid al Adha: Two months after the first feast, the faithful try to visit Mecca's shrine of Abraham and Medina's grave of Mohammed. *Adha* (sacrifice) is celebrated for four days. This feast is to celebrate the Prophet Abraham, who obeyed Allah's order that a sacrifice was needed and proceeded to slaughter his son, Ismael. When an angel descended from heaven with a substitute lamb, Allah ordered Abraham and his followers to sacrifice a lamb in His name on that day as they congregated around his house in Mecca, the *Kaaba*.

Since only two million of the 700 million Muslims perform the Haj to Mecca each year, the remaining Muslims have their own celebration at home. They slaughter a lamb in the name of Allah, which the poor share with another family. These four days of this Islamic feast are spent preparing the lamb to be cooked in a number of ways. Family and friends organize eating parties, for the meat must be consumed within a few days, before it needs refrigeration. Another important activity takes place, similar to the previous feast, visiting cemeteries and hiring sheiks to recite the *Kor'an* at the graves of loved ones.

Public Entertainment: Despite prohibition on religious grounds, public performance by female dancers was witnessed by Lane in 1836, in the streets of Cairo. The "Ghawazee," named after a district tribe, was performed in the court of a house, in the street before the door, or on certain occasions, such as marriage, in the hareem, the section in old mansions reserved for the females of the household. They performed their belly-dance, unveiled with little elegance, first slowly, then with a rapid vibrating motion of the hips, from side to side, accompanied by a rapid collision of brass castanets.

Among other street entertainers were the performers of sleight-of-hand tricks, who would collect a ring of spectators around them as they performed. Some would draw a great quantity of various silk handkerchiefs from the mouth; another would take a large box, put an assistant's skull cap in it, blow on the box, open it, and produce a rabbit.

Other performers were *Bahluwans*, who walked tight ropes and swallowed swords. The rope was sometimes tied to the minaret of a mosque, supported at many points by poles fixed in the ground. The performer used a long balancing pole. Sometimes, a child was suspended to each of the performer's ankles.

The *Kureydatee,* or monkeyman, amused the crowds who would gather for his Friday performances, dressing the monkey as a bride or a veiled woman, putting it on a donkey, and parading it around. The monkey also danced and performed various antics. Other entertainers used trained dogs in their shows.

But all these public festivals and feasts were strictly for men only. As mentioned earlier, there was, and to some extent there still is, the strong practice of public segregation of the sexes, which usually begins taking place at puberty.

Segregation of the Sexes

Many Islamic scholars believe that the strict public segregation between the two sexes was not an original advocation by Mohammed. In fact, he used to have foot races with his wife and allowed women to fight along side men in the many battles of early Islam. Mohammed advocated leisure education for both boys and girls (Sfeir, 1985). Yet this attitude changed over the years and the practice of a harem, isolated in their quarters, is still practiced, albeit to a less extent than during the hegemony of the Ottomans (circa 1453–1908), the last of the Islamic dynasties.

According to Fanny Davis (1986), the life of the wealthy Ottoman women was rich with leisure pursuits despite their segregation. They received other women visitors and were entertained by music, dance, storytelling, and shadow play at their own homes. Julia Pardoe, who visited Constantinople (today's Istanbul) in the early 1800s, wrote the following:

> She twirled the tambourine in the air with the playfulness of a child; and having denoted the measure, returned it to one of the women, who immediately commenced a wild chant, half song and half rec- itative, which at times was caught up in a chorus by the others, and at times wailed out by the dancer only, as she regulated the movements of her willow-like figure to the modulations of the mu- sic. (Davis, 1986, p. 131)

The wealthy women of the Ottoman Empire paid a weekly visit to the public plunge, *hammam,* which we call the Turkish bath. That was her out-of-the-house diversion. In some cities of the vast empire, which extended from the Arabian Gulf to the Atlantic, the public bath had two compartments, one for men and one for women. In other baths, certain days were designed for men or women. Once public swimming pools were built at the urban centers of the dominantly Muslim cities, the same practices were continued. But with the coming of private clubs and international hotels, things began to change.

Winds of Change

Despite the strong opposition from the *Ulma* (Islamic scholars) and the self-appointed fundamentalists, change began to take place slowly, but surely, coupled with reactionary movements, à la Khomeini.

The original allegiance to Islam as the dominant ideology from Morocco to India was punctured by the Napoleonic invasion of Egypt (circa 1798–1801), which revealed the impotence of the Ottoman caliphate. Further annexation of North Africa, of Algeria, Tunis, and Morocco by the French, and of Egypt and the Sudan later by the British, led to the rise of a new ideology and nationalism. "Local nationalism" of the Egyptians, Syrians, Iraqis, etc., coagulated through Gamal Abdel-Nasser's charismatic personality in the early 1950s into Arab nationalism. Surprisingly, Nasser spoke of three circles, Arabism, Africanism, and finally, Islamism. In other words, he underscored secular nationalism over sacred Islamism.

As such, nationalism is an imported ideology which sailed rather obliquely against many old traditions. Should national holidays be as important, if not more important, than the religious ones? Can women ever become equal to men in sport and recreation? Is a community center as important as a mosque? There is no doubt that the struggle between secular ideology–nationalism and sacred ideology–Islam is still continuing. The outcome would have been a toss-up, had Khomeini's Islamic revolution succeeded. Today, nationalism is favored to win. But as is the case in all rapidly changing societies, the expected outcome is not guaranteed. For instance, Arab nationalism, which begat loose alliances among Arabic speaking countries into the Arab League in the late 1940s, failed to produce a United Arab Republic between Egypt, Syria, Yemen, and supposedly Iraq and Libya in the late 1960s. Currently, nationalism is localized into Egyptian, Syrian, Iraqi, and of course, Palestinian nationalism. A rather unique feature of secular nationalism is women's emancipation. While all this started after World War I, particularly in Egypt, small but powerful Islamic fundamentalist movements were beginning. The drive of nationalism continued after WWII, particularly after the Arabs' defeat by Israel in 1948. The continual defeat in subsequent wars with Israel gave an impetus to the fundamentalists.

A strange combination of feminism-fundamentalism is apparent today. For example, in a private club in Giza, a suburb of Cairo, in May 1986, this author saw a young female dressed in her judo attire, barefooted, with a head cover that belonged to her grandmother's generation.

She was not veiled (face-covered), but rather *muhajaba* (hair, ears, and neck covered). Perhaps more intriguing is the fact that she was the only female in a line of about 15 young men (aged 14–16). She practiced falls and all with the team members. Not too far from the judo grounds was the gymnastic team, with females performing in their shorts and leotards.

Yet, this is not a common scene, for as stated in Sfeir (1985), "prohibition against bodily exposure, socializing with men, traveling alone, going out and participating in sports," still predominates in the Islamic countries. Nevertheless, a Moroccan young woman won an Olympic gold medal in 1984 in Los Angeles. Out of 29 countries with two-thirds of the population Muslim, very few sent women to the Olympics. The first was Turkey, in 1936, followed many years later by Iran under the Shah and in 1980, Algeria, Libya, and Syria sent women athletes to Moscow. Egypt participated as early as 1912 in the Olympics, but it was not until 72 years later, in 1984, that it sent six women to the 1984 Games in Los Angeles (Sfeir, 1985).

The Case of Saudi Men: A study was conducted in an administrative zone of 1,760,000 inhabitants in the eastern provinces of Saudi Arabia. The study was the first to reveal the amount of free time among 15,000 young males between the ages of 10 and 15. It also revealed the type of activities these youth prefer and was intended to be used to help planners design suitable programs (Ibrahim, 1988b).

Preliminary questionnaires were constructed from materials provided by UNESCO, the European Centre for Leisure, and the World Recreation and Leisure Association. Two open-ended questionnaires were agreed upon, one for the youth and one for their leaders. A pilot study of 418 youth and 35 leaders was conducted and the questionnaires were modified and applied to 15,000 youth and 1,000 leaders, with the following results:

> Free time among Saudi Arabian young males varies from four hours on the weekday to about seven hours on the weekend and holidays.
>
> Most of the elementary school children spend their free time in the streets. The number decreases as the children grow older.
>
> Soccer is the most participated in leisure activity, followed by watching television.
>
> Most of youth spend their vacations at home.
>
> Those who travel abroad go to Egypt and Syria.
>
> A good number of youth go on outings weekly and/or monthly.

The research team forwarded the following recommendations:

> Youth centers should be erected at the rate of one to each 10,000

residents, at different "levels" (capacity and functions) regardless of affiliation (be it a school, a club, or a structure in a park).

Family recreation centers as well as adult education centers should be established for each 15,000 residents provided they are centrally located.

Literary centers should be established for religious and literary activity.

Mobile recreation units should be established to go to districts void of facilities.

Soccer should be given the top priority as the most preferred sport. Lifelong activities should be encouraged as well.

Outings seem to play an important part in Saudi youth's lives.

Summer resorts are needed since a good number of Saudi youth stay in the country during the summer.

Information pertaining to the countries that are traveled to the most should be provided—Egypt, Syria, Lebanon, Turkey, and Great Britain.

Establishment of Saudi youth hostels in the countries mentioned above.

Cultural attaches of Saudi Arabia in those countries should supervise the visiting Saudi youth.

Egypt's Pursuit of Leisure

In a recent study by Ibrahim et al. (1981), a 24-hour cycle in the life of 400 residents of the Cairo-Giza urban center was compared to a previous study of 12 nations (Szalai, 1972). The data reveal that an urban Egyptian enjoys an average of 298 minutes of free time a day in comparison to 200 for the Hungarian, 231 for the Bulgarian, 233 for the East German, 239 for the Czechoslovakian, 245 for the French, 247 for the Soviet, 262 for the Polish, 264 for the West German, 297 for the Belgian, 301 for the American, 309 for the Peruvian, and 311 for the Yugoslavian. While this may seem surprising to many, there are a number of factors that have led to increased free time in Egypt.

Industrialization

In 1937, the worker in an Egyptian city averaged 52 hours of work per week. In 1964, due to the drastic change in the structure of Egyptian society, the average worker in a commercial or industrial firm averaged 42 hours of work per week. Most of these firms operate on a five and a half day week instead of the traditional six day week. The number of workers in industry and business firms related to industry is steadily increasing. In 1937, out of a population of 16 million, a little over 3 million (18 percent) were in the nonagriculture force compared to 1970, when the population was about 32 million and the nonagricultural workers exceeded 13 million (38 percent). Also, labor laws passed during the past 20 years provided for more and longer vacations for workers. It should be noted that in the countryside, the peasant workers still work long hours each day, using tools that belong to the antiquities.

Urbanization

Egypt suffers from the same fate that befell industrial nations: a large number are moving from their calm, peaceful villages to the cities where there are more work opportunities. The population of Cairo doubled in 10 years, whereas the total population of the country increased only 20 percent. Before World War II, only 25 percent of the population of Egypt lived in the large cities, and now it is over 38 percent. Industry alone did not lead to urbanization, but service provided in the cities drew manpower from the villages and farms to the cities. There are 9,630,000 persons living in cities of over 20,000 population in Egypt compared to less than half that number 20 years ago.

City life is by no means as good as it may have seemed to the farmers. The price paid for living in the cities was great. Delinquency, especially among the juveniles, increased in the Egyptian urban communities. The traditions and customs that ruled the rural communities declined in the city. The control over the behavior of the city dweller was no longer strong. The swift tempo of life and the speed of movement in Egypt's urban centers increased drastically over the last few decades. The number of people escaping the sizzling towns to the seaside resorts during their summer vacations has also increased.

Democracy

For the first time in the fiscal history of the Egyptian government, there was an allocation for cultural and recreational services in the 1960–1961 budget. The amount of 9,000,000 Egyptian pounds was allocated to render these services to the people who had been denied for a long time the enjoyments of club membership, watching an opera, or going to the seashore for a vacation. This money was to provide these services free of charge or for a nominal fee.

Recreation at Home

Watching television is the most participated-in leisure activity enjoyed by all 10 groups in the aforementioned study (Ibrahim et al., 1981). It seems that women, with the exception of female students, spend more time than men in this activity. The data showed 155, 122, 104, 80, and 75 minutes for housewives with high school education, housewives with college education, married working women, unmarried working women, and female students, respectively. Among men, no significant differences existed in watching television. The time men spent watching TV varied from 96 minutes for laborers, 78 minutes for clerical men, 64 minutes for professionals, 52 minutes for students, and 47 minutes for businessmen.

Visiting seemed to be the second most participated-in leisure activity for almost all 10 groups. Among men, professional men spent 40 minutes, laborers 33 minutes, students 32 minutes, clerical men 30 minutes, and businessmen 6 minutes visiting per day. The data showed that housewives spent 41–49 minutes visiting, married working women 23 minutes, unmarried working women 20 minutes, and students spent 4 minutes visiting.

Talking was the third most participated-in leisure activity among most of the groups (at home). Male laborers and married working women spent 36 minutes talking, businessmen 33 minutes, housewives with high school education and clerical men spent 30 minutes talking (per day). Housewives with college education and unmarried working women spent 29 minutes talking, while male students spent 18 minutes, female students 17 minutes, and professional men spent 13 minutes talking.

Listening to the radio was listed as a primary activity among all the groups. Housewives with a high school education listened to the radio 46 minutes, married working women 25 minutes, female students 24 minutes, professional men 21 minutes, clerical and businessmen 11 minutes, male students and unmarried working women 7 minutes, and laborers listened to the radio 3 minutes daily.

Reading is a leisure activity in which professional men and married working women spent 36 minutes a day. Housewives with high school education spent 27 minutes, housewives with college education 19 minutes, male students 16 minutes, unmarried working women 10 minutes, businessmen 8 minutes, laborers 6 minutes, and female students 5 minutes.

Recreation Away from Home

Recreation is defined here as any "autotelic activity in which one participates during his leisure, that is constructive and non-profitable." The types of recreational activities that Egyptians participate in, for purposes of this paper, have been classified as: physical recreation, social recreation, cultural recreation, outdoor recreation, arts and crafts, recreational music, and drama and dancing.

Physical Recreation: As is the case in most of the world, soccer is first, as the most popular game. Field handball is gaining ground very rapidly in spite of the fact that it was introduced into this country only three decades ago. Swimming is the most popular activity among the adult population. The number of swimming pools is not high, but the sea coast of over 1,700 kilometers on both the Mediterranean Sea and the Red Sea provides summer resorts for vacations.

Social Recreation: Social gathering is essential to the Arab way of living. Bedouins enjoy their evenings sitting and chatting around the campfire, as do the village dwellers. In the city, television, as yet, has not affected this sociability. One will find that cafes are still popular places for the Egyptian male to sit with his friends and talk over coffee and tea. In many cases, *Tawla* is played, a game similar to backgammon. Other table games are also played in cafes. Children stay at home to play games that have been passed down from generation to generation and can be traced back to the earliest Islamic era. Those games are played all over the Arab world. They vary from active to quiet games, as well as intellectual ones. At weddings, birthdays, and the birth of babies, special types of food are served and special ceremonies are conducted.

Cultural Recreation: In this ancient land, cultural aspects are of great value to the people. There are cultural institutions in Egypt that are under the supervision of the Supreme Council of Culture: palaces and houses of culture, cinema houses, theaters, national monuments, public libraries, and museums. Television was installed in the Arab Republic of Egypt in July 1960. Two channels offer cultural, educational, and entertainment items for children, youth, and adults. The Egyptian Radio Station started in 1934 by transmitting two hours daily. In 1950, the number of broadcasting hours did not exceed 22 hours a day, in comparison to 198 and 130 hours per day over medium and short waves, respectively. This is still true in 1988.

Outdoor Recreation: The climate of Egypt is mild with little rain. The country enjoys a seacoast over 1,700 kilometers in length. The first two camps for the Boy and Girl Scouts were built in 1923. Additional camps were built in the 1950s. As early as 1930, the Department of Social Activities in the Ministry of Education created an interest in camping and excursion movements, yet the number of participants did not exceed 7,000. Recently, camping was given more support. In 1974, the number of participants in camping and excursions exceeded 300,000. There are 49 camps and camp sites throughout the country, with a capacity of 12,000. The First Conference on Camping and Excursions was held in April 1961. At that conference, it was recommended that camping and excursion services should include workers and farmers as well. The idea of "people's camps" was created, by which any worker or farmer interested in spending his vacation in a camp can join one for a nominal fee for a period of two weeks.

Egyptians are crammed in a narrow valley along the Nile, the rest of the land being desert, yet modern city planners are helping Cairo and other deprived cities to develop parks. Public gardens were built for the opening of the Suez Canal. High fees were charged for entrance to the zoo and botanical gardens. Now, these gardens, as well as the gardens surrounding the ex-kings' palaces, are open to the public. Along the Nile, little parks were built so that the citizens of Cairo could enjoy the summer evenings. There are 412 parks in Egypt; some are as large as 400 acres, some as small as one acre, and some of them provide swings and seesaws for children.

Hosteling was introduced into the country in 1954, and the Egyptian Youth Hostels Association was founded. The Association is a member of the International Association of Youth Hostels. There are ten hostels in Egypt.

Arts and Crafts: Arts and crafts play an important role in the educational system in Egypt. As early as 1960, the Supreme Council of Youth Welfare realized the need for arts and crafts in youth organizations and formed the Committee for Art Education. The committee has suggested that each youth and community center, club, and camp should have an art and craft specialist as a member of its staff. Schools offer students two art and craft lessons a week. In the secondary school, there are two hours of study in practical subjects which include studies in wireless appliances, food industries, etc. The television program "Children's Corner" is designed to teach children how to use their hands and imagination.

Recreational Music: With a beautiful background in music, Egypt should have been a leading country in folkloric music. Unfortunately, it had to follow the modern line, and the entertaining type of songs took the place of group singing; the folkloric songs were apparently rapidly vanishing. A National Committee on Art suggested that such songs should be collected and taught to youth to use in their gatherings. A Center for Folk-Studies was established by the Ministry of Culture to preserve and develop this national heritage.

Drama and Dancing: These two activities are the ones least practiced as recreation. Traditions and customs in Egypt frowned on the activities of the actor and dancer. Children were not allowed to participate in these activities even as hobbies. Only recently have young people been encouraged to enjoy them. Each secondary school has its drama group and some have dancing groups. The students in the universities participate in a competition each year to win the Drama Cup. The Ministry of Education formed a Department for School Theater Activities and they are conducting a competition similar to the universities.

Palaces and houses of culture, youth and community centers, clubs, and camps are encouraged to develop dramatic and dancing groups. Each year, the celebrated October Festivals include competition in the performing arts, which include singing, dancing, acting, and other similar activities.

One in seven persons is a Muslim, and with the rapid growth in the Muslim population, attention should be paid to their aspirations and the changes they have to face if they want to catch up with the modern world. Muslims, and the people who brought about Islam, the Arabs, are trying to regain their place under the sun. Yet they are attached to traditions which go back many centuries. Sometimes, they seem to be unable to reconcile the differences between tradition and modernity. The paradox is clearly apparent in their leisure pursuits. While certain leisure activities that are universally accepted are practiced among Arabs and Muslims (such as men's sports), it is doubtful that other activities such as mixed dancing will be accepted in the near future.

References

Davis, F. (1986). *The Ottoman lady*. Westport, CT: Greenwood Press.

Hitti, P. (1970). *History of the Arabs*. New York: Macmillan Company.

Ibrahim, H., et al. (1981). Leisure behavior among contemporary Egyptians. *Journal of Leisure Research, 13*(2): 89–104.

Ibrahim, H. (1982a). Leisure and Islam. *Leisure Studies, 1*(2): 197–210.

Ibrahim, H. (1982b). Leisure and recreation in Egypt. *Egypt, 1*(5): 10–12.

Ibrahim, H. (1988a). Leisure, idleness and Ibn Khaldun. *Leisure Studies, 7*(1): 51–58.

Ibrahim, H. (1988b). Leisure among young Saudi males. *The International Review of Modern Sociology, 18*(spring): 57–60.

Lane, E. W. (1973). *An account of the manners and customs of the modern Egyptians*. New York: Dover Publications. (Original work published 1836).

Mahdi, M. (1964). *Ibn Khaldun's philosophy of history*. Chicago: Chicago University Press.

Rosenthal, F. (1958). *Ubn Khaldun/The Muqaddimah: An introduction to history*. New York: Bollinger Foundation.

Szalai, A. (Ed.). (1972). *The use of time: Daily activities of urban and suburban population in twelve countries*. The Hague: Mouton.

Sfeir, L. (1985). The status of Muslim women in sport: Conflict between cultural tradition and modernization. *The International Review for Sociology of Sport*, 283–304.

Stewart, D. (1967). *Early Islam*. New York: Time Incorporated.

Section Two

Selected Thoughts

The following selected papers are condensed versions or revisions of presentations delivered at the symposium. Each of the papers serves to identify a distinct and significant area of inquiry in need of continuing investigation. The diversity of topics illustrates the wide scope of meanings associated with the study of leisure and ethics.

What Is the Good of Leisure?

Wes Cooper

Leisure is free time, and the free time of leisure is free, according to the popular view, in the sense that it is free of the obligations of work, family, and society. According to Joffre Dumazedier (1967), for example, "Leisure is activity—apart from the obligations of work, family, and society—to which the individual turns at will, for either relaxation, diversion, or broadening his individual and his spontaneous social participation, the free exercise of his creative capacity" (p. 14). Dumazedier's account has a negative and a positive element. The negative element characterizes leisure as activity in which one is free of obligations, and the positive element characterizes it as activity that one turns to for relaxation and other goods. What I am calling the popular view tends to emphasize the negative element in Dumazedier's definition. It is an impoverished conception of leisure, and I will conclude by proposing a better alternative. For the moment, however, and for the sake of the present argument, I take it for granted in order to raise a question which philosophy has largely neglected: What makes leisure good?[1]

This is a very general question, of course, and really too general to be answered as it stands. So it is necessary to replace it by several more specific questions. One of these is: What makes leisure good for the person who is engaged in it? This is more specific, in the sense that leisure may be good in several different ways without being good for the subject. Goodness (or evil) for a subject will be called *subject-relative*. Leisure might be bad for the subject but good for the economy,

---

[1] I take up a related question, What is leisure? in "The Metaphysics of Leisure," (1989), in *Philosophy in Context, 19,* and in "Some Philosophical Aspects of Leisure Theory," (1989), in *Understanding Leisure and Recreation: Mapping the Past, Charting the Future*, E. Jackson and T. Burton (Eds.), State College, PA: Venture Press.

for instance; perhaps he spends his leisure in expensive and debilitating pursuits which reward entrepreneurs at the same time as they ruin his health. This would not be subject-relatively good leisure, but there would be a subject-neutral sense in which it is good. Of course there is still a subject, in a broad sense, for which the leisure is good, namely, the economy. But I will use the term "subject" in a narrow sense, to denote the person whose leisure is being referred to. If leisure is not good for that subject, but is good in some other respect, then the goodness of the leisure is subject-neutrally good. Subject-neutral goodness does not entail subject-relative evil. A leisure theorist studying the benefits of leisure for society as a whole might be indifferent to the benefit for any particular subject; he is concerned with people collectively rather than a particular individual's welfare. So his claims about subject-neutral benefits would carry no implications one way or the other about the benefits to a given individual.

With the distinction between subject-relative and subject-neutral goodness in hand, I propose the following hypothesis: The goodness of leisure, as such, is subject-relative goodness exclusively. This hypothesis implies that the goodness that is peculiar to leisure is necessarily goodness for the subject who is engaged in it, and that any subject-neutral goodness it may have is accidental to its goodness as leisure. A subject might spend his leisure in self-abnegating good works, for instance, in such a way that his conduct is morally good, perhaps even supererogatory, but not good for him, and therefore not good leisure. His conduct is subject-neutrally good in a moral sense, but not subject-relatively good.

Even the more specific question about what makes leisure subject-relatively good is in need of further specification. Let us distinguish therefore between leisure that is subject-relatively good with reference to some normative value or other, on one hand, and leisure that is good in that the subject enjoys it, on the other hand. Someone might judge jogging good, for example, either because it promotes health, or because she enjoys it. The former may be called value-based goodness, while the latter may be called preference-based goodness. The theorist mentioned above, studying the benefits of leisure, could be engaged in either a value-based or a preference-based study, depending on whether she was measuring subjects' leisure according to some normative standard, such as self-improvement, or whether instead she wanted to find out what forms of leisure people actually liked. The preference-based study would focus on the "perceived benefits" of leisure, whereas the value-based study would be concerned with the benefits that *ought* to be perceived, at least from the perspective of the value-based study. In the example above of expensive but debilitating leisure, characterized as bad for the subject, the badness in question was value-based rather than preference-based. Presumably the subject preferred the debilitating leisure to the alternatives, and so in a preference-based sense the leisure was good for the subject. But by reference to the value of health one judges that the leisure was bad for the subject. This is still subject-relative goodness—it is different, for example, from saying that a person's leisure is bad for public health.

With the distinction between value-based and preference-based goodness in place, I propose the following hypothesis. The goodness of leisure as such is preference-based exclusively. Pursuing or attaining something that is valuable apart from being preferred may make a subject's conduct better for the subject, but not better as leisure. Practicing a musical instrument despite the boredom may be better for the subject than reading the newspaper, because it is helping to gain the subject access to the world of music, and this, we may agree, is a valuable thing. But that is not enough to make the practicing good *qua* leisure. Reading the newspaper, which would be the subject's preference, would be better in that regard.

Value-based goodness may take many forms, corresponding to the many values that may be deemed worth pursuing. But I put these aside in order to attend to preference-based goodness, which is more central to the goodness of leisure. It too may take many forms. Consider first the difference between an egoistic and an altruistic disposition. The altruist's preferences are "about" the welfare of others; he wants the other person to fare well. His altruistic conduct is subject-relatively good in that his preferences are being satisfied, but it normally does not aim at personal benefits in any ordinary sense. This reference to personal benefits can be made more precise by listing some typical ones: pleasure, absence of pain, wealth, power, security, liberty, glory, possession of particular objects, fame, health, longevity, status, self-respect, self-development, self-assertion, reputation, honor, and affection.

By contrast with the altruist, an egoist aims exclusively at personal benefits. I do not think that anyone is a pure egoist, or a pure altruist for that matter. But I do want to hypothesize that a pure altruist would be incapable of good leisure, and that anyone who has a capacity for such leisure—I assume this includes everybody—has a degree of egoistic motivation proportional to this capacity. We have some preferences that ultimately aim at personal benefits, in the way that my preference for an ice-cream cone ultimately aims at my pleasure. Our preferences in these cases, I shall say, are self-directed. The hypothesis then is that good leisure is activity for which one has a self-directed preference; it aims at personal benefits.

Consider next some different temporal interpretations that can be given to preference-based goodness. Acting on the principle "Live your life so that you will have no regrets," one would employ a backward-looking form. What makes one's leisure good now is that, looking back, I would prefer that I do this now. Or acting on the principle "Live your life so as to maximize continuity with your past preferences," past preferences are given priority. What makes this leisure good now is that it is what one would have preferred in the past, or it is more similar than the alternatives to conduct that you would have preferred in the past. Or acting on the principle "Live your life so as to satisfy the desires that you have now," present preference would be relevant.

Given that preference-basedness may be oriented toward past, present, or future preferences, I advance the following hypothesis: What makes leisure good as leisure is present preference. The custodial, backward-looking principle may be the most prudent one to act upon, since anticipation of your future self's judgments may be more likely to promote long-term self-interest than harking to present preference—a contrast that smokers are familiar with, for instance. This shows that the goodness of leisure and the goodness of prudence are distinct, and that they may be at odds, although they need not be. Acting on the past preference principle would induce a kind of unity or continuity to one's life, and perhaps it would satisfy a certain interpretation of the injunction to be true to oneself (Be true to one's past self?), but to the extent that these things are valuable their value is not the value of leisure.

Notice that a present-preference base does not entail some such principle as "If it feels good, do it," for that hedonistic principle is only one of perhaps an infinite number of present preference principles. For example, another such principle is "If it is what you would want if you were fully informed and thinking clearly, do it." Indeed my next hypothesis is that this cognitive principle is the right one for judging the goodness of leisure. That is, a person's leisure is good leisure only when it is what one would want to be doing if one were fully informed and thinking clearly. I shall say that preference under these conditions is cognitively suffused. The conditions of full information and clear thought are not necessarily counter-factual, but often they will be. An exhausted marathon runner may not be thinking clearly, but her running the race may be what she would want to be doing if she *were* thinking clearly: she would not say, "Ah! I should be watching TV." Moreover she would not have said this if she had been informed that her favorite film was on TV, something that as a matter of fact she did not know. The unknown information was relevant to her choice, in the sense that it had some tendency to give rise to a decision to watch TV, but her actual decision to run the marathon would have won out anyway.

As with the other conditions of good leisure hypothesized here, the cognitive suffusion condition is a necessary rather than a sufficient condition. Altruistic activity can satisfy the suffusion condition, presumably, so if good leisure is self-directed activity, hence non-altruistic, then that condition's being fulfilled cannot be sufficient for leisure. The cognitive suffusion condition is one of many necessary, but only jointly sufficient conditions for good leisure.

A final distinction is needed between means-oriented and end-oriented preference. Suppose I plan a holiday, and accordingly I spend a good deal of leisure time—which we are assuming means time off the job, free of obligations—making preparations, only to have the holiday canceled at the last minute. I want to say that the leisure I spent on preparations, being means-oriented, was bad leisure, whereas the leisure of the holiday, had it happened, would have been good leisure, since it satisfies a preference which was end-oriented. When I preferred to prepare for my holiday rather than do the other things I might have been doing, I had this preference because the preferences were necessary means to my end of taking a holiday. The preference was solely instrumental, and apart from the instrumental value I would rather have been doing something else. But my preference for the holiday was not solely instrumental, although one of my reasons for going might have been my belief that the holiday would allow me to return to work refreshed. Apart from this possible instrumental value, however, I wanted the holiday for its own sake: for relaxation, the sun, novel company and good food, etc. This intrinsic, noninstrumental value of the holiday is what would have made it good leisure. Its goodness as leisure, indeed, requires that end-orientation should be the larger part of one's motivation for the activity, even if means-orientation, for example, recreation, plays a part too. I submit this as the last of my hypotheses about good leisure.

I conclude that good leisure is subject-relative, present-preference-based, self-directed, consistent with cognitive suffusion, and predominantly end-oriented. I now want to raise again the question which I put off at the beginning, namely: Might it be a good idea to replace what I called the impoverished conception of leisure—the conception of it as time free of the obligations of work, family, and society—by a conception of it as what I have been calling good leisure? I see no reason not to attempt to reform common thinking about leisure in this direction, and I see several reasons to make the attempt.

For one thing, the proposal would articulate the lingering sense that there is a difference between leisure and idleness, mere freedom from obligation. Leisure is not mere "freedom from," but "freedom for" doing what one prefers doing. This captures the intuitive idea that there is something personally rewarding in leisure, whereas leisure as idleness may be boring and stultifying. There is a nuance of paradox, for instance, in speaking of "the enforced leisure of the unemployed." The present proposal would do justice to this nuance, implying that the so-called leisure is not leisure at all; it's plain unwanted idleness.

There is a "freedom from" of leisure, but this negative freedom is not necessarily freedom from obligations of work, family, and society— after all, it is possible to enjoy the discharge of these obligations instead of suffering them merely as burdens. Nor is the negative freedom of leisure limited to freedom from these obligations when they are experienced as burdens. Also encompassed is freedom from the demands of perfectionist values about what is "good for you." What counts in leisure is one's own perception of one's good, as expressed in end-oriented motivation and conduct. The "as expressed" qualification is important here. I may make a moral or aesthetic demand on myself which I comply with by doing such-and-such, but my motivation for doing it may be entirely instrumental toward doing what I morally or aesthetically ought to do. Only when desire and deed are end-oriented is it right to speak of leisure rather than, say, moral or aesthetic work.

As with everyday obligations, however, leisure does not necessarily rule out perfectionist values. Good leisure may equally be good for one's musicality, good for health, good citizenship, etc. But the value of leisure, the goodness of it, is a distinct value from these others, even when one pursues them in one's leisure.

Also the proposed account draws out the notion, which is not entirely lost to common sense, that there is a difference between leisure and recreation, in that recreation is predominantly means-oriented—a preparation for work—whereas leisure is predominantly end-oriented; what's important to it is that it is desired for its own sake.

The account also brings out the traditional idea that there is something personally valuable in leisure, not by following Aristotle (1953) in identifying leisure with philosophy, which he thought supremely worth doing, nor by identifying it with other values such as Pieper's (1963) "spiritual ecstacy," but rather by characterizing leisure as self-directed activity, aiming at personal benefits that may take many forms.

I recommend the present account as recovering some etymological meanings and traditional associations of the word "leisure" that have been lost to the popular view of leisure or bleached out from it somewhat. But more than an act of recovery, it is a proposal for what I would suggest to be a useful platform for leisure theory and a helpful guide to leisure studies. It is beyond the scope of this essay to make out this suggestion, but I do suppose that I have offered a plausible conception of good leisure. And perhaps I have planted the idea that we should think about leisure in terms of this conception, abandoning the popular view and coming to think that leisure has a positive value of its own, not a mere negative value as freedom from obligations. The present account is at least a place to start thinking about the goodness that is characteristic of leisure as such.

References

Aristotle. (1953). *Ethics* (J. A. K. Thomson, Trans.). Middlesex: Penguin Books.
Dumazedier, J. (1967). *Toward a society of leisure.* New York: The Free Press.
Pieper, J. (1963). *Leisure: The basis of culture.* New York: Mentor Books.

Leisure and Ethics: Ramifications for the Individual and Society

Ann M. Rancourt

Phenomenologists believe that perception is peculiar to each individual. Thus, one's perception of leisure may be different from someone else's. Leisure is an interesting phenomenon to study in reference to ethics for as Parker (1979) states, "the fact that there is no consensus about what leisure is indicates that we need to recognize that we are dealing with a subject which is riddled with value-judgments and preferences" (p. 12).

The writer is in agreement with writers such as Pieper (1963) and Neulinger (1981) that leisure is indeed a state of mind, of being, and a spiritual attitude. The key to leisure is self and self as it relates to others. In leisure, people are concerned with self-realization, self-development, self-fulfillment, self-determination, self-expression, and self-enhancement. To pursue the essence of self is "to leisure." To engage in the pursuit of self—to try to experience the innermost core of one's spirit— is to leisure. To simply or complexly participate in an activity is not "leisuring" unless one is engaged in expressing and enhancing one's spirit—the very essence of who one is at any point in time. What is found to be central to one's essence, for the most part, will drive one's leisure choices. Maximizing a leisure experience or perceiving an experience to be leisure will depend on what is needed to most fully explore the self (Rancourt, 1986). It is important to note that indifference to the end, self-realization, will likely mean indifference to the means, leisure.

Self-Realization in Leisure

Self-realization has often been described as the aim of the moral life. Aristotle gave to the end or final cause of the moral life the name eudaimonia. Aristotle defined eudaimonia as the exercise of a man's soul (or realization of man's capacities) in accordance with "excellence" (or virtue), and if there is more than one excellence, in accordance with the best and most complete excellence. The question raised by this definition is which capacities of our nature are most worth developing? (Lillie, 1961, pp. 196–197)

The unfolding of self is a matter of thinking and being, and it is in leisure where this revelation occurs. Leisure is a vehicle through which one's inner life and outer life may be harmonized. It provides the opportunity to self-examine and to commit to being all that one is capable of. In leisure there is no necessity to juxtapose outward expression and inward belief. Leisure can lead to a deeper understanding of self and others and is a lifelong pursuit that takes fortitude and discipline. Any activity has the potential for self-discovery and self-enhancement, thus any activity provides the potential to leisure. Many activities are options to pursuing leisure. Recreation is a vehicle through which leisure may be experienced, as is parenting, religion, and work that is not merely toil. Leisure takes effort. As Adler (1970) indicates, "we often try to avoid it and turn to playing or idling instead when we have free time at our disposal. ... we often resort to recreational or therapeutic play in order to reduce tensions and fatigues engendered by leisure-work, just as we resort to play to get over effects of subsistence-work" (p. 73).

Leisure optimizes the good life in that "to omit leisuring would be to lead a life devoid of learning, of self-betterment or self-improvement, of growth in the stature of one's person" (Adler, 1970, p. 40). Leisure is a way to integrate insights and experience. Each person is responsible for his/her own self-discovery, and through leisure the individual may corroborate authenticity. Leisure is an opportunity to explore life's meaning and value in relation to self, an opportunity to experience not only what one does but who one is. A life without leisure results in loss of oneself; a life with leisure results in self-discovery, for leisure is a mode of interpreting and understanding.

The following normative argument provides an interesting framework for further normative and metaethical discussion. If one values society, one must value what he/she brings to it. Thus, one must value self. If one values self, then one values leisure for it is in leisure that one's self may be realized. If one comes to realize "self" and one's potential, one, then, in turn, may make a greater contribution to the greater good. One is obliged to leisure only insofar as one believes one has a responsibility to realize virtuous self. Leisure does provide the opportunity to explore and express values in relation to self and others.

Exploring One's Self (Potential) Through Leisure

Does the individual focus on what *others* perceive him or her to be capable of, or does he/she strive to realize the capabilities of self as perceived by *self*? It is each individual's potential and purpose that gives meaning to leisure. One may explore the true self in leisure. In leisure one may learn about whom one is, what one's potential is, and what one may potentially contribute to the larger social order. In leisure one may come to know oneself in relation to one's limitations and possibilities, and one may come to know, enhance, and celebrate one's uniqueness.

Many writers (Adler, 1970; Brightbill & Mobley, 1977; Godbey, 1985; Godbey & Parker, 1976; Martin in Ibrahim & Martin, 1978) have addressed the concept of uniqueness as it applies to leisure. "Most art forms produce something which cannot be translated or substituted. The mystery is partially one of uniqueness. Likewise, in our leisure activity, we must seek our own sense of uniqueness" (Godbey, 1985, p. 280). However, when one works to develop as a person, recognizing one's own uniqueness, one must be aware of becoming so self-centered as to become unavailable to others. Self-exploration requires an awareness of the balance necessary between self-interest and duty.

Leisure is an alternative for experiencing the good life. Schwartz (1982) indicates "an autonomous agent makes certain types of decisions and rational choices informed by an awareness of alternatives; choices are guided by a person's overall conception of his/her own purposes in life" (pp. 635–636). Choices imply the freedom to choose and freedom is often discussed in relation to leisure.

Freedom

Freedom, as it applies to leisure, has been discussed by many writers (Ellis & Witt, 1986; Godbey, 1985; Kelly, 1987; Parker, 1979). As Kelly (1987) indicates, leisure is the "freedom to be." Adler (1970) states that a person has "through freedom of choice, the power of self-determination, the power of creating or forming himself and his life according to his own decisions" (p. 186).

The concepts of free will and moral responsibility became significant matters of concern with the rise of Christianity. Thomas Aquinas identified free will with rational self-determination. Locke saw "will" as the power to decide on actions, and "freedom" as the power to carry out decisions (Edwards, 1967). In discussing Hume's perception of freedoms, Edwards states, "freedom is not a quality of will but a relation between desire, action and environment, such that a man is free when his actions are caused by his own desires and unimpeded by external restraints" (p. 94).

However one defines free will or freedom, it is integral to leisure. "In a society of mass communication and mass dependency, individuality and the kind of nonconformity and free thinking which breed creativeness, although difficult to sustain, must be encouraged if society is to advance" (Brightbill & Mobley, 1977, p. 72). In order to exercise one's abilities one must be free to do so. If society "attaches social sanctions to leisure it similarly interferes with individuals' freedom" (Baier, 1980, p. 90). We are obliged to leisure if we are concerned about contributing to our own and a greater good. We leisure because we believe we are ethically accountable for the care and welfare of self and others. We are responsible, and as such, the source of making moral choices and decisions. We have the freedom to be responsible and accountable. With freedom and self-initiation there is the potential for growth.

If we pursue leisure, we pursue learning and growth and we will bring to the community the fruit we bear. If we do not pursue leisure, we consume what others produce for us, but we produce little or nothing for ourselves or for the good of the community.

Community, Self, and Leisure

The community is as strong and as healthy as its individual members. A society which fosters more vigorous individuals fosters a more vigorous society. There must be balance between individuals and society for favoring one may result in both being weakened.

Persons behaving ethically balance their needs and those of the community of which they are a part. They do not sacrifice one for the other. They serve themselves and they serve their community. If it is ethical to contribute to society all that one can, is it not ethical to pursue just what it is one brings? "How much more promise is in us than we suspect? Are not most of us mere caricatures of what we ought to be" (VanKaam, VanGroonenburg, & Muto, 1968, p. 24).

People and phenomena have value as a means to self and community growth. When we bring our potential for good and others bring theirs, the end result should be a greater contribution than either could make alone. It is by participation with others that each's unique selfhood will emerge, and by being oneself, each can contribute to the selfhood of others. Leisure brings an opportunity for heightened awareness of self and others. Adler (1970), in a discussion of leisure, states:

> Human improvement, individual and social, is the end this activity aims at. Learning in all its forms is the most obvious example of it, since without learning the individual cannot improve himself and with learning he cannot help but do so. Anything that contributes to the growth of the individual as a person, as does anything the individual does that contributes to the improvement of his society, is leisure. (p. 34)

It is because of our interest in contributing to our growth that we choose to leisure, and as we share who we are, we may grow in whom we are. However, if we do not have the energy or caring to attend to ourselves, how will it be that we will have that energy or caring to attend to others?

Reciprocity involves the interaction of giving and receiving. If we are continually receiving more than we are giving, we need to question our intentions and our role as a contributor to the greater good.

> When an individual seeks only those things that are really good for him, he does not infringe on or interfere with the pursuit of happiness on the part of others through their seeking the same real goods for themselves. This insight is confirmed by the consideration of the real goods achieved by leisure-work. Nothing that an individual does when engaged in leisure can injure another man; on the contrary, through his engagement in leisure, the individual not only benefits himself but usually benefits others. (Adler, 1970, p. 174)

The decisions one makes and the paths one follows affect not only the individual but society. If one's choices are based only on what others think is good for one's self, the roles one plays may be less than good for all. Leisure is an opportunity for the individual to discover and rediscover the core of one's being in relation to society. "Despite our phenomenal advances in making life attractive, we are still discontented, ill at ease, and anxious. Few can say with conviction that they have found their place in relation to the universe" (Brightbill & Mobley, 1977, p. 35). A place to begin might be with an assessment of what is valued, followed by a commitment, as best can be done, to live what has been discovered.

Value and Leisure

"Our culture has been brought to a need to redefine its values and, thus, the stage has been set for a return to the concept of leisure as a state of being intimately related to our source of meaning and understanding of experience and life itself" (Martin in Ibrahim & Martin, 1978, p. 19). How do we come to know if the values of a society match our own? We come to know our own values, and we may come to know them through leisure. "If man is to have confidence in values, he must know himself and the capacity of his nature for goodness and productiveness" (Fromm, 1947, p. 7). Leisure is a milieu in which people find themselves and express their worth. That finding and expression is carried into the community. Productivity must cease to be equated only with commodity. It is just as ethical to produce and express self-potential as it is to produce a consumable product. "In a society oriented toward production, the usefulness of persons and things may prevail over a consideration of human values. How can we overcome the tendency to reduce our possibilities for life and leisure to commodity and utility" (VanKaam, VanGroonenburg, & Muto, 1968, vol. 3, p. 61)?

Leisure cannot be viewed as seemingly useless when its potential to contribute to the good of the individual and the good of society is so great. Adler (1970) states "that among the basic activities, there is an order or scale of values, with leisure-work of paramount worth" (p. 68). In a capitalistic society, value is often equated with productivity as it relates to a person's usefulness relative to a given task. It should be kept in mind, though, that "when we praise a person for being functional and practical and disparage his propensity for the nontechnical, for art, poetry, dance and music, we may force him to outbreaks of boredom and frustration, dissatisfaction and despair" (VanKaam, VanGroonenburg, & Muto, 1968, vol. 3, pp. 63–64).

An ethical life is not the result of only thinking about values, it is a result of living them. To live *only* what others value is to bastardize oneself; to live *only* what one values is to bastardize others—balance is necessary. "If we are to make any headway in forming leisure values, we shall have to rid ourselves of the idea that excellence is worthwhile in one socially acceptable endeavor and not in another" (Brightbill & Mobley, 1977, p. 77).

References

Adler, M. J. (1970). *The time of our lives: The ethics of common sense.* New York: Holt, Rinehart & Winston.

Baier, K. (1980). Freedom, obligation and responsibility. In M. B. Storer (Ed.), *Human ethics: Dialogue on basics.* Buffalo, NY: Prometheus Books.

Brightbill, C. K., & Mobley, T. A. (1977). *Educating for leisure-centered living* (2nd ed.). New York: Wiley & Sons.

Edwards, P. (Ed.). (1967). *The encyclopedia of philosophy* (vols. 3, 7, 8). New York: Macmillan Publishing Co.

Ellis, G. D., & Witt, P. A. (1986). The leisure diagnostic battery: Past, present and future. *Therapeutic Recreation Journal, 27*(4), 27–35.

Fromm, E. (1947). *Man for himself: An inquiry into a psychology of ethics.* New York: Holt, Rinehart, & Winston.

Godbey, G. (1985). *Leisure in your life: An exploration.* State College, PA: Venture Publishing.

Godbey, G., & Parker, S. (1976). *Leisure studies and services: An overview.* New York: W. B. Saunders.

Ibrahim, H., & Martin, F. (Eds.) (1978). *Leisure: An introduction.* Los Alamistos, CA: Hwong Publishing.

Kelly, J. R. (1987). *Freedom to be: A new sociology of leisure.* New York: Macmillan Publishing Co.

Lillie, W. (1961). *An introduction to ethics.* New York: University Paperbacks.

Neulinger, J. (1981). *To leisure: An introduction.* Boston: Allyn & Bacon.

Parker, S. (1979). *The sociology of leisure* (3rd ed.). London: George Allen & Unwin.

Pieper, J. (1963). *Leisure: The basis of culture.* New York: Random House.

Rancourt, A. M. (1986). What is the role of leisure in the undergraduate recreation and leisure curriculum? *SPRE Annual,* June, pp. 65–75.

VanKaam, A., VanGroonenburg, B., & Muto, S. A. (1968). *The emergent self* (vols. 1–4). Wilkes Barre, PA: Dimension Books.

Homo Ludens: A Study of the Play Element in Culture

Michael Ruckenstein

Play reinforces, promotes, and perpetuates values and rules inherent in our societies. According to McLuhan, we are becoming a global village reducing dissimilarities among societies. This discrepancy reduction is a consequence of adoption of common play forms such as the Olympic Games, the Pan American Games, and the Commonwealth Games. These are examples of a global society at play sharing values and rules.

Play in this context serves to maintain and sustain civilization.

According to Lee (1964): "Man only plays when in the full meaning of the word he is a man, and he is perfectly human only when he plays" (p. 71).

What is play? Webster's *New World Dictionary* uses the word "play" twenty-nine different ways as a verb and numerous ways as a noun.

The earliest theories of play ranged from the surplus energy theory to the preparation for life, to recapitulation, to instinct, to relaxation, to recreation, to catharsis, and to self-expression. This nucleus of thinking constituted a number of modern explanations of play by various psychologists and educators such as John Dewey, Elmer Mitchell, Bernard Mason, Abraham Maslow, George Herbert Mead, Maria Montessori, Jean Piaget, Erich Erikson, Roger Caillais, and Johan Huizinga.

Kando (1975) states: "Before social scientists could theorize about play, it had to be discovered." He continues that this only occurred two to three hundred years ago in the West and that our contemporary society "has yet to accord to the concept the recognition it grants to, say work, or religion, or law ... " (p. 31).

Huizinga (1950) in *Homo Ludens—A Study of the Play Element in Culture*, opens his treatise with the words: "Play is older than culture, for culture, however inadequately defined, always presupposes human society, and animals have not waited for man to teach them their playing" (p. 1). In commenting that *Homo Ludens* is a classic in the field of leisure, Kaplan (1975) states that: "A theory of leisure is essentially a theory of history" (p. 39).

We have been known as man, the thinker—"Homo Sapiens" and man the maker—"Homo Faber." To Huizinga, we are man the player— "Homo Ludens."

"Civilization arises and unfolds in and as play" (Huizinga, 1950, p. 4). The inference is that in the absence of the play-spirit, civilization is impossible, for then civilization presupposes limitation and mastery of the self. Huizinga further states: "In play there is something 'at play' which transcends the immediate needs of life and imparts meaning to the action. All play means something" (p. 1).

The quality of play is not materialistic but involved with tension, mirth, and fun. Play does not have any rational nexus as its foundation because this would limit it to mankind; thus play "is a thing on its own."

By acknowledging play, one acknowledges the "mind" because play only becomes possible, thinkable, and understandable when man pretends and acknowledges the pretense. Play is a stepping out of "real" life into a temporary sphere of activity with a disposition of its own. It is an interlude in our daily lives which becomes a life function in that it contains meaning, significance, value, and spiritual and social associations. Huizinga noted that "We play and know that we play, so we must be more than rational beings, for play is irrational."

Can play be described as serious? At first one would say "no." Play to the author is used in its broadest sense as the antithesis of serious activity. This is noted by the introduction of words such as laughter, the comic, and folly. On close inspection, one notes that laughter abounds with play; the comic provokes laughter and folly associates with the comic, but the words can scarcely be termed genuine play. However, once stated, one realizes that play indeed can be very serious. Children's games, baseball, or chess are played in profound seriousness.

Is play aesthetic? Certainly one can say that the human body in motion reaches its zenith in play, but again, this is only a connection with play, for beauty is not inherent in play. Thus, the more we try to mark off the form we call "play" from other forms related to it, the more the absolute independence of the play concept stands out.

By investigating the word "play" in a number of languages (Chinese, Sanskrit, Dutch, German), the author notes the elusiveness of the concept for play and that some languages have succeeded better than others in getting various aspects of play in one word. Even the Greeks used different words for contests and for childish play.

Lee (1964) states that:

> The simple word becomes complex when one tries to analyze its varied and numerous meanings. It may be used as a noun or a verb: We can witness a play, but we can also play an instrument, play a game, play fair with the other fellow, play havoc with the state of things, or even play a prank on our neighbor. Perhaps no other word in the English language can be given so many meanings. To one person play may mean the romping and shouting of children in the park; to another, it may mean an afternoon at the races; to a third, it may mean experimentation with a homemade radio set; and to still another person, play is the very highest form of intellectual endeavor as found in literature, science, and art. Perhaps in its own playful way, play eludes precise definition! (pp. 71–72)

Besides the numerous interpretations of the word "play," speech and language are used as a bridge between matter and mind as if it were "playing."

Play is something more than a definition that includes logic, biology, or aesthetics. All play is voluntary and has the quality of freedom. Child, adult, and animal play because they enjoy playing. It is enjoyment, "never a task."

Fackre (1972) discusses Huizinga's concept of play from a philosophical theological view and noted that:

> Play is also food for the starving soul and society, according to Huizinga. It is an ingredient in cultures that keeps them sane. Why? Men need a certain point in their lives which is not controlled by pragmatics, where they do not ask how this contributes to the business of securing food, clothing, and shelter. In these preserves we cultivate a certain nonchalance toward the rat race. Our focus is on doing something nonproductive for its own sake. Both Huizinga and Pieper note the striking similarity and historic connection between play and worship. Both teach us to treat relative things relatively. Both are instruments of a shalom which knits up the raveled sleeves of care which sleep and relaxation cannot touch. (p. 78)

Play is not only "ordinary" or real life. It is a stepping out of "real" life into a temporary sphere of activity with a disposition of its own. Children know that they are "only pretending" or that it is "only for fun." Nonetheless, play is pursued with the utmost seriousness. Try interrupting a child playing house or a sandlotter imitating a Magic Johnson or an Oral Hershiser. According to Huizinga: "Play turns to seriousness and seriousness to play" (p. 8).

Although we tend to be disinterested in play, it is an interlude in our daily lives which becomes a life function in that it contains meaning, significance, value, and spiritual and social associations. For Huizinga, play was a type of activity that met basic needs and should be considered an indispensable element in all civilizations (Roberts, 1970, p. 90).

A third characteristic of play is its secludedness; it is limitless, that is, it contains its own course and meaning. Play begins and then it's "over." It plays itself to an end, but endures as a new-found creation of the mind that is retained. Thus, there is a limitation of time as well as space be it in a material space or ideally.

Another feature of play is that it "creates order, in order," the least deviation from it "spoils the game," robs it of its character. It is this order that also makes play lie in the field of aesthetics, terms we describe to beauty, tension, poise, balance, contrast, variation, solution, that is, a rhythm and harmony.

In play, tension makes for uncertainty. It is this element and the solution that governs all games of skill, be it a crossword puzzle, target shooting, or a team competition that tests the player's prowess: courage, tenacity, resources, and spiritual powers—"fairness," because all play has its rules and despite one's desire to win, one must still stick by the rules of the game.

Frequently a play-community retains its magic beyond the duration of the game in the feeling of being "apart together," of sharing something important from the rest of the world. There is an air of secrecy in that this is for us, not for others.

Godbey and Parker (1976) summarized Huizinga's characteristics of play as follows:

> It is voluntary and free; as an interlude in our daily lives, it is marked by disinterestedness; it becomes traditional and can be repeated; it creates order, rules becoming important for the existence of the playing community; and such a community tends to become permanently established as an "in-group" after the game is over. (p. 5)

Children use their "imagination" to play princes, mothers, a wicked witch, or a tiger—the child is literally beside itself in delight without losing consciousness of reality. In the same manner, archaic culture represents a "play" element.

Rules and contests interested Huizinga in that there was a link between craving for dominance and the role of contests. Huizinga states that:

> The urge to be first has as many forms of expression as society offers opportunities for it. The ways in which men compete for superiority are as various as the prizes at stake. Decision may be left to chance, physical strength, dexterity, or bloody combat. Or there may be competitions in courage and endurance, skillfulness, knowledge, boasting and cunning.... The competition may take the form of an oracle, a wager, a lawsuit, a vow or a riddle. But in whatever shape it comes it is always play, and it is from this point of view that we have to interpret its cultural function. (p. 105)

Contests dominated Greek culture. The Hellenic games and the festivals which were closely allied with religion had a variety of contests; beauty contests as well as contests in singing, riddle-solving, keeping awake, and drinking were held.

The practice of law resembles a contest. Juristic eloquence in the Athens of Pericles and Phidas was mainly a contest in rhetoric dexterity.

The idea of play was evident in philosophy and the Sophists, whose business was to exhibit their knowledge and at the same time defeat their rivals in a public contest.

Even in war, Huizinga illustrates the agonistic element where two Greek cities fought their war as a contest. Rules were laid down beforehand as well as the time and place. All missiles were forbidden— only the sword and lance were allowed.

Huizinga further states that:

> There was no transition from battle to play in Greece, nor from play to battle, but a development *of* culture *in* play-like contest. . . . all rooted in ritual and productive of culture by allowing the innate human need of rhythm, harmony, change, alternation and climax, etc., to unfold in full richness. Coupled with this play-sense is a spirit that strives for honor, dignity, superiority and beauty. (p. 75)

Competition for honor may take place as in China where one demolishes one's adversary by superior manners—an inverted boasting-match since the reason for this display of civility to others lies in an intense regard for one's own honor.

In British Columbia, an Indian tribe practices a curious custom known as "potlatch." Pomp and ceremony take place and gifts are lavishly given for the sole purpose of showing the tribe's superiority. The only obligation lies in the "other" tribe to reciprocate and if possible surpass it within a certain period of time. This donative festival can take place for a birth, a marriage, a death, a tattooing, etc., and dominates the entire communal life of the tribes—their ritual, their law, their art. The action always takes place in the form of a contest.

Thus, it can be seen by the examples illustrated that it is through competition that the higher forms of social play take place. It is the connection between culture and play.

What is of equal importance and should not be lost in these examples and throughout *Homo Ludens* is that one must define beforehand what constitutes winning or what is to be tested.

Kraus (1966) asks the question:

> What is the nature of this appeal? Huizinga, the noted Dutch historian of culture, suggests that mankind's urge to play is fundamental and that, in effect, many of life's most serious rituals and activities represent disguised or sublimated forms of play. Thus,

warfare was for centuries carried out as a sort of deadly game, with
elaborate rules, strategies, and codes of sportsmanship. Huizinga
writes of the practice of law, of art, of philosophy, of poetry, all as
forms of play. In games as such, the essence of the matter is to put
oneself against an opponent or opponents in a mock-serious situation. To try to outguess him, to perplex him, to physically master
him, to defeat him through strategic improvisation—this is the task!
Or, in some games, the object is to cooperate so cleverly that the
coparticipant is enabled to achieve a desired goal, because not all
games are highly competitive. (pp. 71–72)

It is through the fancies of war as a noble game of honor and virtue
that an important part in developing civilization has been played for it
is from them that the ideas of chivalry sprang, and hence became an
important part of international law.

According to Huizinga:

> Its principle of reciprocal rights, its diplomatic forms, its mutual
> obligations in the matter of honoring treaties and, in the event of
> war, officially abrogating peace, all bear a formal resemblance to
> play-rules inasmuch as they are only binding while the game itself—
> i.e., the need for order in human affairs—is recognized. We might,
> in a purely formal sense, call all society a game, if we bear in mind
> that this game is the living principle of all civilization. (pp. 100–
> 101)

In the absence of the play-spirit, civilization is impossible.

Dumazedier (1967), in making reference to *Homo Ludens*, states that
we have inherited a watered-down tradition of play and that "in our
cultural development, competitive games for example, play nowhere
near the part they had in Pindar's time" (p. 21).

Fackre (1975) comments that:

> We take ourselves too seriously in all our talk here about play.
> Huizinga shows conclusively that play is the place where a culture
> says, "Really, now, aren't you wound up a little too tight about the
> whole thing?" He indicates how play and worship meet at this point,
> feeding the spirit with a certain nonchalance about what goes on
> in the rush of daily affairs, each teaching us to keep secondary
> things secondary. (pp. 85–86)

Greenberg (1958) contends that:

> The hobby is play, and play, according to Huizinga, is the mother
> of culture. But play as such, under industrialism, is no longer *serious*
> enough to open the way to the heart of things—is rather a detour
> or escape. Authentic culture must, by definition, not be that. It has,
> instead, to lie at the center, and from there irradiates the whole of
> life, the serious as well as the not serious. It is serious work that
> has become, as I have said, the center of all our lives. If serious

work—not leisure—can be infused with something of the spirit of the hobby, with something of its unseriousness, well and good; but not the other way round—not as long as leisure remains peripheral, as it must, and the hobby finds its only existence there. (p. 41)

Huizinga's *Homo Ludens* has exposed us to the fatal weakness of some of the changes and dynamism that has taken hold of our world in the wake of the triumphs of science and in terms of the break with certain conventions. It is the fact that conventions and a self-discipline belong to culture and to art as much as rules belong to games.

References

Dumazedier, J. (1967). *Toward a society of leisure*. New York: Free Press.

Fackre, G. (1972). The new leisure: Planner and citizen in partnership. In E. J. Stanley & N. P. Miller (Eds.), *Leisure and the quality of life*. Washington, DC: AAHPER.

Godbey, G., & Parker, S. (1976). *Leisure studies and services: An overview*. London: W. B. Saunders Co.

Greenberg, C. (1958). Work and leisure under industrialism. In Larrabee, Eric, and Meyersohn, *Mass leisure*. Glencoe, IL: Free Press.

Huizinga, J. (1950). *Homo ludens*. Boston: Beacon Press.

Kando, T. M. (1975). *Leisure and popular culture in transition*. St. Louis: C. V. Mosby Co.

Kaplan, M. (1975). *Leisure: Theory and policy*. New York: John Wiley and Sons.

Kraus, R. (1966). *Recreation today*. Englewood Cliffs, NJ: Prentice-Hall.

Lee, R. (1964). *Religion and leisure in America*. New York: Abingdon Press.

Roberts, K. (1970). *Leisure*. London: Longham Group Ltd.

Ethics in Management

Larry R. Williams

A high level of ethical controversy indicates our society is undergoing radical change. The last peak of ethical controversy was prior to the industrial revolution when society renegotiated its understandings of work, family, play, church, and government. The function of ethics in our society is to provide a context for considering basic changes, re-looking at operating principles, and restoring order.

Far greater attention and concern must be given to professional ethics, its instruction, and mechanisms for the development, dissemination, and interpretation of ethical behavior and codes for recreation, parks, and leisure services to advance as a profession. All professions have weaknesses in ethical practice.

Professionalism is one of the most valuable elements in our social and organizational structure. In a world where the twentieth century reliance upon the self-determining code of the autonomous individual has broken down, the group becomes increasingly important. Group leadership demands the meeting of professional obligations, responsibility in human relations, and excellence in performance. These elements have a conviction and persuasiveness which neither personal bewilderment nor impersonal outside power can match. But it would be folly not to recognize that the essence of professionalism/ethical behavior—emphasis upon the activity rather than rewards, upon the performance of a service rather than a profit—goes against the grain of the mentality of Western civilization.

It is the responsibility of management to create an atmosphere of integrity, excellence, performance, and achievement reflecting ethical standards of behavior starting at the top and proceeding through all levels. Mere enunciation of a code of conduct (ethics) is not sufficient. Exemplary action is required, as well as an understanding of the conflicts and loyalties and the gray areas of ethical decisions which individual managers face.

Ethical and value commitments of an organization are stronger if they are part of the whole culture of the agency. An organization's value system is strong because it is a part of every performance evaluation system, training program, employee relations policy, and virtually every person-to-person interaction within and outside of the organization. An ethics of open and candid communication can assist in creating a strong value system.

Decision makers are philosophers. All ethical considerations revolve around how we ought to "be" and "act" as humans. And once managers take action, they are deeply involved in ethics all the time, whether they are conscious of it or not. Many professionals tend to think of ethics as a dry subject belonging to professional philosophers who spend their hours splitting verbal hairs. But ethics permeates all human life and activity. Ethical thoughts and resulting behavior are as automatic and involuntary as the beating of a heart, although not as regulated. We can change and grow ethically.

Three of the more important factors in personal and organizational ethics are integrity, purpose, and responsibility. These factors are not easily studied by standard research tools but, in my opinion, are critical to the development of ethical management decision making.

Integrity, which is one of the hallmarks of an ethical person, organization, or business, implies a wholeness or completeness. Integrity is defined as an uncompromising adherence to a code of moral values and involves utter sincerity, honesty, and candor—the avoidance of deception, expediency, or artificiality.

To have genuine integrity involves a flawless integration of all parts of ourselves, a completeness. Of course, this does not imply perfection. Managers must reawaken their feelings regarding ethical decision making. Ethical managers are not afraid to listen to their intuitions and hunches or to ask themselves "does this decision feel right."

A purpose is a way of being or functioning viewed as valuable in itself. A purpose gives an organization a sense of who it is, where its goals come from, and why trying hard matters. Purposes provide continuity for an organization through its inevitable changes in goals, people, operations, structure, and success.

Purpose acts as a foundation—an assurance that decisions and actions have meaning. Once personnel accept the purpose of an organization and its programs as worthwhile, they will assume individual responsibility and work purposefully toward common goals. Management must clearly articulate and reinforce the overall purpose of an organization.

For any purpose to be effective, individuals must accept responsibility for it. Responsibility makes the organization work. Genuine responsibility contains three elements: (a) the ability to act independently of a reward system, (b) the ability to be effective (to do things), and (c) a basis on individual intention (you intended something to happen). People take responsibility for what they intend and create, individually or as organizational members. Genuine responsibility begins where mere response to reward systems ends.

To improve our system, we must first improve ourselves; second, improve our professional ethical code; and third, stress the importance of ethics to those we serve. The essence of ethics is action.

The Language Games in TV Games: Commentary and the Manipulation of Meaning in Televised Sports

David B. Sullivan

T elevision looms large in the American leisure experience. While media consumption in general occupies 30 percent of adult leisure time, people spend more time watching television than doing anything else between sleeping and working; in the average American household, a television set is turned on for over seven hours each day, and the average daily viewing time for individual members is about three hours (Morgan & Signorielli, 1989).

Given such consumption patterns, television's influence has been given wide attention in the popular press, and has been the object of much academic and government-sponsored study (Pearl, Bouthilet, & Lazar, 1982). The bulk of television effects research has focused on a handful of programming genres, especially news, advertising, primetime entertainment programs, and children's programs. The paucity of effects research on televised sports is curious given the pervasiveness of sports programming.

Sports traditionally has dominated network weekend afternoon programming and, since the inception of ABC's Monday Night Football in the early 1970s, has been a regular feature of weeknight primetime schedules. The rise of professional and college team "networks" of independent local stations has brought a wide array of nightly regular-season and playoff games to most of the top markets. Cable television offers, both in basic service and on premium channels, a wide array of sports programming at all hours.

The popularity of televised athletics provides further testimony of the importance of sports to society. According to a Simmons Market Research Bureau study (Schlosberg, 1987), the audiences for team sports are huge: 63.2 million adults, representing 37 percent of the adult population, watch pro football frequently; 62.7 million watch pro baseball regularly; 49 million watch college football regularly; and between 35 and 37 million adults are frequent viewers of boxing, college basketball, and professional basketball. Given such demand, the broadcast networks increased the total hours of sports programming 63 percent in a 10-year period beginning in 1973 (Schlosberg, 1987).

Sports programming is not merely one alternative among many for viewers; sports frequently is synonymous with television leisure activity. Given sports television's privileged position in Americans' "quality time," the larger question that social science research should pose is, what contributions does sports television make to social attitudes, beliefs, and behavior? This discussion examines the potential consequences of sports commentary on audience perception, moral reasoning, and meaning construction.

Televised Sports and Socialization

In American society, as in most societies, sports are considered important to the socialization of individuals (Dunning, 1971; Edwards, 1973; Eitzen, 1984; Furst, 1971; Goldstein, 1979; Goldstein & Bredemeier, 1977). At a broad level, sports activities may be symbolic representations of social functions that influence individual behavior and consciousness (Goodger, 1985). Real (1975) showed how audience needs are satisfied by sport within a ritualized context, the mythic spectacle. Jhally (1984) characterized the sports spectacle as "the ritualized mass activity of modern industrialized societies" serving to celebrate idealized structures and providing socialization into these structures (p. 51).

Television plays a crucial mediating role in the transmission of the value-laden messages of sports to society. The electronic arena conveys an entirely different reality about the sports even than is experienced by the spectator first-hand. The television messages that define the sports environment have been characterized as dramatizing a cultural sense of order (Novak, 1976). Exposure to sports television, particularly contact team sports such as football and hockey, operates as a socializer of conservative political values (Prisuta, 1979), and sports coverage acts as "mass propaganda" sustaining and reinforcing male domination and authoritarian structure (Real, 1975).

Although sports programming is not overtly political, it may transmit conservative values as an implicit agent of socialization via incidental learning. Seen from this perspective, authoritarian individuals, for example, may endorse centralized power as a means of maintaining a sense of place, and sports television viewing may provide both a cause for and reinforcement of that endorsement. Taken as a whole, sports television programming disseminates a coherent set of messages that, following a hypothesis in cultivation analysis (Gerbner, Morgan, & Signorielli, 1986), defines dominant, mainstream assumptions about society.

TV Sports Text: Camera and Commentary

Researchers have, with few exceptions, treated camera visuals and commentary narrative as independent message sources. The camera, for example, reveals either too much or too little in large-field sports such as football, focusing on individuals while butchering the wide geometry of the game (Oriard, 1981). The use of overhead, wide-angle shots in the manner of the "game" film lends only a modicum of realism; although these camera shots take in most or all of the field, they are used to diagram the "backstage" of sports performances (Morse, 1983). Players are objectified into "Xs" and "Os" that are superimposed on the videotape to chart offensive and defensive alignments.

Morse finds little that is "real" about the visual images of televised sports. In compressing space with the zoom lens, stretching time via slow motion, and continually displacing the viewer's perspective, television coverage obliterates the viewer's appraisal of linear time, gravity, and spatial dimensions in relation to the live sports event.

One may pursue the relationship between the visual television text and the live sports site further. The game and its live site have been transformed to mimic the television environment. Those who produce and deliver television content sometimes say that what they do is hold a mirror to society; in the case of sports, the events come to mirror television. Sports audiences, it would appear, have grown so accustomed to the mediated event that they are uneasy with the raw, live event. The reproduction is deemed more trustworthy and more real than the original.

Current theories of the functions and effects of commentary examine the link between viewer enjoyment and commentary portrayals of affective player relationships and player aggression. Enjoyment of contact sports contests is facilitated by roughness, enthusiasm, and violence of play, and commentary can alter viewer perceptions of rough play (Comisky, Bryant, & Zillmann, 1977).

Similar relationships appear to hold for coverage of some noncontact sports, in which viewers consider intimidation to be a component of competitiveness and feel that commentators encourage them to enjoy player aggression (Sullivan, 1988). Further, commentators' hesitancy to explicitly condemn player aggression extends tacit approval to violent acts committed for the sake of winning.

To summarize, both the camera and commentary transform the signifying material of the live event from sport to spectacle. The camera, in its totality, lends plot to what is an unpredictable, unscripted story by enhancing the imaginary (Morse, 1983). Commentary contributes to the transformation by creating story lines to fit within the plot provided by the visual representation of the live event. The visual and aural texts are designed to produce a narrative that attracts and maintains viewership.

Sports Spectacle, Myth, and Ideology

The moral implications of the camera-commentary text depend on how audiences receive the text. The televised player is, from the viewer's perspective, in an ambiguous position. In spectator sports, players fluctuate between dramatic and sports roles, engaging in play one moment and in display the next (Stone, 1955). The televised representation of the contest merges player with character (Fiske, 1987) and blurs the distinction between what is play and display, and what is real and fictional.

Viewers, however, are likely to know the difference between the showboating player and the "quintessential professional," and might enjoy the performances of both types of players while distancing themselves critically from the former's behavior and from television's interpretation of it. This would appear to pose a problem for determining what meanings are accepted by viewers, for even if sports television conveys a coherent set of cultural messages, this message system still does not in itself constitute evidence that sports television cultivates in viewers specific attitudes and assumptions about society. What is needed is a theoretical link between the unidirectional meanings provided by the televised text and how the cultivation of those meanings skirts viewers' critical assessment and shapes moral reasoning.

Barthes (1957) provided such a bridge in mapping the transformation of symbolic meaning to myth. Whereas, in Saussurean semiology, the relation between concept (the signified) and mental image (the signifier) is constituted by primary language (the sign), mythology takes the sign as its starting point. Barthes' mythic signifier is a duplicitous form that contains the sign's meaning yet is receptive to a new concept that distorts the reality of the original sign. As a second-order semiology, myth is metalanguage superimposed over a given text; that is, myth operates beyond the literal sign, but must depart from it. As Barthes described it, metalanguage is to primary language what the gesture is to the act.

So whereas sports can be divided into narrative form and the game as concept, the sports spectacle is, following Barthes, the relation between form and concept; that is, the meaning of sports as spectacle is mythic. Since, for the audience, myth is constituted by the inextricable whole made of meaning and form (Barthes, 1957), the symbolic may be spun into social usage that is ideological in function. The mythic meaning slips easily into acceptance, for the symbolic appears to summon up the concept naturally, "as if the signifier *gave a foundation* to the signified" (p. 130, emphasis original). Mythic meaning is not easily thwarted, for it is preemptive of critical assessment: "[It] does not matter if one is later allowed to see through the myth, its action is assumed to be stronger than the rational explanations which may later belie it" (p. 130).

The connection between televised sports as spectacle and the cultivation of moral attitudes and assumptions about society is clearer when it is recognized that myth smuggles ideology into the reception of the television sports text. As Jhally (1984) noted, for example, sports mediates a social dialectic between work and leisure in capitalist societies. Sports provide both an escape from the rigorous demands of the workday, or work week, and socialization into the cultural structures supporting capitalist conditions (p. 51). Sports reconciles these contradictory functions by presenting them as one dialectic—sports as a dramatic life-world (Lipsky, 1979).

In Barthes' terms, sports is a duplicitous dramatic form that allows for such a juxtaposition in functions. Sports drama, however, is itself mediated by television. The television text can be divided into the narrative itself and the game as concept defined by the narrative (Morse, 1983). The perceptual distortion occasioned by television's narrative techniques corresponds with the ideological distortion of the sports drama.

The enmeshment of textual and cultivation perspectives allows us, citing questions raised by Jhally, to determine what values viewers internalize from televised sports and how this movement is structured. An analysis of the dramatic function of commentary indicates how commentary cultivates specific attitudes and accomplishes its ideological work. Television as a medium flattens the experience of the sports contest; commentary reinvigorates the experience by conveying information about the players and the game that the camera cannot convey. In this role, commentators tell the story of the game using a set of descriptive narrative modes: objective, interpretive, and historical (Morris & Nydahl, 1983).

In fulfilling its objective role, commentary complements the camera by summarizing what has occurred in the game. In the interpretive mode, commentary assigns motivations to player and team performance and player behavior. Commentary which places players, teams, and games in a historical perspective typically relies on biographical material and on statistical comparisons to previous games, previous years, to lists of all-time leaders, etc.

Descriptive, interpretive, and historical forms blend when sports commentators engage the dramatic mode, which is used to emphasize events that may amuse viewers and to enhance the suspense inherent in sports contests by focusing on player and team conflict. Following Goffman's (1959) dramatistic metaphor for the construction of social reality, commentators define game situations and the range of appropriate viewer responses to performance and behavior.

In the case of contact sports, at points where commentary's goals are intertwined, references to acts of display and conflict (that is, player aggression) are often one and the same. For the viewer of contact sports, commentary helps maintain a sense of place; the viewer can easily correlate displays of courage and daring with intimidation and aggression (Coakley, 1984). Commentary's treatment of display and conflict in the case of some noncontact sports, especially basketball, may displace viewer assessment of play; for, following theory from Meyrowitz (1985), the television settings for some noncontact sports have merged with the television settings of contact sports with extended television coverage.

Objective, Narrative, and Interpretive Modes

At least three compelling dimensions underlie the contribution made by the objective narrative mode to the blurring of television sports settings and corresponding transformations in meaning. First, the objective mode is best represented by "jock talk," which translates sports experience into lockerroom elocutions and circumscribes the sports experience within a set of values that support traditionally masculine characteristics of male domination and authoritarianism. Second, much descriptive language used by commentators in some noncontact sports is borrowed from the contact sports lexicon. Third, commentators tend to borrow terms from contact sports jargon to define player roles in noncontact sports.

Such is the case with the emergence in basketball of the expendable, heavily-muscled reserve player whose game mission usually is to "lay a body" on a high-scoring opponent. Commentators find an analogous role in ice hockey and have appropriated from hockey the descriptive term "enforcer." By using this term, commentators direct the viewer to connect the role with a function: intimidation. As even the casual sports fan is likely to know that the chief motive of the hockey "enforcer" is to intimidate opponents even to the point of beating them up (Swift, 1986), it is likely that the basketball viewer will infer that the primary goal of a player commentators call an "enforcer" is to intimidate opponents.

Among the most visible symptoms of changing player norms in some noncontact sports is the increasing occurrence of overt player aggression, ranging from the flagrant foul in basketball to the bench-clearing brawl in baseball. In dealing with such incidents, commentators avail themselves of the interpretive mode. Commentators have long justified such player behavior in contact sports as occurring in the "heat of battle." In an interpretive mode, commentators of both contact and noncontact sports punctuate for the viewer incidents of aggression, ascribing antecedents to player actions that escape the camera's eye. Lacking information that would confirm or deny the commentators' rationales, viewers may perceive the player as justified in "striking back."

Historical Mode

The historical mode is essentially the realm of the color commentator. While his or her colleague calls the shots, as it were, the color commentator is expected to provide insightful analysis that *goes beyond the action at hand*. The demonstration of conflict between individuals or groups is crucial to the dramatic story structure. Where that conflict exists, as is the case with player aggression, the dramatic story structure calls for the narrators to punctuate the action with some sense of closure; that is, given their job to dramatize sports events, commentators feel compelled to suggest a resolution to the conflict. Seeking closure, commentators frequently align speculative remarks about player motivation with references to a player's past behavior or rumors about a player's temperament. Through references to past behavior, the commentator judges whether a player's aggression is unusual or typical.

Patterned commentary narrative can transport the televised game to a more abstract level of mythic signification. Fusing the historical-interpretive treatment of specific incidents of player aggression with the dramatic story structure's requirement for characterizations yields the probability that commentators identify for the viewer heroes and villains at those points in the story when conflict becomes most intense. The noncontact sports hero, like the contact sports warrior, "can take a hit as well as give one," the commentators assure us. The hero "isn't afraid to fight anyone," or "won't back down from anyone," and, by virtue of his aggression, "sends a message" to his opponents. Conversely, the villain is a "cheap-shot artist," a "goon," or a "thug."

Operating far more subtly but relating to the dramatic context of television sports stories are commentators' references to player or team rivalry. In college basketball, historical-interpretive commentary treatment can make entire league seasons appear to operate on the revenge motif; such was the case with the 1985 Big East Tournament when fights between players during the regular season prompted the Entertainment and Sports Programming Network (ESPN) to dub the St. John's vs. Georgetown final as "Armegeddon III." Play gave way to conflict during the season and the conflict, in the commentator's own terms, grew to mythic proportions by season's end.

Descriptive and Elaborative Modes

The descriptive and elaborative modes interact to define the intense nature of contests and define for the viewer the rules which govern play. Like their counterparts in contact sports, commentators in non-contact sports blend interpretive and historical forms into sweeping generalizations to explain how games get rough and how player behavior is controlled. In NBC coverage of a March 4, 1989 men's college basketball game between Arizona and UCLA, which featured aggressive play but not aggression, commentator Buckey Waters hinted nonetheless that player aggression was imminent. When a loose ball play resulted in a jump ball situation, Waters remarked, "Officials tend to uptempo the call on such plays for fear that it may result in a fracas." Moments later, Waters added, "In an emotional environment officials are liable to be quick with the whistle (cautious) on loose balls, especially since one guy has already been put on his back." The colloquialism is especially value-filled in this context. The player didn't trip and fall accidentally; Waters implies, with no visual evidence, that the player had been shoved to the floor intentionally, in clear violation of the rules, and he implies the officials were aware of this aggressive act and will enforce player rules the remainder of the game.

Mixed Messages

Viewers may infer from the preceding examples a metamessage that aggressive behavior is good. The "overly-aggressive" player may overreact to a pressure situation, but the commentators imply that less overt aggression would be acceptable. Indeed, aggressive behavior in basketball—including actions which marginally violate game rules such as elbowing—is expected behavior.

The blending of descriptive modes regarding rough play may send contradictory messages about the game and about the sport being played. On the one hand, commentators enhance conflict between players and teams to enhance the program's ratings—this sends a message that player aggression is part of the game. On the other hand, commentators seek to assure viewers that game officials will ensure that player behavior remains within the scope of game rules.

An almost certain consequence of these mixed messages is that viewers of noncontact sports are not at all sure what player behavior is deemed acceptable. In basketball, for example, commentary's mixed signals about player behavior reflect the probable conclusion that basketball is perceived ambiguously between its traditional acceptance as a noncontact sport and contemporary reality which indicates "hoop" is as physically rugged as any contact sport.

In complementing the plot of sports stories reconstructed for the viewer by the camera, dramatic commentary simplifies what is complex in sports and lends excitement to what might be dull. But what does commentary *tell* the viewer? The story commentary reflects mainstream American myths: American society consists of winners and losers; domination and aggressiveness should be valued above equality and fair play; women's roles are subordinate to those of men in the competitive world of capital culture; individualism provides richer rewards than cooperative effort, but still, the individual must bow to authority; being fiercely competitive is always admirable; and intimidation is a preferred means toward success.

Television sports commentary bespeaks ideology in reinforcing the normative assumption that society *ought* to work this way; for in the end, television sports celebrates the sports experience both as a good story to cover and as *the* story about what American life is about.

References

Barthes, R. (1957/1972). Myth today. In R. Barthes, *Mythologies* (pp. 109–158). New York: Hill and Wang.

Coakley, J. J. (1984). The sociological perspective: Alternate causations of violence in sport. In D. S. Eitzen (Ed.), *Sport in contemporary society: An anthology* (2nd ed.) (pp. 98–111). New York: St. Martin's Press.

Comisky, P., Bryant, J., & Zillmann, D. (1977). Commentary as a substitute for action. *Journal of Communication, 27*(3), 150–153.

Dunning, E. (Ed.). (1971). *Sport: Readings from a sociological perspective.* London: Frank Cass.

Edwards, H. (1973). *Sociology of sport.* Homewood, IL: Dorsey.

Eitzen, D. S. (Ed.). (1984). *Sport in contemporary society: An anthology* (2nd ed.). New York: St. Martin's Press.

Fiske, J. (1987). *Television culture.* New York: Methuen.

Furst, R. (1971). Social change and the commercialization of professional sports. *International Review of Sport Sociology, 6*, 153–173.

Gerbner, G., Morgan, M., & Signorielli, N. (1986). Living with television: The dynamics of the cultivation process. In J. Bryant & D. Zillmann (Eds.), *Perspective on media effects* (pp. 17–40). Hillsdale, NJ: Erlbaum.

Goffman, E. (1959). *The presentation of self in everyday life.* New York: Anchor.

Goldstein, J. H. (Ed.). (1979). *Sports, games, and play.* Hilldale, NJ: Erlbaum.

Goldstein, J. H., & Bredemeier, B. J. (1977). Socialization: Some basic issues. *Journal of Communication, 27*(3), 154–159.

Goodger, J. M. (1985). Collective representations and the sacred in sport. *International Review for the Sociology of Sport, 20*, 179–187.

Jhally, S. (1984). The spectacle of accumulation: Material and cultural factors in the evolution of the sports/media complex. *The Insurgent Sociologist, 12*, 41–57.

Lipsky, B. (1979). Political implications of sports team symbolism. *Politics and Society, 9*, 61–88.

Meyrowitz, J. (1985). *No sense of place: The impact of electronic media on social behavior.* New York: Oxford University Press.

Morgan, M., & Signorielli, N. (1989). Cultivation analysis: Conceptualization and methodology. In N. Signorielli & M. Morgan (Eds.), *Cultivation analysis: New directions in media effects research* (pp. 13–34). Newbury Park, CA: Sage.

Morris, B. S., & Nydahl, J. (1983). Toward analysis of live television broadcasts. *Central States Speech Journal, 34*, 195–202.

Morse, M. (1983). Sport on television: Replay and display. In E. A. Kaplan (Ed.), *Regarding television: Critical approaches—an anthology* (pp. 44–66). Frederick, MD: University Publications of America.

Novak, M. (1976). *The joy of sports: End zones, bases, baskets, balls, and the consecration of the American spirit.* New York: Basic Books.

Oriard, M. (1981). Professional football as cultural myth. *Journal of American Culture, 4*, 27–41.

Pearl, D., Bouthilet, L., & Lazar, J. (Eds.). (1982). *Television and behavior: Ten years of scientific progress and implications for the 80's.* (DHHS Publication No. ADM 82-1196). Washington, DC: Government Printing Office.

Prisuta, R. H. (1979). Televised sports and political values. *Journal of Communication, 29*(1), 94–102.

Real, M. (1975). Super Bowl mythic spectacle. *Journal of Communication, 25*(1), 31–43.

Schlosberg, J. (1987, February). *American Demographics*, 45–49.

Stone, G. (1955). American sports: Play and dis-play. *Chicago Review, 9*, 83–100.

Sullivan, D. B. (1988, November). *Commentary and viewer perception of player hostility: Adding punch to televised non-contact sports.* Paper presented at the Speech Communication Association Conference, New Orleans.

Swift, E. M. (1986, February 17). Hockey? Call it sockey. *Sports Illustrated*, 12–17.

Exploring Ethics Through Sports and Leisure: A Writing Seminar

Kathleen Cordes

This paper presents a model of a class that integrates a freshman writing seminar with the topic of ethics and values in a controversial area provoking thoughtful and purposeful writing. This provocation is brought about by focusing on the world of sports and leisure, which is replete with ethical and moral dilemmas. The course promotes the crystalization of the student's value system and the development of sound ethical choices supported by clear rational thinking.

The freshman year is ideal for a class in critical thinking combined with ethics and morality. Freshmen are generally experiencing a new independence, making value judgments on their own often for the first time, and are influenced by a new group of friends in a new atmosphere. They are planning a major field of study, a future life, and rediscovering and recreating their own identity. Fresh ground has been broken. Their educational training has often emphasized learning the subject and memorization of the material so that it can be tested. Less attention has been given to deriving solutions to problems, achievement of insight into a situation, or the development of an inductive reasoning process. This year is a crucial time for the student to develop this ability to think critically. If the skill is developed as a freshman it can be exercised throughout the college experience.

The goal of the program is to initiate students into the practice of college level discourse in reading, thinking, writing, and discussions. The primary objectives are to attain basic proficiency in writing, to appreciate the idea of writing to learn, and to develop critical thinking skills such as analysis, synthesis, and evaluation. Other objectives are to explore the ethical, cultural, historical, and social issues which help relate the topic of the seminar to one's realm of knowledge and life experience. Significant interaction, both written and oral, occurs between peers and the professor.

The sports world is a favored metaphor where the factual world of rules and scores evokes questions of right and wrong. The course is an inquiry into ethics and morality in the sports and recreation setting. Competition, sportsmanship, spectator violence, interpersonal power, gambling, drugs, and environmental issues are some of the concepts examined. Various ethical approaches are explored with abundant opportunities provided to write, followed by debate and discussion. A daily journal is required and students also make formal and informal recommendations by assuming the roles of the athlete, coach, administrator, recreation director, or spectator. The typical pattern of the class each week includes one day of lecture and two days for discussion of case studies, analysis, and evaluation of controversial current subjects and class debates.

With the sports and recreation world often viewed as a microcosm of the larger world, topics for debate often touch on areas that an individual faces in any path in life. Values play a very important role in any social system including the system of sports and games. Related to values are norms which are looked upon as specific guides for behavior. Attached to these components are the enforcement elements of goals on one side and sanctions on the other. An interactive relationship must exist among all these components to produce an effective social outcome, such as a good sports system. Today some of the outcomes of sport are not only ineffective, they are destructive. The class will decide through case studies and debate how and if the American sport system is going awry.

Efforts are not made to indoctrinate students toward solutions but rather to stimulate the process of making ethical choices. Each individual must formulate an ethical standpoint through reflection after conducting research, interviews, debates, and discussions. The instructor does challenge ethical sensitivity and helps to construct sound theory, legal standards, critical thinking, and the ability to adequately state and defend one's moral arguments. Ethical decisions are developed through the study of the effect of the incident, the motives, the intentions, and the parties involved.

Schools are charged with the mission of educating the whole student which includes the personal, social, and moral dimensions. Questions of good and bad or right and wrong arise as a natural consequence of social interaction, and they occur in all aspects of school life. Students confronted with issues seek answers, and it is important that a competent attempt be made to satisfy those needs. Programs are needed not to indoctrinate the student into society's standards, but rather to promote rational thought and examine moral principles that eventually will result in spontaneous actions. Through logical reasoning and careful examination of ethical situations students will develop a set of defensible principles that may be used to judge and guide their actions. For some students, the school or classroom may be the only source of ethical training.

This class, however, embraces the experiential approach; students, therefore, are actively constructing, discovering, dissecting, and exploring ethical situations and ethical frameworks. It is a laboratory class in ethics: sport and leisure situations are the subject of dissection. The purpose of the assignments is to introduce the students to one another; to create an environment where they can be supportive of one another; to learn to work together and to begin to develop a trust; to learn to think as "the other side" might; to learn to respect and relate to the other side; to begin to learn elements of debate; to learn how to research; to develop and promote their opinions; to learn to work with others to make a value decision in a social setting; to develop critical thinking; to be open to the opinion of others; to learn how to sway others to their opinion; and to begin to open up other issues that could be incorporated in class contents, for example, violence, steroids, the purpose of sport and leisure, and the meaning of ethics and morality.

The effectiveness of this class can be attributed to several factors. First, the subject matter of sports and recreation is quite common to many people. It has an everyday quality and is not threatening. In other words, the student is comfortable with the subject. Ethics is abstract, whereas sports and recreation is tangible. Dealing with one intangible is often more than enough for a freshman to address.

Second, the atmosphere of the class is cooperative and nonthreatening. The emphasis on group interaction and interdependence allows for the risk taking which is necessary for a student to express and support an ethical or moral point of view. To express one's own opinion is to be personally at risk. Initially stretching the student to express an ethical standpoint which is not necessarily their own assists in breaking down the risk of someone disagreeing with the adopted position. The speaker is not personally at risk.

Third, the extensive writing in journals and formal and informal writing followed by debate and discussion stimulates the thought process necessary so that all sides of an issue can be evaluated prior to the step of making an ethical choice.

Character Education: Something's Missing— Whose Responsibility?

Nila M. Ipson and L. Dale Cruse

From the beginnings of formal education, a primary aim of schooling has been the development of sound character. In his collection of eloquent and wise essays, *Wise Men Know What Wicked Things Are Written on the Sky*, Russell Kirk further observed that "the end of true education is ethical; and that end is to be attained through intellectual means" (cited in Gow, 1989).

The true purpose of education is the cultivation of wisdom and virtue. Clearly today, in our institutions of learning and social structures we need to reemphasize the kind of education that cultivates minds and character. Conventional wisdom says that the family is the chief agent of character education, but we are seeing a real transition in the values that many of our children and youth are absorbing within their home environments. Moral character is given scant regard, and increasingly, ethics and morality have come to be understood as subjective and relative. As this transition takes place, students today are arriving at school and university seemingly more prepared for, and in need of, hearing issues of morality and ethics discussed and more prepared for the notion that life is a difficult process in which choices are continuous rather than occasional (Lewis, 1987). There is still need to be explicit and public about the values which shape our society. Other social forces must serve as surrogate agents in trying to supplement or stand in for parents and families as providers of character education. Schools and universities, therefore, need programs to assist and protect youth against the ravages of social disorganization and family collapse, to nurture the growth of personality as well as intellect and physical well-being.

Scholastic achievement is but one side of the learning coin. The other side is ethics, morality, and integrity. This is supported by Hogness (1989) when he states: "If erudition is the result of education, then morality ... learning right and wrong ... is the essence of education. This is because wisdom is a moral sensibility which facts and information will not provide and knowledge unchecked by wisdom and moral judgement is easily corrupted" (p. 693). Ethics and ethical behavior are more than a matter of knowing and adhering to the informed precepts. It is what has in earlier times been referred to as "character"—a respect for self and others, a willingness to sacrifice for the common good, a sense of civic responsibility, the relentless pursuit of truth, basic honesty, and an intolerance to anything less than adherence to the highest standards (Rosken, 1988).

Schools, teachers, and social leaders cannot, of course, assume full responsibility for moral development and character education; but they should at least try not to shun it! There has been of late a cynical attitude toward ethics, and there seems to be a rising tide of mediocrity that threatens our very future as a people and a nation (Hearn, 1988). Ethics and values are not just taught, but rather they are "caught" and developed over time and affected by human relationships and life's experiences. Nothing is, therefore, any more important than the impact that teachers and social leaders can have on young lives in this crucial period when their adult values are being established and ambitions formed (Sand, 1988).

The purpose of this paper is to discuss the role of leisure and recreation academicians and professionals in the enhancement of personal ethics and character education of today's youth. The paper provides a rationale for the teaching and reinforcing of ethics and civic responsibility to our academic institutions and leisure programs, and suggests ways for park and recreation professionals to assist in the advocacy of social consciousness and social responsibility.

Character Education: An Ethic of Responsibility

Character education as used here refers to two things: (a) education in civic virtue and in the ethical rules of citizenship in a just society and (b) education in personal adjustment to life's encounters. The formation of one's character has to do with the development of values, personal identity, and development, which is intricately related to one's life experiences. Youth cannot achieve these ends without a sense of altruism, achievement, integrity, self-control, or self-esteem. They certainly cannot succeed if they are drunk, drugged, depressed, or anxious; if they are parents before they can be breadwinners; or if they must abandon school to escape brutality, neglect, or despair at home (London, 1987).

The issues that plague the lives of young people are more than personal problems. They are not simply signs of health and welfare of youth, but of the character of the society, the quality of civilization, and the prospects of the future. London (1987) further admonishes that schools and social programs must rethink what they see as their only relevant unit of concern; they must provide outright assistance to children and youth, but they must also attend to families. Schools and social agencies must lead the battle against the worst psychosocial epidemics that have ever plagued our youth. It is time to pay more than lip service attention to the principles by which we would live. In the end, the quality of our civilization and the heritage we leave for our young people will depend upon it (Rosken, 1989).

Youth are shaped by what they encounter and wrestle with, in the home, in the classroom, and in their relationships with friends, teachers, and social leaders. There can be no doubt that as teachers and leaders we do have a concrete responsibility to assist in the ethical and character education of today's young people. Zumberge (1989) endorses this when he stated "If we hold dear the enduring values of truth telling, reliability, loyalty, self-discipline, respect for others, tolerance and reasoned resolution to conflicts, why shouldn't we affirm these values at every opportunity?" (p. 202).

Although our ethic foundation has never totally collapsed, there are today definitely new moral dilemmas being poised by advanced technology and the great social changes in society. Individuals have gradually become indiscriminant in their attitudes and actions, because of not being taught to think about the many issues until they are confronted with the problems or not given help in solving real problems and learning to make decisions where principles conflict.

A major task of moral and character education today is to enable youth to acknowledge and to some extent become tolerant of differences in moral codes without being led into an extreme moral relativism—a concern and criticism levied at some systematic approaches at teaching values clarification and character education. Despite differences among various schools of thought regarding the valuing process, one message comes through loud and clear from the modern movement in moral/value education. Students should not have values imposed on them, but rather should (a) be introduced to certain general procedures for arriving at values and (b) be exposed to various ideas and arguments in the area of values as a stimulus to thought and personal obligation (Beck, 1979).

There is a great deal of commonality in the ultimate life goals pursued by most human beings, and even where there are differences in life goals, there is a great deal of room for objective inquiry into how best to pursue them. There is much more to moral education than the study of values. It does seem, however, that other aspects of moral and character development could take place much more quickly and assuredly if students were helped to grow in their understanding of values, under the tutelage of caring leaders and teachers rather than through the powerful impact of television.

The major concern in character education is with helping people come to live in accordance with their own values (Beck, 1979). "Talking about values and principles is not a substitute for experiencing their operation in life and working through the tough decisions where principles conflict" (Kelly, 1982, p. K3). The basic philosophy of leisure and recreation is "freedom"—freedom of choice and efficacy! Freedom is not free! "To remain free the individual must recognize the attendant personal obligations, costs and self sacrifices ... free societies cannot survive unless the values on which they are founded are fully comprehended and practiced by each generation" (Duttera, 1980, p. 5).

The Role of the Profession

How does all of this apply to the profession of leisure and recreation? Leisure education and recreation programs provide opportunities to introduce topics for values clarification in leisure and recreational situations (i.e., personal and social values in general): the need to look ahead, pollution control and the environment, prejudice against races and social classes, worthwhile personal goals to pursue in one's life, balancing the work and leisure ethic, the need for self-control, service and helping others, international protection policies, and the effects of alcohol and drugs, to name but a few (Beck, 1979).

Leisure educators and recreational programmers have significant influence on the lives of young people in important ways. They are in a position to teach leadership, cooperation, discipline, dedication, and respect for others (Hearn, 1988). Hearn remarks: "teamwork is a lesson in cooperation which is more important than competition in sport and in life" (p. 21). Leisure and recreation professionals have the opportunity to teach the civic virtue side of character—the issues and duties of citizenship in a democracy, as well as providing lifelong guidance in the areas of fitness, health, and well-being. Our programs can provide skills in managing differences and develop incentives to draw people out of themselves through service to others. Our programs demonstrate understanding about different cultures, customs, and events, provide hands-on self-governing, and foster intergenerational cohort involvement.

While home, church, and school have not been keeping pace with moral development and character education of today's citizens, young people have, nevertheless, been indiscriminately bombarded with values through other very powerful influences. Never before has society been so saturated by means of mass media communication and subliminal persuasions from so many clashing value systems. Television has become a major influence in the molding of our ethical values. Repeatedly, survey studies on leisure participation name television watching as the number one leisure involvement. Today society is being jaded by complacent values which teach that any major problem or concern can be resolved in 30 to 60 minutes, that disrespect for others is justified for personal gain and satisfaction, and that wilful and wanton destruction and disregard for nature and our natural resources doesn't matter. Synnestvedt (1989) explains that children and youth who watch TV violence act violently, accept violence as a means, and are discouraged from cooperating with others. This is because of the desensitizing, role modeling, and apparent approval of such actions and behaviors. "It isn't only what young people watch that damages them—it is that they watch!" (Synnestvedt, 1989, p. 209). People must play or recreate in order to develop physically, socially, and mentally. Television retards development because it holds individuals as passive captives before a lot of bright moving images. How can people learn to be responsible participants when they are being trained to be passive viewers of amusing spectacles? Television is hypnotic—it is literally physically addictive. We have an obligation as a profession to educate about the powerful impact of television and its imbalanced use or abuse as a leisure pursuit.

Another major value concern directly related to our profession deals with our perceived responsibility to our natural resources—to the environment. In our pursuit of leisure and enjoyment, are we displacing the value of our national resources? Are we destroying our natural "playgrounds" for future generations? We must become active vanguards in the preservation of our society and our environment!

Conclusion and Recommendations

As educators and professionals we might ask what can we do? How can we influence the education and character development of citizens within our society? How can we make our contribution to the improvement of society's concerns? Let us begin with ourselves, by first examining our own lives and our own values. Do we believe that our actions can make a difference, and that what we do or do not do now affects the next generation?

As professionals in leisure and recreation, we have been negligent in our responsibility by allowing the number one leisure pursuit to be carried on with little or no input by our profession into the shaping of its purposes or influence upon society. We have also been guilty of contributing to the demise of our environment and natural resources by our unsatiated desire for leisure pursuit. The challenge facing us is to become more actively involved as major advocates in support of responsible, disciplined television programming and viewing, and the active recycling programs and restorative conservation programs. We can, as individuals and as a collective association of professionals, encourage corporate sponsors to be more selective in the types of values they promote through their sponsorship of television programming. As a large national association of concerned leisure professionals, we should sponsor and promote the production of television programs and promotional advertisements and materials that serve to develop moral and character education, and present a positive option to what now exists. As professionals, concerned citizens, and consumers, we should levy concerted pressure on corporations to protect the environment through better control of emissions and waste products and to support protection and revitalization programs.

In conclusion, our goal and responsibility must be to demonstrate an honest and dedicated effort in helping to develop individuals with a strong sense of human values, civic responsibility, and respect for others: By our example and by applying value processing and clarification techniques in leisure situations, and by means of our advocacy role in citizenship and civic matters, we can make a difference. We can only succeed, however, through sincere honest desires, self-assessment, and dedication. Then, with a firm philosophical foundation, we can direct our attention and efforts toward helping to fortify society, by contributing to the development of individuals with character, civic responsibility, personal values, and sound leisure ethics.

References

Beck, C. (1979). *Moral education in the schools: Some practical suggestions*. Profiles in Practical Education No. 3. Ontario, Canada: The Ontario Institute for Studies in Education.

Duttera, M. J., Sr. (1980). *Ideas for a minimum curriculum for education for excellence in citizenship*. San Antonio, TX: American Institute of Character Education.

Gow, H. B. (1989) The true purpose of education. *Phi Delta Kappan, 70*(3), 545–546.

Hearn, T. K., Jr. (1988). Sports and ethics. *Vital Speeches of the Day*, 55(1), 20–22.

Hogness, J. R. (1989). The essence of education. *Vital Speeches of the Day*, 52(7), 201–203.

Kelly, M. J. (1982). The value of teaching ethics. *The Baltimore Sun*, May 23, pp. K1–K3.

Lewis, A. C. (1987). A word about character. *Phi Delta Kappan*, 68(6), 724–725.

London, P. (1987). Character education and clinical intervention: A paradigm shift for U. S. schools. *Phi Delta Kappan*, 68(5), 667–673.

Rosken, R. W. (1988). Ethical leaders. *Vital Speeches of the Day*, 56(22), 692–695.

Rosken, R. W. (1989). Integrity. *Vital Speeches of the Day*, 55(16), 511–512.

Sand, P. O. (1988, November). Business ethics: A trend toward ethical cynicism. *Vital Speeches of the Day*, 55(3), 85–87.

Synnestvedt, J. (1989). T.V. No! Let's get off the couch. *Vital Speeches of the Day*, 55(7), 209–211.

Zumberge, J. H. (1989). Ethical and moral responsibilities as faculty: Enduring values. *Vital Speeches of the Day*, 55(7), 199–202.

The Contribution of Leisure to Moral Development

James S. Leming

Given the pervasiveness of leisure in contemporary society it is inconceivable that it does not in some significant way contribute to the many dimensions of human development. From the child's earliest experience of play with a parent until the days preceding one's death, leisure is a central part of everyone's life. It is within the domain of leisure as well as within the more instrumental aspects of life that one's understanding of the self and one's understanding of the social world develops. It is the social nature of leisure that logically and psychologically relates it to moral life. This paper proposes to examine the dynamics that contemporary psychology has identified that contribute to moral development and examine the construct of leisure from this perspective. The goal of this analysis is to move the study of leisure's contribution to moral development from a theoretical analysis to a perspective based on contemporary psychological research.

The terms "moral development" and "leisure" are frequently used in myriad ways by different individuals. Both terms refer to broad areas of human experience and scholarly interest where disciplined inquiry must be framed within clear understandings of the terrain. Therefore, the first section of this paper is an attempt to develop a clear understanding of the nature of the language of morality and moral development as well as a review of the dominant perspectives on the psychology of moral development. Next will be presented those factors that contribute to moral development. This framework will then be used to analyze the potential for leisure activities to contribute to moral development. The following section will discuss the implications of the above analysis for the training and practice of leisure professionals.

The final section of the paper will consist of suggestions for further research into moral development and leisure.

Morality—Basic Concepts

Morality in its broadest sense can be defined as interpersonal behavior that involves the rights, duties, or welfare of either party. The function of morality is to regulate our behavior in particular ways when the rights and well-being of others are involved. Morality is a necessary component of any social organization. Social organization (society) requires rules or norms of appropriate behavior so that an acceptable level of stability and personal security is achieved. Those norms and principles that regulate relations between individuals and between individuals and groups are properly called moral and comprise the content of morality. If the society is a just society, then those norms and principles will be considerate of others' rights and well-being. Examples of such norms are: eschewing violence in the pursuit of one's desires, telling the truth, respecting the property of others, etc.

Another term frequently encountered in discussions of morality is value. Values are principles or ideals that people feel strongly about and that impel us toward and guide our action. Values are composed of beliefs and attitudes. Beliefs are a conviction about the truth of particular ideas or states of affairs. Attitudes are an enduring organization of beliefs around an object or situation that generate affect and predispose one to respond in some preferential manner. Beliefs, attitudes, and values may be moral or nonmoral. A moral value is a deeply held judgment regarding what is morally good with reference to persons, motives, intentions, character traits, etc. Questions of moral value do not consider questions of moral action (what we should do). Questions of moral action are functions of judgments of moral obligation or responsibility, not moral value. For the purposes of this paper, it is important to note that many values one finds discussed in the literature on leisure are nonmoral in nature. To the extent that leisure results in intrapersonal benefits (for example, sense of well-being, reduction of tension, enhanced self-worth), the results are nonmoral in nature. To the extent that the results of leisure activities are other-regarding or interpersonal (for example, development of a sense of responsibility or improved sensitivity to others' needs), the leisure activity can be said to have contributed to the development of moral values.

Moral Development—Two Contemporary Perspectives

In psychology, moral development has been a topic of increasing interest over the past six decades. As noted by Gibbs and Schnell (1985), "moral development had ascended from the status of an 'odd' topic in the 1960s to a major theoretical and research area" (p. 1071). Today the research field is marked by great complexity and disagreement regarding how best to understand moral development. Even the term moral development has different meanings depending upon the research perspective under consideration. This section presents two perspectives that are most useful in attempting to understand the relationship between leisure and moral development. A brief set of research-based generalizations, regarding the conditions under which moral development occurs, is presented.

What is meant by the term "moral development"? Moral development refers to the process by which the child moves from being an egocentric selfish being with little awareness of socictal norms to the state where the individual regulates his/her own behavior in such a way that he/she will conform to society's norms and will do so from a moral point of view. That is, the person chooses to obey society's norms because he/she recognizes that those norms are just and fair. Thus, moral development occurs on a number of levels. First, on a behavioral level, society through parents, peers, schools, and the like slowly socializes the child. Second, the child's understanding of social organization also develops. Finally, affect, a part of both socialization and cognitive development, is also refined. The child learns to feel good about doing good and feel bad about doing bad. Affect is also a part of the deliberative process with regard to the individual's need to maintain integrity between his/her reasons and behavior.

In this paper, a pluralistic but somewhat selective viewpoint is adopted. That is, the focus is on the two perspectives on moral development that have dominated the research of the past 40 years. They have the most developed research base and offer the most explanatory power in the attempt to understand the relationship between leisure and moral development. These two perspectives to be considered are the social learning theory, which has been reflected in the work of Aronfreed (1968), Bandura (1977), Hoffman (1963), Miller and Dollard (1941), Sears, Maccoby, and Levin (1957), and Whiting and Whiting (1975), and the cognitive developmental theory, which has been based on the pioneering work of Piaget and more recently Kohlberg.

The basic concepts of social learning theory—reinforcement, generalization, discrimination, habit strength, drive, mediation, and the stimulus and response associationist base—are well known. Within the moral development literature, the terms "moral socialization" and "internalization" are frequently used to define this perspective on moral development. Most social scientists agree that individuals do not go through the life span viewing society's moral norms as external and coercively imposed. These norms initially may be external and conflict with one's desires, but eventually they become a part of one's motive system and help guide behavior even in the absence of external authority. When the individual comes to shape behavior so that it is consistent with society's moral codes, we say those norms have been internalized and the individual has been socialized. The classical social learning interpretation of how overt moral action occurs in conditions of temptation and lack of surveillance holds that such behavior is the result of conditioned anxiety, that is, the pairing of unpleasant sensations with antisocial norms. This perspective on moral conscience has much in common with the psychoanalytic perspective.

The most current perspective on the development of moral character (learned moral habits or virtues) from the social learning perspective is based on the pioneering work of Bandura and Walters (1963). It was their contribution to document that a substantial portion of a person's moral responses are acquired through observation and imitation of a model without direct reinforcement. Clearly, parents play an important role in both discipline and in serving as models, but it is through the process of modeling that the potential range of influences (both positive and negative) on moral development is expanded. Through the process of observation and imitation such forces as peers, media, significant others, etc., become potential sources of appropriate and inappropriate social and moral behavior for children.

Whereas the social learning perspective emphasizes behavior in moral contexts, the focus of the cognitive developmental perspective is on moral reasoning. The debate over the nature of moral development in this century has its historical roots in the seminal work of the French sociologist Emile Durkheim. Durkheim (1925/1973) understood moral development as a process of cultural "impression" upon the child accomplished by an emotional transmission of society's values to the child. The salient features of this transmission were its emotional nature through the use of authority and discipline in the early years and later the child's natural attachment to groups. This perspective was sociological in nature, but the dynamics and outcomes are highly consistent with the social learning analysis that was to follow later in the century. Piaget (1932/1965) rejected the view of Durkheim and argued instead that moral development was best understood as a cognitive understanding which was constructed by the individual as a result of experiencing conflicts of social interaction natural to growing up in any society. Piaget's initial perspective was based on his observation of children playing a game of marbles, in effect a leisure setting, where children are removed from supervision by authorities and where they had to solve real social conflicts. In Piaget's first stage, children feel an obligation to obey rules because they are sacred and unalterable. They judge an act as right or wrong on the basis of its consequences, whether it conforms to established rules and whether it is punished. At the more advanced stage, rules are created through reciprocal agreement. Actions are judged right and wrong on the basis of interactions as well as consequences, and duty and obligation are defended by maintaining peer expectations. Piaget placed the child and his/her interactions with the social environment as the dynamic that explained moral development. The child was not a passive recipient of the socialization process but was the creator of moral meaning.

Kohlberg, like Piaget, rejected the perspective that moralization was a matter of individual accommodation to society. Instead Kohlberg saw moral development as the development of reasoning around a sense of justice that enabled the individual to isolate the legitimate moral claims of individuals in a situation and to balance these perspectives in a way that takes into account the perspectives of all the individuals in the situation. Kohlberg saw moral development as occurring in a seires of five qualitatively distinct stages, with each stage a homogeneous form of moral reasoning that builds on, reorganizes, and encompasses the preceding one. Based on Kohlberg's pioneering longitudinal data (Colby, Kohlberg, Gibbs, & Lieberman, 1983), it was found that all individuals go through the stages in the same order and they vary only in how quickly and how far they eventually move through the sequence.

The key to understanding how individuals progress through the stages is the experience of cognitive disequilibrium and the opportunity for role taking. The experience of moral conflict produces a tension which is the result of the individual's attempt to make sense of the contradiction. If the experience of cognitive conflict is accompanied by exposure to stages of moral reasoning that are moderately higher than the individual's current level, then research suggests that the individual will begin to utilize the higher reasoning. Central to the individual's attempt to make sense out of moral conflict are successive changes in role-taking ability. The ability to take the perspective of others is crucial in the development from egocentric reasoning to more socially oriented reasoning. An impressive body of evidence collected in instructional settings supports the claim that disequilibrium accompanied by exposure to higher reasoning results in moral development (Enright, Lapsley, Harris, & Shawer, 1983; Leming, 1985; Schlaefli, Rest, & Thoma, 1985). The above studies summarize the research on deliberate educational interventions where the teacher, through the use of class discussion of moral dilemmas, achieved upward movement in stages of moral reasoning among students.

After this brief survey of the research on moralization, what are we left with that can be applied to examining the topic of leisure and moral development? In a nutshell, we have two perspectives on moral development, one with a focus on behavior, the other emphasizing reasoning. From the social learning perspective, to the extent that a situation involves the individual in moral behavior and that behavior is rewarding to the individual, that behavior will be strengthened. Alternatively, observation and imitation of others' behavior may also constitute powerful dynamics. From the cognitive developmental perspective, to the extent that experiences offer opportunity for role taking and cognitive disequilibrium with exposure to the next higher stage of moral reasoning, development in moral reasoning will occur. We now turn to an analysis of leisure activity and the characteristics of the leisure experience that may or may not facilitate moral development.

Analysis of the Research Base

As Gunter (1987) has aptly noted, "As a topic for research in the social sciences, leisure contains more than its share of problems, of which the most significant seems to be a lack of definitional consensus" (p. 115). Since the remainder of this paper is based on available research, the interpretation of leisure is somewhat dictated by that body of research; however, what emerges from the literature is a conception of leisure that has its origins in Aristotle. According to Aristotle, the proper use of leisure includes contemplation, music, art, community service, and physical fitness (*Ethics*, Book X, Ch. 7; *Politics*, Book VIII, Chs. 4– 6). Research exists on three contemporary forms of leisure that are informative with regard to the potential influence of leisure activity on moral development. These emerging bodies of research focus on community service, popular culture, and sports and are rough approximations of Aristotle's music and art, community service, and physical fitness. In the remainder of this section, the research base on each of these leisure forms will be described and analyzed for its potential effect on moral development.

Community Service
One informative body of research is based on programs designed to involve youth in service activities and contribute in a general way to their social or moral development. The available research on the influence of these programs on students is taken from two careful reviews of the field.

First, Conrad and Hedin (1981, 1982) evaluated the impact of experiential education programs on the social, psychological, and intellectual development of secondary school pupils. In the late 1970s, approximately 1,000 students in 27 nationwide experiential education programs were administered a questionnaire to assess the impact of those programs. All students were pre- and posttested near the first and last days of the program. Six of the experiential samples had comparison groups from nonexperimental programs drawn from comparable populations. The various types of experiential programs studied were: volunteer community service (N = 400), career internships (N = 244), community study/political action (N = 241), and outdoor adventure education (N = 152). The discussion below is based primarily on the findings from the one community service (N = 41) and two community study programs (N = 51, N = 94) for which there existed comparison groups.

In the community service and community study programs, self-esteem increased; however, these increases were slight and the comparison group in one of the community study programs also gained in self-esteem. To assess moral reasoning, the Defining Issues Test (Rest, 1979) was administered to students of two experiential programs and one comparison group. The type of program(s) is not reported. Both experiential groups attained small significant gains, while the comparison group did not. This finding, however, must be qualified by two related studies. Corbett (1977) found that over a two-year period with students in a community involvement program involving the out-of-school solution of social problems, there was no impact on moral reasoning. Reck (1978), however, found that some students involved in in-school service programs did experience statistically significant moral development, namely, those students with the longer experience (105 hours or more).

With regard to social development, Conrad and Hedin used a researcher-constructed Social and Personal Responsibility Scale (SPRS). This scale assessed the extent to which a student: (a) feels a sense of personal duty; (b) feels a concern for the welfare of others; (c) feels competent to act responsibly; (d) has a sense of efficacy; and (e) acts responsibly. The overall results from the SPRS showed a statistically significant movement for the experimental programs and no movement or negative movement for the comparison groups. On the subscales of the SPRS, it was found that the strongest gains were recorded for sense of competence and performance, followed by social efficacy and sense of duty. Additionally, it was found that students in community service and community study programs showed large, consistent changes toward more positive attitudes toward adults. This was especially pronounced in students' evaluations of people they came into contact with in the process of their community participation. It was also found that community service and community study students increased in their attitude toward being involved in the community. Over the entire range of experiential programs studied, the strongest gains in social development were by students involved in community study/social action programs.

Three additional findings by Conrad and Hedin are deserving of comment. First, the social growth of students was greatest in those programs where there was a regularly scheduled time for collective reflection on the experience. Second, the impact on students was greater in those programs of longest duration. Third, characteristics of the individual experience, rather than program characteristics or individual characteristics, were the most important in accounting for student growth. What students reported as characteristics of their individual experience accounted for 15 to 20 percent of the variance in pre- and postgain, whereas program characteristics and individual characteristics accounted for not more than 8 percent of the gain. Among the most significant characteristics reported by students were discussing the experience with teachers and doing things on one's own.

A second source of information on the impact of community service programs is found in the review by Newmann and Rutter (1983). Unlike the Conrad and Hedin review, this review was limited only to an examination of community service programs. In this tightly controlled study, eight schools were identified where there existed on-going community service programs in which students were given academic credit for the experience and were involved in at least four hours per week of service in the community. Comparison groups were drawn from each of the schools and both groups were pre- and posttested at the beginning and end of the spring 1983 semester. The program and comparison groups consisted of 150 students each. Demographic data were collected on each student, and selected students were interviewed regarding their motivations for entering the programs and their perceptions of the experience. Data collection consisted of a questionnaire that assessed the range of developmental opportunities provided within the programs, as well as six measures of social development.

The measures of social development used by Newmann and Rutter were researcher-constructed multiple-item Likert scales. The six areas measured were sense of community and school responsibility, sense of social competence, political efficacy, anticipated future community involvement, and anticipated future political participation. The study concluded that community service programs increased students' sense of community responsibility and sense of personal competence in a very modest way (about 1.5 percent on a 5-point scale), but had no impact on the other variables studied. In studying the specific developmental activities that differed from program to program, it was found that these variations within programs failed to account for those changes that accrued to individual students. Thus, community service programs, regardless of the experiences provided, were found to have no discernable impact on sense of school responsibility, political efficacy, and anticipated future involvement in community and political affairs.

Overall, the findings of research on programs involving community participation and social action can be considered tentative and only slightly encouraging. All of the findings are based on results of a very small effect size. Reasons why researchers are unable to find strong consistent significant social and political development as a result of participation in such programs is puzzling, especially in light of the enthusiasm that staff and students show for the programs and their conviction that the programs have an effect (Newmann & Rutter, 1983). One possible explanation is that the time period covered by the majority of the studies is only one semester. It may be that given the nature of the dependent variables, longer treatment time is necessary to observe growth. It also could be that the results of the experience only manifest themselves later in life. Another possible reason for the failure to detect mean growth for program students may be that each individual field experience is perceived idiosyncratically by the student. The net result is a wide range of response, both positive and negative, with the mean response relatively unaffected. Whatever the reasons for the pattern of findings reported above, this is an area in which careful systematic research is clearly called for. The potential effect of involvement in community life on student development is a question of supreme importance to leisure research.

Popular Culture

Popular culture, the expression of a people's or group's salient concerns, attitudes, and values, through music, television, literature, humor, cinema, etc., has increasingly received attention by the general public and scholars with regard to its role in the socialization process of youth. While popular culture may either be representative of the prevailing culture or present an alternative to that culture, it is the latter conception that has stimulated much recent interest. The concern in the United States is that popular culture, especially rock music and television, is teaching youth a set of values that contradict traditional cultural values—and thereby threaten society's very existence and the ability of youth to develop so as to lead happy and productive lives. One recent example of this concern regarding the deleterious effect of popular culture can be illustrated by a quote from the best selling and highly influential author Alan Bloom. In *The Closing of the American Mind*, Bloom (1987) makes the following observations about the role of rock music in the socialization of youth: "Rock music has one appeal only, a barbaric appeal to sexual desire (p. 73) ... the inevitable corollary of rock sexual interest is rebellion against the parental authority that represses it (p. 74) ... life is made into a nonstop, commercially prepackaged masturbational fantasy (p. 75) ... it ruins imagination and makes it difficult to have a passionate relationship to the art and thought that are the substance of liberal education (p. 79) ... after addiction to rock music, the pleasures have been so intense, the rest of life is a disappointment—life may be accepted, but it is something harsh, grim and essentially unattractive, a mere necessity (p. 80)."

If the effect is as damaging as Bloom's lament would indicate, then certainly this is an area in need of careful study and reflection. As calls for public policy in this area increase, it becomes vitally important to understand the phenomenon as completely and as objectively as possible. There are two central and related questions surrounding the alleged relationship between popular culture as leisure activity and the value socialization of youth: (a) What is the nature of the influence of popular culture on the values of youth and (b) What is the mechanism, in terms of psychological dynamics, by which this influence is best understood? The available research on these two questions is examined below.

Among the many dimensions of popular culture, music and television occupy the central place in terms of youths' leisure time. In the United States, studies have reported that adolescents spend approximately 20 hours per week watching television (Merrow, 1985; Leming, 1987; Lawrence, Tasker, Daley, Orhiel, & Wozniak, 1986) and in excess of 20 hours per week listening to music (Leming, 1987; Schwartz & Mannella, 1975). Some recent studies of European youth (East Germany and Sweden) indicate that although the amount of time spent is only half that of American youth, it still results in over two hours per day spent with TV and music (Wicke, 1985; Roe, 1985). Generally, television watching tends to decline as youth move into and through adolescence, but time spent with music remains fairly constant across adolescence. Because youth spend more time with television and music than other forms of popular culture, this paper will focus on these two forms.

The review below on the influence of television on youth will be limited to two areas that have well-developed bodies of research: violence and sex-role stereotyping. The majority of the research on television's influence has focused on children's aggressive behavior. According to the Neilson index, the average American child watches 18,000 television murders before he or she graduates from high school (Rothenberg, 1975). In addition to murder, other types of violence are regular fare on American television. Does watching all this violence have any discernible impact on youth? Listen to the conclusions of two recent reviews: "At this time, it should be difficult to find any researcher who does not believe that a significant positive relation exists between view- ing television violence and subsequent aggressive behavior under most conditions" (Huesmann, 1982) and "there is little convincing evidence that viewing violence on television in natural settings causes an increase in subsequent aggressiveness" (Freedman, 1984).

It is beyond the purview of this paper to review the voluminous literature on this issue, but a number of observations about the field as a body of research appear to be warranted. First, the studies on the link between television viewing and aggression that utilize an experi- mental design were conducted in laboratory settings. The major short- comings of these studies is the artificial setting and the measurement of only short-term effects. The studies that were conducted in real- world settings and attempted to measure persisting relationships be- tween viewing violence and violent behavior all preclude causal claims since they can not rule out alternative interpretations such as the di- rectionality of causality or the possibility of a third underlying factor causing both the selection of violent programs and real world aggres- siveness. Even when positive correlations are found, television viewing seldom accounts for more than 10 percent of the variance in explaining aggression in children (Zuckerman & Zuckerman, 1985).

The research on the impact of sex role portrayal on television is not nearly as extensive as that associated with violence and aggression, but there are similarities. First, reviewers of the field disagree considerably with respect to the findings in the field. For example, Greenberg (1982) argues that children learn the stereotypes presented on television while Durkin (1985), after reviewing the literature, asserts that there is no strong and convincing evidence of a relationship between viewing sex role stereotypes and the child's sex role beliefs or attitudes. In addition, the problems associated with research designs and drawing warranted conclusions based on the evidence are similar to those noted above with respect to aggression.

The literature on popular music's influence on youth behavior has been long on rhetoric and very short on empirical inquiry. In addition to Bloom's jeremiad cited above, rock music has been accused of fos- tering drug usage, alcoholism, sexual immorality, rebellion, and vio- lence. Two studies that claim to have determined a link between lis- tening to rock music and alcohol use (Lewis, 1980, 1981) used a correlational design and must be interpreted cautiously due to the di- rectionality and third variable questions raised above. Other studies such as Greeson and Williams (1986) found that after viewing selected music television videos (MTV) for less than one hour, seventh and tenth grade adolescents were more likely to approve of premarital sex and violence. This study, however, was conducted in a laboratory setting and only measured immediate responses.

The research briefly discussed above has, in my judgment, resulted in an equivocal body of knowledge whose claims add little to an understanding of the phenomenon. The problem in my judgment is that the research programs have been based on two faulty assumptions regarding how youth learn from popular culture. The first misconception, popular among the general public and many researchers, is what Howitt (1982) refers to as the hypodermic model of learning. According to this model, the various forms of media inject into the audience a dose of persuasive communication (values) and this injection has a fairly uniform effect. Related to the hypodermic model, as a corollary principle, is the linear effects assumption: the greater the exposure to the stimulus, the greater the effect (Williams, 1981). This model and assumption have considerable appeal to the lay public and have even begun to be accepted by policy makers.

I believe that the study of popular culture's influence on youth needs now to move beyond the social learning perspectives described above and to begin to look at the phenomenon differently. Due to complex methodological problems in studying real life experiences and behavior changes over time, it is unlikely in the future that a social learning perspective will contribute new insights.

In one of the early studies of the place of television in the lives of children by Schramm, Lyle, and Parker (1961), the suggestion was made that studies should include not only what television does to children but also what children do with it. I want to build on this suggestion and sketch out what I see as a potentially more powerful way of studying the phenomenon that is built on the observation that children are not passive receptors of popular culture, but rather themselves determine what meaning popular culture will have. This approach to the study of popular culture's influence on youth is built around three related assumptions: constructivism, interactionism, and developmentalism.

Constructivism holds that by thinking about and acting in the world individuals construct meaning for themselves; as they interact with the world, they actively construct and reconstruct reality. Unlike the hypodermic and linear effects models of learning, constructivism holds that minds create reality, not that reality creates minds. Although each response to the environment is an individual action of the moment and experience, its form is constrained or determined by the person's current developmental level. These two assumptions, constructivism and developmentalism, have been most carefully explicated in the work of Piaget and Kohlberg.

Interactionism (Magnusson, 1981) holds that culture's influence is not unidirectional but rather is bidirectional. Its influence on youth is mediated, even determined, by the way it is perceived and handled as subjectively experienced. The experience, therefore, of popular culture would involve two clusters of components (Salomon, 1985): one's anticipatory schema and one's specific perceptions and emotional reactions to what was past experienced. In some cases, perceptions will appear to reflect the medium's "reality," yet in other cases, perceptions will reflect more strongly people's pre-existing notions and schemata.

If the position is accepted that popular culture is subjectively experienced and meaning is personally constructed, then what predictions would follow and is there any evidence to support these inferences? First, it should be noted that the nature of the research methodology will change. In the future it will be essential to gather data on how youth personally experience and interpret popular culture. Simply looking for links between exposure and subsequent behavior will not provide the required information. Use of interview and ethnographic methodologies would seem most appropriate. The available evidence is sketchy and suggestive at best; however, there are some studies whose methodology and results are consistent with this new perspective. Collins (1983) has found that with young children the social influences of television are not a simple function of on-screen content: age and previous experience influence what is perceived. Sutherland and Siniowsky (1982) found that college students neither seek nor take advice from soap operas. In addition, they found the content of soap operas to represent much more traditional values than many of the medium's critics recognized.

With regard to popular music (rock and roll), three recent studies (Leming, 1987; Prinsky & Rosenbaum, 1987; Rosenbaum & Prinsky, 1987) have found: (a) lyrics are relatively unimportant to youth in the experience of music, (b) in approximately 30 percent of the cases youth have no idea regarding the meaning of the song, (c) adult and youth interpretations of songs vary widely with adult interpretations containing more antisocial content, and (d) youth interpretations of songs and the meaning assigned are highly individual and related to development and experience. Although at this time the research base for this constructivist perspective is eclectic, it is suggestive that this represents a promising new way of studying the nature of youth experience of popular culture.

Sport/Athletic Participation

A final area of leisure research to be examined, that of athletic participation, is also long on speculation and without a solid research base. Three approaches to the relationship between sports and morality have been pursued by researchers: sportsmanship (character traits), social behaviors, and cognitive moral development. First, the research on the character traits associated with sportsmanship, because of a lack of a common understanding of the construct, has been uninformative (Shields & Bredemeier, 1984). Second, research, derived from a social learning perspective, has focused on specific social behaviors such as altruism, honesty, and cooperation. This research has not provided encouraging data with regard to the effect of sport on moral development. Generally, participation in sport has been shown to be associated with decreased prosocial behavior (e.g., Kleiber & Roberts, 1981) and increased anti-social behaviors (e.g., Gelfand & Hartman, 1978).

A third research perspective on the relationship between sport and morality is derived from cognitive developmental theory with a focus on the development of social cognition, that is, how individuals develop in their understanding of the rights and responsibilities of self and others. The most developed perspective on the relationship between sport and moral reasoning is that of Shields and Bredemeier (1984). In a study of the level of social reasoning of 46 male and female college basketball players, Bredemeier and Shields (1984) report that their sample's level of moral reasoning was substantially below that reported for other college samples. In addition, they report that stage of moral reasoning was related to athletic aggression as measured by coaches' evaluations and actual fouls in games. Using Haan's interactional model of moral development, Bredemeier and Shields (1986a) found no moral reasoning differences between high school basketball players and non-athletes. In the same study, using a college sample, nonathletes' moral reasoning was found to be significantly more advanced than athletes' moral reasoning. In both cases, the females in the samples were significantly more advanced in moral reasoning than the males. Using the same sample, Bredemeier and Shields (1986b) also found that moral reasoning about sport is more egocentric than moral reasoning about everyday life. In a related study, Bredemeier (1985) found that high school and college basketball players' moral reasoning levels were inversely related to the number of intentionally injurious sport acts they perceived as legitimate.

Thus it would appear that with regard to sport's influence on character, social behavior, or cognitive moral development, there is no evidence to suggest that it in any consistent or significant way contributes to moral development. Rather the research reviewed found that the moral reasoning of athletes is significantly lower than their peers at the college level, and that among athletes, lower stages of moral reasoning are associated with increased aggression and judgments that intentionally injurious acts are legitimate. In the next section, we turn to some possible reasons for these findings and offer some suggestions for evaluating the potential of different leisure activities for moral development and what leisure professionals might do to enhance this potential.

Conclusions and Discussion

Despite the common adage that popular culture shapes one's values, community service develops social responsibility, and sport builds character, the research reviewed above suggests no such clear effect. The reason for the persistence of these misconceptions lies in overly simplistic understandings of the experience of the leisure activity, the highly variable nature of leisure experiences, and the failure of many leisure experiences to include the dynamics essential for moral development to occur.

The value structure of popular culture is far from monolithic in the United States. While one may find within popular culture examples of egocentrism reaping rewards, rampant violence, and other forms of antisocial behavior, one can also find many examples of concern for others, prosocial actions, and traditional American values. When one adds to the diversity of the value content of popular culture the diversity of the individual experience of culture it is little wonder that clear trends do not emerge regarding its influence on individuals. To the extent that popular culture influences youth, it most likely reinforces existing values of family and/or peer group. The hypodermic model of value transmission that holds that popular culture injects unsuspecting youth with the virus of destructive values is not warranted by the research.

In many respects, the experience of community service is similar to that of popular culture. Clearly not all community service experiences are of equal quality and individuals' motivations and experiences of such service also differ. Motivations for community service may range from to gain rewards (meet girls, get a grade), to parental pressure, to fight for social justices, to help others, etc. While inadvertent learnings may result from community service experiences, they likely will be judged to be successful or unsuccessful by the extent to which they meet personal goals. It is not unusual for youthful naivete regarding social realities to be challenged in community service activities. The result may be cynicism. Of course, some individuals find community service experiences rewarding and productive and as a result have lifelong values shaped. The point is that, just as with popular culture, there is no single type of community service and no uniform experience of that service. As a result, there is no clear effect on moral development found in the research.

The experience of sport is also just as likely to vary widely with regard to the content of the experience and the meanings that are derived by participants. Clearly some sport experiences can be morally developmental to the extent that they contain moral examples and require cooperative endeavor. On the other hand, as Shields and Bredemeier (1984) suggest, sport can be viewed as "bracketed morality," that is, sport can provide a temporary release from the constant demand to coordinate one's own sense of morality with the needs, interests, and perceptions of others. Sport, thus interpreted, frees participants to concentrate on personal goals to the relative neglect of others' interests. A simple example might be a golfer of modest income with a large family who spends, to the detriment of the family, time and money on his golf game. In such a case, sport provides the opportunity for the development of immoral behavior.

Finally, two propositions follow from the above analysis regarding the potential of the leisure experience to foster and moral development and the role of the leisure professional in this process.

First, there is no intrinsically moral dimension to leisure activity. While leisure may, under some circumstances, have morally developmental characteristics, it may just as likely be nonmoral or immoral with regard to its potential to influence moral development. Leisure professionals need to be able to analyze existing leisure experiences in terms of their moral characteristics and potential. Especially, leisure professionals must be able to identify cases where individuals must accommodate self-interest to the interests of the group, where leisure poses cognitive conflict around moral questions, or where clear moral examples or messages are being communicated in speech or action. Professionals must be trained so that they can optimize opportunities for positive moral development and minimize opportunities for negative moral development. In the design and implementation of leisure activities, leisure professionals should have the ability to incorporate those characteristics that would provide the best possible opportunity for moral growth.

Second, since the meaning derived from the leisure experience is personally constructed, leisure professionals must be able to provide opportunities and guidance for leisure participants to reflect on those experiences. One of the strongest predictors of positive student change in experiential education has been the opportunity to engage in discussion with adults and others about the experience (Conrad & Hedin, 1981, 1982). Some degree of skill at aiding reflection and leading discussions is crucial. Knowledge of the language of morality and of different levels of students' moral development would appear to be an important component of the education of leisure professionals.

It is the conclusion of this paper that the experience of leisure activity may, under certain conditions, contribute to moral development; under other conditions, it may not. The knowledge base for leisure professionals to optimize this potential is emerging and, at this time, is sufficient to begin to inform practice. To achieve the potential of leisure activity to foster moral development will require building into the training of leisure professionals a strong emphasis on morality and moral development.

References

Aronfreed, J. (1968). *Conduct and conscience.* New York: Academic Press.

Bandura, A., & Walters, R. H. (1963). *Social learning and personality.* New York: Holt, Rinehart, and Winston.

Bandura, A. (1977). *Social learning theory.* Englewood Cliffs, NJ: Prentice-Hall.

Bloom, A. (1987). *The closing of the American mind.* New York: Simon and Schuster.

Bredemeier, B. (1985). Moral reasoning and the perceived legitimacy of intentionally injurious sport acts. *Journal of Sport Psychology, 7,* 110–124.

Bredemeier, B., & Shields, D. (1984). The utility of moral stage analysis in the investigation of athletic aggression. *Sociology of Sport Journal, 1,* 138–145.

Bredemeier, B., & Shields, D. (1986a). Moral growth among athletes and non-athletes: A comparative analysis. *Journal of Genetic Psychology, 147*(1), 7–8.

Bredemeier, B., & Shields, D. (1986b). Game reasoning and interactional morality. *Journal of Genetic Psychology, 147*(2), 257–275.

Colby, A., Kohlberg, L., Gibbs, J., & Lieberman, M. (1983). A longitudinal study of moral judgment. *Monographs of the Society for Research in Child Development, 48* (1–2, Serial No. 200).

Collins, W. A. (1983). Interpretation and inference in children's television viewing. In J. Bryant & R. Anderson (Eds.), *Children's understanding of television: Research on attention and comprehension* (pp. 125–150). New York: Academic Press.

Conrad, D., & Hedin, D. (1981). *Executive summary of the final report of the Experiential Education Project.* St. Paul, MN: University of Minnesota, Center for Youth Development and Research.

Conrad, D., & Hedin, D. (1982). The impact of experiential education on adolescent development. *Child and Youth Services, 4,* 57–76.

Corbett, F. (1977) The community involvement program: Social service as a factor in adolescent moral and psychosocial development. Doctoral dissertation, University of Toronto.

Durkheim, E. (1925/1973). *Moral education: A study in the theory and application of the sociology of moral education.* New York: Free Press.

Durkin, K. (1985). *Television, sex roles and children: A developmental social psychological account.* Philadelphia: Open University Press.

Enright, R. D., Lapsley, D. L., Harris, D. J., & Shawer, D. J. (1983). Moral development interventions in early adolescence. *Theory into Practice, 22,* 134–144.

Freedman, J. L. (1984). Effect of television violence on aggressiveness. *Psychological Bulletin, 96*(2), 227–246.

Gelfand, D., & Hartman, D. (1978). Some detrimental effects of competitive sports on children's behavior. In R. Magil, M. Ash, & F. Small (Eds.), *Children in sport: A contemporary anthology* (pp. 165–174). Champaign, IL: Human Kinetics.

Gibbs, J. C., & Schnell, S. V. (1985). Moral development "versus" socialization. *American Psychologist, 40,* 1081–1089.

Greenberg, B. S. (1982). Television and role socialization: An overview. In D.

Pearl, L. Bouthilet, & J. Lazar (Eds.), *Television and behavior: Ten years of scientific progress and implications for the eighties.* Rockville, MD: National Institute for Mental Health.

Greeson, L. E., & Williams, R. A. (1986). Social implications of music videos for youth: An analysis of the content and effects of MTV. *Youth and Society, 18*(2), 177–189.

Gunter, B. G. (1987). The leisure experience: Selected properties. *Journal of Leisure Research, 19,* 115–130.

Hoffman, M. (1963). Child rearing practices and moral development: Generalizations from empirical research. *Child Development, 34,* 295–318.

Howitt, D. (1982). *Mass media and social problems.* Oxford: Pergamon Press.

Huesmann, L. R. (1982). Television violence and aggressive behavior. In D. Pearl, L. Bouthilet, & L. Lazar (Eds.), *Ten years of scientific progress and implications for the eighties.* Rockville, MD: National Institute for Mental Health.

Kleiber, D., & Roberts, G. (1981). The effects of sport experience in the development of social character: An exploratory investigation. *Journal of Sport Psychology, 3,* 114–122.

Lawrence, F. C., Tasker, G. E., Daly, C. T., Orhiel, A. L., & Wozniak, P. H. (1986). Adolescents time spent viewing television. *Adolescence, 21*(82), 431–436.

Leming, J. S. (1985). Research in social studies curriculum and interaction: Interventions and outcomes in the socio-moral domain. In W. B. Stanley (Ed.), *Review of research in social studies education: 1977–1983* (pp. 123–213). Washington, DC and Boulder, CO: National Council for the Social Studies and Social Science Education Consortium.

Leming, J. S. (1987). Rock music and the socialization of moral values in early adolescence. *Youth and Society, 18*(4), 363–383.

Lewis, G. H. (1980). Popular music, musical preference, and drug use among youth. *Popular Music and Society, 7*(3), 176–181.

Lewis, G. H. (1981). Toward a uses and gratifications approach: An examination of commitment and involvement in popular music. *Popular Music and Society, 8*(1), 10–18.

Magnusson, D. (1981). Wanted: A psychology of situations. In D. Magnusson (Ed.), *Toward a psychology of situations: An international perspective* (pp. 9–35). Hillsdale, NJ: Lawrence Erlbaum Associates.

Merrow, J. (1985). Children and television: Natural partners. *Kappan, 67*(3), 211–214.

Miller, N. E., & Dollard, J. (1941). *Social learning and imitation.* New Haven, CT: Yale University Press.

Newmann, F. M., & Rutter, R. A. (1983). *Effects of high school community service programs on students' social development.* Final Report to the National Institute of Education (Grant No. NIE-G-81-0009). Madison WI: Wisconsin Center for Educational Research.

Piaget, J. (1932/1965). *The moral judgment of the child.* New York: Free Press.

Prinsky, L. E., & Rosenbaum, J. L. (1987). "Leer-ics" or lyrics: Teenage impressions of rock and roll. *Youth and Society, 18*(4), 384–397.

Reck, J. (1978). *A study of the relationship between participation in school service programs and moral development.* Doctoral Dissertation, St. Louis University.

Rest, J. R. (1979). *Development in judging moral issues.* Minneapolis: University of Minnesota Press.

Roe, K. (1985). Swedish youth and music: Listening patterns and motivations. *Communication Research, 12*(3), 353–362.

Rosenbaum, J., & Prinsky, L. (1987). Sex, violence, and rock and roll: Youth's perceptions of popular music. *Popular Music and Society, 11*(2), 79–89.

Rothenberg, M. B. (1975). Effects of television violence on youth. *Journal of the American Medical Association, 234*, 1043–1046.

Salomon, G. (1985). The study of television in a cross-cultural context. *Journal of Cross-cultural Psychology, 16*(3), 381–397.

Sears, R. R., Maccoby, E. E., & Levin, H. (1957). *Patterns of child rearing.* Evanston, IL: Row, Peterson & Co.

Schlaefli, A., Rest, J., & Thoma, S. (1985). Does moral education improve moral judgment? A meta-analysis of intervention studies using the DIT. *Review of Educational Research, 55*, 319–353.

Schramm, W., Lyle, J., & Parker, E. B. (1961). *Television in the lives of our children.* Palo Alto, CA: Stanford University Press.

Schwartz, D. C., & Mannella, C. J. (1975). Popular music as an agency of political socialization: A study in popular culture and politics. In D. C. Schwartz & S. K. Schwartz (Eds.), *New directions in political socialization* (pp. 209–315). New York: Free Press.

Shields, D., & Bredemeier, B. (1984). Sport and moral growth: A structural developmental perspective. In W. Stroub & J. Williams (Eds.), *Cognitive sport psychology.* New York: Sport Science Associates.

Sutherland, J. C., & Siniowsky, S. J. (1982). The treatment and resolution of moral violations on soap operas. *Journal of Communication, 32*(2), 67–74.

Whiting, B. B., & Whiting, J. W. M. (1975). *Children of six cultures: A psychocultural analysis.* Cambridge, MA: Harvard University Press.

Wicke, P. (1985). Young people and popular music in East Germany: Focus on a scene. *Communication Research, 12*(3), 319–325.

Williams, T. M. (1981). How and what do children learn from television? *Human Communication Research, 7*, 180–192.

Zuckerman, D. M., & Zuckerman, B. S. (1985). Television's impact on children. *Pediatrics, 75*(2), 233–240.

Private vs. Public Recreation Ethics: Is the Vision Different?

Robert M. Wolff

This article has been colored by the incidents that took place since the tanker Exxon Valdez strayed off course and ran aground in Prince William Sound in 1989. Although not all the evidence is in, it appears that Exxon felt it was easier to mislead the Alaskans, break the law, and pay the fines, rather than actually be prepared to deal with a spill of the magnitude of the Valdez spill.

Before the Exxon Valdez, it was a lot easier to believe public and private recreation served similar masters, that the two run parallel tracks, that the two can easily coexist, just as the two Alaskas have: the one that is "America's last frontier, a place of wonder that is virtually unspoiled and a priceless treasure that is largely unspent," and the other, "a land of mining towns, lumberjacks and tourists boats, of developers and exploiters" (Church, 1989). But the oil spill may have shattered the idea that either can easily coexist.

The spill, the response, the attitude, and the government's inaction make it harder to defend the private sector, the benefits provided, or the ability of the private sector to serve (not necessarily better, just serve) the needs of our people.

On the surface, private and public recreation appear to be quite different and apparently traveling different roads. Each seems guided by a different set of acceptable behaviors. Public recreation, in its most basic form, operates within a system supported by taxes and grants and, although certainly affected by an eroded support base, is not usually concerned with survival. Public sector ethics have historically been based on resource management issues, public needs, societal benefits, enrichment of community, promotion of leisure opportunities, enhancement of desirable leisure values, and equity issues of accessibility. The central focus has been the welfare of the entire society, with a certain noble pursuit of preservation and the development (improvement) of the behavior of all residents (Wolff, 1988).

The study of private sector recreation and entrepreneurship changes the focus of ethical and acceptable behavior to the role of the corporation and business ethics. Common belief would have us believe that ethics are somehow inappropriate to any study of business, whether in corporate America or recreational entrepreneurship, that business ethics is an oxymoron, and that the pursuit of profits takes precedent over any concern with ethics. Scandals, kickbacks, environmental abuses, insider trading, etc. certainly support this attitude and make the public wary of the way corporations conduct their business.

A 1985 Roper poll points out that: 65 percent of the public believe that business executives do everything they can to make a profit, even if it means ignoring the public's needs ... and 75 percent of the public agree that business neglects the problems of society (Hennessy, 1986). But still others are quick to point out that it has been that self-interest, that pursuit of profits in our capitalistic society, that has produced the greatest goods at the least cost for the consumers of our society. Bowie (1982) believes it is this pursuit of profits and the ensuing competition that "serves as a meritocratic device allocating scarce resources ... and enables efficient high quality production and hence brings the greatest good for the greatest number." "By meeting consumer demand, business firms are contributing to the public welfare" (1982). To those critics of the private sector, Seligman (1985) warns: "people who counterpose profits and the public interest are not helping the public as much as they think."

We must remember the function of the corporation and subsequently the recreational entrepreneur. Unlike the public sector whose ethics hinge on public welfare, the role of private business, in simple terms, is the satisfaction of consumer wants for goods and services. That role is helping the consumer enjoy the good life, increasing access to a wide variety of choices and not asking them to spend more than necessary (Wolff, 1988).

DeGeorge (1982) thinks that moral responsibility and the application of ethics is only relevant in the macro sense. He cautions: "moral language must be used with care and caution when applied outside the realm of human individuals." A recreational entrepreneur is not just an individual acting morally or immorally but he/she is more akin to a corporation, with Bowie (1982) defining the ethics of a corporation as the maximization of profits while being consistent with universal moral norms of justice and with respect for legitimate individual rights.

The corporation is given its charter by society and, as stated above, its role is to satisfy the wants of society by providing goods and services at a profit. Bowie (1982) continues that although "chartered by society to promote the common good ... it is not chartered to promote its own survival regardless of the cost to society ... there are certain limits to the measures one can take to win the game. When corporations begin to take moral shortcuts, either the government steps in and further constrains business or a Hobbesian state of nature develops in which each business ends up trying to cut the throat of its competitors ... either result undermines the conditions of capitalism." It would seem that Exxon and Eastern Airlines have created both states of affairs.

While most would define murder, lying, and cheating as unethical, that same universality is not apparent when applied to a business venture to determine the role of profits or the protection of the environment (DeGeorge, 1982). Although any given business may have or want to have an enlightened long-term view of morality, ethics, and social responsibility, business conditions may force the firm to focus on the immediate survival of the firm. When only one firm, out of a sense of morality or ethics, embarks on a campaign to address a perceived social responsibility, that firm's products or services are subjected to higher costs because of the time and energy devoted to the project.

In addition, we are subjected to the by-products of successful businesses, like the crowding that takes place on our highways, the pollution caused by our cars, the clear cuts made to support the housing and paper industry or the oil spills made by Exxon. These by-products, called external diseconomies, are a cost that is borne by society (Bowie, 1982). Although we are outraged at the size of the Exxon spill, the response of the company, and the practices that would allow Captain Hazelwood to act as he did, how many of us will give up the lifestyle (cars, books, homes, jets, etc.) that would allow the pipeline to be shut down?

To allow business to meet our demand for products and services, we seem willing (no matter how outraged we are, or how many of us send back our Exxon cards, or vow never to pump gas at Exxon again) to absorb these costs. The individual firm can not and usually does not absorb these costs and stay competitive in the marketplace.

The by-products of a successful commercial recreation operation may be trampling, exceeding carrying capacity, overcrowding, noise, etc. and although the cost is produced by the commercial activity, we as a society should be willing to absorb that cost so the individual firm can continue to meet our need to recreate (Wolff, 1988).

The recreational entrepreneur could make a recreational experience safer, less damaging to the environment, or more developmental; but at what cost?

While it may be in the best interest of a given firm to do any or all of the above, we must recognize that "corporate responsibility requires collective action." Bowie (1982) also tells us that a firm can only "be held morally accountable for events that are within its power," and any "cost that puts it at a competitive disadvantage and hence threatens its survival . . . lies beyond the capacity of the company."

But, while profits may seem to reign supreme, Stroup, Neubert, and Anderson (1987) believe there is "a newly emerging era of corporate responsibility," an era described by DeGeorge (1982) "to weight more factors in their actions than only financial ones." Today, many corporations view social responsibility as investments in the future. Exxon may not have responded as many would have liked and were clearly wrong in this case. At what price is the environment worth protecting? As long as we demand oil, there may never be a completely safe way of delivering it to the pump.

This new era has been ushered in because of an enlightened self-interest, one that looks to the long-term enhancement of company profits. Any company that wishes to survive into the future must look to the future. The business literature is full of tips to enhance repeat business, customer satisfaction, and social responsibility.

The new era is typified by the long-term view Johnson and Johnson took in their 1979 revised code of ethics after one of their products was implicated in the deaths of several people. The code stated that "their primary responsibility was to protect consumers, above the interests of stockholders, employees and others." Johnson and Johnson is not alone as "most major companies have taken the first step in constructing ethics programs by developing written codes" (Hennessy, 1986). There is also good news for the environment as Hennessy notes that "environmental auditing is perhaps the fastest growing type of company self-regulation practiced in today's business world . . . in an attempt to anticipate future environmental problems."

The "buyer beware" philosophy has seen better days. For business to survive, to remain possible, most businesses must behave with a certain morality, creating trust in the marketplace; otherwise, business transactions would become difficult, expensive, and perhaps impossible (Bowie, 1982). Firms can not let the "buyer beware" if they are to establish or maintain any kind of reputation. Our society is too information rich for most firms to be successful in the long run without a policy concerned with customer satisfaction and trust. As long as businesses have this view then the concern of Dustin, McAvoy, and Schultz (1987) that parks and recreation in its current market-oriented mode is drifting toward a "merchant mentality," losing sight of such things as preservation and the development of the individual, is not really a concern.

To the question "Are the overriding ethical guidelines different in the public and private sector?" it would seem the differences are minor and the gap is closing. The biggest problem exists when an individual firm is put at a competitive disadvantage; but there too, just as we address certain concerns by public action, we can and should respond with collective action when an action threatens an important or valuable part of our world.

Suffice it to say that both public and private providers are serving recreational needs expressed in the marketplace and that is what both public and private recreation has always been in the business of doing: serving recreational needs no matter how small when expressed in the marketplace. Any good recreation text (public or private) will have as its center piece a section on assessing market needs and wants to provide the services and products that best serve select target markets.

From a macro point of view, who can place a greater value on "one river runner" vs. 100 riders on a commercial raft? Both are exposed to the outdoors, both experiences contribute to the leisure welfare of the population, and both will provide the participants stories to carry home. As stated earlier, "people who counterpose profits and the public interest are not helping the public as much as they think."

The individual river runner is rewarded for his/her independent functioning and the commercial users may be getting their first exposure to a lifelong experience. We all benefit when more people are exposed to the grandeur of the great outdoors, because it is an enlightened and exposed populace that empowers us in both the public and private sector by providing leisure dollars and tax dollars to enable us to continue to enjoy recreational experiences. Who is to say the commercial raft rider of today will not be tomorrow's defender of our recreational land and wildlife.

References

Bowie, N. (1982). *Business ethics*. Englewood Cliffs, NJ: Prentice-Hall, Inc.

Church, G. J. (1989, April). The big spill. *Time, 133*(10), 38–42.

DeGeorge, R. T. (1982). *Business ethics*. New York: Macmillan Publishing Co.

Hennessy, E. L. (1986, October). "Business ethics: Is it a priority for corporate America?" *FE: The Magazine for Financial Executives, 2*, 14–19.

Seligman, D. (1985, October). The Menace of Ethics. *Fortune, 112*, 197–198.

Stroup, M. A., Neubert, R. L., & Anderson, J. W. Jr. (1987, March-April). Doing good, doing better: Two views of social responsibility. *Business Horizons, 30*, 22–25.

Wolff, R. M. (1988, October). Beware the public mentality: Ethical dilemmas for the recreational entrepreneur. *Leisure Today*, 56–58.

Methods for Teaching Ethics in Leisure Studies Curricula

Leandra A. Bedini and
Karla A. Henderson

A renewed concern has surfaced within higher education during the past twenty years regarding the university's and educator's responsibility for the ethical development of students. As Fleischaur (1984) and others have noted, educators have a stake in preserving the social order and, thus, helping people confront their daily personal and professional decisions about right and wrong and good and bad. Since students today will be citizens and professionals in the future, it is beneficial to address how ethical behavior can be developed through using appropriate teaching methods. The purpose of this paper is to delineate strategies and to describe specific methods that may be used in leisure and recreation studies curricula to develop both professional and personal ethics in university students.

Two dimensions of ethics, professional and personal, have relevance for leisure studies. The essence of professional ethics is the guidance of conduct and what an individual or a professional perceives to be right and good (Callahan, 1980). Professional ethics relates to what one ought to do, one's duty, as a member of a socially responsible profession, which includes one's responsibility to consumers, to the profession, and to society (Pelegrino, Hart, Henderson, Loeb, & Edwards, 1985). Personal ethics refers to moral values as they may or may not affect one's role as a professional. Morality often refers to an individual's definition of right and wrong. To act morally or ethically is to act according to principles held by an individual as the "right" thing to do. Thus, ethics not only encompasses beliefs and attitudes, but also represents behaviors as they are embodied in professional and personal living.

Justification for Teaching Ethics in Higher Education

In today's society, it appears that while the development of useful skills is a reasonable expectation of higher education, universities and colleges ought also to produce thoughtful citizens with moral character, and not just technically trained workers, if all human lives are to be enriched (Morrill, 1980; Robertson & Grant, 1982). While salable skills are important, the devotion to truth and critical intellect, as well as moral obligation and personal responsibility (Lahey, 1985), are also important.

Studying ethics, however, does not result in a moral life any more than studying medicine assures health (Loewy, 1986). Through structured educational processes and specifically designed methods, it is possible to develop ethical behavior within students that will become tacit knowledge. One does not learn professional ethics by "on-the-job" training alone.

According to Frazer (1986), the ultimate goal of education is that students should put their opinions and beliefs into action. Educators can present ways to enable students to evaluate and reevaluate their own personal and professional ethical behavior. By presenting a variety of perspectives, by providing critical skills for analyzing behavior, and by providing opportunities to practice one's beliefs and commitments, educators can help students to examine their personal and professional ethical responsibilities. According to Callahan (1980), the goal in teaching ethics is not to seek behavior change but to assist students in development of their insights, skills, and perspectives that set the stage for a life of personal and professional responsibility.

Strategies for Teaching Ethics in Higher Education

Students tend to oversimplify many of the problems they encounter. Further, while many students can articulate their own value system, many are not aware of the ethical issues that may confront them as professionals. They also may have trouble articulating the reasons for the moral judgments that they make. Students, therefore, need to develop skills in thinking carefully, asking relevant questions, articulating the basis for their decisions, and testing their decisions for consistency (Carroll, 1986). For the educator to teach ethics effectively, she/he will need to provide information along with analytical skills and the opportunity for the student to put this knowledge to use under structured supervision (Loewy, 1986).

Different opinions exist regarding whether students should take a separate course on ethics within a field of study or whether ethics should be included within each professional course. For the field of leisure studies, the latter solution is preferable given the limited resources available and because of the breadth of issues that need to be explored. One course alone is not sufficient to address the personal and professional ethical dilemmas that a student may encounter as a professional and as a citizen.

Educators' behavior can affect the learning of ethics by how they set the tone, establish what is important, ascertain what is legitimate, and delimit what merits the time and attention of students. Unfortunately, faculty are often so focused on the transmission of knowledge and skills within their chosen discipline that they neglect helping students become more mature, morally perceptive human beings (Bok, 1988). A commitment is needed on the part of the instructors to enrich their own ethical understanding so that means for accomplishing the goals of teaching ethics to students can be found. The educator will want to create an environment within which students can address the basic question, "What, all things considered, ought to be done?" (Howe, 1986).

For students to answer this question, specific areas need to be addressed through instruction. It is not difficult to uncover ethical issues that the leisure studies instructor can present for classroom analysis and individual consideration. Personal skills that are related to ethics in all areas of leisure services include: compassion, truth-telling, competence, social responsibility, and behavior control. In addition, therapeutic recreation professionals often are concerned with client-oriented issues such as confidentiality and nonmalfeasance. The community recreation administrator must be concerned with issues related to drug and alcohol abuse among employees and crowd control. Basically, any decision that one might encounter in one's personal or professional life that addresses right or wrong could be a potential ethical issue to be discussed. The purpose of addressing the issues is to help students identify ethical situations, to enable them to ask the relevant questions about the situations, and to assist them in applying reasoned solutions to the ethical dilemmas. It is particularly important that students understand that the end results are not justified by the means in most personal and professional situations.

The goal of ethical development is to enable students to make tacit and implicit decisions concerning professional and personal issues. This is a long-term teaching goal that may be undertaken through various activities during a given academic term. Merely telling students "what's right" and what one "ought to do," however, is not enough. One cannot learn values/morality through only lectures, books, or "mind to mind" encounters. The affective aspects of ethical behavior as well as the

cognitive aspects can be addressed through consciousness-raising activities, experiential opportunities, democratic classrooms, and decision-making exercises (Evans, 1987). These might include the use of
role playing, case studies, and other problem-solving techniques. Prac-
tical/participatory methods are also needed that can be accomplished
by allowing students to experience social responsibility through assignments (Lickona, 1980). Supervised practical experience in the community through advocacy, community service, and internships may be
a way to teach specific skills and to help future professionals develop
a social conscience and a social consciousness (McGothlin, 1970). The
following methods are offered as examples of how personal and professional ethics might be emphasized using experiential activities both
inside and outside the classroom.

Advocacy

Advocacy is the process of speaking or acting on behalf of another.
Advocacy is directed toward the support of an individual or group
viewpoint, program, or ideological position (Edginton, Compton, & Hanson, 1980). The process of advocacy allows students to act on their
values and experience first hand the potential for social responsibility
within their communities and their profession. By assuming different
advocacy roles, students have an opportunity to test their convictions
and ability to initiate social change and empower others for whom they
are advocating.

Within a classroom, the instructor can help students understand advocacy roles through class discussion. These roles might include the
initiation of community programs, investigation or fact-finding, lobby-
ing, or being a mediator. The instructor may also assist students in
finding advocacy possibilities and encouraging them to become involved
in these roles. As an assignment within a course, a written and oral
advocacy report might be required by the instructor. Processing an
advocacy project, from the identification of the need to the evaluation
phase, can help students integrate the social responsibilities that they
have as citizens and as professionals.

Community Service

Community service and volunteering are beneficial to society and the
individual and provide opportunities for personal and professional development for students. Many values are evident in having community
service assignments as part of the leisure and recreation studies course-
work. The biggest short-term outcome is the experience a student will
get in "people" skills. If the student is a leisure and recreation studies

major, the volunteering can be valuable as experience for future employment. Further, students usually have had little experience in community service and can gain practice in skills related to future vocations and avocations. Skills learned will enable them to volunteer in future situations.

Whether an instructor in a leisure studies curriculum selects community service as an experiential education learning option will depend upon the course objectives, the community, the cooperation of volunteer agencies, the time available, and the willingness of the instructor to integrate the experiences into the classroom. The effort is well worth the time invested if the development of social responsibility and ethical behavior in students is really sought.

Practicums and Internships

For many leisure studies students, practicums, internships, and fieldwork provide the culminating experience of their professional preparation. Ethics is only one of many issues that may arise as a result, but ethical issues can be "teachable moments" for the leisure studies educator before, during, and after such experience.

Instructors should make sure students understand the issue of ethics prior to the internship, that ethical issues are addressed directly and not ignored during the course of the internship, and that opportunities are given for students to share their experiences in a summative manner for analysis at the completion of the internship. As was indicated before, practicing ethical behavior is one of the best ways to become good at it.

Case Studies

The case study is a method that has been used effectively by many disciplines in addressing ethical situations that students may encounter as future professionals. The technique involves presenting scenarios or situations which involve ethical dilemmas and allowing students to apply standards of practice to these real situations. These cases help to address the affective-attitudinal dimensions of ethics as well as the cognitive aspects of the standard of practice (Howe, 1986). Students find case studies interesting, of practical significance, realistic, and illustrative of the complexity of issues. The "absolutes" that may be apparent concerning professional ethics may take on a different perspective when they are presented in a situational context. Therefore, it is important that the students understand the principles surrounding the practice in which they are involved and are able to make informed judgments concerning how they will address particular situations within case studies.

Problem-solving Techniques

Related closely to case studies are other problem-solving techniques. McMinn (1988) found that a computer simulation program using case studies was effective in allowing students to work with alternatives that they might encounter in addressing a particular situation. Computer programs may be designed to pose alternatives within ethical dilemmas from which the student can choose. These simulations also help them to analyze the consequences of particular alternatives chosen. This technique might be considered as a method of teaching ethics by trial and error within a problem-solving context.

Another problem-solving method that might be used is the nominal group technique (NGT). This is a structured group activity in which qualitative information is obtained from a target group of individuals. The leader must be a task master in ensuring that each individual is involved in identifying issues that may surround a problem. For example, McElreath (1982) used the nominal group technique in her public relations class. She presented a lecture on ethics, used NGT to determine issues, used NGT to develop strategies for addressing these issues, and discussed and critiqued the strategies at the end.

Role Playing

Role playing may also be used as an instructional method to enhance ethical decision making and problem solving. Similar to the case study, a situation must be developed; but rather than using discussion, the students will act out the situation. The ethical dilemma is given to the student and he/she is asked "What would you do?" In this way, students experience the actual conflict as they attempt to resolve the situation. These role plays may be done in high stress/quick reaction situations wherein the students have to make a spur of the moment ethical decision (Herring, 1985) or the role playing may be used after a more structured problem-solving discussion is held. The instructor must allow sufficient time for the class to analyze the situation, determine the issues, explain why the judgments were made, and discuss how the ethical decisions might be applied with consistency in other situations.

Conclusions and Recommendations

Methods that faculty in leisure studies curricula can use to enhance ethical behavior in students have been identified. Units in courses that address ethics can help define and clarify ethical issues; students who take courses that encompass units on ethical issues report that they feel more confident about their abilities to make ethical decisions (Pelegrino et al., 1985). The argument has been made that higher education, and particularly curricula in leisure studies, have an obligation to address personal and professional issues as an important part of education for professional competence as well as for informed citizenship.

The goal of professional education ought to be the development of the capacity not only to think ethically, but also to act ethically (Lickona, 1980). The university of the future must find connections between knowledge and human values or it will fail to provide students with the lifelong skills that they need (Muscatine, 1970). Educators have an obligation to transmit information that will improve society, practice, and individuals. Teaching personal and professional ethics through experiential methods may be one way to assure that leisure studies will make a contribution to "the preservation of civilization and the social order" (Fleischaur, 1984, p. 114).

References

Bok, D. (1988, March). *The university's responsibility in ethics teaching.* Paper presented at Duke University, Durham, NC.

Callahan, D. (1980). Goals in the teaching of ethics. In D. Callahan & S. Bok (Eds.), *Ethics teaching in higher education* (pp. 61–74). New York: Plenum Press.

Carroll, M. A. (1986, August). *A philosophical perspective on teaching ethics to undergraduate psychology majors.* Paper presented at the Annual Convention of the American Psychological Association.

Edginton, C. R., Compton, D. M., & Hanson, C. J. (1980). *Recreation and leisure programming: A guide for the professional.* Philadelphia: Saunders College.

Evans, N. (1987). A framework for assisting student affairs staff in fostering moral development. *Journal of Counseling and Development, 66*(4) 191–194.

Fleischaur, J. (1984). Back to the cave: Social responsibility in liberal arts education. *Liberal Education, 70*(2), 113–119.

Frazer, M. J. (1986). Teaching styles. In M. J. Frazer & A. Kornhaurer (Eds.), *Ethics and social responsibility in science education* (pp. 141–147). Oxford: Pergamon Press.

Herring, D. (1985). Role playing shows pitfalls of quick decisions. *Journalism Education, 40*(2), 27–30.

Howe, K. R. (1986). A conceptual basis for ethics in teacher education. *Journal of Teacher Education, 37*(3), 5–12.

Lahey, M. (1985). Training in values and ethics in the health and human services fields—Research update. *Parks and Recreation, 20*(4), 28–33.

Lickona, T. (1980). What does moral psychology have to say to the teacher of ethics? In D. Callahan & S. Bok (Eds.), *Ethics teaching in higher education* (pp. 103–132). New York: Plenum Press.

Loewy, E. H. (1986). Teaching medical ethics to medical students. *Journal of Medical Education, 61*(8), 661–665.

McElreath, M. P. (1982, July). *Using the NGT to teach ethics in public relations.* Paper presented to the Association for Education in Journalism, Athens, OH.

McGothlin, W. J. (1970). *Patterns of professional education.* New York: G. P. Putnam's Sons.

McMinn, M. R. (1988). Ethics case study simulation: A generic tool for psychology teachers. *Teaching of Psychology, 15*(2), 100–101.

Morrill, R. L. (1980). *Teaching values in college.* San Francisco: Jossey-Bass Publisher.

Muscatine, C. (1970). The future of university education as an idea. In A. S. Nash (Ed.), *Choice before the humanities* (pp. 1-25). Durham, NC: Regional Education Laboratory for the Carolinas and Virginia.

Pelegrino, E. D., Hart, R. J., Henderson, S. R., Loeb, S. E., & Edwards, G. (1985). Relevance and utility of courses in medication ethics/A survey of physicians' perceptions. *Journal of the American Medical Association, 253,* 49–53.

Robertson, E., & Grant, G. (1982). Teaching and ethics. *Journal of Higher Education, 53*(3), 345–357.

The Recreational Context of Moral Development for Adolescents

Kelly Wilhelm

How does recreation contribute to the moral growth of adolescents? To answer this question, the writer analyzed data, including reports, newsletters, press releases, and daily records collected over a ten-year period of work in four different therapeutic recreational settings with adolescents. Qualitative methodology was used and data were analyzed inductively. This study concludes with a call to recreators who work with youth.

Peter Blos (1941) said the tasks of adolescence are emancipation from family, acceptance of sex role, and economic independence. Blos stated that the most important contribution toward an adolescent's growth lies in social experiences, community participation, and vocational planning. A teenager needs to learn to think through potentialities, needs, and aspiratións as a sexually mature person, as a family member, and as an individual.

Maria Harris (1981) underscored two main issues concerning adolescence and moral development. The first is that the environment of youth, with its political, social, and cultural dynamic, is the starting point for understanding young people. The second is that human beings know far more than they are able to say. Awe, exultation, ecstasy, and death shatter the boundaries of speech and silence. The most profound of life's happenings cannot be stated.

Recreation programming contributes to the accomplishment of the tasks of emancipation from family, acceptance of sex role, and economic independence. Recreation programming acts as a moral force in the lives of youth by providing opportunities for social interaction, for learning leisure and work skills, and for participating in the community.

Different contexts shift the foci of developmental issues for youth. This study examined adolescents in acute clinical settings who experience a crisis of health, adjudicated adolescents residing in a youth home, multihandicapped adolescents who participate in a community recreation program, and adolescents who participate in a youth ministry program. Each context, the youth involved, and the types of recreation programs were described. The contribution of recreation to the moral development was shown.

The programs for multihandicapped adolescents were designed to be fun as well as to learn social amenities, to increase physical abilities, and to function competently in the community. Youth were challenged to be all they could be while challenging fellow citizens of the city to accept them for all they could contribute. Mainstreaming and normalization in recreation programming demanded growth in physical, social, emotional, and moral domains for these young people. They were learning to be part of a wider community.

The other three groups had different needs. The youth in the hospital demanded psychological and physiological support. Juvenile delinquents needed support, discipline, and structure. Kids in youth ministry programs wanted the spiritual dimension of their lives addressed.

What united these disparate groups? What was similar in these different programs with different goals? How did recreation contribute to the moral development of these youth?

Recreational activities contributed to fulfillment of the legitimate needs, drives, and desires of teenagers. Recreational activities provided an avenue for youth to express the pain and the ecstasy in their lives. Recreational activities grounded youth in their own time and place with social opportunities, work opportunities, and freedom opportunities.

Thus, recreation contributed to the moral development of youth. Teenagers develop physically, psychologically, and socially as they engage in normal activities. The moral dimension of growth is addressed implicitly because contribution to normal growth in context is contribution to the moral growth of youth.

This paper ends with a call to recreation professionals to continue recreation programs for youth which address their developmental needs and thus contribute to their moral development. Consideration of context is important. Caring leadership is crucial. Attention to the goal of becoming a contributing member of local, national, and world communities is vital.

References

Blos, P. (1941) *Adolescent personality*. New York: Appleton Century Croft.
Harris, M. (1981). *Portrait of youth ministry*. New York: Paulist Press.

An Ethical Perspective of Recreation and Leisure Services in a Northern Cross-Cultural Environment

Gerald A. Bruce

History is being written in the Canadian North, right now as we speak. Northern Canada, and specifically the Yukon Territory, is at this writing attempting to achieve what few have ever achieved—a fair and equitable land claim settlement with the aboriginal peoples of the territory.

A land claim agreement is close. At this writing only the signature of the Canadian government is needed for the settlement to go to band to band final agreements. Now, as never before, people are talking about and discussing the following issues: Who amongst us have rights that may differ from others? If their rights are defensible, then upon whose shoulders falls the duty to meet the obligations that will satisfy the rights? If a right is determined and a duty designated, what entitlements follow, and who ought to be responsible to provide for the entitlements? If entitlements are determined, to what extent and for what time period will those entitlements be valid and binding on the dutyholders? What scope of compensation is fair and what external organizational structures and controls are required to ensure that the entitlements are delivered to those deserving?

The people of the Yukon are on the brink of significant change. They will soon be faced with the mighty task of translating ethical considerations into practical administrative policy and procedure and, more importantly, melding two peoples into one harmonious whole. It will require the best efforts of the entire community.

What role if any will the recreation and leisure field have in such a scenario?

One purpose of this paper is to argue that recreation and leisure services do have a role. That role is to play a part in the larger community development process, that purpose being, "to create a safe, healthy, happy and stable community." Further, I will argue that to accomplish this task, this field must be based on values consistent with meeting the human needs of our society. Third, I will argue that recreation and leisure services can legitimately be encouraged and funded by governments as an ethically proper thing to do.

In the process of discussing these topics I will address two major ethical questions:

1. Does nonnative society intervene in the development of the native people of the Canadian North?
2. Should government utilize recreation, parks, and leisure services as a "tool" in the larger process of overall community development?

Historical Perspective

There are two primary players in the land claims process, the native and the nonnative, who function under significantly different value systems and thus view the past from different perspectives. This is not unreasonable when you consider that the native people in the Yukon have had very short exposure to white culture.

In some parts of the Yukon, native people saw white people for the first time as late as the early 1940s and the arrival of the Alaska Highway. It is important to realize that less than 50 years ago, our northern natives were in effect free, nomadic, self-sufficient people living literally from the land and trading periodically with white people. To some of the people of the southern Canadian provinces and to the people of the United States this may be new information. The northern natives have not been exposed to the white society for very long in comparison to the exposure the southern natives have had. Since this initial exposure they have undergone dramatic change. They are no longer nomadic, no longer self-sufficient, no longer proud, and certainly no longer masters of their own destiny.

Beginning earlier, throughout Canada, the impact of exposure to white civilization and the resultant diseases, the reserve system, residential school system, and the Indian Act all combined to destroy native Indian culture. Native people, by government fiat, were made wards of the government of Canada, and personal basic rights and privileges were removed supposedly for their own benefit. Indian agents were assigned, the privilege of voting withheld, children legislated to white religious schools, their language taken from them, their ways of worship taken, and substituted in their place were the white Victorian belief systems and the values of the white culture.

During the time this was happening to native people the nonnative population of settlers, believing the land was open for grabs, moved into tribal areas and settled. Nonnative interests developed the land, cut down the trees, dug up the resources, and raised the Canadian to one of the highest standards of living in the Western world from land that was never properly acquired from the native people.

It is important to note here that the Yukon native people never were defeated in battle and never entered into any treaties with Canada.

Residential schools, the Alaska Highway, major hydro-electric projects, petroleum megaprojects, pipelines, and the ancillary commercial developments brought northern native people into real contact with the white culture.

Native people believe the white leadership "stole" the land from the native people and has never properly compensated native people. Second, through a "reserve" system and a "residential school system" it is claimed that cultural genocide would be a more accurate definition of the intent of the Canadian government for the Indian people instead of their salvation. The native people lost touch with their own nativeness without surrender and without their consent.

The Canadian educational system to this day does not teach the history of our native peoples and how the native lands were acquired. Thus there is significant ignorance of these issues, which has contributed greatly to a lack of understanding of what is involved in the current land claims issues by the nonnative public in general.

The issues at stake are as follows: Who owes what to whom? And how much is owed? What is the debt or duty of the Canadian people to make a proper settlement with the native communities of the Yukon? What price is to be paid in 1989 for land seized in 1871?

In short, what duties and obligations ought to be recognized to compensate for lost "rights"? Such a settlement is designed to recognize and define aboriginal title and privileges that have previously gone undefined.

As the duties and obligations are defined, and as rights are recognized and translated into entitlements and obligations, we will see the evolution of new forms of governance in Canada and experience the impact of significant change.

In the Yukon, the settlement talks have been under way for the last 16 years. Now, in 1989, the government of Canada, the Yukon territorial government, and the Council of Yukon Indians are about to settle.

Previous negotiations have created a framework agreement acceptable to all parties, and the next two years are set aside for band to band final agreements that will achieve, in detail, a document agreeable between the respective governments and the native people of the Yukon.

It is in such a milieu that we will consider the potential role of recreation and leisure services.

Values Inherent in Recreation and Leisure

Recreation as a tool in the overall development of a community can significantly contribute by offering positive values and healthy attitudes to citizens on a daily basis. Healthy alternatives to alcohol and drugs, breaking and entering, unemployment, unsupervised parties, loneliness, and feelings of low esteem are essential to developing healthy communities.

This writer believes that a strong and ethically sound emphasis on recreation and leisure service values would be a positive investment in the development of any community. What are some of the values we in the recreation and leisure field ought to encourage?

Basic to recreation and leisure services is the concept of fair play and voluntary activity. Exposure to the values inherent in the pursuit of creative and performing arts, music, physical education, sports, and outdoor and wilderness adventure is badly needed. In essence, the values inherent in the leisure experience are ethically "good" values, values that contribute to healthy individuals and ultimately healthy communities.

We would indeed be remiss not to note here that the recreation field can benefit from the values traditional to native communities. In my experience those values would include a continuing love of children, a true belief in the value of the family unit, and a firm belief in the need to nourish and care for the environment.

The value of recreation and leisure opportunities specific to native people of the Canadian North appears when we realize that currently the native people do not have the training or resources to assist themselves fully to develop their communities. It is primarily the nonnative that has the necessary resources. Therefore, through the government, we ought to assist with leadership, programs, and facilities delivered in a community development framework.

In many cases alcohol and the television set have become the major recreation activity in native communities. The recreation and leisure field offers a great deal more.

To be frank, I see no better way for us to bridge the cultures in an unthreatening and positive way than through recreation and leisure opportunities.

Back to the Ethical Questions

Ethics, morality, fairness, proper behavior. Choose any of these words and you will find that you can use them interchangeably. In essence the concept of ethics is based on the idea of there being some rules of conduct by which we judge our actions. The proper action ought to bring happiness, security, fairness, and social equity to those involved. Improper action will cause hurt and inequity in the same circumstance.

One cannot discuss the word "ethics" without the word "moral" coming up. Moral introduces the notion of distinguishing between right and wrong behavior and dealing with the regulation of conduct founded on current laws of the society.

Why then is it right for you or me to intervene in anyone's life? And in terms of this paper, why should any "field of endeavor" feel some compulsion to intervene?

Ina Corrine Brown discussed this issue in a 1950 paper (Murrow, 1952). She felt several values to be critical to life. One was her need to be concerned with her own positive perception of herself; a second was the idea that the one thing that really matters is to be bigger than the things that can happen to you. She felt that nothing that can happen to you is half so important as the way in which you meet it.

She noted that "nobody can be sure when disaster, disappointment, injustice or humiliation may come to him through no fault of his own. Nor can one be guaranteed against one's own mistakes. But the way we meet life is ours to choose and when integrity, fortitude, dignity and compassion are the choices, the things that can happen to us lose their power over us."

Of relevance to this paper was her next statement, because she expanded her comments from individual responsibility for our own ethical behavior to a level of community responsibility:

> It is one's duty and obligation to help create a social order in which persons are more important than things, ideas more precious than gadgets, and in which individuals are judged by their personal worth. Moreover, for this judgement to be fair, human beings must have an opportunity for the fullest development of which they are capable. One is thus led to work for a world of freedom and justice through those social agencies and institutions which make it possible for people everywhere to realize their highest potentialities.

In a separate article in the same publication, Carroll commented "I don't think I'm my brother's keeper. But I do think I am obligated to be his helper. And he has the same obligation to me" (Murrow, 1952).

A final thought may be offered by Nelson Glueck: "It has become ever clearer to me that danger is far from disaster, that defeat may be the forerunner of victory, and that, in the last analysis, all achievement is perilously fragile unless based on enduring principles of moral conduct" (Murrow, 1952).

Justice, fairness, honesty, integrity, and keeping and fulfilling one's agreements are the stuff ethics is made of. How we assist in building a world to secure these things is a challenge to all of us. I believe the recreation and leisure services field is uniquely positioned to assist in this task.

Ethical Questions

1. *Should society intervene in the development of the native people of the Canadian North?* The answer, simply put, is yes! We have already intervened. It is too late to change that. That intervention has in many cases had a very negative impact on the native people.

A practical example is the effect that television channels from the South can have promoting pop, chips, chocolate bars, and other high profile profitable items. In northern communities, nutrition is a problem. The long winters plus the difficulty of isolation means that fresh fruit and vegetables are expensive when available. Children and adults alike watch television and are significantly influenced; when given the choice, they will often choose pop and chips, of no food value, over fruit and juices.

Parental guidance, or pleas from educators and the health profession, are to date no competition for advanced media advertisements.

In addition, from an economic development and business perspective, the mark-up on pop may be as much as 150 percent while on an orange or apple it may be a nominal 30 percent. Do we sacrifice profit and financial stability for a healthier population? In a country of free choice, where individual free choice is king, economic realities and values related to financial success currently outweigh the value of healthy eating.

Canadian research on Indian reserves has clearly shown that malnutrition has a significant impact on school performance. Pop, chips, and chocolate bars do not a student make!

Of even greater importance is the effect of videos. In the North, where the long nights are real, the television and VCR have become the major recreation diversion. Videos, some good, but some pure uncut pornography, are available to all on a 24-hour basis. Their use is, in my opinion, in direct proportion to the lack of healthy recreational alternatives available throughout the community and to the lack of competent leadership to assist people to deal with their leisure time.

With few organized and healthy opportunities for youth or adults, and with the reality of excess alcohol easily available, it is not difficult to recognize the resultant sexual violence evident. It is only recently that this topic has even been raised, let alone dealt with!

Alcohol, pornography, and potent advertisements to buy the things important to a southern economy all combine to be a tremendous influence on northern populations.

It is my contention that our choices now lie in the wise choice of actions we "ought" to take to best overcome the negative impacts of the past and assist the native people to cope with the long-term future.

2. *Should government utilize the recreation, parks, and leisure field as a tool in the process to overcome the negative impacts from the past by encouraging and supporting values that will strengthen the native people in the future?* Yes!

The role of recreation and leisure so critical in these times of stress ought to be as a tool in the larger community development process.

The North is in a crisis in my judgment, and for the government to utilize the leisure field for positive human purposes is ethically sound and defensible in our society.

I believe that history teaches us that previous governments have felt the need to support recreation and leisure opportunities during times of crisis or depression as a legitimate government service. Government interaction utilizing recreation as a tool in assisting communities is not new. Richard Kraus (1983), in his paper to the Academy of Leisure Services, outlined a critically important aspect of one of the issues here, the issue of the role of government.

Kraus suggested that the recreation, parks, and leisure field has essentially departed from the human goals evolving from the 1960s. He stated that the current leadership in the field values goals concerned with the efficient management of park and recreation facilities and other management functions. His basic message was a call for new approaches to organized community-based recreation, park, and leisure services and more sharply defined values unique to this field.

It is the opinion of this writer that as we drift from meeting basic human values as the justification of this field to valuing the "business" model of efficiency and productivity, we lose the support of the ordinary people. A return to valuing "ways of achieving a fuller sense of community, integrating the generations and people of varying backgrounds, enriching the quality of life, and numerous other outcomes of this kind" (Kraus, p. 80) is critical.

In regard to the recreation and leisure field, the government ought to be encouraged to see recreation and leisure opportunities as significant players in bridging the cultures. For example, to encourage the arts in particular as the vehicle through which the native culture, mores, traditions, myths, and language can be promoted in a healthy fashion— this is right! This is good! Also, to encourage the sports in which native people excel and experience the personal pride and dignity attached to performing well—this is right! This is good!

In my opinion, the values mentioned previously are more easily taught in the recreation environment than in any other environment.

Conclusion

Identifying the value base for recreation, parks, and leisure services is of critical importance so that the field can in fact stand for something.

Right now I agree with Richard Kraus, that the citizens of my country and yours are wondering why they should support this field. It is our challenge to answer this question.

When this field was "ought" oriented it appeared to have public support. For example, we ought to have playgrounds for kids, we ought to have programs for seniors, we ought to have places for people to breathe in the middle of large cities, we ought to involve people in decisions that affect their leisure. The field was "ought driven" and in return received community recognition and support.

When the field became more professional in nature and appeared less value-driven from a public perspective I believe public support was to some degree lost. When expediency and businesslike behavior became its reason for being it became "expediency driven." It is more expedient for us to make the decisions for the people instead of involving them. We are the professionals; it is our business to plan for leisure. The issue of professionalism discussed in Goodale and Witt (1980) addressed this point to some extent.

I believe we ought to speak loudly and clearly about what we believe to be the oughts in life—in this case, the oughts as they relate to safety, health, nutrition, sporting behavior, care of the wilderness, concern for single parent families trying to raise children in a high-cost/high-pressure society, to name but a few.

In addition, it is critically important to realize that in all of this we are only a "part" of the larger "whole." Recreation people ought not to isolate themselves behind programming and facilities as their reason for being, when programming and facilities are simply "tools" or methods by which we develop people and communities.

Recreation people are really "community developers" using recreation as their tool for intervention, as much as the planners and economic developers are really "community developers" utilizing their unique training, background, and abilities to create safe, happy, healthy, and stable communities. Some would believe this is a noble role in a troubled world.

In terms of the Canadian North, the role of the recreation, parks, and leisure services is to actively assist government and native leaders to bridge the gap between cultures, to utilize the unique opportunities we offer during leisure time to build people and communities.

I believe we "ought" to be held accountable for what we say we believe in. If we do not identify with morally sound and ethically right societal values, we have no right to solicit public funds and perpetuate a valueless profession.

I will close with Ina Corrine Brown's previous comment: "One is thus led to work for a world of freedom and justice through those social agencies and institutions which make it possible for people everywhere to realize their highest potentialities." It is my contention that the recreation and leisure services field can do just this.

References

Goodale, T. L., and Witt, P. (Eds.). *Recreation and leisure: Issues in an era of change*. State College, PA: Venture Publishing Inc.

Kraus, R. (1983). *Values and leisure: Trends in leisure services*. State College, PA: Venture Publishing Inc.

Murrow, E. R. (1952). *This I believe, the personal philosophies of 100 thoughtful men and women*. New York: Simon and Schuster Inc.

Section Three

Epilogue

It is reasonable to expect that here, at the end, there should be some closure or synthesis to the diverse set of writings included in the text. Yet, this expectation is unfounded in that the authors were not asked to collaborate in the construction of a single or coherent thesis. In contrast this text represents the interpretation of individuals who have given thought to the ideas associated with leisure, ethics, and philosophy. The value or sturdiness of any particular chapter or idea will therefore remain self-evident as it becomes the subject of continued reflection and work.

This section does include the 1990 Jay B. Nash Scholar Lecture, along with a brief closing comment. The Nash lecture presents a challenge to those who find their work in the study of leisure. Perhaps ending with this challenge is an appropriate reminder that there is little hope for the advancement of leisure unless those of us who study it are willing to admit the profound limits of our knowledge and experience.

Moral Leisure: The Promise and Wonder

Gerald S. Fain

The ability to note change, as part of human experience, is a universal. Yet recent world events promise to make this past year especially memorable. In reflection, our collective memory is shaped by actions both within and beyond the control of people.

The weather brought Hurricane Hugo and a San Francisco earthquake which struck at the start of the third game of the World Series and killed 67 people. The 11 million gallons of oil spilled in Prince William Sound, Alaska will not soon be forgotten or cleaned up. We think nearly 50 million people died last year and more than 135 million babies were born. Malcolm Forbes, the magazine publisher died, but not before giving himself a 70th birthday party in Tangiers. He invited 700 guests at a cost of two million dollars.

Events in the Soviet Union, Hungary, Poland, East Germany, Czechoslovakia, Bulgaria, and Romania forecast the emergence of a new Europe. The European Community will begin free trade in 1992 and the founding purpose of the 40-year-old North Atlantic Treaty Organization (NATO) to provide military support for Western European allies becomes less essential.

The world is changing at such an accelerated pace one can only wonder if school teachers can rely on textbooks to teach our children anything but the way things used to be. Television, radio, and computer networks bring news of changes to us so quickly that it has become impossible to rely on the printed newspaper as a definitive source of current events.

Jay B. Nash, born on October 17, 1886, would be 103 years old today. We can only imagine what he would be doing and thinking about had he lived to 1990. Based upon his writing, we can with confidence predict that he would be calling us into action, to become part of world events, compelling each of us to consider how we can use the relatively few days of our lives to advance the public good.

Each of us, as an individual, has the freedom to choose a life spent in front of the television, watching the world change before us, resting on our certifications, tenure, and accreditations, or we can choose to go beyond what those around us say is the good and shape the future. In the moral sense we ask ourselves, if we should live to see our 103rd birthday, what will we have done to address the serious need to do good in our time?

In a like way, you may recall the now famous challenge issued by Apple Computer genius Steven Jobs to John Sculley, who at the time was the president of Pepsi-Cola. Jobs was trying to convince Sculley to leave Pepsi and join him in the business of computers when he asked, "Do you want to spend the rest of your life selling sugared water or do you want a chance to change the world?" (Sculley, 1987, p. 90).

In essence, it is this idea, the role of the individual as a reflective initiator and agent of change, that I ask you to consider.

Heritage of Concern

The moral imperatives that drive the study of leisure are embedded in the ideals of participatory democracy, personal freedom, and human potential. These are imperatives that may be uniformly embraced without regard to cultural background, orientation to profession, or political ideology. Yet it is not adequate, from a moral point of view, for any field of inquiry to rest on its assertion of virtue. People, and the ideas they wish to represent, are obligated to act in ways that evidence and advance the moral imperatives they wish to be associated with.

Those in the fields of leisure and recreation historically have taken great pride in actions to advance the public good. The contributions of the early founders of the profession include the creation of urban playgrounds for immigrant children where the moral meaning of play was inextricably joined with the ideals of participatory democracy. These same individuals worked to support the settlement house and progressive school movements of the early 1900s. A study of this earlier history also reveals the development of youth serving agencies, creation of national parks and protection of open spaces. During the Depression, leaders in the field of recreation supported the New Deal and its many "make work" programs. The Federal Emergency Relief Administration, Works Progress Administration, and Civilian Conservation Corps en-

listed thousands of volunteers and professionals who constructed recreation facilities and developed recreation programs and activities.

This history, dating back more than 100 years, is rich in both ideals
and actions. The moral imperatives that attracted Jane Addams, Joseph
Lee, Luther Gulick, Stephen Mather, George Butler, George Hjelte, Charles
Brightbill, and Harold Meyer to support the recreation movement were
tied to the issues of their day. As a result, one who studies this history
cannot help but sense the strong feelings of fulfillment these individuals
took in the contributions made toward the creation of a higher social
order. In summary, the early years of the recreation, park, and leisure
service professions were marked by the creation of institutions and
social structures designed to support the clearly defined economic,
political, and cultural agenda.

However, over the past 20 years the complexities of American culture
have made the defining of public agenda problematic. Major shifts in
the culture brought by civil rights, human rights, technological innovation, the "cold war," and the wars fought on battlefields, including
those in Southeast Asia and the Middle East, have created a more global
and complex world. Perhaps due in part to the growing awareness that
we live in an evolving global culture, the past few decades have not
been marked by significant advancement of a moral agenda by those
in the recreation, parks, and leisure service fields. Changes in social
structures should not be considered the primary cause for the decline
of these professions in shaping an agenda rooted in moral meaning. A
more important source of the problem may be found by studying what
has been happening to the fundamental structure of recreation, park,
and leisure services as a unified field.

As a result of ongoing work across this field, it is now becoming
clearer that the value structure which has presumed to unify may no
longer be sturdy enough to support the diversity of interests and mis-
sions. Those in parks are committed to fighting for clean air, conservation of resources, protection of wild lands and the ecology essential
to support all forms of life. Simultaneously, many municipal recreation
and park agencies, faced with the realities of financial reorganization,
are working to find the funding essential to the continuation of culturally
sensitive service delivery to an increasingly diverse clientele. Clinically
oriented therapeutic recreators are preparing for written examinations
as part of progress made toward credentialling, while academicians in
higher education struggle in finding ways to recruit and educate highly
capable and energetic students with the potential to assume the next
generation of leadership.

This quality of diversity is a problem only if a common set of unifying
values is unclear to the practitioner and the public. It is, for example,
a problem when those in natural resources find little to study jointly

or even discuss as a matter of mutual interest with those in community or clinical settings. The degree to which organizational and conceptual diversity is a primary source of moral alienation, is the degree to which the field needs to accept the possibility of conceptual reformulation. Is it possible to continue to think of these professions, with their proliferation of specialities, as realistically united under any particular banner? This question seems especially relevant should we be interested in knowing more about the ways in which recreation, parks, and leisure, as intellectual inquiry and fields of public service, are unified. It is at this juncture where study of the question of moral leisure has utility, for it is through study of moral leisure that we hope to find a common moral mission and mutuality of virtue.

Moral Leisure

Leisure is more than time—it is the freedom to choose how one "ought" live.

What "ought" I do?
What "ought" I be?
What "ought" I become?

These are questions of personal reflection that precede the act of leisure.

The ideal of leisure rests at the core of the recreation, park, and leisure services fields. Leisure, as a conceptualization of freedom, individual liberty, creative expression, and developer of human potential, represents the virtue in professional action. It is toward this end, the celebration of leisure, that the potentiality for shared moral meaning is evidenced. However, this commonality of like-mindedness cannot only be wished. Commonality of moral meaning must be achieved through both thought and action.

The classical and well-established conceptualizations often attributed to leisure in our textbooks, journals, professional meetings, and popular culture have increasingly less to do with the lives of most citizens in this and other social orders. There is all too little evidence to support leisure as either a field of study, or a professional field of service, that joins public agenda in a timely and rigorous way.

Leisure has been thought of and studied from varied perspectives and in numerous ways. Numerous scholars have provided thoughtful contributions to this inquiry (e.g., Charles Brightbill (1960), Sebastian de Grazia (1962), Max Kaplan (1975), Seppo Iso-Ahola (1980), James Murphy (1981), John Neulinger (1981), John Kelly (1987), Thomas Goodale and Geoffrey Godbey (1988), and others). For some leisure is defined as a state of mind, a way of living or type of experience. For some it is delimited to a period of time, while still others, including those in labor and economics, view it as a commodity or as specific types of activity. We therefore know it as leisure activities or leisure time, as well as psychological experience. There are also leisure villages, leisure magazines, leisure amusements, and the unforgettable leisure suit. People take leisure time, play golf for leisure, retire to a state of leisure, and complain that they never have enough of it. This thoughtless use of the word has had a pervasive influence on the field of study. Despite all of the professional meetings held, research studies completed, and scholarly journals published, the promises of the early days, where public support and professional understanding were high, have faded. I think it was the leisure suit that broke the meaning of this wonderful word. Like the last straw on the back of the camel, the leisure suit was an insult that made those to follow of no particular consequence.

Is there no hope for recovery of the word? In my view, recovery is possible. But for the recovery to occur, a vision is needed that can be joined by the public along with the collective professions. The type of vision to which I am referring attracts people like the young J.B. Nash, who devote their lives to the serious study of leisure—a life that others, without orientation to such ideals and values, would be unable to experience and therefore properly understand.

In consideration of the diversity of interests across these fields, this search for meaning will hold promise only so far as it focuses on the naturalness by which this phenomenon occurs. Again, the meanings cannot be wished or invented. This idea for which we search, if it is to reflect human condition as it must, is simply part of our experience and therefore available for discovery and explanation.

To illustrate this concept of naturalness we could select most any of the things we know and love in the world of human experience. For me, my thoughts have turned to snow.

I live in New England, a part of the world where there is snow during the winter months. I recently had the occasion to shovel snow from my driveway with my daughter. The first snow that fell was quite wet. It stuck together and easily formed into snowballs and snow sculptures. As often happens, in my part of the world, the snow kept falling and within a few hours I was out again with my daughter shoveling snow from my driveway. This time the snow had changed. It was light and dry. It was not possible for us to make snowballs and snow sculptures.

The snow had changed. Those who shovel snow and make snowballs know what I am describing. Yet, to the newscasters, weathermen, and most citizens who watched the snow, what had fallen over the course of this time was simply snow. But to those of us in it, there is more than one kind of snow. Eskimos and others who live in winter climates not only know the difference, but find the necessity for creating specific names for what many of the citizens in Massachusetts routinely call snow.

Observations of this kind bring to question the rationale for attributing so much meaning to words which, as natural occurrences, vary so significantly. This is particularly important when the consequences associated with variable meanings affect our actions and experience. In the world of children and snow, the difference is in knowing whether it will be possible to build a snow fort or not. In the realm of leisure, the difference could be time spent in the study of Aristotle's Nicomachean ethics or a night of dining and dancing.

The problem is therefore much greater than it may first appear. The issue is not fundamentally semantic. And as an observation, it is not easily dismissed by assuming that all experience associated with leisure is for the good. While we may be able to live quite well calling all of snow, snow, I argue that all of what has been called leisure is not of equal virtue.

To illustrate, most among us will agree that leisure has embodied within it the essence of liberty and freedom. From the Latin word, *licere*, it means to be permitted freedom from occupation. It is here, within the context of scholarly inquiry and professional life, that we may begin the pursuit of moral meaning.

A basic principle of liberty, articulated by John Stuart Mill in his essay *On Liberty*, asserts,

> ... the sole end for which mankind are warranted, individually or collectively, in interfering with the liberty of action of any of their number, is self-protection. That the only purpose for which power can be rightfully exercised over any member of a civilized community, against his will, is to prevent harm to others. His own good, either physical or moral, is not a sufficient warrant. He cannot rightfully be compelled to do or forbear because it will be better for him to do so, because it will make him happier, because, in the opinions of others, to do so would be wise, or even right. (Reiser, 1977, p. 186)

Mills reminds us that our personal freedom and liberty extend only so far as our action begins to interfere with the welfare of others. At the point where there is interference, we are obligated to stop. Furthermore we are compelled to stop the actions of others who interfere with the freedom of others.

One ought not, in a moral sense, tolerate all actions of individual freedom as being equally good. Swinging one's arms as an act of free expression has limits. Similarly, we ought not accept all that may be considered leisure to be equally worthwhile. Knowing that an activity experience is freely chosen, during "leisure" is pleasing to self, is not sufficient in determining moral acceptability. Acts which we know interfere with the rights of others can, and in a moral sense ought, be viewed differently from those acts which support the rights of others. Crimes where there is injury to an individual, while the perpetrator claims a pleasing state of mind having completed said act, are in no way consistent with attributes of leisure assumed by the field. Who among us would want to use the word leisure to characterize criminal acts? Yet, if one were to read some of the literature in the field it would be impossible to disqualify criminal acts from the conceptualizations of leisure presented. Taken out of their natural contexts, the meanings associated with recreation experience and countless activities freely chosen during unobligated time are fundamentally valueless ideas. Those who read in this literature can easily find evidence of authors who do not struggle to discriminate against the destructive and morally unacceptable acts of personal freedom that adversely affect self and others.

In contrast, and by example, it would seem reasonable for this field to publicly support efforts to prevent the abuse of alcohol and drugs. However, such a position may not be believable or even possible until there is publicly recognized thoughtfulness by the profession on fundamental ideals associated with the moral meaning of leisure. One can only imagine the extraordinary conversation a beginning student, armed only with a vacuous notion of leisure, stated in terms of time, activity, or state of mind, would have with an addict who claims to use drugs as his form of leisure expression. Too often I am afraid the student, unable to discern the position of the profession at such critical times of thoughtfulness, is without the moral meaning provided by the early history of this field. If we are to believe that consumption of drugs degrades individuals' personal freedom of choice and destroys human potential, thereby obviating the ideal of leisure, then we ought to take action against drugs and instruct our students to follow.

For some, taking such positions creates problems. Based upon the belief that personal freedom is best left unexamined, thoughtfulness on questions of "ought" are not part of their professional lives. Yet I cannot imagine such individuals finding fulfillment in the study of leisure. For it is in the examination of leisure that one is made aware of the inescapable ethical question about what we "ought" to be and to do in our lives. Leisure is the occasion of ought in that it has no single form or virtue. It holds only possibility. In leisure, one encounters the existential meaning of life where the assertion of one's will defines the substance of their life. What I choose to do with leisure, in the moral sense, marks my past, my purpose, and my future.

On this occasion, it is particularly relevant to note that J.B. Nash had no problem with this idea. Approaching this lecture required my revisiting of J.B. Nash. I had studied his writings during the course of my education and I also encountered his influence upon professionals who had known him as their teacher. Among the most enduring influences of J.B. Nash were his strong character and his firmly stated belief that one not only could, but must, distinguish on the basis of ideals between various uses of leisure.

In the presentation of his well-known triangular figure, "Man's Use of Leisure Time," he places in hierarchy levels of leisure. At the lowest level are acts performed against society. Next higher, but still without virtue, are acts detrimental to self. The four levels to follow, in order, are "spectatoritis" type activities, emotional participation, active participation, and the highest level, which he calls creative participation. In making this presentation, he asserts: "There is a wide scale of values to be applied to the activities chosen for one's leisure" (Nash, 1960, p. 93).

In my review of history in this field, J.B. Nash stands as a distinguished voice called those around him to think more critically about the use of leisure. For him, it was not only a call to participation in life, but an essential opportunity for personal growth and development.

Nash lived with colleagues and a public that believed in the positive possibilities of leisure and recreation. This belief was strong, and largely without question. A kind of logical positivism seemed to pervade those times that gave occasion to speculate on the possibilities of a leisure society.

The world in which we live today is complex and rapidly changing. And while the moral philosophic questions of "ought" endure, the possibilities for creating a leisure society are in need of reconsideration. Nonetheless, the demand for living a virtuous life, one characterized by moral reflection, is unabated. The call for moral leisure could not be less compelling today than it was in the days of J.B. Nash.

The Promise

There is, by necessity, a social contract that each and every profession makes with the society in which it lives. That contract, written on the soul of the professional, contains the moral imperatives that promise to benefit the citizens of the society. The extent to which these imperatives are embraced by the public determines in large measure the virtue of the individual and the collective group. It is a contract dependent upon mutual consent.

In a practical way, and as a point of moral reflection, there is an obligation to ask what this field has been doing to advance the public interest. Local and world news, reported each day, provides an ample framework for the assessment.

In our communities, we are struck by the need to attend to the problems and conflicts of homelessness, poverty, abortion, violence in the streets, drug abuse and gun control. Globally, we care about apartheid, the events in Tiananmen Square, our fouled seas, air pollution, the dismantling of the Berlin Wall, and the end to the cold war. Peace is breaking out all around the world yet our children are afraid to play in their neighborhoods. As a result, many don't know how to jump rope, or play four-square, and they don't know the other children they are growing up with because they don't play outside after school. Many adults in our urban centers are afraid to walk in their parks after dark. One of every five adults in this country is illiterate.

The promises made by this profession more than 100 years ago are still in need of keeping. Systemic economic, social, cultural, and political problems associated with violence, racial and ethnic discrimination, and poverty still manifest themselves on our streets. The promise was no less than working toward the creation of a better world. There were even forecasts on the possibilities of a leisure society.

The Wonder

In Book A (1) of *Metaphysica*, Aristotle explains that after the utilities of life have been invented, men first began to have leisure. "That is why the mathematical arts were founded in Egypt; for there the priestly caste was allowed to be at leisure" (McKeon, 1968, pp. 690–691).

Imagine with me, what that act of wonder may have been like. Egyptians asked about their world, without the press of utility.

"Do you see that tree over there?

"How far do you think that is from here?"

"What do you mean by far?"

"The space from here to there."

"Do you think it is farther away than the one over there?"

"How shall we decide which of the two is a greater distance?"

"You walk in that direction and I will walk in the other and we shall see who takes more paces."

"But your pace is not the same as mine."

"How shall we determine which pace to use as the rule?"

And so it continues. ... the act of wonder. ... the act of creative transcendence. ... taking a leap into the unknown, without the press of utility and restrained only by the limits of human potential and reflective morality. It is here in acts of creative transcendence, where the courage of human experience is called to reach beyond its known limits, that the future becomes possible. To me, this is the essence of leisure.

Perhaps the most fundamental of purposes in the study of leisure is

directed at understanding the prerequisites for the experience of wonder. What is it that enables and precedes wonder?

As a qualification, wonder, as leisure experience, is not available to
all. Small children, without experience in the world, can no more easily
understand this type of wonder than they can understand the concept
of political freedom, economic independence, or the realities of living
in their own adult anatomy. Nor is this experience possible for those
who, because of intellectual inabilities, or health and economic conditions, find themselves overwhelmed by temporal experience, which
supersedes the essential process of personal reflection.

Having now set some boundary for the idea, the stating of what
wonder cannot be, it is possible to give some thought to what it is. I
ask for your consideration of the following four preconditions to wonder. They are not presented in a hierarchy nor should they be considered
mutually independent. For the present, they serve as illustrative points
for discussion.

The first precondition is the active deciding to become. In the adult
world, we celebrate those who decide to become. In the existential
sense, these are individuals who know that they are what they do. As
a society, we especially respect them as citizens because they shape
the world by taking the matters of life seriously and respond in thoughtful action with the intention to improve themselves. These are the people
who are influenced by ideas, seek truth, and defend the necessity to
abandon what was once comfortable, because they believe in the power
of ideas. Like Socrates in his dialogue with Crito (Church, 1908), there
are ideals worth dying for and when we truly commit ourselves to the
freedom required to know and protect these ideals we find thoughtful
self-interest.

In making this point, it is essential to distinguish between those who
seek to improve themselves solely on the basis of personal happiness
and those who demonstrate by their actions that personal happiness is
inextricably tied to the personal happiness of fellow citizens. One, in a
moral sense, ought not be happy without knowing and freely paying for
the right to be happy. The payment, in the manifest form of ongoing
reflection, may never be settled. In a mature adult world, consideration
for fellow human beings is both an obligation and a privilege. It is the
kind of reflection which may bring happiness. In this deciding, one
chooses to do what is right, what one ought do with one's life. This is
not a career decision. It is not a major in college.

The second condition is deciding to know. My friend Larry Neal (1983)
is right. Leisure has no enemy but ignorance. Not only do the ideas
themselves reveal the promise and wonder, but they require study and
reflection.

Knowing how to communicate, the actions of literacy, are fundamental to human transactions. While not necessarily fixed in a particular set of cultural tenets, the tools used in human transactions provide the vehicles to mutuality of understanding essential to knowing moral meanings. As a prerequisite, deciding to know is embedded in both the mastery of these tools and the commitment to using them.

The third precondition is deciding to be healthy. This is both a public and private decision. The cigarette smoked in public announces to others that personal health is being sacrificed. A lack of physical conditioning, combined with overeating, makes an impression of a similar kind. In contrast, when one decides that life is to be lived in the fullness of opportunity, one works to ready oneself for the challenge presented by the unknown. What a disappointment it would be if one were to discover the possibility of wonder but fail to have the prerequisite health to run after it.

The fourth and final decision is deciding to live with less. Searching for happiness through materialism is both vulgar and impossible. Just as one learns that there are limits to the world's resources, one also ought learn that there are limits to what one ought desire in material wealth. The result of coming to rest with this decision is the freedom to know and understand what is present. It is the act of lifting one's head from the desk and looking out at the world. It more fully allows the celebration of family, community, and participation in one's culture.

The kind of wonder to which I am referring is a personal experience that unifies the self in morally reflective and creative action, transcending the limits and utilities of daily living. It is in the teaching, study, and reflection that the moral imperatives which drive and unite this field may be found.

What would it be like if an individual were to accept the challenge of moral leisure? I support they would take more walks for hunger, volunteer in the soup kitchen, fight the abuse of drugs and alcohol, teach literacy to children and adults, fight with those who discriminate against minorities, and advance the human potential of all individuals including those with the most severe disabilities. They would be a friend to those who advance education and health. I don't suppose they would have a lot of time free of wonder.

Epilogue

Professionalization often breeds a type of excessive bonding and promotion of self that undermines public interest. It may also support overspecialization at the expense of the clientele it purports to serve. However, an even greater danger of professionalization is the timidity which drives the intellectual self into a position of powerlessness out of the fear that others might be offended. Doing good requires a tenacious appetite for competence, energy, and reflection on moral mission.

People can wonder about war, poverty, world hunger, environmental pollution, and violence on their streets. Professionals in this field can also wonder whether or not they are working hard enough to advance the public's interest in creating a society marked by personal liberty, respect for humanity and human potential, and the wonderment of personal happiness.

If we want a profession of public value it must do more than administer competency tests, accredit university curriculum, engage thoughtless philosophic dialogue, and conduct research filled with jargon, statistics, and technique. There is simply too much at stake to squander the most unique and vital of all human resources. While leisure, as reflective moral action, does not belong to any particular field, it is within the realm of responsibility for those who study leisure to know its worth and articulate its contributions toward the advancement of civilization.

The refrain of Steven Jobs is haunting. Do you want to spend the rest of your life selling sugared water or do you want a chance to change the world?

In my university teaching it is not uncommon for students to ask me if I commute to work in a single passenger car, volunteer to feed the hungry, or recycle my household trash. I like these questions, and I like these students. For they have begun the reflective process that indicates the possibilities of personal growth. Moreover, it is through the asking of these questions that we begin to build our hope for the future.

References

Brightbill, C. (1960). *The challenge of leisure*. Englewood Cliffs: Prentice Hall.

de Grazia, S. (1962). *Of time, work and leisure*. New York: Twentieth Century Fund.

Church, F. J. (Ed. and Trans.) (1908). *The trial and death of Socrates*. London: Macmillan.

Goodale, T., & Godbey, G. (1988). *The evolution of leisure: Historical and philosophical perspectives*. State College, PA: Venture.

Iso-Ahola, S. (1980). *The social psychology of leisure and recreation*. Dubuque, IA: Brown.

Kaplan, M. (1975). *Leisure: Theory and policy*. New York: Wiley.

Kelly, J. (1987). *Freedom to be: A new sociology of leisure*. New York: Macmillan.

McKeon, R. (Ed.). (1968). *The basic works of Aristotle*. New York: Random House.

Murphy, J. (1981). *Concepts of leisure*. Englewood Cliffs, NJ: Prentice-Hall.

Nash, J. B. (1960). *Philosophy of recreation and leisure*. Dubuque, IA: Wm. C. Brown.

Neal, L. (Ed.). (1983). *Leisure: No enemy but ignorance.* Reston, VA: American Alliance for Health, Physical Education, Recreation and Dance.

Neulinger, J. (1981). *To leisure: An introduction.* Boston: Allyn and Bacon.

Reiser, S. J., Dyck, A., & Curran, W. J. (Eds.). (1977). *Ethics in medicine: Historical perspectives and contemporary concerns.* Cambridge: MIT Press.

Sculley, J., with Byrne, J. (1987). *Odyssey: Pepsi to Apple—A journey of adventure, ideas, and the future.* New York: Harper & Row.

Reflections

Gerald S. Fain and Kimberly A. Gillespie

Before outlining his particular philosophy, Aristotle generally presented a review of the philosophical claims of scholars whose ideas had come before him. After presenting this historical review, he then proceeded to state what was correct and incorrect about their claims. Regardless of whether he thought their claims were correct, he had respect for each scholarly idea, even the ones he rejected outright. Each scholar had "hit the side of the barn" and gotten at the truth a little. Through all their stumbling, they got hold of something valuable.

> The investigation of the truth is in one way hard, in another easy. An indication of this is found in the fact that no one is able to attain the truth adequately, while, on the other hand, we do not collectively fail, but every one says something true about the nature of things, and while individually we contribute little or nothing to the truth, by the union of all a considerable amount is amassed. Therefore, since the truth seems to be like the proverbial door, which no one can fail to hit, in this respect it must be easy, but the fact that we can have a whole truth and not the particular part we aim at shows the difficulty of it. (Aristotle, *Metaphysica*, Book a)

We are all driven by the desire to know the truth, the truth about life—the truth about leisure. This desire to know the truth is what compelled the contributors to this book to explore aspects of leisure and ethics. Aristotle, in the *Metaphysica*, emphasized the difficulties in investigating the truth, but he also noted the value of each effort made on its behalf.

This book represents a wide range of scholarly efforts on the topic of leisure and ethics. Some chapters represent the continuation of considerable thought over time, while other chapters are presentations of initial scholarship. Each, in its own way, contributes to our understanding of leisure and ethics. As Aristotle noted, individually we are not able to adequately attain the truth, but collectively we do not fail. From the union of all ideas and contributions, a considerable amount is amassed. Through the Symposium on Leisure and Ethics and the publication of this book, we have amassed a considerable amount, but its virtue can only be realized through future scholarship. Collectively we cannot fail, but collective effort is not a finite, contained pursuit, such as one article, collection of papers, book, or symposium. It must be ongoing, sustaining inquiry of sufficient depth and breadth if we are to understand the most fundamental truths about leisure and ethics.

The conceptualization of this work rested on five themes. They are:

Leisure, Ethics, and Philosophy
Moral Life and Professional Practice in
Leisure Science and Service
Moral Development and Leisure Experience
Global Perspectives on Leisure
Multidisciplinary Works in Leisure and Ethics

The five themes have been useful in constructing a template for the study of leisure and ethics. The connections and relationships between leisure and ethics are multidimensional and provide a distinct and robust way to think about things and ideas. Conceptualizations that are useful in structuring questions and relationships are fundamental to the advancement of our knowledge and the pursuit of what we come to know as truth.

This is a time in history when citizens across the globe are actively exercising their hope for increased freedoms. This love of freedom as an ideal, be it from economic, social, or political repression, is inextricably tied to the pursuit of the "good life." From this vista we can see the coming of a new leisure age from which there can be no turning back. The more we know about the possibilities of living in ways that are less dependent on the unfulfilling drudgery of work, the greater the demand on knowing about the unique freedoms that constitute leisure.

The growing demand to know more about leisure will test scholars, professional organizations, and those who practice in related fields. While we may predict that there will be more books, meetings, symposiums, and discussions, predicting substantive contributions to science and matters of practical social importance remains uncertain. The outcome of these efforts will in large measure be dependent upon the scholarship, discipline, and character of individual contributors. Therefore, in addition to encouraging the continuing dialogue, the need to recruit and nurture the next generation of leisure scholars is arguably our greatest single challenge. And to meet this need, by attracting students with these interests, will undoubtedly require the reformulation of what is presently perceived to be the academic study of leisure.

The contributions made to the symposium and this text give one indication of where the field of leisure studies is headed. Some of those who presented papers at the symposium were quite surprised to find others engaged in scholarly work related to their own particular topic of interest. Others were simply gratified to find that they were not alone in their views that ethics and philosophy were fundamental to the study of leisure.

The scholarship presented in this book is the type of work that can be done in isolation, but it cannot be done well in isolation. By providing the opportunity to collectively study and challenge our individual thoughts and ideas, we find the hope of discovering something of greater value.

About the Authors

Leandra A. Bedini, Ph.D., lecturer and project director of professional preparation training grant in the Curriculum in Leisure Studies and Recreation Administration, University of North Carolina at Chapel Hill. Scholarship and grant work is focused on leisure education and community integration of people with disabilities. Professional service includes committee work on national (National Recreation and Park Association, American Therapeutic Recreation Association) and local levels.

Gerald A. Bruce, B.A. Recreation Administration, M.A. Community Development. Currently president of Bruce Community Development Consultants, Whitehorse, Yukon, Canada. A graduate of the University of Alberta, Edmonton, Alberta, Canada, Bruce spent nine years as an instructor in leisure education at Mount Royal College in Calgary, Alberta and was a recreation consultant to the governments of Alberta and British Columbia. More recently, he is involved in strategic planning for the Yukon Territorial Government Municipal Affairs and the city of Whitehorse. Bruce consults in the area of land use dispute resolution and economic development planning.

John M. Charles, Ed.D., associate professor in the Physical Education Department at the College of William and Mary in Williamsburg, Virginia. Born in England, with an undergraduate degree from Westminster College, Oxford, and terminal degree from the University of Oregon. Scholarship and teaching are focused on philosophical, sociocultural, and cross-cultural aspects of play, sport, and leisure.

William Coe, Ph.D., professor of philosophy and coordinator of the humanities program, Fort Lewis College, Durango, Colorado. Scholarly interests comprise the history of philosophy, contemporary continental philosophy, philosophy of the self, moral philosophy, philosophy of leisure, and logic. Publications include the book *Concepts of Leisure in Western Thought,* with Byron Dare and George Welton; memberships include the American Philosophical Association, the Society for Phenomenology and Existential Philosophy, the International Association for Philosophy and Literature, and the Mountain-Plains Philosophy Conference.

Wes Cooper, Ph.D., professor, Department of Philosophy, University of Alberta, Edmonton, Alberta, Canada; managing editor, *Canadian Journal of Philosophy.* His articles in moral philosophy, philosophy of mind, and theory of work and leisure have appeared in such journals as *Philosophy and Phenomenological*

Research, Ethics, Philosophy In Context, Journal of the History of Philosophy, and *Dialogue.* His professional service includes acting as co-chair for Canada of the North American Society for Social Philosophy.

Kathleen Cordes, assistant professor, Department of Physical Education, Whittier College, Whittier, California. Past department chair, she taught outdoor recreation in the graduate program at the Pan America Institute at the Universidad del Zulia, Maracaibo, Venezuela, 1990. Scholarship is focused on history, philosophy, and ethics in physical education and recreation. Professional service has included vice president of Whittier YMCA Executive vice president of Girls and Women in Sport of the California Association of Health, Physical Education, Recreation and Dance, editor and chair of the National Association of Girls and Women in Sport *Tennis Guide,* 1986–88.

L. Dale Cruse, Ed.D., chair and professor, Department of Recreation and Leisure, University of Utah, Salt Lake City. Scholarship is focused on management and leadership skills and special populations, especially, minorities and Native Americans. Professional service has included president of American Association for Leisure and Recreation, president of Utah Association for Health, Physical Education, Recreation and Dance, National Recreation and Park Association accreditation teams, and service to both state and regional associations for recreation and parks as well as health, physical education, recreation, and dance.

Byron Dare, Ph.D., professor and chair, Department of Political Science and Philosophy, Fort Lewis College, Durango, Colorado. Primary co-author of *Concepts of Leisure in Western Thought: A Critical and Historical Analysis.*

Gerald S. Fain, Ph.D., professor, School of Education, Boston University, Boston, Massachusetts; chairman, Department of Special Education, and coordinator of Leisure Studies and Health Education Programs. Creator and director of the SCHOLE telecommunications network. Scholarship is focused on leisure, moral philosophy, and professional ethics. Professional service has included chairman, American Association for Leisure and Recreation Committee on Ethics, intern for the National Recreation and Park Association, president of the National Therapeutic Recreation Society, and service to various professional societies in the fields of leisure, health, and special education.

Karen M. Fox, Ph.D., assistant professor, Faculty of Physical Education and Recreation Studies, University of Manitoba, Winnipeg, Manitoba. Teaches outdoor recreation and education. Scholarship is focused on environmental ethics, outdoor education, and ethical outdoor leadership. Professional service has included reviewer for the Leisure Research Symposium and service to various professional societies in the fields of interpretation, outdoor leadership, and wilderness emergency medicine.

Kimberly A. Gillespie, doctoral candidate at Boston University; M.S., The Pennsylvania State University; manager of SCHOLE telecommunications network 1988–90. Professional experience in therapeutic recreation. Scholarship is focused on moral philosophy, professional ethics, and therapeutic recreation.

Richard Gull, Ph.D., associate professor of philosophy, Philosophy Department, University of Michigan-Flint, Flint, Michigan. Co-director, Center for New Work, Project for Urban and Regional Affairs, University of Michigan-Flint. Scholarship has recently focused on philosophical foundations of work and the transformation of work by technology, economic globalization, and ideology. Co-produced (with Frithjof Bergmann) a video series titled "The Future of Work."

Serves on the Board of Directors of the National Coalition for Innovative Housing and Jobs. Teaches a course titled "Philosophy, Work, and Economic Freedom."

John L. Hemingway, Ph.D., assistant professor, Department of Physical Education, Recreation, and Sport Science, St. Cloud State University, St. Cloud, Minnesota. Research focuses on the philosophical investigation of leisure and play and on the nature of leisure inquiry, with current efforts directed at the role of play and play concepts in late nineteenth and twentieth century thought. Publications include discussions of Aristotelian leisure, distributive justice and therapeutic recreation, the therapeutic element in recreation, and hermeneutic inquiry in leisure studies. Professional service includes twice chairing the NRPA Symposium section on leisure and the humanities and serving as associate editor of *Leisure Sciences.*

Karla A. Henderson, Ph.D., associate professor and graduate coordinator, Curriculum in Leisure Studies and Recreation Administration, University of North Carolina-Chapel Hill. Scholarship is focused on women's leisure, constraints to leisure, social psychological perspectives on leisure, volunteerism, and professional preparation. Professional service has included the Board of Directors of American Camping Association, Society of Park and Recreation Educators, and Wisconsin Park and Recreation Association as well as serving on the editorial boards of several publications in the field of recreation, leisure, and camping.

Hilmi Ibrahim, professor of physical education and recreation at Whittier College, Whittier, California. Serves on the Board of the Research Consortium of AAHPERD and on the Editorial Board of *Leisure Today* of AALR. He has served as president of the California Association of Park and Recreation Commissioners. His recent publications include *Leisure and Society: A Comparative Approach* (Wm C. Brown, 1990), *Pioneers in Leisure and Recreation* (AAHPERD, 1989), and *Effective Park and Recreation Commissions* (AAHPERD, 1987). He received a grant from Whittier College to study the role of citizens in local, state, and national policies pertaining to recreation.

Nila M. Ipson, M.S., assistant professor, Division of Leisure Studies, coordinator of campus recreation, athletics and recreation services, Dalhousie University of Halifax, Nova Scotia. Director of Western Laboratory for Leisure Research, University of Utah, 1988–89. Scholarship is focused on aging and campus recreation activities. Professional service has included member of Canadian Parks and Recreation Conference Program Planning Committee, host organizer, Invitational Women's Hockey Tournament, Halifax, and member of the Canadian National Intercollegiate Basketball Championship Finals Organizing Committee (1984 and 1985).

Max Kaplan, Ph.D., degrees in music (B.E. and M.Mus.) and sociology (M.A. and Ph.D.-Illinois), university professor for 43 years: Colorado, Illinois, Florida, Maryland, Massachusetts. Author of 26 volumes in leisure, the arts, aging (examples: *Leisure in America,* 1960: *Leisure, Lifespan and Lifestyle,* 1979; *The Arts, a Social Perspective,* 1990); about 200 articles and 40 chapters in American and foreign publications. Lectures and consultations in most western and eastern nations; consultant to Lincoln Center for Performing Arts, SPEBSQSA, Canadian Arts Council, Israel, Puerto Rico, and Japanese research groups; former president, ISA Leisure Research Commission. Violinist with symphonies, university faculty quartets, and with New Southern Trio. Home in Senoia, Georgia.

Gerald S. Kenyon, professor, Department of Sociology, University of Lethbridge, Alberta, Canada. Held a number of academic and administrative posts at the Universities of Wisconsin, Waterloo, and Lethbridge. Research interests have included the sociology of sport, leisure, and the arts. Currently studying the social construction of taste in the arts, with special reference to corporate-art world networks. Member of Canadian, U.S., and international sociological associations and related organizations.

Victor Kestenbaum, Ed.D., associate professor, Department of Philosophy, College of Liberal Arts; associate professor, Department of Curriculum and Teaching, School of Education, Boston University, Boston, Massachusetts; chairman ad interim, Department of Philosophy. Scholarship is concerned with American philosophy and its relationship to hermeneutics and phenomenology, philosophy and the professions, and the philosophy of higher education. Associate editor, *Human Studies: A Journal for Philosophy and the Social Sciences.*

James S. Leming, Ph.D., professor, Department of Curriculum and Instruction, College of Education, Southern Illinois University, Carbondale, Illinois. Coordinator of Graduate Programs in Social Studies Education. Research interests include the moral development of adolescents, moral education in the schools, and social studies education. Professional service has included chair of the College and University Faculty Assembly of the National Council for the Social Studies and chair of the Research in Social Studies Education Special Interest Group of the American Educational Research Association.

Leo H. McAvoy, Ph.D. Primary area of research and teaching is in outdoor recreation and outdoor education, specifically studying the personal and social benefits of participation in environmentally related activities and the management of human behavior in outdoor recreation resources. This applied research has been supported by federal, state, and local agencies as well as published in a variety of scholarly and professional journals. Professional service has included serving as associate editor for *Leisure Sciences*, as chair of the Leisure Research Symposium, board member for the Society of Park and Recreation Educators, and as a research and training consultant on a number of projects for public and private outdoor recreation and outdoor education agencies.

Ann M. Rancourt, Ph.D., associate professor/coordinator, Department of Recreation and Leisure Studies, SUNY-Brockport, New York. Scholarship is focused on leisure as a personal and social issue, recreation and leisure for persons with disabilities, and professional preparation. Professional service has included president, Greater Grand Rapids Therapeutic Recreation Association; chair, Research Committee, Therapeutic Recreation Section, New York State Recreation and Park Society; president-elect, Genesee Valley Recreation and Park Society; associate editor, *Therapeutic Recreational Journal*; and service to various professional societies and community agencies in recreation, leisure, and therapeutic recreation.

Michael Ruckenstein, Ed.D., professor, Community Recreational Leadership Training (CRLT) Department, Dawson College, Montreal, Quebec, Canada. Coordinator of physical education and athletics, Dawson College; associate coordinator of CRLT Department. Presentations and research on leisure pursuits of the English and French in an urban population. Member of AAHPERD, CAHPER, and NRPA; chairman, Young Men's and Young Women's Hebrew Association (YM-YWHA), Montreal, Canada. Service in the fields of leisure and physical education.

Debra Shogan, Ph.D., associate professor, Faculty of Physical Education and Recreation, University of Alberta, Edmonton, Alberta. Teaches courses in professional ethics, philosophy of leisure, ethics and sport, and feminist ethics. Her book *Care and Moral Motivation* was published in 1988 by OISE Press.

David B. Sullivan, visiting assistant professor of communication at the University of Hartford, West Hartford, Connecticut. He is also a doctoral candidate in the Department of Communication, University of Massachusetts-Amherst (M.A., University of Hartford, 1987). Editorial assistant for the *Journal of Broadcasting & Electronic Media.* Background in print journalism as reporter and editor complements research interests in meaning construction and mass mediated news, politics, and sports.

Margaret Trunfio, Ed.D., professor of leisure studies, Gordon College, Wenham, Massachusetts. Creator and coordinator of leisure studies and recreation major at Gordon College. Master Certified Leisure Professional. Scholarship is focused on leisure philosophy and Christian theology, sociology of leisure, and lifestyle ethics. Service and consultation regarding leisure and lifestyle management to various church-related and nonprofit organizations.

David Whitson, Ph.D., associate professor, Department of Recreation and Leisure Studies, University of Alberta, Edmonton, Canada. Scholarly interests include gender and leisure, the professionalization of leisure, leisure studies and cultural theory, and popular culture in Canada. Co-author of a major new work entitled *The Game Planners: Transforming Canada's Sport System* and author of articles appearing in *Leisure Studies, Society & Leisure, Quest, Theory, Culture & Society,* and *Canadian Public Policy.* Member of Editorial Board of *Sociology of Sport Journal.*

John R. Wilcox, Ph.D., associate professor of religious studies, Manhattan College, Bronx, New York. Founder and director of the Center for Professional Ethics at Manhattan College. Center focus: a pervasive approach to ethics in the curricula of the schools at Manhattan College. Teaches business and engineering ethics. Engaged in research on ethical issues in higher education and higher education administration. Initiated and directed a values audit of Manhattan College. Professional service includes board membership in the American Association of University Administrators, convener of the Interest Group on Christian Ethics and the Professions (Society of Christian Ethics), chair of the Board of Ethics, Westchester County, New York.

Kelly Wilhelm, Ph.D., recreation, University of Maryland. Has worked as a practitioner and educator in therapeutic recreation since 1974. At present, she is vice president of Storyfest Journeys, which leads pilgrimages to England, Ireland, and Italy.

Larry R. Williams, Ph.D., coordinator of leisure services, College of Education, University of South Alabama, Mobile, Alabama. Professional endeavors focus on professional management training in ethics, international training of leisure professionals, marketing research, resource and community development. Scholarly pursuits focus on ethics, the community college, and hospitality/tourism. Professional service includes leadership and membership in numerous leisure/tourism/educational related international, national, regional, state, and local association/societies.

Robert M. Wolff, Ph.D., associate professor and coordinator of the parks and recreation management curriculum at Florida International University, Miami, Florida. Academic and research interests are in commercial recreation, travel and tourism, conflict resolution, and services marketing. Received a Ph.D. in recreation management, M.B.A. in marketing from The Ohio State University, and B.S.B.A. in marketing from the University of Akron.

Index